Handbook of

Market Risk

HANDBOOK OF
Market Risk

CHRISTIAN SZYLAR

WILEY

Published by John Wiley & Sons, Inc., Hoboken, New Jersey
Published simultaneously in Canada

Library of Congress Cataloging-in-Publication Data:

Szylar, Christian.
Handbook of market risk / Christian Szylar, Marshall Wace LLP.
pages cm
Includes bibliographical references and index.
ISBN 978-1-118-12718-6 (cloth) – ISBN 978-1-118-51494-8 – ISBN 978-1-118-51492-4 (ePDF) – ISBN 978-1-118-51493-1 (ePub) – ISBN 978-1-118-51490-0
1. Risk management. 2. Financial risk management. 3. Capital market. I. Title.
HD61.S99 2013
332.64'5–dc23

2013018808

To my wife and my two beloved sons

Contents

Foreword

Market risk is a field of great importance both to firms managing risk and supervisors alike. It embraces a huge field, made more complex as innovations lead to an ever-expanding variety of financial instruments, and which needs to cover many fields of activity from banking to asset management.

Christian Szylar has written an excellent exposé of the field, which manages to retain an inherent readability for the nontechnical reader, with a rigorous technical approach for those wishing to go into more depth.

The book helps to reduce inherent complexities into a field better understood and makes a valuable contribution for all those interested in the area of managing risks. At a time when we are living with the aftermath of financial crisis, it deserves to be widely read.

Sir Andrew Large
Former Deputy Governor, Bank of England

Acknowledgments

My first acknowledgment is of course to Ruey S. Tsay and Steve. Quigley for giving me this opportunity to work on this handbook. It was a great honor for me that both of them thought about me for this project. I owe a very special debt of gratitude to both of them.

My thanks go to Paul Marshall and Ian Wace from Marshall Wace LLP. I hope they appreciate the merits of this work. I thank them for creating an environment where their risk team can freely challenge and discuss with the investment teams all matters of market risk.

My sincere thanks to Sebastian Ceria and Alessandro Michelini from Axioma; they gave me access to some of their internal documents and in particular their *Axioma Robust Risk Model Handbook*. Their extracts were crucial for this handbook, especially on building the fundamental multifactor model.

Sincere thanks to John Carter at Marshall Wace LLP for his support and review of my mathematical formulations, which have been extremely valuable especially for the volatility estimates. His constructive remarks helped to improve the content of this book.

Sincere thanks to Alessandro Orsaria at Marshall Wace LLP for his valuable research on correlation estimates; I hope this work will help him in furthering his studies.

Finally, my biggest debt is to my friend Clement Menace, whose support was essential for this book and especially regarding Basel II/III. His inputs have been invaluable.

C.S.

About the Author

Christian Szylar is currently Global Head of Risk and Performance Measurement in a global leading asset management company Marshall Wace LLP. Christian worked at Kinetic Partners LLP as a Partner, where he headed a risk and valuation solution to asset management firms and banks. Prior to this, he was Managing Director of RBS Portfolio Risk Services, where he developed a portfolio of risk management services tailored to worldwide asset managers, and was also a conducting officer at RBS Luxembourg offering independent management company services. He was also Vice President at Mizuho Financial Group.

Christian holds a Ph.D. in Management Science from University of Law, Economics and Management at Nancy. He furthered his studies at MIT/Sloan School of Management and participated in a number of Harvard Economics programs. He teaches in various Masters degree programs in Finance, and for some time he headed the MBA program in Luxembourg.

Christian also acted as a senior official expert for the ATTF, and as such he advised many financial institutions and Central Banks. He was Vice President of the IAS Luxembourg, an organization aiming to promote corporate social responsibility in Europe.

Christian has published many articles on risk, finance, macroeconomics, and economic intelligence in reviews and several books. He recently published *Risk Management under UCITS III/IV—New Challenges for the Fund Industry* (ISTE/Wiley) and also edited the *UCITS Handbook* (ISTE/Wiley).

Introduction

The last five years have been driven by the credit crisis that started in the United States in 2008 before spreading all around the globe and affecting all of major economies. The severity of this crisis can be compared to the 1929 crisis. Charles Kindelberger,[1] a professor at the Massachusetts Institute of Technology (MIT), analyzed all financial and economic crises since the seventeenth century, and it seems that all crises seem to follow the same steps: (1) a boom (often driven by new product(s); (2) keen interest/enthusiasm/frenzy and transaction speed and volume until its maximum, and then the crisis starts; (3) fear and mess/chaos, and behavior/reference marks are lost; (4) a consolidation phase where we decrease what has increased in an overly excessive way and has contaminated the entire economy—recession starts; and finally (5) the recovery with usually public and state support. The 2007 crisis is not different from this pattern formalized by Charles Kindelberger. The amplitude and severity of this recent crisis has nevertheless something that is different from the other ones. The big difference is that all of the models, assumptions, and practices we knew from the past about investing and managing market risk will not be working again. This crisis led to a new investment paradigm, hence modifying our market risk perception and management. This is a major change for the investment community, and today's investors and those who manage money try to identify how best to manage this new paradigm. The pre-2008 era is profoundly different from the post-2008 years.

What have we learned from the 2008 financial crisis?

- Capital requirement for financial institution is not enough to protect against bankruptcy.
- Stress testing was faulty and not run properly.
- We have misunderstood the links between some over-the-counter (OTC) products.
- Liquidity risk was not properly monitored.

[1]Kindelberger, Charles, *Manias, Panics, and Crashes: A History of Financial Crisis*, Wiley, 2000.

- The value-at-risk (VaR) method has created a false sense of security and comfort for regulators and all market participants. In the wake of the most recent troubles, critics have noted VAR's reliance on normal market distributions and its fundamental assumption that positions can be readily liquidated.
- Correlations have not been managed properly, especially in credit derivative products.
- Risk management was not always part of the full investment process, and there was over-reliance on some mathematical models.
- Risk governance was not working properly in many financial institutions, which led to excessive risk.

Over the last five years, we have seen some of the most significant changes in financial markets that have ever been witnessed. Correlations and the way that risk should be handled have changed dramatically. For example, recent high correlations between asset classes have led the market to become obsessed with the idea of risk on–risk off (RoRo). The concept of risk on–risk off is based on the market's view of the future state of the world: Either the market believes that future prospects are good, in which case risk is on; or the market believes that future prospects are bad, in which case risk is off. This recent polarization of the market participants implies a high degree of synchronization between the movements of different assets and consequently a high degree of correlation. Within this risk-on–risk-off framework, the nuances between different assets have disappeared, which makes diversification extremely difficult. From 2009 to the start of 2010, the degree of correlation between markets progressively increased until the beginning of 2010, when most markets were highly correlated. Relative value is extremely difficult to identify, and finding uncorrelated assets is extremely difficult. Correlations between asset classes appear to be on a long-term upward trend, which may reflect the growing internationalization of financial markets, the improvements in information technology, and the spectacular development of the Exchange Traded Funds (ETF) which mechanically reinforce this phenomenon. As a consequence, we should not expect correlations to fall back to levels seen in the mid-2000s. Correlations rise during most, but not all, crisis periods and fall back once the crisis has passed. The rise in correlations associated with the credit crisis which started in 2007 is, of course, the most dramatic and has the longest duration. Correlations also tend to rise during weak macroeconomic conditions, and they fall back when growth is stronger. High correlations tend to be associated with high levels of volatility, and vice versa. However, correlations have stayed high in recent months despite declines in volatility. This suggests that a structural change could be taking place in markets.

It is in this challenging context that Ruey S. Tsay and Steve Quigley asked me if I would be interested in writing a handbook on market risk. I have to say that I was honored that they thought about me for such a book, but I also felt immediately the difficulties I would face in writing on such a hot topic because we had not yet found all the solutions to cope with all the lessons learned from this financial crisis. I have to admit that it did not take a long time for me to accept this challenge, and I hope that this book will meet their expectations.

The goal of this handbook on market risk is to provide a one-stop source that investors, whether institutional or retail investors, senior executives of financial institutions (banks and asset management firms), board directors, students, and practitioners can use to gain the necessary knowledge about tackling market risk in this difficult period. If there is only one lesson to learn from this financial crisis is that market risk needs to be managed in a professional manner and in a holistic approach. Holistic market risk management is the sole way that financial institutions and asset management firms will protect their assets and ensure a sustainable development. Failure in market risk management will have dramatic consequences. I also have to mention that this book is not a pure quant book because I wanted to introduce the key concepts for each selected topic. To target a larger audience, I also tried to make it as simple as possible so that every reader can get a reasonable understanding. Pure quant books exist for most of the topics I tried to explain in this handbook. Last but not least, I also have to point out that market risk is a very broad subject, especially since the beginning of the recent financial crisis. Therefore I also had to be selective because it was not possible to mention everything in a single book. I voluntarily tried to focus on key topics as raised by the current market situation. The other reason for being selective was the size limitation for this handbook.

It is difficult to write about market risk without writing about risk management and I would anticipate that this is also expected by the readers. Market risk is intimately linked with risk management. Recent market risk events have pushed the limits of traditional risk management practices. One main difficulty when dealing with risk is to define the concept of risk. Risk is often related to the occurrence of an event that one cannot predict which has a significant impact on the bank's balance sheet or on a portfolio for an asset management firm. Making an investment is a sacrifice of a certain and immediate advantage in the hope of uncertain future benefits. Thus, we can say the risk is exposure to uncertainty. The banking industry is exposed to financial risk, and its primary objective should be to control this uncertainty as much as they can in relationship with a risk tolerance. The evolution of risk management is a relatively new function in banks as well in asset management firms. In order to understand its evolution, it is essential to have some historical landmarks: The 1930s marked the beginning of the empirical research on the price of assets with the creation of the Cowles Commission for Research in Economics[2] in 1932 and the journal *Econometrica* by Joseph Schumpeter in 1933. These researches focus more specifically on price formation, market efficiency, and detection of profitable strategies (i.e., on the anticipation of shares price). It was only in the 1950s that researchers (Markowitz, Lintner, Sharpe, etc.) undertake substantial work on the risk side. These lead to the modern portfolio theory choice based on the famous CAPM (Capital Asset Pricing Model) and APT (Arbitrage Pricing Theory) models. In 1973 the famous Black–Scholes formula was introduced to value a

[2]http://cowles.econ.yale.edu/

European option. This can be considered as the starting point to the intensive development of the research on valuation (pricing) of financial derivatives, whose growth will be exponential. The Basel Capital Accord of 1988 also raises a new vision of risk being more regulatory risk. This was a significant development, and measuring market risk became formalized and required for banks. The publication in 1994 by JP Morgan RiskMetrics methodology allows a very wide dissemination of the Value-at-Risk method (VaR) among both academics and professionals.

The evolution of the prudential regulations on the control of financial risks is a direct consequence of the various financial crises and their impact on their solvency. During important financial crises (e.g., Mexican crisis, Russian crisis, Asian crisis, and more recently the 2008 Credit Crisis), the establishment of a lender of last resort is very expensive to prevent a systemic crisis as the world has just realized. Similarly, the failure of one financial institution can lead to a contagion to other financial institutions because of the financial panic as happened with the collapse of Lehman Brothers.[3] The implementation of risk regulation aims initially to limit systemic risk, and then to avoid individual failures of financial institutions. On the asset management side, the implementation of risk regulations aims to protect investors against too much high risk-taking. Recently and as a consequence of the 2007 financial crisis, the European regulator also aimed to regulate alternative management to limit systemic risk with the next coming AIFM Directive.[4] Prudential regulation has considerably evolved in recent years under the leadership of the work of the Basel Committee. Even if it has no decision-making authority, its recommendations are taken up by different authorities in different countries. For example, the concept of value-at-risk was also transposed into the requirements for measuring the global exposure of any UCITS fund since the UCITS III Directives (2001). UCITS stands for Undertaking for Collective Investment in Transferable Securities. They usually target retail investors as opposed to alternative investments. The equivalent type of investments in the United States is called "Mutual Funds."

Risks are manifold and multidimensional. We need to list them and define them as best as we can if we want to measure, follow, and monitor. Market risk is a particular category of risk.

Credit risk is the risk of not being repaid at maturity of the credit risk is the risk inherent in banking. Credit risk is also, in a wider and more nuanced way that degradation of a borrower's financial situation. This is a critical risk because the failure of a small number of major customers can be sufficient to put a facility in serious trouble. The risk of credit depends on:

- The nature of credit.
- The credit time horizon, medium- and long-term loans are considered more risky that short-term loans.

[3]Lehman Brothers filed for Chapter 11 bankruptcy protection on September 15, 2008.

[4]The Alternative Investment Fund Managers Directive is a European Union Directive that will put hedge funds and private equity funds under the supervision of an EU regulatory body.

Credit risk is comprised of default risk, credit spread risk, and downgrade risk. Each can have a negative impact on the value of a debt security.

Default risk is the risk that the issuer will not be able to pay the obligation, either on time or at all.

Credit spread risk is the risk that there will be an increase in the difference between the interest rate of an issuer's bond and the interest rate of a bond that is considered to have little associated risk (such as government guaranteed bond or treasury bill). The difference between these interest rates is the so-called "credit spread." Corporate bonds are sensitive to movements in credit spreads, which reflect changes in market perceptions of the possibility of defaults. Credit spread changes are approximately log normally distributed.

Downgrade risk is the risk that a specialized credit rating agency, such as Standard & Poor's, Moody's Investors Services, and so on, will reduce the credit rating of an issuer's securities. Downgrades in credit rating will decrease the value of those debt securities.

Operational risks or technical risks are due to a bad management and management systems. They are subject to organizational and logistical measures—for examples, systems of transfer of means of payment, back-office system, and so on. If the documentation on transactions, on their contractual clauses, and on the associated guarantees is not well known or recorded, risk measures are wrong. If the back office does not work correctly, the reliability of operations, delays, and accounting will directly face the consequences. Operational risks include the risk of disaster, the risk of fraud, processing risk, settlement risk, technological risk, and legal risk.

Liquidity risk is defined as the risk that the credit institution cannot fulfill, under normal conditions, its obligations as they come due. The liquidity risk is considered to be a major risk, but it is the subject of various meanings: the extreme illiquidity, safety that provide liquid assets, or the ability to raise capital at a "normal" cost or ability to refinance on the markets or with the Central Banks. A situation of extreme illiquidity causes the bankruptcy of an institution. In this sense, liquidity risk can be fatal. On the portfolio management side, liquidity risk is the ability of the fund to repay any investors who want to redeem from the fund. Therefore, the portfolio has to be liquid enough if the manager has to sell some assets to get the proceeds of cash to face any redemption. Funds that deal with retail investors have to offer daily liquidity. For alternative funds the situation may vary because some strategies invest in illiquid assets, which makes those strategies also more risky for investors.

Market risk refers to the risk of losses in the bank's trading book due to changes in equity prices, interest rates, credit spreads, foreign-exchange rates, commodity prices, and other indicators whose values are set in a public market. This definition is mainly used for the banking industry. In general, the market risk is the potential loss that will be incurred by investors following changes on the market. The main factors of market risk are, among others:

- Change in equity prices
- Change in interests rates

- Changes in foreign exchange rates
- Changes in commodity prices

From an asset management perspective, market risk is the risk that a stock will drop because some event, such as a hike in interest rates, may cause the stock market as a whole to fall. Market risk is common to all securities of the same class. For example, all stocks always have the same market risk. The risk cannot be eliminated by diversification. Market risk is also known as systematic risk. Market risk is the risk that investments will lose money based on the daily fluctuations of the market. Bond market risk results from fluctuations in interest. Stock prices, on the other hand, are influenced by factors ranging from company performance to economic factors to political news and events of national importance.

How we measure market risk will depend on a number of variables, which depend on the financial instrument types, on the institution culture, on how regulations require us to measure and report market risk, and so on. To manage market risk, banks deploy a number of highly sophisticated mathematical and statistical techniques. Chief among these is value-at-risk (VaR) analysis, which over the past 15 years has become established as the industry and regulatory standard in measuring market risk. Despite these accomplishments, VaR and other risk models have continually come up short. The 1998 crisis at Long-Term Capital Management demonstrated the limitations of risk modeling. In the violent market upheavals of 2007–2008, many banks reported more than thirty days when losses exceeded VaR, a span in which 3 to 5 such days would be the norm. In 2011, just before the European sovereign crisis got under way, many banks' risk models treated eurozone government bonds as virtually risk-free.

The demands placed on VaR and other similar techniques have grown tremendously, driven by new products such as correlation trading, multi-asset options, power-reverse dual currency swaps, swaps whose notional value amortizes unpredictably, and dozens of other such innovations. To keep up, the tools have evolved. For example, the number of risk factors required to price the trading book at a global institution has now grown to several thousand, and sometimes as many as 10,000. Valuation models have become increasingly complex. And most banks are now in the process of integrating new stress-testing analytics that can anticipate a broad spectrum of macroeconomic changes.

In order to meet the objective of this publication, the handbook has been divided into 14 chapters.

Chapter 1 introduces the concept of financial markets and introduces the main financial markets: the money market, the capital market, the stock market, the futures and options market, the foreign exchange market, and the commodity market.

Chapter 2 is about the efficient market theory, which is probably the most debated theory ever since financial markets came into existence. This chapter will start by defining the efficient market theory and explaining the different type of forms this theory can have. We will also review the criticisms regarding this theory. If this theory is true, then how is it possible to beat the markets? Thus, we will also discuss the different methods that managers use to beat the market—mainly the fundamental and technical methods.

Chapter 3 is about return and volatility estimates. We will explain these two important concepts. This is followed by an explanation of different techniques to capture, measure, and monitor the volatility and how best volatility can be forecasted.

Chapter 4 studies the fundamental concepts of diversification benefits, the efficient frontier, and the correlation. Correlations have been under the spotlight since the beginning of the 2008 financial crisis, and therefore we focus on correlation estimates and assess how these methods can help in improving our market risk practices.

Chapter 5 deals with two important founding theories before introducing the fundamental multifactors in the next chapter. These two important theories are the Capital Asset Pricing Model, commonly referred to as the CAPM, and the Arbitrage Pricing Theory, mostly known as APT. This will allow us to introduce a key concept for market risk: beta.

Chapter 6 is devoted to the equity fundamental multifactors model. In order to illustrate our purpose, we use a fundamental risk model called Axioma to go through all the components of such a model. We do believe that companies will benefit when using a multifactors model to measure their market risk.

Chapter 7 provides a historical approach that helps to understand how we tackled the problematic links with market risk. It is mainly due to the improvements made in the field of mathematics and statistics of course, but also because of some important market events. Market events were an important catalyst for improving regulations but also market risk practices. This will guide us until the creation of the value-at-risk (VaR), which became so popular (and not at the same time because of its supposed failure during the 2008 financial crisis) among market participants. The different methods to calculate the VaR are also presented and explained.

Chapter 8 deals with financial derivatives instruments as a result of the fantastic development over the last 20 years in creating new instruments. This chapter presents and introduces the most commonly used derivatives for hedging or investment purposes and their related risks, with a particular focus on Options. We also explain how exposure to these instruments is calculated using the commitment approach.

Chapter 9 is about fixed income and interest rate risk. In this chapter we review the basics of bond pricing as well as the main risk indicator when holding a bond and how best to determine hedging ratios.

As mentioned at the beginning of this introduction, liquidity risk was not extensively managed prior the 2008 financial crisis. Regulators around the world have therefore dedicated a lot of energy to make sure that such a risk will be properly managed in the future. Therefore Chapter 10 takes a more strategic view about liquidity risk and introduces some of the traditional methods to monitor this risk and also focus on innovative approach such as the liquidity-at-risk.

Chapter 11 looks at the active management versus the passive management. Alternatives such as hedge funds were also under the spotlight during the 2008 financial crisis because many of them have not delivered the expected return to their investors but also failed to exhibit uncorrelated return with the markets because they were supposed to target alpha. We will present some of the key metrics used when dealing with alternatives without being completely exhaustive, and this chapter could have been a book topic on its own.

Chapter 12 is about stress testing and back testing. Deficient stress testing was identified as one of a number of failures that exacerbated the recent financial crisis. The regulators and internal management at financial institutions have strengthened stress testing regime. In this chapter we emphasize the quality of a firm's stress testing frameworks involving scrutiny and assessment of a stress testing framework against the regulators' expectations and how a stronger stress testing framework can provide deeper insight into portfolio performance and identify uplifts to capital planning buffers. We also introduce the different stress tests methods. The concept of back testing is also explained, and different approaches are proposed.

Chapter 13 introduces Basel II/III, which was released in December 2010 and is the third in the series of Basel Accords. These accords deal with risk management aspects for the banking sector. Basel III is the global regulatory standard (agreed upon by the members of the Basel Committee on Banking Supervision) on bank capital adequacy, stress testing, and market liquidity risk. (Basel I and Basel II are the earlier versions of the same and were less stringent). In this chapter we introduce what Basel II/III is all about, the objectives of these measures, the key requirements, and the main changes between Basel II and Basel III.

Finally, concluding remarks are presented in Chapter 14.

CHAPTER ONE

Introduction to Financial Markets

Markets are constantly in a state of uncertainty and flux and money is made by discounting the obvious and betting on the unexpected.

—George Soros

Traditionally, a market is a place where people go to buy or sell things to meet their needs. Financial markets are very similar except that we find stocks, bonds, and other things. A financial market is a market in which financial assets are traded. In addition to enabling exchange of previously issued financial assets, financial markets facilitate borrowing and lending by facilitating the sale by newly issued financial assets. Examples of financial markets include the New York Stock Exchange (resale of previously issued stock shares), the U.S. government bond market (resale of previously issued bonds), and the U.S. Treasury bills auction (sales of newly issued T-bills). A *financial institution* is an institution whose primary source of profits is through financial asset transactions. Examples of such financial institutions include discount brokers, banks, insurance companies, and complex multifunction financial institutions.

Traditionally, financial markets serve six basic functions. These functions are briefly listed below:

- *Borrowing and Lending.* Financial markets permit the transfer of funds (purchasing power) from one agent to another for either investment or consumption purposes. Borrowers can be either government or companies. Borrowers are driven by costs when accessing financial markets where Investors (institutional or non-institutional investors) are looking for return and profit. Financial markets bring them together.
- *Price Determination.* Financial markets provide vehicles by which prices are set both for newly issued financial assets and for the existing stock of financial assets. An asset is any item of value that can be owned. A financial instrument is an asset that represents a legal agreement. There are numerous

Handbook of Market Risk, First Edition. Christian Szylar.

financial instruments—for example, stocks, bonds, T-bills, personal loans, futures, forwards, options, swaps, and so on. An asset class is a group/ classification of financial instruments that share similar characteristics—for example, equity-based assets, debt-based assets, and cash-based assets (money market, etc.).

- *Information Aggregation and Coordination.* Financial markets act as collectors and aggregators of information about financial asset values and the flow of funds from lenders to borrowers.
- *Risk Sharing.* Financial markets allow a transfer of risk from those who undertake investments to those who provide funds for those investments.
- *Liquidity.* Financial markets provide the holders of financial assets with a chance to resell or liquidate these assets.
- *Efficiency.* Financial markets reduce transaction costs and information costs.

In attempting to characterize the way financial markets operate, one must consider both the various types of financial institutions that participate in such markets and the various ways in which these markets are structured (Figure 1.1). Thus, a financial market is a marketplace in which financial instruments are traded.

There are four admitted primary financial markets, but we will see that there are also other important markets:

- The stock (equities) market
- The bond (fixed-interest) market

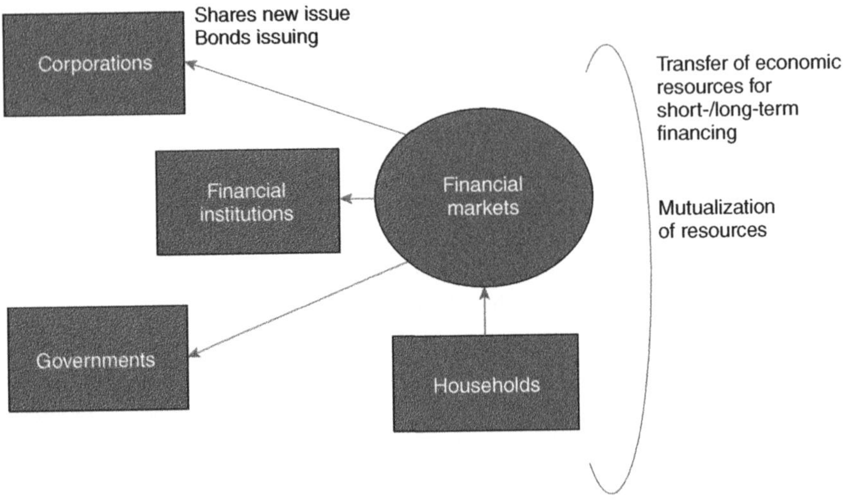

FIGURE 1.1 The financial markets.

- The derivatives market (futures, options, etc.)
- The foreign exchange market

Many companies either occasionally or regularly must raise money for either (a) operations purposes such as covering payroll, adjusting inventory level, or managing any other operating expenses or (b) expansion purposes such as purchasing real estate (land, buildings, factories, etc.), purchasing equipment (e.g., an airline company wants to buy some additional aircrafts), purchasing raw materials, or hiring new employees. How can companies raise money?

In the area of debt financing, a company may borrow some money from an outside source with the promise to repay the principal and interest. Thus they can borrow money either from a bank or from issue such as bonds, bills, or notes. Borrowing money is not necessarily a bad decision, because debt is also a form of leverage and is a common and often cost-effective method of raising money. Corporate balance sheets of all companies, even the healthiest ones, include some level of debt. Another form of corporate financing is equity financing. A company sells a portion of itself to an outside source. Actually, it is selling shares of the company. A share is a unit of ownership in a company. The company decides how many shares to authorize when it incorporates. Usually, some of the authorized shares are issued to the founders, and some shares are retained by the corporation.

Here is an easy example to understand:

Example. Let's imagine that a new corporation is formed. This corporation authorizes 2,000,000 shares of stock. If the total combined value of the corporation's asset is $200,000, then how much is each share of the company worth? This is not complex to calculate, and the following formula answers that question.

$$\text{Company}_{\text{share value}} = \frac{200{,}000}{2{,}000{,}000 \text{ shares}} = \$0.10 \text{ per share}$$

Each of these markets is highly regulated (even if for some individuals they are never enough!). Regulation of the U.S. financial markets is the responsibility of the U.S. Securities and Exchange Commission, the SEC.[1]

The SEC was formed during the Great Depression after the stock market crash of 1929. It has been created by the Securities Exchange Act of 1934. It is headquartered in Washington, D.C. and currently employs approximately 4000 people. The original purpose if the SEC is to regulate the stock market and prevent corporate abuses relating to the reporting and sale of securities. Trust is the backbone for all financial markets. The SEC was given the power to license and regulate stock exchanges, companies that issue stock, stockbrokers, and dealers.

[1]http://www.sec.gov/

Currently, the SEC is in charge for overseeing eight major laws that govern the securities industry:

- Securities Act of 1933
- Securities Exchange Act of 1934
- Trust Indenture Act of 1939
- Investment Company Act of 1940
- Investment Advisers Act of 1940
- Sarbanes–Oxley Act of 2002
- Credit Rating Agency Reform Act of 2006
- Dodd–Frank Wall Street Reform and Consumer Protection Act of 2010 as a result of the credit and financial crisis[2]

The SEC can bring civil enforcement actions against individuals or companies who are alleged to have committed fraud, engaged in insider trading, or violated any other securities law.

In Europe this task is spread among national regulators and a pan-European authority called ESMA.[3]

1.1 The Money Market

The term *money market* refers to the network of corporations, financial institutions, professional investors, and governments that deal with the flow of short-term capital. The money market is for transactions up to one year. It is an over-the-counter market. When a professional requires cash for a short period, when a bank wishes to invest money for a while, when a government needs to meet its payroll, and so forth, a short-term liquidity transaction occurs in the money market.

The money markets have expanded significantly in recent years because of the general outflows of money from the banking industry, a process referred to as *disintermediation*. Financial deregulation has caused banks to lose market share in both deposit gathering and lending. Consequently, market forces rather than regulators determine interest rates. However, it has to be noted that central bank's intervention in short-term rates may have their undoubted impact on the markets.

There are numerous types of short-term instruments apart from plain deposits and loans.

[2]There are many pieces to it, and some are overseen by the Fed, Treasury, FSOC, FinCen, the SEC, and the CFTC. However, the parts most well known (and applicable to asset management) relate to the pieces under the authority of the SEC and CFTC.

[3]http://www.esma.europa.eu/

Deposits and Loans. For deposits and loans, quotes are given with bid[4] and offer rates—for example, 3.25–3.35 for a given period, which means that the bank is inviting you to place money at 3.25 less its margin and will allow you to borrow at 3.35 plus its margin.

Periods are standard, and the computation of interest is done on an exact day count basis. The computation of interest is done in the eurozone on a basis of 360 days.

Commercial Paper. It is a short-term debt obligation of a private-sector company or government-sponsored corporation. In most cases, the paper has a lifetime between 3 and 9 months.

Bankers' Acceptances. A promissory note is issued by a nonfinancial company to a bank in return for a loan. The bank resells the note in the money market at a discount and guarantees payment. Acceptances usually have a maturity of less than six months.

Treasury Bills (T-Bills). These are securities with a maturity of one year or less, issued by national governments. Treasury bills issued by an AAA country are generally considered the safest of all possible investment until now. Those securities account for a larger share of the money market trading than any other type of instrument.

Certificate of Deposit (CD). CDs are negotiable interest-bearing deposits that cannot be withdrawn without penalty before a specific date.

Repurchase Agreements (Repos). Repos play a critical role in the money markets. A repo is a combination of two transactions. In the first transaction, a security dealer sells securities it owns to an investor, agreeing to repurchase the securities at a specified higher price at a future date. In the second transaction, days or months later, the repo is unwound as the dealer buys back the securities from the investor. The amount the investor lends is less than the market value of the securities in order to ensure that there is sufficient collateral if the value of the securities should fall before the dealer repurchases them. For the investor the repo offers a profitable short-term use for unneeded cash.

1.2 The Capital Market

The capital market comprises transactions beyond one year.

[4] The bid rate is the rate a bank is willing to pay to attract a deposit from another bank.

1.2.1 THE BOND MARKET

The predominant instrument for raising long-term capital is bond. A bond is an interest-bearing security mainly issued by governmental entities or large companies. An alternative to issuing shares or taking out a bank loan, bonds are a further way to raise capital. A bond is issued in the primary market. The bond market is a part of the capital market. It is divided in two different types known as the primary bond market and the secondary bond market. The primary bond market is also referred to as debt market, credit market, and fixed income market.

In the primary bond market, the companies or the government will offer the new bonds and the fund generated through the process will go to the issuer of the bond. The total size of the global bond market is about $100 trillion. The United States shares a major portion of the global bond market revenue.

There is a certain process of offering these bonds for the first time in the primary bond market. The process of offering bonds to the public is similar to the offering of the stock. For the purpose of offering bonds in the primary market, a company or a firm needs the assistance of an investment bank. The investment bank provides all the necessary experience and expertise for the purpose. The investment bank provides its suggestions regarding the creation of the issue.

At the same time, the bank also provides an estimate of the expected yield from the issue. The maturity period of the bond is also suggested by these banks. The bank also helps in selling the bonds in the primary bond market. At the same time, the bank may also purchase the whole issue through firm commitment underwriting.

For the marketing of the new issue in the primary bond market, the investment bank uses its own network. The bank forms a syndicate—or, at certain times, forms a selling group—to sell the bonds to the investors through the primary bond market. The institutional investors or the individual investors lend their money to the particular company through these bonds. Once these are purchased from the primary bond market, these can be further traded in the secondary bond market.

These bonds provide a fixed income source to the investor. At the same time, the offering companies or the government will also get the very necessary money for their projects.

The bond generates a series of periodic interest payments, called coupons. A bond's yield is the interest rate (or coupon) paid on the bond, divided by the bond's market price. Bonds may be issued for a period of up to 30 years, as in the United States. A bond is considered to be a long-term bond if it is issued for a period of over 10 years. Years ago, Great Britain issued perpetual bonds—that is, without final maturity.

The capital market is subject to the same laws of perception, demand, offer, and choices as the money market, even more so because of the time element. The clearest illustration of this is in long-term bonds, whose value decreases substantially with increasing inflation—that is, increasing interest rates. Bear in mind that there is a correlation between interest rates and inflation rates.

As an instrument, bonds come in all sorts of versions. The capital market is a sophisticated market in which to raise long-term money. Both governments and corporations have tapped the market significantly, to the tune of trillions of euros. Imagination, in the field of issuance of types of bonds, is only limited by the mathematics.

Few of the millions of daily capital-market transactions involve the issuer of the security. Most trades are in the secondary markets, between investors who have bought the securities and other investors who want to buy them—in contrast to money markets, where short-term capital is raised or for pure speculation purposes.

Bonds are generally regarded as a lower risk investment. Government bonds, in particular, are highly unlikely to miss their promised payments. Corporate bonds issued by the blue chip "investment grade" companies are also unlikely to default; this might not be the case with high-yield "junk" bonds issued by firms with less healthy financials.

How are bond prices usually determined?

Assume that you are the holder of a bond but wish to sell it; you would certainly like to obtain as high a price as possible whereas the purchaser would like to pay as little as possible. How then are prices fixed? The easy answer at this stage would be *by demand and offer*. However, there is an additional concept: the present value concept. It is a key concept in finance. Let us take some time to have a look at it without developing too much on this, considering that this concept has already been largely explained in many manuals and books dealing with basic in finance and investing.

1.2.1.1 The Present Value Concept. Let us assume that you are purchasing a 10-year bond. You are only going to do this if you recover your 100 units plus something more called a coupon (profit). Let us assume that you get 5 units per annum out of this investment. That would mean that during the period of 10 years ahead, you get 10 times 5 units, plus, at the end of the ten years, you get your money back.

However, is the last payment of 5 units worth as much as the first payment of 5 units? Will the last 5 units allow you to purchase the same amount of goods as the first five units? Those 5 units have a different purchasing power. What will be the purchasing power of the 100 units you get back 10 years from now? The difference in purchasing power is due to inflation, which generally erodes the purchasing power of money. Money loses its value in an impressive way. Charlie Chaplin's film *Modern Times* in 1936 was considered expensive, with a cost of USD 1,500,000, whereas James Cameron's *Titanic* cost USD 1,000,000 per minute!

Let us then summarize this: In an inflationary environment, the present value of 5 units to be received in one year is smaller than 5 units now. In that type of environment a monetary unit of today is worth more than a monetary unit of tomorrow. A monetary unit of today can be invested and start producing income immediately. The level of income will be linked to the level of inflation. This is one of the basic principles of finance.

Example. Suppose that we place 100,000 for one year at 5% a year.

We all know that we will have 105,000 at the end of the year.

The PV (present value) is 100,000 and the FV (future value) in this case is 105,000.

Put this into an equation:

$$105{,}000 = 100{,}000 + 5\% \text{ of } 100{,}000$$

or

$$105{,}000 = 100{,}000 + 100{,}000 * 0.05$$

or, by isolating 100,000,

$$105{,}000 = 100{,}000(1 + 0.05)$$

$$105{,}000 = 100{,}000(1.05)$$

Here 105,000 represents the future value of 100,000 with an interest rate of 5% during one year.

What is the simple interest rate formula? The discount formula is derived from the above formula by dividing both parts of the equation by (1 + 0.05).

Let us now pose the following question:

What is the present value of 105,000, which will be paid out to us in a year's time, assuming a 5% interest (discount) rate?

Computing is easy. By employing the reverse interest formula—that is, the discount formula—we have

$$105{,}000 * \frac{1}{1 + 0.05} \quad \text{or} \quad 105{,}000 * \frac{1}{1.05} = 100{,}000$$

Assuming now that we place the same amount at the same interest rate for one more year (i.e., for two years), determine the future value?

For the first year, one calculates this as follows using simple interest rate computation:

$$100{,}000 * 1.05 = 105{,}000$$

For the second year, one calculates this as follows:

$$105{,}000 * (1.05) = 110{,}250$$

By replacing 105,000 by 100,000 (1.05), one gets 100,000 * (1.05)*(1.05)—that is,

$$100{,}000 * (1.05)^2 = 110{,}250$$

For an investment with a compounded interest rate, it is sufficient to take the initial amount being invested and then multiply it by the given interest rate raised to the power which represents the number of years during which the amount is placed.

The future value of 100,000 bearing interest at 5% during 2 years is 110,250. The present value of 110,250, which we will receive in 2 years' time, with a discount rate of 5% is 100,000; the formula is $110,250 * 1/(1+0.05)^2$.

Thus, the present value of a delayed payoff may be found by multiplying the payoff by a discount factor. If C1 denotes the expected payoff at a period 1 (one year hence), then the present value is

$$\text{Present value (PV)} = \text{C1} \times \text{Discount factor}$$

Let us see how the simple concepts of present and future value are useful with regard to our understanding of bonds.

Assuming that an investor has a 3-year bond with a value of 100,000 (called the face value), providing us with 10,000 a year, our successive cash flows would be

10,000 at the end of the first year
10,000 at the end of the second year
10,000 at the end of the third year + the initial capital of 100,000 = 110,000

We know that 10,000 in 1 year's time will not have the same value as 10,000 today, and even less so 3 years from now. If we do not want to compare unequal elements, it is absolutely necessary to put all these amounts on the same basis—that is, the present value (PV). Once we have done that, all these amounts can be added as they have been put on the same basis. It is thus necessary to discount these amounts to obtain their present value.

The discount rate should at least represent the inflation rate, or rather our perception of the inflation rate during the lifetime of the bond. Let us say, in this case, that it is 7%.

The future cash flows discounted at 7% are as follows:

PV(C1): $10{,}000 \times 1/1.07 = 9{,}346$
PV(C2): $10{,}000 \times 1/1.07^2 = 8{,}734$
PV(C3): $(10{,}000 + 100{,}000) \times 1/1.07^3 = 89{,}793$

Therefore, the total present value is:

$$9346 + 8730 + 89{,}760 = 107{,}836$$

which is definitely less than 130,000. This bond will be quoted at 107.83% of the par value—that is, its price at the issuance.

$$\frac{10{,}000}{1.07}+\frac{10{,}000}{(1.07)^2}+\frac{10{,}000}{(1.07)^3}+\frac{100{,}000}{(1.07)^3}$$

As a result of this way of computing bond prices, one will notice the following characteristics of bonds:

An increase in the interest rates (and/or inflation) will result in decreasing bond prices. Long-term bonds are more sensitive to interest rate fluctuations than short-term bonds. Bonds with high-interest-bearing coupons are less sensitive than bonds with low-interest-bearing coupons.

1.2.1.2 Types of Bonds. Since the beginning of the 1980s, so many new versions of bonds have been issued—even more so than shares—which makes it virtually almost impossible to draw up an exhaustive list. Some versions are much more widespread than others.

Fixed Rate Bonds. The traditional fixed-rate bonds can be divided into two types of bonds dependent upon the selected amortization formula. The simplest structure is the entire amortization at the end of the lifetime of the obligation. It is the simplest structure and easiest to manage for the issuer. However, it is usually not in line with the cash flow of the issuer. Certain issuers prefer an amortization by constant annual installments. Each payment includes interest due and the repayment of a fraction of the principal. Bonds are reimbursed as they are selected on the basis of a lottery. This represents a definite risk for the bearer. A similar method consists of amortization per equal series. Each year the same quantity of bonds is being repaid.

Variable Maturity Bonds. The simplest version of a bond with a variable maturity is a bond with an extendable maturity. The bearers may require the extension of the maturity date to a later date when the original maturity date has been reached.

Bonds with a Subscription Certificate. Bonds with a subscription certificate are bonds to which a subscription right is attached as of the issuance of the loan. This right constitutes in itself a transferable security and is quoted separately. This right gives to its holder the right to subscribe, at a predetermined date and at a predetermined price, to a new issue of bonds or shares.

Zero Coupon Bonds. This type of bond only generates two flows of funds, one at the issuance and one at the maturity when principal and interest are repaid in one single transaction. The bonds with a zero coupon offer the advantage that the risk related to the reinvestment of the coupons has been eliminated. The subscriber knows, as of the issuance, what the exact actualized yield will be.

Therefore, the rate of interest is lower than that of a traditional bond issued at the same time. The issuer benefits from the fact that interest can be carried forward until the maturity date.

Bonds with Variable or Revisable Rates. The interest rate risk incurred, throughout the lifetime of the bond, by the issuer (if the interest rate drops) and by the investor (if the interest rate rises) has been partially neutralized by the introduction of a clause allowing for a periodical adjustment of the interest rate. Obviously, one observes, in that case, a commonly agreed-upon reference date. Thus, some bonds have a market interest rate as reference, like the "London inter-bank offered rate" (LIBOR) or the rate for other bonds such as the 10-year U.S. government bond.

Indexed Linked Bonds. The principal is repayable as a function of a well-specified reference, unlike the bonds with variable or revisable interest rates. This is a bond in which payment of income on the principal is related to a specific price index—often the Consumer Price Index. This feature provides protection to investors by shielding them from changes in the underlying index. The bond's cash flows are adjusted to ensure that the holder of the bond receives a known real rate of return.

This type of bond is valuable to investors because the real value of the bond is known from purchase and the risk involved with uncertainty is eliminated. These bonds are also less volatile than nominal bonds and they help investors to maintain their purchasing power. For example, assume that you purchase a regular bond with a nominal return of 4%. If inflation is 3%, you will actually only receive 1% in real terms. On the other hand, if you buy an index-linked bond, your cash flow will be adjusted to changes in inflation and you will still receive the full 4% in returns.

Convertible Bonds. The convertible bond offers the bearer, during a predetermined period and at his request, the opportunity to convert the bond into a previously agreed-upon, number of shares of the issuer. The conversion right is not quoted separately but is included in the price of the bond. The bearer pays for this privilege by accepting a lower rate of return for the bond. Convertible bonds combine the features of bonds and stocks in one instrument. It is a bond that gives the holder the right to "convert" or exchange the par amount of the bond for common shares of the issuer at some fixed ratio during a particular period. As bonds, they have some characteristics of fixed-income securities. Their conversion feature also gives them features of equity securities.

A convertible bond is a security, typically ranging between 25 and 30 years in term, that gives its' owner the right to acquire the issuers common stock directly from the issuer rather than purchasing it in the open market. The terms under which this exchange can occur are detailed out in the bond indenture. The optionality component of this security, which allows for the bond holder to convert debt into equity, results in the bond holder receiving lower yields as compared to nonconvertible securities.

Typically, convertible bonds will be classified as subordinated debt and therefore more risky than unsubordinated debt. Subordinated debt holders are lower on the totem pole as far as principal repayment during times of distress for the issuer. In the event of bankruptcy, "senior" bond holders will be paid their credit balance before subordinated debt holders.

Convertible Bond Structure. A convertible bond has a few key additional features in structure as compared to a typical bond:

Conversion Price. Price paid per share to acquire the common stock of the issuer

Conversion Ratio. This ratio determines the number of shares the bond holder will receive per bond they exchange. The formula for the conversion ratio is: par value of convertible security divided by conversion price.

Parity. Conversion parity is the point at which a profit, or loss, would be made at conversion. Basically, parity exists when the conversion ratio at issuance is equal to the convertible security price divided by the market value of the stock. When the price of the stock increases above the conversion parity price, the convertible security would be subject to price changes relative to the movements of the stock. When this condition exists, stock price appreciation will be reflected in the price of the bond which will allow the bond holder to sell the convertible security for a profit rather than performing a conversion and then selling the stock for a gain.

Conversion Premium. The conversion premium measures the spread between the conversion price and the current market value in percent. For example, if a stock is currently trading at $50 per share and the bond conversion price is $60, the bond would be said to be trading with a 20% conversion premium.

Advantages and Disadvantages to Issuers. Convertible securities tend to be offered by issuers as a means to achieve lower fixed costs for borrowing. Issuers save an average of 2% on the yield that they give their convertible bond holders. For a start-up firm, this is especially helpful; rather than issuing common stock at a 15% to 20% discount to market value on IPO, firms can issue convertible securities which offer lower upfront yields to their borrowers and a conversion premium of 20% to 30% above market value at that time.

Secondly, through the issuance of convertible debt, issuers avoid dilution of their common shares and, therefore, higher stock prices for their shareholders. The analysis would need to be done for the issuer to understand if the interest expense of the convertible debt issuance would be less than the cost of diluting the common stock. For start-up companies with lower revenues, this is most likely the case.

Issuers may even add their own call protection feature into the bond, allowing them to call the bond back in the case that the company starts to increase their earnings, thereby increasing the stock and the price of the bond. The call feature would allow the issuer to force the bond holder to convert their bonds at a lower price.

For example, suppose the indenture stated that the convertible bond could be exchanged for 10 shares of common stock and also assume that the issuer built in a call provision that would allow them to call the bond away at a bond price of 110. When the bond was issued, the stock was trading at $100/share. After a few years of rapid growth, the earnings per share increased dramatically and propelled the stock much higher to $120 per share, which also moved the bond price to 120. In this scenario, the issuer would be able to make the bond holder sell the bond back at 110, or $1100 per bond. The value of the conversion is now $1200. Remember, the issuer uses convertibles rather than equity in order to avoid equity dilution, which lowers stock price. In this case, the issuer has borrowed funds at a lowered rate, avoided equity dilution, and forced the bond holder to sell the bond at a discount to market. If equity needs to be raised, it can now be done at a higher price.

One key disadvantage to the issuer of a convertible exists if the stock price increases so rapidly that the conversion takes place in a relatively short amount of time. This indicates that the company did not do a good job of valuing themselves; however, it is a win–win for both parties nonetheless. A second, more negative scenario exists when the common stock actually moves lower after issuance. In this case, the bond holder will not convert to equity as the issuer had hoped.

Advantages and Disadvantages to Convertible Investors. Convertible bonds are a safer investment than buying common stock but can provide the stock-like returns. They are less volatile than stocks, and their value can only fall to a price where the yield would be equal to that of a nonconvertible bond of the same terms. They offer strong downside protection in a bear market, but also allow the investor to take part in the profits as a stock moves higher.

Convertibles can be disadvantageous in the sense that the bond holder will be receiving substantially lower yield to maturity in comparison to the nonconvertible equivalent. This is only a concern when the issuer's equity does not achieve the upward price projections that would make taking the lower yield speculation worthwhile.

Additionally, the ability for speculation is greatly reduced when a call provision is attached to the convertible bond. This limits the upside and will force the bond holder to give up their bond at a discount to market.

Convertible bonds provide the investor with a vehicle that has lower risk and lower yields, yet allow the investor to take advantage of a higher stock price. Upfront research should be done, however, to understand if the security will work for you. Remember, a convertible sells at a premium to the value of the stock. The bond holder is making a tradeoff: lower yields upfront for anticipated gains in the stock price. If those gains are not achieved, the bond holder will have given up the yield spread between the convertible and nonconvertible security.

Total market size:	$185.6B
Average market yield:	3.66%
Average conversion premium:	52.23%

FIGURE 1.2 **The convertibles market in 2012. Source: Bank of America Merrill Lynch as of 12/31/11.**

Today's Convertibles Market. The convertibles market provides access to capital for a wide variety of companies. Convertibles have become particularly beneficial to small and midsize companies whose low credit ratings, limited earnings history, or small market cap may limit their ability to access the straight equity or debt markets at levels attractive to them. The market also has become increasingly attractive to investment-grade companies, given the relatively low cost of capital associated with issuing convertibles and the diversification of funding sources that convertibles provide.

The overall market for convertibles today is balanced in terms of supply and demand (Figure 1.2), with the makeup of issuers changing dramatically over time. Demand is both strong and broad-based, as dedicated convertible investors and crossover fixed-income and equity investors have replaced speculative hedge funds as the dominant market participants. At the start of 2012, convertibles were cheap relative to their theoretical value, and they continued to offer downside protection along with the potential to participate in a market rally.

Advantages for Investors. Convertible securities offer four main advantages to investors:

1. For many investors, managing portfolio risk means limiting volatility. Convertible securities offer a unique way to accomplish this. In a falling stock market, the debt portion of the convertible typically cushions the effects of a market decline, often allowing convertibles to outperform equities. In a rising stock market, convertibles also can provide the opportunity for capital growth, albeit to a lesser degree than common stock. In volatile markets, such as the one experienced in 2007 and 2008, the underlying call options embedded in convertible securities tend to rise in value, adding to the price of convertible securities.
2. It is important to point out that although convertible investors do not typically participate in 100% of the movements in the underlying stock, historically they have generally participated in a greater proportion of upward movements than downward movements (absent meaningful credit deterioration) because of the downside protection provided by the instrument's bond component. Adding convertible securities to an all-equity portfolio reduced portfolio standard deviation over the past 10 years. Furthermore, while most convertibles can be exchanged for shares of common stock, there is most often no obligation to do so.

3. Convertibles generally represent a lower level of principal risk than common stock, since convertibles are more senior in the capital structure. In the event of corporate bankruptcy, convertible holders are repaid ahead of common shareholders. That said, there are times when convertibles tend to underperform. Specifically, during downturns in the credit cycle, convertibles tend to lag behind the broader equity market due to a higher proportion of lower-credit-quality issuers in the convertibles market. Convertibles also tend to underperform in certain equity bull markets, where performance is driven by a narrow range of stocks.
4. Also, convertible bonds are usually less volatile than regular shares. Indeed, a convertible bond behaves like a call option. Therefore, if C is the call price and S is the regular share, then

$$\Delta = \frac{\delta C}{\delta S} \Rightarrow \delta C = \Delta \cdot \delta S$$

Consequenctly, since $0 < \Delta < 1$ we get $\delta C < \delta S$, which implies that the variation of C is less than the variation of S, which can be interpreted as less volatility.

Special Bonds. Up to this point we have been describing ordinary bonds, technically called "straight bonds." There are other types of bonds with special characteristics:

- Bonds with a call option give the issuer the possibility to redeem the bonds prior to the maturity date.
- Bonds with a put option give the holder the possibility to ask for redemption of the bond before the due date, either at a previously agreed-upon price or at par.

Junk Bonds. These bonds are below the threshold commonly considered as a "good investment" and contain consequently speculative components. Their return will thus be higher than bonds with a comparable maturity. The key issue here is the level of risk. However, experience has shown that, with some exceptions, the rate of nonpayment is not alarmingly high for these kinds of instruments. These instruments may sometimes offer quite attractive opportunities.

The global default rate for speculative-grade debt increased 0.1 percentage point during the third quarter to 3 percent in September 2012, the highest level in almost two years, according to Moody's Investors Service. The ratings company's trailing 12-month global speculative-grade default rate increased from 2.9 percent in the second quarter and compares with 1.8 percent a year ago, according to Moody's. The rate remains less than a historical average of 4.8 percent in data going back to 1983 and is the highest since 3.2 percent in December 2010.

U.S. junk-rated defaults increased to 3.5 percent in September 2012 from a 3.2 percent rate in the second quarter. In Europe, the pace of high-yield defaults fell to 2.6 percent last month from 2.8 percent in the second quarter, still according to a Moody's statement.

1.2.2 THE STOCK MARKET

A share is a representative fraction of the net worth of a corporation. A share may generate a dividend. The subscription or the purchase of a share implies a participation in the profits generated by the company but also the acceptance of risk sharing. However, the nature and legal status of a limited company limits the risks taken by the shareholders to the amount invested in the company.

A shareholder is entitled to a number of rights, one of which is a right to a fraction of the distributed profits, called dividends, each year following the approval by the (ordinary) general meeting—the annual meeting of the shareholders—upon the recommendation of the board. The dividends are not automatic and depend on the good fortune of the business—in other words, on a positive cash flow.

Other shareholder rights include:

- A preferential right of subscription for all new share issues
- A voting right at the ordinary and extraordinary general meetings
- A right to check on the management and the accounts
- A right of participation in the liquidation of the company in the event of sale or a dissolution

There are various ways of issuing shares on the market:

- *Via a Prospectus*: This is the most popular way to privatize state-owned entities; this method is widely used.
- *Via a Public Offer*: Everyone is invited to buy shares. In other words, everyone is free to make an offer beyond a fixed minimum price.
- *Via Private Placements*: This method is followed mainly for small and medium-sized companies that want to raise new capital. In view thereof, the shares are placed with brokers or institutional investors and are accessible to the public only on the secondary market.
- *Via Registration Fees*: This method of raising capital implies that only the existing shareholders can subscribe at a preferential rate, in proportion to the number of shares they already hold. The great advantage of this formula is that the percentage of the shareholding is not amended.

Being quoted on the stock exchange constitutes a cumbersome and expensive operation. However, it enables a company to increase its equity in order to finance its expansion. It is a convenient way to finance expansion when the original shareholders do not wish to put fresh money on the table or if they do not mind seeing their shareholding being diluted. Figure 1.3 and Figure 1.4 give an overview of the main domestic equity market capitalization performances and the largest domestic equity market capitalization in the world.

Region	USD bn End June 2012	End Dec 2011	End June 2011	% Change, end Dec. 2011 (in USD)	% Change, end-June 2011 (in USD)
Americas	21,361	19,587	22,582	9.1%	–5.4%
Asia Pacific	15,396	14,670	17,384	4.6%	–11.8%
Europe Africa Middle East	12,978	12,942	16,305	0.3%	–20.4%

FIGURE 1.3 **Regional and total WFE domestic equity market capitalization performances. Source: World Federation of Exchanges, Market Highlights for First Half-Year 2012.**

	Exchanges	USD bn End June 2012	End Dec 2011	End June 2011	% Change, end Dec. 2011 (in USD)	% Change, end-June 2011 (in USD)
1	NYSE Euronext (U.S.)	13,028	11,795	13,791	10.5%	–5.5%
2	NASDAQ OMX (U.S.)	4,475	3,845	4,068	16.4%	10.0%
3	Tokyo Stock Exchange Group	3,385	3,325	3,655	1.8%	–7.4%
4	London Stock Exchange Group	3,332	3,266	3,849	2.0%	–13.4%
5	NYSE Euronext (Europe)	2,460	2,447	3,248	0.5%	–24.3%
6	Shangai Stock Exchange	2,411	2,357	2,804	2.3%	–14.0%
7	Hong Kong Stock Exchange	2,376	2,258	2,712	5.2%	–12.4%
8	TMX Group	1,860	1,912	2,231	–2.7%	–16.6%
9	Deutsche Borse	1,212	1,185	1,622	2.3%	–25.3%
10	Shenzhen Stock exchange	1,149	1,055	1,283	8.9%	–10.4%

FIGURE 1.4 **Ten largest domestic equity market capitalization at mid-year 2012. Source: World Federation of Exchanges.**

In order to be considered a company acceptable for quotation on the stock market, a considerable number of formal requirements must be met.

The stock market is divided in two different markets known as the primary equity market and the secondary equity market. The primary equity market is used for offering new equity issues in the market. This market provides the companies the source of generating funds for the business purpose. It is also interesting to look at the concentration level in the main equity markets as the dispersion between the top 10 companies can be very large. It is particularly important to be aware of the concentration level when analyzing any equity market (see Figure 1.5).

Exchange	2011 Market cap. of top 10 companies	2011 Turnover value of Top 10 companies	2010 Market cap. of Top 10 companies	2010 Turnover value of Top 10 companies
Americas				
Bermuda SE	97.8%	NA	84.6%	NA
BM&FBOVESPA	53.1%	47.7%	55.4%	50.3%
Buenos Aires SE	70.1%	71.1%	69.9%	70.2%
Colombia SE	79.1%	68.7%	79.3%	86.6%
Lima SE	61.6%	64.2%	64.3%	68.6%
Mexican Exchange	65.9%	62.1%	66.1%	60.6%
NASDAQ OMX	38.1%	36.9%	35.8%	33.5%
NYSE Euronext (US)	18.0%	24.4%	19.2%	20.4%
Santiago SE	45.0%	52.0%	46.7%	53.2%
TMX Group	40.1%	24.8%	23.7%	25.9%
Asia - Pacific				
Australian Securities Exchange	43.6%	41.8%	41.7%	42.7%
Bombay SE	30.8%	20.1%	27.3%	14.5%
Bursa Malaysia	37.1%	36.5%	37.0%	37.4%
Colombo SE	36.9%	19.1%	41.9%	12.7%
Gretai Securities Market	21.7%	29.4%	21.0%	21.0%
Hong Kong Exchanges	37.3%	30.5%	36.9%	29.6%
Indonesia SE	44.3%	44.8%	40.6%	42.3%
Korea Exchange	33.4%	21.4%	32.0%	20.9%
National Stock Exchange India	31.4%	27.6%	27.9%	21.9%
Osaka Securities Exchange	42.4%	59.6%	50.6%	65.8%
Philippine SE	41.2%	43.8%	42.9%	45.7%
Shanghai SE	39.7%	9.1%	36.0%	9.6%
Shenzhen SE	10.9%	7.5%	10.6%	7.1%
Singapore Exchange	25.7%	28.6%	28.1%	59.3%
Taiwan SE Corp.	37.1%	25.7%	33.9%	20.0%
Thailand SE	47.2%	38.8%	45.4%	38.1%
Tokyo SE Group	17.0%	16.6%	17.1%	18.2%
Europe - Africa - Middle East				
Amman SE	71.2%	43.7%	69.9%	49.3%
Athens Exchange	59.8%	86.2%	63.5%	88.2%
BME Spanish Exchanges	37.2%	86.2%	37.3%	84.9%
Budapest SE	95.6%	97.8%	95.6%	99.2%
Casablanca SE	70.4%	74.9%	74.3%	74.1%
Cyprus SE	82.1%	99.6%	82.9%	95.0%
Deutsche Börse	45.1%	50.8%	45.6%	48.8%
Egyptian Exchange	46.4%	45.1%	44.4%	47.8%
Irish SE	88.0%	89.0%	77.7%	85.0%
IMKB[1]	44.9%	43.6%	47.5%	34.7%
Johannesburg SE	25.2%	12.1%	26.4%	34.6%
Ljubljana SE	80.9%	94.2%	79.9%	90.4%
London SE Group	35.1%	35.8%	32.9%	37.8%
Luxembourg SE	95.0%	91.4%	96.6%	96.8%
Malta SE	92.6%	97.7%	93.6%	95.7%
Mauritius SE	56.6%	85.7%	52.9%	84.7%
MICEX	62.1%	96.0%	60.4%	95.5%
NASDAQ OMX Nordic Exchange	36.8%	44.2%	37.9%	41.6%
NYSE Euronext (Europe)	39.2%	31.9%	34.6%	32.0%
Oslo Børs	75.6%	93.3%	62.8%	83.5%
RTS Stock Exchange	62.1%	99.5%	59.0%	99.6%
Saudi Stock Market - Tadawul	58.2%	32.9%	61.8%	47.2%
SIX Swiss Exchange	64.4%	67.5%	60.6%	69.6%
Tel Aviv SE	54.5%	55.6%	52.2%	48.1%
Warsaw SE	53.3%	68.2%	53.4%	68.9%
Wiener Börse	61.7%	78.1%	64.2%	78.6%

FIGURE 1.5 Top 10 companies, concentration per equity markets. **Source:** World Federation of Exchanges.

At the same time, the primary equity market along with the secondary market help the investors to get a share in the company that is offering the shares. The investor can also make a good amount of money from this market. The primary that market is also termed as the New Issue Market (NIM) because the Initial Public Offerings (IPOs) are meant for this market.

This market is a source of long-term debt for the companies; because of this, the market can also be termed a long term debt market. The securities that are designed for the public and are introduced through the primary equity market are of two types.

When any new stock is introduced in the market, it is called the Initial Public Offering. At the same time, offering new issues of existing stocks to the purchasers is known as underwriting.

The growing number of companies offering IPOs in the primary equity market represents the growth of the global equity market itself. The growth of the primary equity market is dramatic in the developed countries, and at the same time the numbers of IPOs are rising in the developed countries. Along with this, the mechanism of the primary equity markets has also developed and the competition between various primary equity markets are rising rapidly. This growth of the IPOs also represent the fact that the companies are preferring to generate funds through the primary equity market rather than go to the financial organizations or commercial banks.

Introducing of IPOs in the primary equity market is done through a particular process. According to this process, a syndicate of the securities dealers should perform the job. Because of their services, the securities dealers receive a certain amount of money as their commission. The price at which the IPO is offered in the primary equity market includes the dealer's commission also.

It is important to know if a few companies are dominating the stock exchange's market capitalization and the respective weight of the first 10 corporations to avoid any concentration risk. This can reveal some dispersion between stock exchanges.

1.3 The Futures and Options Market

The futures market as it currently stands rose from humble beginnings. Futures trading began in the eighteenth century in Japan. It was originally designed for trading in silk and rice. In the 1850s the Unites States developed a futures market to trade agricultural commodities including cotton, corn, and wheat. A futures contract is an agreement between two parties to engage in a transaction involving physical commodities or financial instruments that will be delivered in the future at a predetermined price. It is a kind of financial contract or derivative instrument. When a person buys a futures contract, they are agreeing to buy a product from the seller at a set price. The product has not yet been produced. The futures market does not necessarily involve large deliveries of commodities because transactions are usually entered into by people wanting to speculate or hedge their risks. This means that physical goods are not always exchanged. This feature makes the financial instruments of the futures market popular for speculators as well as producers and consumers.

Investors generally agree that the futures market is an important hub of the financial world which allows for competition in trading in products, as well as being an outlet in which price risks can be managed. It is a very complicated and risky market, but breaking it down and considering how it functions can help us to understand it. Futures are a useful trading tool for many different types of people. This information is designed to help you understand the way that the futures market functions, who uses this market, and what strategies work best when trading in futures.

The futures market in North America originated approximately 150 years ago. Before it began, farmers would physically bring their crops to market to sell their inventory. This system meant that they had no idea of the demand; and, if they brought too much with them, any excess in supply would often be left to rot. Another problem was that goods made from crops that were out of season would become very expensive. To deal with these problems, central grain markets and a centralized marketplace were established as places for farmers to sell their products. They could either sell the commodities for immediate delivery (also known as spot trading) or sell for forward delivery. Contracts for forward delivery were the first type of what are now known as futures contracts. Forward contracts prevented a lot of wasted products and profits and also stabilized the supply and prices of off-season products.

The futures market today has grown into a global marketplace that trades all sorts of products, not just agricultural commodities. Currencies and financial instruments are also traded on the futures market. Participants in the futures market include farmers, manufactures, importers, exporters, and speculators. Technological advances mean that prices of various commodities can be communicated throughout the world, connecting buyers and sellers from different countries.

A futures contract is just what it's called—a contract. It is *not* equity in a stock or commodity. It *is* a contract—a contract to make or take delivery of a product in the future, at a price set in the present. If you agree in April with your Aunt Sue that you will buy two pounds of tomatoes from her garden for $5, to be delivered to you when they're ripe in July, you and Sue just entered into a futures contract.

In formalized trading of futures contracts on exchanges, standardized agreements specify price, quantity, and the month of delivery. Futures markets have their roots in agriculture, but today futures and options on futures are traded on a wide range of products from wheat to stock indexes, precious metals, and currencies.

Options on futures can be thought of like insurance. An option buyer (the insured) pays a premium to an option seller (the insurance company) for the right to buy or sell a futures contract at a specific price. However, just like with insurance, the option buyer may or may not exercise his right (use his insurance).

Why do futures and options markets exist? Two reasons: risk transfer and price discovery.

Professionals such as grain merchants, energy firms, and portfolio managers use futures and options to reduce the risk to their business associated with volatile prices. For example, a flour miller might use a futures contract to set a price now for wheat that he knows he will need to purchase in the future, rather than face the chance that prices could be even higher when he buys the wheat. Similarly, a natural gas producer might use a futures contract to set a price now for gas he will sell in the future, locking in a profit rather than being exposed to the possibility of lower prices. These types of futures and options users are known as *hedgers*, and they are in the market specifically to reduce risk.

People who assume risk take it on in exchange for the opportunity for profit. Thus the futures and options markets serve the important function of risk transfer.

Futures and options markets also provide the economy with *price discovery.* Futures prices are determined by supply and demand. An exchange itself does not set prices; it simply provides a place where buyers and sellers can negotiate. If there are more buyers than sellers, the price goes up. If there are more sellers than buyers, the price goes down. The prices discovered through futures markets offer valuable economic information about supply and demand in a competitive business environment.

Similar to stocks, gains and losses in futures trading are the result of price changes. If you have sold a futures contract, your trade will show a profit if prices fall. If you have bought, higher prices will produce a profit. To make a profit on a futures trade, you can first buy low and then sell high, or reverse the order and sell high, then buy low.

It is important to understand that losses may be highly *leveraged.* This means that if the price moves in the direction you anticipated, you could realize large profits in relation to your initial investment. Conversely, if prices move in the opposite direction of what you anticipated, you could realize large losses in relation to your initial investment.

Options on futures are different from futures themselves in that the most a buyer can lose is the cost of purchasing the option, known as the *premium*, along with transaction costs. An option seller, however, has unlimited risk. Think of the insurance example we used earlier. The option buyer is like the insured and is paying only the insurance premium for his protection. The option seller is like the insurance company and is taking on unlimited risk in hopes that he can collect the premium and the insurance will not be used.

Should an investor decide to participate in futures or options trading, just as with stocks, there are a number of factors to consider. Similar to trading stocks, in futures you can trade your own account—with or without the recommendations of a brokerage firm. Another alternative is an account that is still your individual account, but you give someone else written power of attorney to make and execute trading decisions on your behalf. You can also choose to use an individual or firm that for a fee provides advice on commodity trading. Yet another choice is to participate in a commodity pool, similar in concept to a stock mutual fund. Your money is combined with other participants and traded as a single account, and you share in profits or losses in the pool.

1.4 The Foreign Exchange Market

We are not living in a closed economy. Consumers purchase what they need in another economy or country that has a different currency. He will need to exchange his national currency into the foreign currency. Alternatively, the seller will accept the purchaser's currency but will have to exchange it in his country.

The foreign exchange market is by far the largest market in the world. It is an over-the-counter market regulated by a strict code of conduct. The daily turnover is close to an estimated USD 2,500,000,000,000. This largest market in the world is scarcely predictable, although there is a fundamental link between interest rates (reflecting inflation rates), the short- and long-term inflows and outflows of the countries concerned, and the exchange rates of their currencies.

A quotation on the foreign exchange market would be given as follows:

EUR / USD 1.23341–1.23348

where 1.23341 is the buying side being the rate at which the market maker is willing to purchase EURO and sell USD and 1.23348 is the selling side being the rate at which the dealer is willing to sell EURO and purchase USD. This rate is called the *spot rate.*

You could conclude this transaction with delivery three months from now, and it would be called a forward transaction. The foreign exchange markets underpin all other financial markets. They directly influence each country's foreign trade patterns, determine the flow of international investments, and affect domestic interest and inflation rates.

1.5 The Commodity Market

Commodities are traded in both spot and forward markets. They are physical as opposed to financial assets, creating the need for storage and shipping. Because commodities are generally not perishable and can be stored, they are also an asset and can be used as a store of value. Gold and silver have been units of account and numeraires of the entire financial system, as well as a medium of exchange and a store of value. Forward markets for commodities have existed for centuries because, with high volatility, risk-adverse producers and consumers have attempted to hedge their inventories in forward and future markets.

Risk managers in any market have a special interest in the pricing forward contracts. One key observation regarding commodities is that the term structure of the forward curve has often been downward sloped, despite the fact that there are nontrivial storage and other transaction costs. Backwardation of commodity markets is something of a puzzle, since storage costs would normally be expected to raise future prices above spot prices.

Commodities are divided into four types:

- Metals
- Softs
- Grains and oilseeds
- Livestock

These are generally traded in the spot markets and most have evolved forwards, futures, and option-based contracts. The metals can be decomposed into base metals, such as nonferrous metals (e.g., zinc, aluminum, lead, and nickel); strategic metals, such as bismuth and vanadium; minor metals, such as cobalt and chromium; and precious metals, such as gold, silver, and palladium. The London Metals Exchange (LME) is one of the key spot-trading centers for base, nonferrous metals, steel, and certain minor metals. Gold, silver, platinum and other precious metals are traded over-the-counter (OTC) between producer and consumer in markets such as the London Bullion Market, an informal OTC market. The buyers tend to be the automotive, aerospace, pharmaceutical, and electrical corporations.

The softs include cocoa, sugar, and coffee, and minor softs include rubber, tea, and pepper. Most trading of soft commodities involves processors, roasters, refiners, distributors, and traders who are "inventory flow traders" or speculators. The grains and oilseeds category spans most edible agriculture products. It can be further decomposed into the grains, such as wheat, barley, rice, and oats; oilseeds, such as soybeans, rapeseed, palm kernel, and flaxseed; fibers, such as wood, cloth, and silk; and finally, livestock and other, including live animals and meat products such as pork bellies. Also included in the latter category are dairy products, such as milk and cheese, and citrus and tropical fruits, such as orange juice.

The most important commodity exchanges belong to the Chicago Mercantile Exchange (CME) Group, such as the Chicago Board of Trade (CBOT); the New York Mercantile Exchange (NYMEX); the Intercontinental Exchange (ICE); the London International Financial Futures and Options Exchange (LIFFE); and the London Metals Exchange (LME).

Irrespective of whether the commodity is traded spot, forward, or futures, the delivery and settlement methods are critical in determining the actual spot, forward, or futures price. There are at least six characteristics of delivery mechanisms:

1. *In Store.* The simplest form of physical delivery. The seller is responsible for the delivery to an agreed-upon warehouse. As in all physical deals, quality,

quantity, and location are all negotiated or embedded in the terms of a standardized (futures) contract. It is used, for example, in softs such as coffee and cocoa.

2. *Ex Store.* It is identical to in store except that the seller prepays the storekeeper for loading onto the buyers' transportation network. Thus the price will be more expensive than the former.
3. *Free on Board (FOB).* Once the goods have passed over the ship's rail, the seller has fulfilled his obligations. The onus of risk is shifted onto the buyer once goods are loaded, and hence an FOB price will be cheaper by the insurance premium for damage while on board along with the transportation costs.
4. *Free Alongside Ship (FAS).* It is similar to FOB, whereby the goods are delivered alongside the shipping vessel instead of being loaded. The FAS price will be lower than the FOB price by the cost of loading.
5. *Cost, Insurance, and Freight (CIF).* This involves FOB delivery plus the costs of insurance and transportation. The following simple arbitrage equation relates the FOB to the CIF price: $CIF = FOB + F + I$, where F is the freight cost and I is the insurance premium.
6. *Exchange of Futures for Physicals (EFP).* It is possible to swap a physical position for a future position, and this will be subject to off-exchange negotiations.

As a risk manager it is important to recognize the transactions' characteristics of the different types of commodities, which focus on delivery and settlement mechanisms for heterogeneous commodities. The key arbitrage equation which links spot prices with forward prices is the commodity equivalent of covered interest arbitrage in foreign exchange or interest parity in bonds. Unlike other markets, the arbitrage equation for commodities contains a convenience yield which reflects the importance that is sometimes placed on immediate access to supply. This feature of commodity markets is no doubt related to the importance of commodities as factors of production and possible delays in supply/shipping. It is the presence of convenience yield, along with its variability, that makes commodity risk management unique. Failure to properly appreciate these aspects of commodity markets can have disastrous consequences.

Energy Markets. Energy trading began in 1978 with the first oil futures contract in NYMEX. During the 1980s and 1990s, NYMEX and the International Petroleum Exchange (IPE), now called ICE Futures, successfully launched futures contracts for oil and gas futures trading. These successful energy future exchanges have survived the trading debacles of recent years, of which Enron was the most notable. Oil companies and financial houses now provide the necessary trading liquidity through market-making on both the established government-regulated futures exchanges and OTC energy derivatives markets that can clear on the futures exchanges. They have considerable skill in the management of financial energy risks and the risks in the emerging global environmental markets.

The energy complex trades the following products on established futures exchanges, OTC markets, and the internet: crude oil, gasoline, naphtha, gasoil, jet fuel, home heating oil, residual heating oil, bunker fuels, freight-rate swaps, natural gas, electricity, liquefied natural gas (LNG), petrochemicals, coal, emissions such as sulfur dioxide and nitrous oxides, greenhouse gases (i.e., carbon credits), renewable energy credits, and megawatts (value of energy efficiency).

Energy commodities are subject to numerous risks, including credit or counterparty risk, liquidity risk, event risk, cash-flow risk, basis risk, legal and regulatory risk, operational risks, tax risk, and most evidently geopolitical and weather risks. There are also tremendous variations over time in many energy markets. The weather (seasonal) impacts supply and demand so that risks increase in the mid-summer and winter seasons as more energy is required for heating, cooling, and transportation. Of all the different types of risks that affect the energy markets, market risk is still preeminent. Price volatility is caused by fundamental factors such as supply/demand, as well as by weather and financial factors such as technical trading, speculators, and market imperfections. These factors are very well defined in energy markets, and as a result they are the most volatile commodity markets ever created.

A standardized energy futures contract always comprises certain characteristics. It has an underlying physical commodity or price index upon which the energy futures contract is based. There is a certain size for the amount of the underlying item covered by each futures contract. There is a predetermined and specified time given in months for which contracts can be traded. There is an expiration date. Finally, there is a specified grade or quality and delivery location for oil and coal future contracts. Whereas oil varies by grade/quality, natural gas (methane) and electricity are more homogeneous commodities, obviating the need for the grade/quality to be specified in the contract. The settlement mechanism can be either physical delivery of the underlying item or cash payment.

A few decades after the first successful oil futures contracts, we are now seeing the development of a true multicommodity market that encompasses oil, gas, power, coal, freight rates, weather, and green trading. Energy commodity trading is evolving into many areas of the energy complex and extending into emerging markets such as coal, emissions, and weather trading. Convergence (a term often much overused) is actually now upon us as multicommodity arbitrage is the watchword of today's energy trader. High price volatility, the extra liquidity provided by financial institutions, and a greater risk appetite are three major factors that make the present time the real dawn of energy trading. Energy risk management has become not only a fiduciary responsibility but also a core competency of energy companies. Broader penetration into the emerging markets of the developing world, and particularly Asia, shows that there are no barriers to entry in trading on the internet. The true financialization of the energy markets is upon us.

FURTHER READING

Burton, M., Nesiba, R., Brown, B., *An Introduction to Financial Markets and Institutions*, second edition, M.E. Sharpe, Armonk, NY, 2009.

Choudhry, M., *An Introduction to Bond Markets*, fourth edition, The Wiley Finance Series, John Wiley & Sons, Hoboken, NJ, 2010.

Garner, C., *A Trader's First Book on Commodities: An Introduction to the World's Fastest Growing Market*, second edition, Pearson Education, New York, 2013.

Pilbeam, K., *Finance & Financial Markets*, third edition, Palgrave Macmillan, London, 2010.

Pike, R., Neal, B., Linsley, P., *Corporate Finance and Investment*, seventh edition, Pearson Education, Harlow, 2012.

The Financial Times Guide to Investing, second edition, Pearson Education, Harlow, 2009.

Rutterford, J., *An Introduction to Stock Exchange Investment*, third edition, Palgrave Macmillan, New York, 2007.

Valdez, S., Molyneux, P., *An Introduction to Global Financial Markets*, sixth edition, Palgrave Macmillan, New York, 2010. *An Introduction to Financial Markets and Institutions*, second edition, M.E. Sharpe, Armonk, NY, 2010.

Weithers, T., *Foreign Exchange: A Practical Guide to the FX Markets*, Wiley Finance, John Wiley & Sons, Hoboken, NJ, 2006.

CHAPTER TWO

The Efficient Markets Theory

I'd be a bum on the streets with a tin cup if the markets were efficient.
—Warren Buffett

In this chapter we will examine a fundamental question about financial markets. This question has raised a lot of debates among practitioners and academics about its reality. The question is about market efficiency, along with the following questions: How do financial markets match providers with users and, more importantly, how efficiently does the market determine prices?

The financial markets perform much the same function as the markets for other goods and services. They bring large numbers of buyers and sellers together, thus relieving each party of the need for a potentially long and expensive search for a counterpart with exactly equal but opposite needs to his or her own. The existence of such a market improves price transparency, encourages competition, and improves efficiency generally.

But the financial markets can also be highly volatile. The stock market is possibly the most volatile of them all. Some investors will win and some will lose. Is it just a matter of luck or skill? Or does it depend on a mixture of the two?

A fair return on investment is one that offers the investor just the right level of compensation for the expected risk of the investment (in addition to the time preference rate and an adjustment for expected inflation). But why is it so important at the end whether market prices for investments in fact offer fair returns? Could we argue that the pricing of investments is a zero-sum game in which one investor's loss is another's gain? For every investor who loses by buying at the top of the market and selling at the bottom, there must be another who profits by doing the opposite. So we can argue that if a particular investment offers either an excessive or an inadequate return, total income and wealth are neither increased nor reduced but simply redistributed among the market participants.

Handbook of Market Risk, First Edition. Christian Szylar.

On the other hand, if it could be demonstrated that markets do price investments fairly, this would have genuinely radical consequences. It would tell us that all the time, money, and efforts expended by investors on trying to do the right stock-picking would be so much time and effort wasted. The converse argument would apply to organizations' efforts to spot windows of opportunity to finance their operation when funds are apparently cheap, because such cheapness would be in fact an illusion. The rate demanded by the market would be a fair one in relation to the risks involved.

It brings up the question about whether there are any successful managers. Is it realistic, through the exercise of skill and/or experience, to predict the movement of share prices in such a way that excess returns or "alpha" can be earned not just occasionally but consistently? It is somewhat shocking to note that around 80% of the long-only portfolios do not beat their reference benchmark. And what can we say about the hedge funds industry, which has also disappointed more than one investor?

Before we consider whether financial markets are indeed efficient in the sense of offering fair prices, we need to have a closer look at the definition of an efficient market. The best starting point for this is the concept, in general economic theory, of a perfectly competitive market (also called pure competition).

The degree to which a market or industry can be described as competitive depends in part on how many suppliers are seeking the demand of consumers and the ease with which new businesses can enter and exit a particular market in the long run.

The spectrum of competition ranges from highly competitive markets where there are many sellers, each of whom has little or no control over the market price, to a situation of pure monopoly where a market or an industry is dominated by one single supplier who enjoys considerable discretion in setting prices, unless subject to some form of direct regulation by the government.

In many sectors of the economy, markets are best described by the term oligopoly, where a few producers dominate the majority of the market and the industry is highly concentrated. In a duopoly, two firms dominate the market, although there may be many smaller players in the industry.

Competitive markets operate on the basis of a number of assumptions. When these assumptions are dropped, we move into the world of imperfect competition. These assumptions are discussed below.

2.1 Assumptions behind a Perfectly Competitive Market

1. Many suppliers each with an insignificant share of the market—this means that each firm is too small relative to the overall market to affect price via a change in its own supply—each individual firm is assumed to be a price taker.

2. An identical output produced by each firm—in other words, the market supplies homogeneous or standardized products that are perfect substitutes for each other. Consumers perceive the products to be identical.
3. Consumers have perfect information about the prices all sellers in the market charge—so if some firms decide to charge a price higher than the ruling market price, there will be a large substitution effect away from this firm.
4. All firms (industry participants and new entrants) are assumed to have equal access to resources (technology, other factor inputs), and improvements in production technologies achieved by one firm can spill over to all the other suppliers in the market.
5. It is assumed that there are to be no barriers to entry and exit of firms in long run, which means that the market is open to competition from new suppliers; this affects the long-run profits made by each firm in the industry. The long-run equilibrium for a perfectly competitive market occurs when the marginal firm makes normal profit only in the long term.
6. No externalities in production and consumption, so that there is no divergence between private and social costs and benefits.

In a perfect market, there would be no barriers or even temporary delays to the formation of perfectly fair prices; that is, prices would instantaneously and universally reflect all available and relevant information. What conditions would have to be met in order to produce this ideal state of affairs? Here are the most important.

- There are so many individual buyers and sellers in the market that no one participant (or group of participants acting in concert with each other) can manipulate prices.
- All participants can gain all the information on which to base their purchases at no cost and as soon as it is available.
- There are no barriers to entry or exit.
- There are no transaction costs. This is a very wide concept in the context of financial markets. It embraces the following factors:
  - Stamp duties.
  - Broker's commissions.
  - Exchange fees.
  - Tax regulations affecting either the relative attractiveness of different investments or the timing of purchases and sales.
  - Accounting practices that either affect the relative attractiveness of different transactions or cause significant differences in the timing of the recognition of profits and losses.
  - Regulatory constraints, for example, preventing particular classes of investor from acquiring a specific type of investment.
  - Adverse impact on market prices of an attempt to buy or sell.

In the real world, no investment market meets all of the above conditions, because there are (a) delays in the dissemination of information and (b) transaction costs and taxes. It clearly appears that markets are not really perfect. The next question is then how far are they from being perfect? Are they still sufficiently close to the status of perfect markets that it is still impossible to profit systematically (and not just occasionally and coincidentally) from mispricings that offer excess returns?

Research into the workings of the stock market began by examining this question in its simplest form: Are there patterns in share prices, so that future movements can be predicted from past history? The earliest relevant research (Bachelier, 1900) looked not at stock-market prices but at commodity prices and concluded that there were no discernible trends in historic prices. In the 1950s and 1960s, these findings were extended to the stock markets, because successive research studies suggested that there was little or no correlation between successive movements in share prices. This observation was called the "random walk theory," because it likened the progress of share prices to the walk of a drunken man; you cannot predict the direction of his next step from the last one.

Observers of the random walk in share prices naturally sought to explain their findings in terms of the efficiency with which new information was incorporated into prices. They reasoned that if there were delays as new relevant information became disseminated through the market, the price of the affect share would not move instantaneously to the new equilibrium level reflecting the information, but would trend toward the new level over time. This might happen gradually or quite rapidly, but would still not be instantaneous. If this were the case, then there would be periods (immediately following the release of new information) when price trends could be discerned. This in turn would mean that excess returns could be made, by either (a) buying the shares before the price had finished moving up to the new equilibrium level justified by good news or (b) selling before the price had finished moving down to the new equilibrium level justified by bad news. The fact that these early studies found no such trends or correlations was seen as powerful support for the argument that the markets were efficient. It seemed to be the case that at any point in time, all available information was reflected in the price; the next move could not be predicted from the last one, because the next piece of news would not be genuine news if it was already implied in past prices. This finding was the central feature of what became known as the Efficient Markets Hypothesis (EMH)—the theory that the major stock markets, in particular those of the USA and UK, while not perfect, are at least efficient.

2.2 The Efficient Market Hypothesis

In George Gibson's book *The Stock Markets of London, Paris, and New York*, published in 1899, we find one of the first references to the question of market efficiency. He writes, "*in an open market, when the shares become publically know, the value they obtain may be considered to reflect the most intelligent appreciation possible.*"

The Efficient Market Hypothesis (EMH) was first formally proposed in University of Chicago professor Eugene Fama's 1970 paper "Efficient Capital Markets: A Review of Theory and Empirical Work." In a series of publications, Eugene Fama became the father of market efficiency. To beat the market, stock pickers need to discover mispricings in stocks, but the EMH claims that the market is a ruthless mechanism acting instantly to arbitrage away such opportunities, claiming that the current price of a stock is *always* the most accurate estimate of its value (known as "informational efficiency").

The EMH has evolved into a concept that a stock price reflects *all* available information in the market, making it *impossible* to have an edge. There are *no* undervalued stocks, it is argued, because there are smart security analysts who utilize all available information to ensure *unfailingly* appropriate prices. Investors who seem to beat the market year after year are just *lucky*.

> An efficient market is defined as a market where there are large numbers of rational, profit maximisers actively competing, with each trying to predict future market values of individual securities, and where important current information is almost freely available to all participants. In an efficient market, competition among the many intelligent participants leads to a situation where, at any point in time, actual prices of individual securities already reflect the effects of information based both on events that have already occurred and on events which, as of now, the market expects to take place in the future. In other words, in an efficient market at any point in time the actual price of a security will be a good estimate of its intrinsic value. (Fama, 1970)

Fama identified three distinct levels (or "strengths") at which a market might actually be efficient.

2.2.1 STRONG EMH

In its strongest form, the EMH says a market is efficient if all information relevant to the value of a share, whether or not generally available to existing or potential investors, is quickly and accurately reflected in the market price. For example, if the current market price is lower than the value justified by some piece of privately held information, the holders of that information will exploit the pricing anomaly by buying the shares. They will continue doing so until this excess demand for the shares has driven the price up to the level supported by their private information. At this point they will have no incentive to continue buying, so they will withdraw from the market and the price will stabilize at this new equilibrium level. This is called the strong-form EMH. It is the most satisfying and compelling form of EMH in a theoretical sense, but it suffers from one big drawback in practice. It is difficult to confirm empirically, because the necessary research would be unlikely to win the cooperation of the relevant section of the financial community—insider dealers.

2.2.2 SEMI-STRONG EMH

In a slightly less rigorous form, the EMH says a market is efficient if all relevant publicly available information is quickly reflected in the market price. This is called the semi-strong EMH. If the strong form is theoretically the most compelling, then the semi-strong form perhaps appeals most to our common sense and is closer to the real world. It says that the market will quickly digest the publication of relevant new information by moving the price to a new equilibrium level that reflects the change in supply and demand caused by the emergence of that information. What it may lack in intellectual rigor, the semi-strong EMH certainly gains in empirical strength, because it is less difficult to test than strong EMH.

One problem with the semi-strong EMH lies with the identification of "relevant publicly available information". Neat as the phrase might sound, the reality is less clear-cut, because information does not arrive with a convenient label saying which shares it does and does not affect.

2.2.3 WEAK-FORM EMH

In its third and least rigorous form (known as the weak form), the EMH confines itself to just one subset of public information, namely historical information about the share price itself. The argument runs as follows. "New" information must by definition be unrelated to previous information, otherwise it would not be new. It follows from this that every movement in the share price in response to new information cannot be predicted from the last movement or price, and the development of the price assumes the characteristics of the random walk. In other words, the future price cannot be predicted from a study of historic prices.

Each of the three forms of EMH has different consequences in the context of the search for excess returns—that is, for returns in excess of what is justified by the risks incurred in holding particular investments.

If a market is weak-form efficient, there is no correlation between successive prices, so that excess returns cannot consistently be achieved through the study of past price movements. This kind of study is called technical or chart analysis, because it is based on the study of past price patterns without regard to any further background information.

If a market is semi-strong efficient, the current market price is the best available unbiased predictor of a fair price, having regard to all publicly available information about the risk and return of an investment. The study of any public information (and not just past prices) cannot yield consistent excess returns. This is a somewhat more controversial conclusion than that of the weak-form EMH, because it means that fundamental analysis—the systematic study of companies, sectors and the economy at large—cannot produce consistently higher returns than are justified by the risks involved. Such a finding calls into question the relevance and value of a large sector of the financial industry, namely investment research and analysis.

If a market is strong-form efficient, the current market price is the best available unbiased predictor of a fair price, having regard to all relevant information, whether the information is in the public domain or not. As we have seen, this implies that excess returns cannot consistently be achieved even by trading on inside information. This does prompt the interesting observation that somebody must be the first to trade on the inside information and hence make an excess return. Attractive as this line of reasoning may be in theory, unfortunately it is nearly impossible to test it in practice with any degree of academic rigor.

2.3 Critics of Efficient Markets Theory

Following the publication of Fama's classic statement in 1970, the efficient markets theory was extraordinary popular among the academic and business world. A series of research papers and studies, empirical or theoretical in approach, seemed to confirm this hypothesis. As Jensen (1978) wrote: "There is no other proposition in economics which has more solid empirical evidence supporting it than the EMH." Not less than this!

However, as Schleifer (2000) put it, "strong statements portend reversals"; and in the two decades following Jensen's statement, a growing volume of theoretical and empirical work either contradicted the EMH outright or sought at least to show that its case was "not proven."

One of the first serious reviews of the market efficiency hypothesis came from Sanford J. Grossman and from Joseph E. Stiglitz. They showed that it is impossible for a market to be perfectly efficient on the informational level since the information is costly. The prices cannot perfectly reflect the information available since the investors who hire resources in order to obtain privileged information want to be compensated. When the informed investors take a stand on the market, this is reflected on the prices and therefore makes the information universal.

In 1989 Robert J. Shiller published the book *Market Volatility*. In this book, Shiller used statistical evidence to illustrate the causes of price fluctuation in a speculative market. He challenged EMH by questions such as: Why does the market crash from time to time? Why does the real estate market change during periods of boom? Why do long-term bonds have sudden reversals? He presented the consequences of popular models that provoke incorrect reactions toward the economic data, and he stated that changing these models is enough to provoke changes in prices. Such movements have nothing to do with EMH.

In 2000, Shiller published the first version of *Irrational Exuberance*, which continued to defy EMH.

Critics of EMH have produced a wide range of arguments, of which the following is a summary.

1. EMH makes predictions that are not in accord with the reality.
2. Both the Tech Bubble and the Credit Bubble/Crunch show that that the market is subject to fads, whims, and periods of irrational exuberance (and despair) that cannot be explained away as rational.

3. Furthermore, contrary to the predictions of EMH, there have been plenty of individuals who have managed to outperform the market consistently over the decades.
4. The assumption that investors are rational and therefore value investments rationally—that is, by calculating the net present values of future cash flows, appropriately discounted for risk—is not supported by the evidence, which shows instead that investors are affected by
   - Herd instinct
   - A tendency to churn their portfolios
   - A tendency to underreact or overreact to news (Schleifer, 2000; Barber and Odean, 2000)
   - Asymmetrical judgments about the causes of previous profits and losses

Furthermore, many alleged anomalies have been detected in patterns of historical share price such as the small firm effect, the January effect, and the mean reversion. The mean reversion is the name given to the tendency of markets, sectors, or individual shares following a period of sustained under- or outperformance to revert to a long-term average by means of a corresponding period of out- or underperformance. This was picked up in detailed research by De Bondt and Thaler (1984), who showed that, if for each year since 1933 a portfolio of "extreme winners" (defined as the best-performing U.S. shares over the past three years) was constructed, it would have shown poor returns over the following five years, while a portfolio of "extreme losers" would have done very well over the same period.

Some are also finally questioning the rationality or efficiency of investors. Prices are formed in function of the investors "rationale forecasts" of what future profits/earnings will be. The history of markets easily demonstrates that some stocks valuation in some points in time were absolutely not driven by rationale drivers or driven by the firm's fundamentals. Tobin tried to demonstrate it with its famous *Q* ratio.

A ratio which hypothesized that the combined market value of all the companies on the stock market should be about equal to their replacement costs. The *Q* ratio is calculated as the market value of a company divided by the replacement value of the firm's assets:

$$\text{Q ratio} = \frac{\text{Total market value of firm}}{\text{Total asset value}}$$

For example, a low *Q* (between 0 and 1) means that the cost to replace a firm's assets is greater than the value of its stock. This implies that the stock is undervalued. Conversely, a high *Q* (greater than 1) implies that a firm's stock is more expensive than the replacement cost of its assets, which implies that the stock is overvalued. This measure of stock valuation is the driving factor behind investment decisions in Tobin's model.

This other factor is speculation, and speculation amplifies considerably (according to Tobin) the dividend and earnings variance. In other words, speculation adds some further variance to the normal and natural variance that has to exist on the market.

2.4 Development of Behavioral Finance

Behavioral finance is one of the areas of the new "behavioral economics" that is to apply psychology to finance. Born 30 years ago, this theory was recognized officially in 2002 with the awarding of the Nobel Prize in economics to Daniel Kahneman and Vernon Smith for their theory. Their study focuses on the behavior of investors in their decision making.

As opposed to the base of the efficient-market hypothesis, this theory will seek to highlight situations in which the markets are not rational and will attempt to explain the causes by studying the psychology of investors. In other words, it will identify human behavior as well as its effects on the market for use in investment strategies.

According to the standard financial theory, financial markets lead to economically more efficient equilibria as if they were purely rational rules. The premise of behavioral finance is totally different.

Indeed, it considers that the investor is not always rational and that his feelings are subject to errors of systematic judgments (called "cognitive bias") or emotional factors, such as fear or overconfidence, which interfere in its decision making.

At this time, much proof has accumulated to the point where it is difficult to believe that the markets are perfectly and totally efficient.

2.5 Beating the Market: Fundamental versus Technical

A company's share return can be measured using different methods that will all result in different outcomes. They all share the same objective—namely, to detect some increase in value (in absolute or relative terms), or decrease in value in the case of those investment strategies allowing the shorting of stocks.

In a short-term perspective, stock prices follow a random walk. Some valuation methods have a high degree of complexity, but complexity is not always a guarantee of success or convenience. All methods have to deal with financial flows, and these flows depend largely on macroeconomic factors. A good approach to select a particular stock consists of estimating what one can expect in the market in the future. A stock's value depends on current liquidity and future flows to generate dividends. Profits are at the origination of potential future dividends. Therefore it is necessary to consider the dividend in the computation of a stock's return.

Methods of stock valuation link the discount rate with the return of a "risk-free" asset or with a bond without uncertainty on the nominal flow. The key issue with valuation is to identify what is the most convenient in the past to predict future and in which conditions one can expect a change in the trend pattern. On the contrary, technical analysts try to select some stocks by means other than the estimation of future cash-flows.

The methods used to analyze securities and make investment decisions fall into two very broad categories: fundamental analysis and technical analysis. Fundamental analysis involves analyzing the characteristics of a company in order to estimate its value. Technical analysis takes a completely different approach: It doesn't care one bit about the "value" of a company or a commodity. Technicians (sometimes called chartists) are only interested in the price movements in the market.

2.5.1 FUNDAMENTAL METHODS

Price multiples are amongst the most widely used tools for valuation of equities. Comparing stocks' price multiple can help an investor judge whether a particular stock is overvalued, undervalued, or properly valued in terms of measures such as earnings, sales, cash flow, or book value per share.

The method of comparable values evaluates a stock based on the average price multiple of the stock of similar companies. The economic rationale for the method of comparables is the Law of One Price, which asserts that two similar assets should sell at comparable price multiples (e.g., P/E). This is a relative valuation method, so we can only assert that a stock is over- or undervalued relative to benchmark value.

Example: ABC Global Technology Ltd. shares are selling for 120. Earnings for the last year end were 10.00 per share. The average P/E ratio for firms in the technology industry is 18. ABC is relatively undervalued because its observed P/E ratio (120/10 = 12) is less than the industry average P/E ratio (18).

Method Using Dividend or Earnings Growth on an Absolute Basis. If one considers that the value of a stock is the sum of gains realized when it is sold and its chain of dividends D1 to Dn, the discounting becomes (considering that dividends are distributed the next year in Europe)

$$V_{\text{stock}} = D_0/(1+t) + D_1/(1+t)^2 + D_2/(1+t)^3 + \cdots + D_{n-1}/(1+t)^n + V_n/(1+t)^n$$

The sole benefit of this method is to help visualize the way a stock's price moves. Indeed, it is unusual and also very difficult to get access to expected dividends above 5 years. Despite the fact that roughly 85% of the value resides in the last term, the stock's price continues to gain as long as expected dividends continue to grow. This is one of the reasons why this method is not frequently used. Nevertheless, this method appears useful for integrating sectors with expected growth on the long term. These are the ones that maximize V_n, namely 85% of the stock's valuation.

One way to look at this is to refer to the Gordon Shapiro model. In this model, growth is supposed to be constant and equal to g, from year 1 to year N.

$$D_1 = D_0 \times (1+g)$$
$$D_2 = D_1 \times (1+g)$$
$$\vdots$$
$$D_{p+1} = D_p \times (1+g)$$

If t is the required rate of return for the stock, then the value of that stock is

$$V_{\text{stock}} = D_0 / (t-g)$$

This formula has a lot of weaknesses, particularly when t and g are close. Additionally, the growth rate is never constant and infinite, which obviously is a serious drawback for this method. Some researchers tried to tune and improve this method by proposing, for example, to set up g until a certain time horizon and another g' above this limit.

2.5.1.1 Price Earnings Ratio. A price multiple/valuation ratio of a company's current share price compared to its per-share earnings is a measurement of earning power. The P/E ratio can therefore alternatively be calculated by dividing the company's market capitalization by its total annual earnings.

The price-to-earnings ratio is a financial ratio used for valuation; a higher P/E ratio means that investors are paying more for each unit of net income, so the stock is more expensive compared to one with a lower P/E ratio. The P/E ratio can be seen as being expressed in years, in the sense that it shows the number of years of earnings which would be required to pay back purchase price, ignoring inflation and time value of money. The P/E ratio also shows current investor demand for a company share. The reciprocal of the P/E ratio is known as the earnings yield. The earnings yield is an estimate of the expected return from holding the stock if we accept certain restrictive assumptions.

Based on how earnings (the denominator) are calculated, there are three versions of the P/E ratio.

Historical P/E uses year-end declared audited earnings in the denominator.

Trailing P/E uses earnings over the most recent 12 months, or four quarters in the denominator.

Forward P/E uses next year's expected earnings, which is defined as either (a) expected earnings per share (EPS) for the next four quarters or (b) expected EPS for the next fiscal year.

2.5.1.2 Price to Book. A price multiple/valuation ratio is calculated as price per share divided by audited NAV per share. Book value is an accounting term denoting the portion of the company held by the shareholders—in other words, the company's total tangible assets less its total liabilities. The calculation can be performed in two ways, but the result should be the same each way. In the first way, the company's market capitalization can be divided by the company's total book value from its balance sheet. The second way, using per-share values, is to divide the company's current share price by the book value per share (i.e., its book value divided by the number of outstanding shares).

As with most ratios, it varies a fair amount by industry. Industries that require more infrastructure capital (for each unit of profit) will usually trade at *P*/*B* ratios much lower than, for example, consulting firms. *P*/*B* ratios are commonly used to compare banks, because most assets and liabilities of banks are constantly valued at market values. A higher *P*/*B* ratio implies that investors expect management to create more value from a given set of assets, all else equal (and/or that the market value of the firm's asset is significantly higher than their accounting value). *P*/*B* ratios do not, however, directly provide any information on the ability of the firm to generate profits or cash for shareholders.

This ratio also gives some idea of whether an investor is paying too much for what would be left if the company went bankrupt immediately. For companies in distress, the book value is usually calculated without the intangible assets that would have no resale value.

2.5.1.3 Price to Cash Flow. A price multiple/valuation ratio is calculated as price per share divided by operating cash flow per share. The price/cash flow ratio (also called price-to-cash flow ratio or *P*/*CF*) is a ratio used to compare a company's market value to its cash flow. It is calculated by dividing the company's market capitalization by company's operating cash flow in the most recent fiscal year (or the most recent four fiscal quarters); or, equivalently, divide the per-share stock price by the per-share operating cash flow. In theory, the lower a stock's price/cash flow ratio, the greater the value that stock.

2.5.1.4 Return on Equity. Return on equity (ROE) is a profitability ratio calculated as audited net income divided by audited NAV. ROE is equal to a fiscal year's net income (after preferred stock dividends but before common stock dividends) divided by total equity (excluding preferred shares), expressed as a percentage. As with many financial ratios, ROE is best used to compare companies in the same industry. High ROE yields no immediate benefit. Since stock prices are most strongly determined by earnings per share (EPS), you will be paying twice as much (in Price/Book terms) for a 20% ROE company as for a 10% ROE company.

2.5.1.5 Price to Earnings to Growth Ratio. The price to earnings to growth ratio (PEG) is a valuation metric for determining the relative tradeoff between the price of a stock, the earnings generated per share (EPS), and the company's expected growth. In general, the *P*/*E* ratio is higher for a company with a higher growth rate. Thus using just the *P*/*E* ratio would make high-growth companies appear overvalued relative to others. It is assumed that by dividing the *P/E* ratio by the earnings growth rate, the resulting ratio is better for comparing companies with different growth rates.

The PEG ratio is considered to be a convenient approximation. It was popularized by Peter Lynch, who wrote in his 1989 book *One Up on Wall Street* that "the *P/E* ratio of any company that's fairly priced will equal its growth rate"—that is, a fairly valued company will have its PEG equal to 1.

2.5.2 TECHNICAL ANALYSIS

Despite all the fancy and exotic tools it employs, technical analysis really just studies supply and demand in a market in an attempt to determine what direction, or trend, will continue in the future. In other words, technical analysis attempts to understand the emotions in the market by studying the market itself, as opposed to its components.

2.5.2.1 Average True Range. Average true range (ATR)[1] is an indicator that measures volatility. It reflects volatility as absolute level. In other words, ATR is not shown as a percentage of the current close price. Because of this, ATR values of different stocks are not comparable.

Calculation: Typically, the ATR is based on 14-day period and can be calculated on an intraday, daily, weekly, or monthly basis. One can use daily data to calculate ATR and 15-day period in calculation of ATR. Because there must be a beginning, the first TR (true range) value is simply the high price minus the low price, and the first 15-day ATR is the average of the daily TR values for the last 15 days. After that, a smoothing technique is used by incorporating the previous period's ATR value.

$$\text{Current ATR} = ((\text{Prior ATR} \times 14) + \text{Current TR}) / 15$$

ATR is not a directional indicator, such as MACD or RSI. Instead, ATR is a unique volatility indicator that reflects the degree of interest or disinterest in a move. Strong moves, in either direction, are often accompanied by large ranges, or large true ranges. This is especially true at the beginning of a move. Insignificant moves are usually accompanied by relatively narrow ranges. As such, ATR can be used to validate the enthusiasm behind a move or breakout. A bullish reversal with an increase in ATR would show strong buying pressure and reinforce the reversal. A bearish support break with an increase in ATR would show strong selling pressure and reinforce the support break.

2.5.2.2 Rate of Change. Rate of change (ROC) measures the percentage increase or decrease in price over a given period of time. It is a pure momentum oscillator. Many leading indicators come in the form of momentum oscillators.

---

[1]This indicator was developed by J. Welles Wilder, Jr. in his book *New Concepts in Technical Trading Systems* (Trend Research, Edmonton Albertar, Canada) in 1978.

Generally speaking, momentum measures the rate of change of a security's price. As the price of a security rises, price momentum increases. The faster the security rises (the greater the period-over-period price change), the larger the increase in momentum.

Calculation:

$$\text{ROC } (n \text{ period}) = ((\text{Close} - \text{Close } (n \text{ period})) / \text{Close } (n \text{ period})) * 100$$

There is no upward boundary on the ROC. There is, however, a downside limit. The minimum value of ROC is −100% because securities can only decline by 100% to have zero value. The most common period for the ROC is 12 periods for short-term signals, while 25 periods is popular among mid-term investors.

In general, prices are rising as long as the ROC remains positive. Conversely, prices are falling when the ROC is negative. That's why investors will buy a security when the ROC crosses above the 0 line and sell when the indicator crosses below 0. But the best method for trading the ROC is to look at previous peaks and troughs for the indicator. By comparing the current ROC value to recent levels, an investor will know what to expect in terms of price movement relative to the most recent trading activity.

2.5.2.3 Relative Strength Index. Relative strength index (RSI) is an extremely popular momentum oscillator that measures the speed and change of price movements. It can also be used to identify the general trend.

Calculation: RSI is calculated for a specific period. The smaller the period, the quicker it moves with market movement. We can use, for example, a 15-day period in calculating RSI of individual stocks. For a 15-day period, it is calculated in the following ways:

$$\text{RSI} = 100 - \frac{100}{1 + \text{RS}}$$

$$\text{RS} = \text{Average gain/Average loss}$$

The very first calculations for average gain and average loss are simple 15 period averages:

$$\text{First average gain} = \text{Sum of gains over the past 15 periods/15}$$

$$\text{First average loss} = \text{Sum of losses over the past 15 periods/15}$$

After the first 15 periods, subsequent calculations are based on the prior averages and the current gain loss:

$$\text{Average gain} = [(\text{Previous average gain}) \times 14 + \text{Current gain}]/15$$

$$\text{Average loss} = [(\text{Previous average loss}) \times 14 + \text{Current loss}]/15$$

We can also calculate RSI for different sectors using the weighted average technique. For each sector, RSI is calculated in the following formula:

$$\text{Industry RSI} = \sum (\text{M.cap. weight} * \text{Respective company RSI})$$

where M.cap. stands for market capitalization.

RSI fluctuates between 0 and 100. A stock is deemed to be overbought once the RSI approaches the 70 level, meaning that it may be getting overvalued and is a good candidate for a pullback. Likewise, if the RSI approaches 30, it is an indication that the stock may be getting oversold and likely to become undervalued. Investors can also use a bull market range and a bear market for RSI. RSI tends to fluctuate between 40 and 90 in a bull market with the 40–50 zones acting as support. RSI tends to fluctuate between 10 and 60 in a bear market with the 50–60 zone acting as resistance. These ranges may vary, depending on RSI parameters, strength of trend, and volatility of the underlying stock.

2.5.2.4 Money Flow Index. Money flow index (MFI) is an oscillator that uses both price and volume to measure buying and selling pressure. It is also known as volume-weighted RSI. It moves between 0 and 100.

Calculation: We can use, for example, a 15-day period in calculating MFI of different stocks. A 15-day MFI is calculated as follows:

$$\text{Typical price} = (\text{High} + \text{Low} + \text{Close})/3$$

$$\text{Raw money flow} = \text{Typical price} \times \text{Volume}$$

$$\text{Positive money flow} = \text{Sum of positive raw money flow over 15 periods}$$

$$\text{Negative money flow} = \text{Sum of negative raw money flow over 15 periods}$$

$$\text{Money flow ratio} = (\text{Positive money flow}) / (\text{Negative money flow})$$

$$\text{Money flow index} = 100 - 100/(1 + \text{Money flow ratio})$$

As a volume-weighted version of the RSI, the MFI can be interpreted similar to RSI. In simple terms, MFI above 80 is considered overbought and MFI below 20 is considered oversold. More robust signals can be recognized with charts. A bullish swing occurs when MFI becomes oversold below 20, surges above 20, holds above 20 on a pullback, and then breaks above its prior reaction high. A bearish failure swing occurs when MFI becomes overbought above 80, plunges below 80, fails to exceed 80 on a bounce, and then breaks below the prior reaction low.

2.5.2.5 Moving Averages. Moving averages smooth the price data to form a trend following indicator. They do not predict price direction, but rather define the current direction with a lag. Moving averages lag because they are based on past prices. Despite this lag, moving averages help smooth price action and filter out the noise. They also form the building blocks for many other technical indicators and overlays, such as Bollinger bands, MACD, and the McClellan oscillator. The two most popular types of moving averages are the simple moving average (SMA) and the exponential moving average (EMA).

Calculation: A simple moving average is formed by computing the average price of a security over a specific number of periods. Most moving averages are based on closing prices. A 5-day simple moving average is the 5-day sum of closing prices divided by 5. As its name implies, a moving average is an average that moves. Old data are dropped as new data become available. For a 5-day simple moving average, the first day of the moving average simply covers the last 5 days. The second day of the moving average drops the first data point and adds the new or sixth data point. This causes the average to move along the time scale.

The longer the moving average, the more the lag. That's why short moving average (5–20 periods) are best suited for short-term trends and trading. Long-term investors will prefer moving averages with 100 or more periods. The direction of the moving average conveys important information about prices. A rising moving average shows that prices are generally increasing. A falling moving average indicates that prices, on average, are falling. A rising long-term moving average reflects a long-term uptrend. A falling long-term moving average reflects a long-term downtrend.

Two moving averages can be used together to generate crossover signals. A bullish crossover occurs when the shorter moving average crosses above the longer moving average. A bearish crossover occurs when the shorter moving average crosses below the longer moving average. There is also a triple crossover method that involves three moving averages. However, these crossovers produce relatively late signals.

Another variant of the moving averages exists. It is called an exponential moving average. This moving average calculation uses a smoothing factor to place a higher weight on recent data points and is regarded as much more efficient than the linear weighted average. Having an understanding of the calculation is not generally required for most traders because most charting packages do the calculation for you. The most important thing to remember about the exponential moving average is that it is more responsive to new information relative to the simple moving average. This responsiveness is one of the key factors of why this is the moving average of choice among many technical traders.

FURTHER READING

Bachelier, M.L., *Theorie de la speculation*, Gauthier-Villars, Paris, 1900.

Barber, B.M., Odean, T., Trading is hazardous to your wealth: the common stock investment performance of individual investors, *Journal of Finance*, **55**, 2000, pp. 773–806.

Colby, R. W., *The Encyclopedia of Technical Market Indicators*, 2nd edition, McGraw-Hill Professionals, New York, 2003.

De Bondt, W. F. M., Thaler, R., Does the stock market overreact?, *Journal of Finance*, **40**(3), Papers and Proceedings of the Forty-third Annual Meeting of the American Finance Association, Dallas, Texas, December 28–30, 1984.

Fama, E., Random walk in stock market prices, *Financial Analyst Journal*, September–October, 1965.

Fama, E., The behaviour of stock market prices, *Journal of Business*, January 1965.

Fama, E., Efficient capital markets: a review of theory and empirical work, *Journal of Finance*, **25**(2), May 1970.

Fama, E., Efficient capital markets, II, *Journal of Finance*, **46**(5), December 1991.

Fama, E., Fisher, L., Jensen, M., Roll, R., The adjustment of stock prices to new information, *International Economic Review*, February 13, 1969.

Frank, R., *Microeconomics and Behavior*, 7th edition, McGraw-Hill, New York.

Gibson, G., *The Stock Markets of London, Paris, and New York*, G.P. Putman & Sons, New York, 1899.

Grossman, S. J., Stiglitz, J., On the impossibility of informationally efficient markets, *The American Economic Review*, **70**(3), June 1980.

Jensen, M., Some anomalous evidence regarding market efficiency, *Journal of Financial Economics*, **6**, 1978.

Pinto, J. E., Henry, E., Robinson, T. R., Stowe, J. D., *Equity Asset Valuation*, 2nd edition, CFA Investment Series, Wiley, Hoboken, NJ, 2010.

Schleifer, A., Inefficient markets, in *An Introduction to Behavioral Finance*, Oxford University Press, New York, 2000.

Sewell, M., History of the efficient market hypothesis, UCL Research note, RN/11/04, January 2011. This article contains an exhaustive bibliography about the efficient markets theory.

Shiller, R. J., *Market Volatility*, MIT Press, Cambridge, MA, 1989.

Shiller, R. J. *Irrational Exuberance*, Princeton University Press, Princeton, N.J., 2000.

Summers, L., Does the stock market rationally reflect fundamental values? *Journal of Financial and Quantitative Analysis*, September 1985.

Tobin, X. Y., 1985.

CHAPTER THREE

Return and Volatility Estimates

October: This is one of the peculiarly dangerous months to speculate in stocks. The others are July, January, September, April, November, May, March, June, December, August, and February.

—Mark Twain

The concept of return may have different acceptations according to investors. When referring about return obtained by an investor on a stock, we usually mean not only the net dividend generated by the stock but also the potential value-add when selling the stock. Therefore, the rate of return comprises the yield obtained by the dividend (net dividend) as well as the value-add or not in capital scaled to the purchase price of the stock.

$$R_t = \frac{D_t + P_t - P_{t-1}}{P_{t-1}}$$

where R_t is the rate of return of the stock i during period t, D_t is the dividend paid during period t, P_t is the stock price at the end of period t, and P_{t-1} is the stock price at the end of the period $t - 1$.

This formula does not take into account any tax requirements. It is the gross return for the investor. This formula assumes that dividends are paid at the end of each period or that dividends are not reinvested before the end of the period.

Example:

$$P_{t-1} = \text{USD } 200.00$$

$$P_t = \text{USD } 210.00$$

$$D_t = \text{USD } 5.00$$

$$R_t = (5 + (210 - 200))/200 = 7.5\%$$

Handbook of Market Risk, First Edition. Christian Szylar.

The cumulative return under this method is given by the formula

$$R_t = \prod_{t-1}^{t}(1+R_t)-1$$

Lognormal Return:

$$R_t = \ln[S_t/S_{t-1}]$$

The cumulative return under this method is given by the formula

$$R_t = \sum_{t=1}^{t} rt$$

Geometric Mean. The geometric mean formula is the correct version to use when considering rates of change/growth rate, where $\bar{x}$ is the mean and x_n is the rate of growth or change in each time period, expressed as a decimal.

$$\bar{x} = \sqrt[n]{(1+x_1)X(1+x_2)X(1+x_3)X\ldots X(1+x_n)}-1$$

Geometric fund's return can also be obtained using the formula

$$R_{\text{Fund}} = \exp\left(\sum_{i=1}^{n}\log(1+R_i)\right)$$

To annualize the fund's return, the following equation can be used:

$$AR_{\text{Fund}} = (1+R_{\text{Fund}})^{\frac{252}{\text{Days}}}-1$$

What is risk? In simple terms, risk measures how volatile an asset's return are. Volatility is a measure of how much the price of an asset fluctuates around its mean. The more volatile the asset, the greater the potential to make large profits or large losses.

Investors sometimes begin a quantitative screening by stating that they want a fund with a "low risk." Because of the historical ties between risk and standard deviation in the world of traditional investments, they equate high standard deviation with high risk and then use standard deviation as a comparative statistic. However, in truth, standard deviation is merely a statistic that measures predictability. A high standard deviation means that the fund is volatile, not that the fund is risky or will lose money, while a low standard deviation means that a fund is generally consistent in producing similar returns. A fund can have extremely low standard deviation and lose money consistently, or have high standard deviation and never experience a losing period.

Let's consider, for example, two portfolios with 250 daily returns:

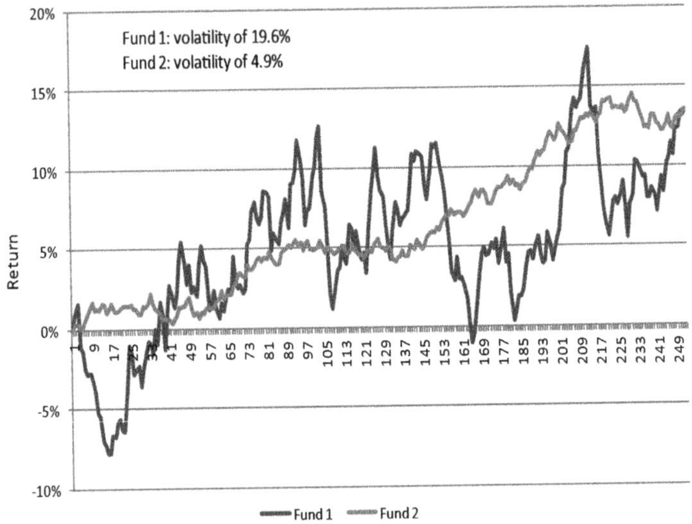

FIGURE 3.1 **Fund returns with different risk profiles.**

Both funds have the same return with 13.49%. Nevertheless, they do not have the same level of risk. Fund 2 has returns that are very close to the mean (the mean is 0.06% daily return). If the past is any guideline, then the future returns can almost be predicted to be very close to the mean. Fund 2 would contain a relatively low risk because volatility is low. The standard deviation for fund 2 is indeed very low with 4.92%. (Figure 3.1). The standard deviation is simply a statistical term that measures how volatile the portfolio is. On the contrary, in fund 1, although the mean return is the same at 0.06%, some data points vary considerably from the mean, and as a result the standard deviation is much higher. Its standard deviation is indeed much higher (19.59%) than that of fund 2—almost four times higher. Fund 1 is considered to be a higher-risk portfolio.

One can then assimilate the investment risk to its dispersion or variability around an anticipated value. The measure of the variability of a time serial as historical data is done using standard deviation or identically its square root, called variance.

Standard deviation in its simple form is given by the formula

$$\sigma(x) = \sqrt{V(x)}$$

And variance is given by

$$V(x) = \frac{\sum_{i=1}^{n} (x_i - \bar{x})^2}{n}$$

or

$$\overline{x} = \frac{\sum_{i=1}^{n} x_i}{n}$$

Volatility estimation is of central importance to risk management, pricing, and portfolio construction, and a number of attempts have been made in the last 25 years to improve upon the classic standard deviation of daily returns as an estimator of asset volatility. Volatility has been one of the most active and successful areas of research in time series econometrics and economic forecasting in recent decades. This chapter provides a selective survey of the most important theoretical developments and empirical insights to emerge from this burgeoning literature, with a distinct focus on forecasting applications.

3.1 Standard Deviation

As just mentioned, one of the most commonly used measures of volatility is a statistical measure referred to as the standard deviation. It quantifies the level of dispersion of an asset or portfolio using only the historical returns data. These returns can be the change in asset price or level over any time period—for example, daily price changes.

$$r_t = \ln\left(\frac{P_t}{P_{t-1}}\right) \tag{3.1}$$

where r_t is the return of the asset over the period $t - 1$ one to t (typically, an appropriate risk-free rate is subtracted from this return) and P_t is the price of the asset at time t.

Given two or more return data points, the asset volatility (σ) can be calculated with the standard deviation as

$$\sigma = \sqrt{\frac{1}{N_{T-1}} \sum_{i=1}^{N_T} (r_i - \overline{r})^2} \tag{3.2}$$

where r_i is the ith return; N_T is the number of returns, r_i; and $\overline{r}$ is the average of the returns, r_i.

The $N_T - 1$ in Eq. (3.2) denotes that this is the *sample* standard deviation, recognizing that not all of the returns data may be accounted for. The number of observed returns can vary and is typically a tradeoff between sampling error and relevance. The more data points that are used, the lower the standard error of the measurement. However a large number of data points imply using returns further back in time. Very old data may not be relevant in the current market environment. The units of σ are consistent with the returns; so, for example, if the returns are daily, then the volatility will be a daily volatility. Typically the volatility will be quoted as an annualized figure by multiplying by a factor that accounts for the number of periods in a year. For example, a daily volatility will be annualized by multiplying by $\sqrt{250}$ because there are approximately 250 trading days in a calendar year. Likewise, monthly volatility will use an annualization factor of $\sqrt{12}$.

Standard deviation as a measure of volatility is formulaically straightforward to implement and interpret. It is not, however, a particularly robust metric and is susceptible to large outliers. The downside returns are treated as equally as upside returns, leading to a symmetric measure that does not accurately reflect the skew empirically observed in financial returns data. Despite these concerns, the standard deviation has become an integral part of the language of volatility.

3.2 Standard Deviation with a Moving Observation Window

The standard deviation measure of volatility given by Eq. (3.2) provides a single volatility estimate over an entire set of returns. For example, the annualized volatility of the S&P 500 Index using the daily returns between January 2000 and December 2011 is 21.53%. The daily returns over this period are illustrated in Figure 3.2, where it is immediately clear that the dispersion exhibited by the returns are not constant; there are periods where the returns are notably more volatile—for example, in the third quarter of 2008 when the financial markets were under significant duress.

It is clear that a single measurement does not capture the time-varying nature of volatility, and a simple modification to the application of the standard deviation method can yield far more intuitive results. Rather than use the entire set

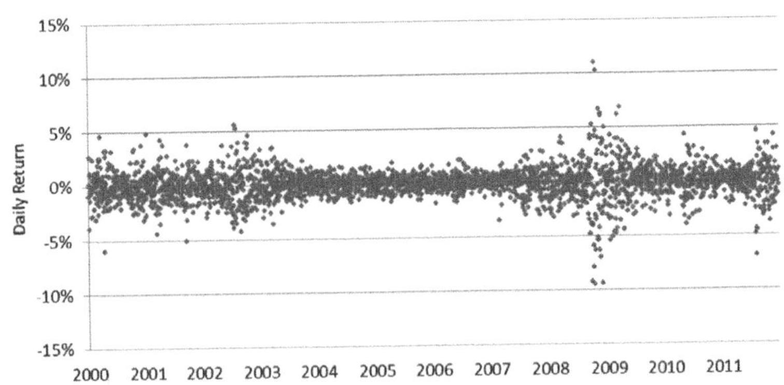

FIGURE 3.2 Daily returns of the S&P 500 Index from January 2000 to December 2011.

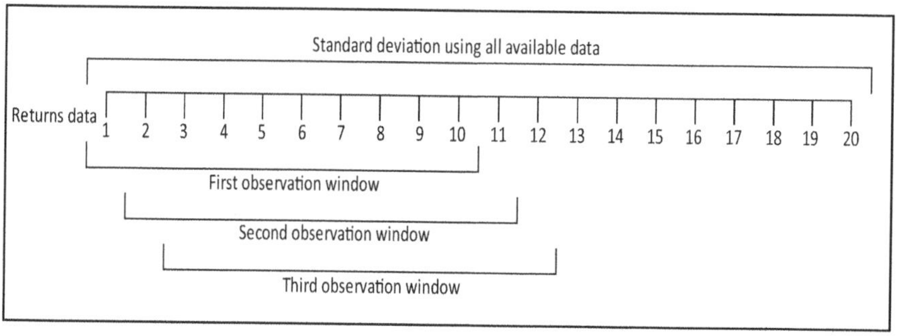

FIGURE 3.3 Comparing a moving window that observes 10 data points to an inclusive volatility measure using all 20 data points.

of returns data, it can be useful to instead observe a smaller set of the data such that the volatility measurement is more relevant to the prevailing environment. The number of returns, N_T, in Eq. (3.2) is therefore replaced by M_T, the number of returns in the *observation window* such that $M_T < N_T$:

$$\sigma = \sqrt{\frac{1}{M_{T-1}} \sum_{i=1}^{M_T} (r_i - \bar{r})^2} \tag{3.3}$$

where r_i is the ith return; M_T is the number of returns, r_i, in the observation window; and $\bar{r}$ is the average of the returns, r_i, in the observation window.

The first volatility estimate is computed using the first M_T of the returns. The second volatility estimate moves the observation window along by 1 period such that the first return is removed and the latest return is added. A simple example is illustrated in Figure 3.3, where the data set consists of $N_T = 20$ returns and a moving observation window of $M_T = 10$ returns. On closer inspection, both Eq. (3.2) and Eq. (3.3) can be interpreted as taken the average of the squared deviation beyond the mean return. The former takes the average over all N_T data points whereas the latter only uses a subset, M_T.

Applying this to technique to the S&P 500 Index daily returns and using an observation windows of $M = 60$ days yields the time-varying volatility shown in Figure 3.4.This method quite clearly highlights different periods of time as being more volatile for the S&P 500 Index.

It's worth noting, however, that the level of structure observed in the volatility over time will depend on the size of the observed window. Using a larger value for M_T can cause changes in volatility to be less reactive to the point where $M_T = N_T$, and there is a single estimate and hence no structure to the volatility. Using a smaller value for M_T can lead to a higher degree of variability of volatility to the point where a very small value of M_T can cause the metric to be highly erratic and difficult to draw conclusions from.

The nature of a moving window can lead to sudden increases in the volatility when a large data point enters the window. The volatility will stay elevated until

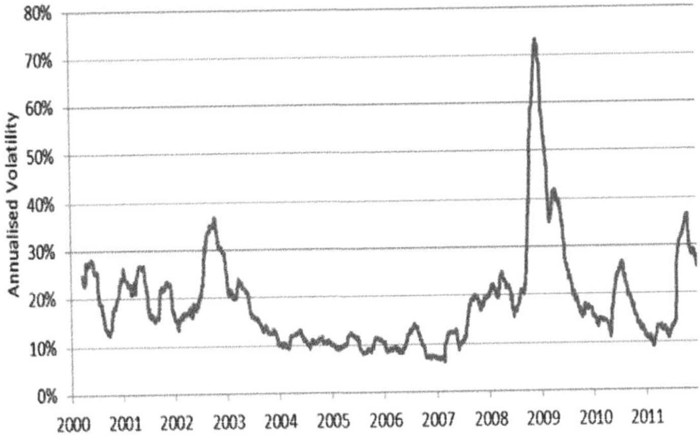

FIGURE 3.4 Volatility of the S&P 500 Index using an observation window of 60 trading days.

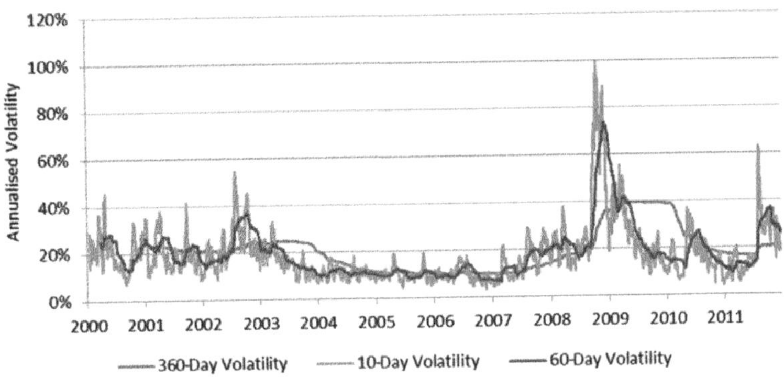

FIGURE 3.5 Comparing volatility computed using observation windows of 10, 60, and 360 days.

the large data point leaves the window, at which point a large drop will be recorded by the volatility estimate. This is illustrated by Figure 3.5 by using a randomly generated set of returns and augmenting a single data point to represent an extreme return.

3.3 Exponentially Weighted Moving Average (EWMA)

The Moving Average method assigns an equal weight to each data point in the observation window, thereby placing equal importance on each. An exponential weighting scheme is a commonly used alternative, popularized by RiskMetrics.

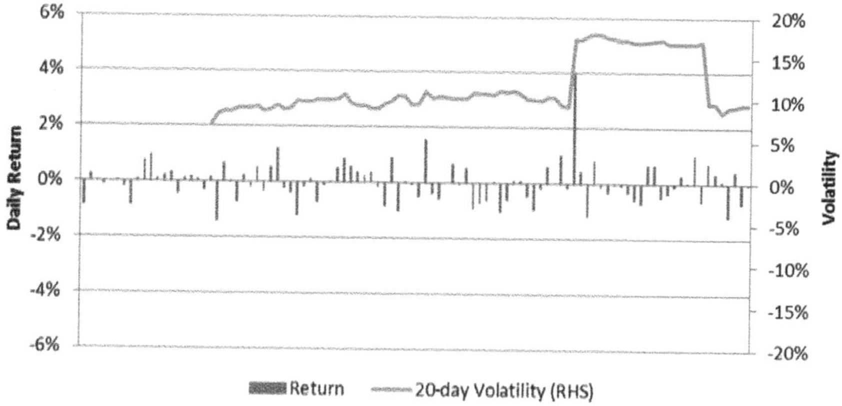

FIGURE 3.6 Example of temporary elevation in volatility due to a single data point.

As can be seen from Figure 3.6, the weights decay exponentially such that the most recent data points have the highest weighting. The rate of decay can be parameterized by either a *smoothing parameter* or a *half-life*. These parameters can be used interchangeably because they have a deterministic relationship:

$$\lambda = 1 - \frac{\ln(2)}{\tau_{1/2}} \tag{3.4}$$

where λ is the smoothing parameter and $\tau_{1/2}$ is the half-life.

The weight w_t applied at time t can then be found using

$$W_t = \frac{(1-\lambda)\lambda^{M_T - t}}{1-\lambda^{M_T}} \tag{3.5}$$

where λ is the smoothing parameter and M_T is the total number of return observations.

Note that the denominator in Eq. (3.5) is used to normalize the sum of all weights to equal one. This is not required if the observation window is particularly long, but is especially important for short observation windows.

The half-life can be interpreted as the time taken for the weight to drop to half the value. The RiskMetrics approach is to use a smoothing value of 0.94, equivalent to half-life of approximately 11.5 periods. This is evident in Figure 3.7, where the weight has fallen from ~6% to ~3% after ~11 data points.

Using Eq. (3.3) and replacing the weighting fraction with Eq. (3.5) yields the EWMA volatility estimator:

$$\sigma = \sqrt{\sum_{i=1}^{M_T} W_i (r_i - \bar{r})^2} \tag{3.6}$$

where w_i is the ith weight.

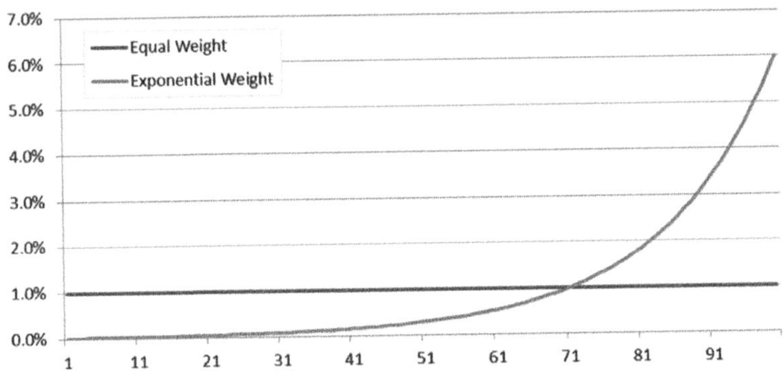

FIGURE 3.7 **Equal and exponential weighting schemes.**

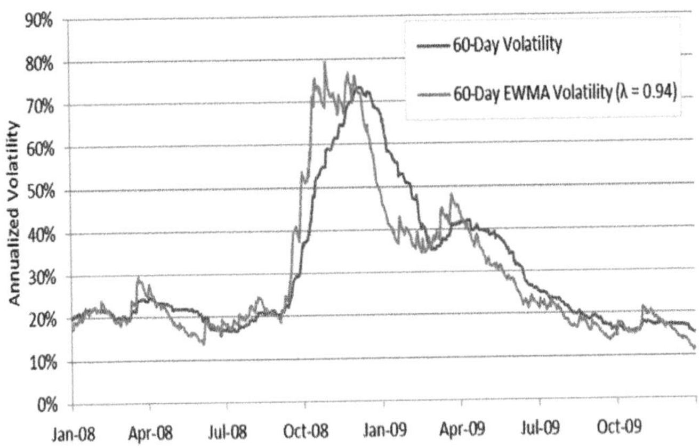

FIGURE 3.8 **Volatility estimated from EWMA compared to standard deviation.**

An alternative formulation exploits a recursive feature of the EWMA. The variance at time t is a function of the smoothing parameter and the volatility and return on time $t-1$:

$$\sigma_t^2 = \lambda\sigma_{t-1}^2 + (1-\lambda)r_{t-1}^2 \tag{3.7}$$

It should, however, be noted that this recursive formulation does not normalize the weights as in Eq. (3.5). It also assumes that the return distribution has a zero mean.

The 60-day standard deviation and EWMA methods are compared in Figure 3.8 over the two-year period from January 2008 to December 2009 where the EWMA estimate can be seen to have a faster reaction time.

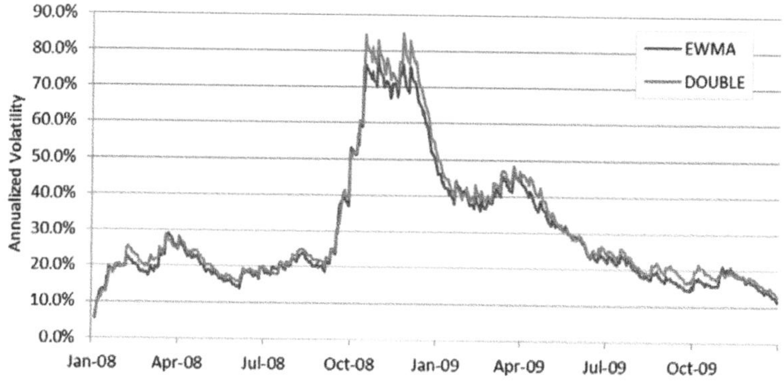

FIGURE 3.9 EWMA versus DES.

3.4 Double (Holt) Exponential Smoothing Model (DES)

The double exponential smoothing model is an extension of the EWMA method that attempts to smooth trends within the data. The EWMA recursive formulation shown in Eq. (3.7) can be updated with an adjustment to the returns:

$$\sigma_t^2 = \lambda\sigma_{t-1}^2 + (1-\lambda)(r_{t-1} + \beta_{t-1})^2 \tag{3.8}$$

where β_t is the trend adjustment and is given by

$$\beta_t = \gamma(r_{t-1} - r_{t-2}) + (1-\gamma)\beta_{t-1} \tag{3.9}$$

where γ is the trend smoothing parameter.

A comparison of EWMA and DES is shown in Figure 3.9.

3.5 Principal Component Analysis (PCA) Models

Principle Component Analysis models are statistical multifactor models that decompose a correlated set of assets into a number of orthogonal principal components, or factors. The number of factors is typically much less than the number of assets resulting in large reduction in dimensionality, facilitating computation of risk metrics of large portfolios with the model.

The PCA models are built on a factor returns model:

$$r - r_f = r^* = Bf + \varepsilon \tag{3.10}$$

where r is the $N_A \times 1$ vector of asset returns, r_f is the risk free rate, r^* is the $N_A \times 1$ vector of excess asset returns, B is the $N_A \times$ K matrix of factor loadings,

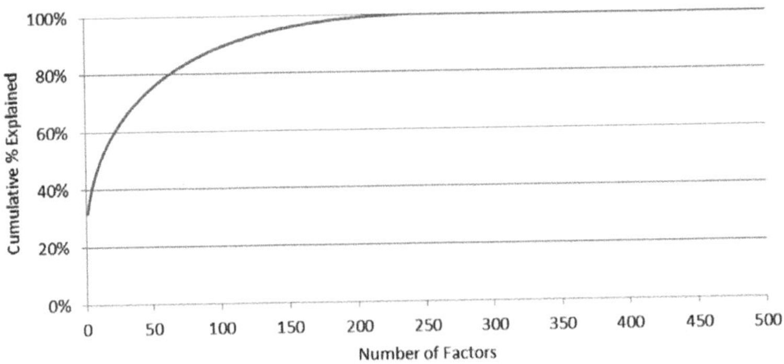

FIGURE 3.10 Number of factors versus the total explained variance for a 500 asset model.

f is the $K \times 1$ vector of factor returns, and ε is the $N_A \times 1$ vector of idiosyncratic asset returns.

Using the assumption that idiosyncratic returns are uncorrelated, the returns model given in Eq. (3.10) implies that the covariance of the excess returns can be expressed as

$$V = BFB' + \Omega \tag{3.11}$$

where V is the covariance matrix of the excess asset returns, F is the covariance matrix of the factor returns, and Ω is the diagonal covariance matrix of idiosyncratic returns.

Modeling Eq. (3.11) with a principal components model results in F being a diagonal factor covariance matrix. The PCA can be performed with a range of techniques including singular value decomposition (SVD) and eigendecomposition.

When the number of principal components (K) is set to the number of assets (N_A), the total variance explained by the factors will be 100%. Each factor explains marginally less variance, and trimming the number of factors to be less than N_A will result in a tradeoff between dimensionality reduction and explanatory power. Figure 3.10 shows how the percentage of variance explained approaches 100% as the number of factors is increased.

Typically the number of factors will be chosen based on a fixed percentage of variance explained. In the example given in Figure 3.9, it would be possible to retain 90% of the variance with only 102 factors, representing a dimensionality reduction of nearly 80%.

3.6 The VIX

The volatility index (or VIX) is a weighted measure of the **implied volatility** for real-time $SPX put and call options (Figure 3.11). The puts and calls are

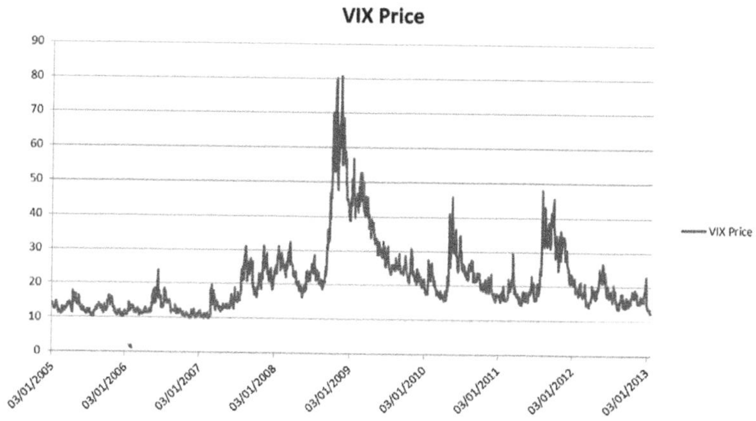

FIGURE 3.11 The VIX value: Period 01/01/2005–23/01/2013.

weighted according to time remaining and the degree to which *they are in or out of the money*. From this is created a hypothetical at-the-money option with a 30-day expiration time period. In this way, they are trying to set a value that is equal to the equivalent value of the $SPX's current price. (When a stock's option strike price is "at the money," it is theoretically the same as the price the stock is trading for at that moment.) So what does that mean? It means that the VIX really represents the "implied volatility" for the hypothetical $SPX put/call options on an "at the money" option value.

Simply put, the VIX is a key measure of market expectations in the near term. For almost 20 years, the VIX has been considered as a valuable barometer of investor sentiment and volatility. Another way to look at it is that it measures perceived risks of investors. The greater the perceived risks investors have about stocks, the more they buy "protection put options," which means that the VIX will therefore be moving higher. When the VIX moves higher, the market moves lower because they are inversely related.

3.7 Geometric Brownian Motion Process

A geometric Brownian motion process for an asset with price S evolves as follows:

$$dS_t = \mu S_t \, dt + \sigma S_t \, dZ_t$$

where μ is the asset drift, σ is the volatility (assumed constant), and Z_t is a Weiner process. From Ito's lemma the the log asset price is

$$d \ln S_t = \left(\mu - \frac{1}{2}\sigma^2\right) dt + \sigma dZ_t$$

3.8 GARCH

GARCH is an acronym for generalized auto regressive conditional heteroscedasticity. This is an econometric model used for modeling and forecasting time-dependent variance, and hence volatility, of stock price returns. It represents current variance in terms of past variance(s). It was proposed by Bollerslev[1] in 1986.

GARCH now comprises different variations (EGARCH, NGARCH, IGARCH, FIGARCH, etc.), but the simple one is GARCH(1,1). In this model the variance v_n of stock returns at time step n is modeled by

$$v_n = (1-\alpha-\beta)w_0 + \beta v_{n-1} + \alpha v_{n-1} B_{n-1}^2$$

where w_0 is the long-term variance, α and β are positive parameters, with $\alpha+\beta<1$, and B_n are independent Brownian motions—that is, random numbers drawn from a normal distribution. The latest variance, v_n, can therefore be thought of as a weighted average of the most recent variance, the latest square of returns, and the long-term average.

3.9 Estimator Using the Highest and Lowest

3.9.1 PARKINSON ESTIMATOR

Michael Parkinson, a physicist, in 1980 showed that the trading range of a security (stocks, currencies, etc.) contains significantly more information about the return generating process than about the simple period to period return, that is, market close-to-close.[2]

Parkinson's number attempts to estimate the volatility of returns for an asset following a diffusion process (geometric random walk) by using only the high and low of the period. Essentially, the simple formula gives the distribution of the maxima and the minima of the asset returns. Parkinson's number N for an asset, say a stock or Treasury futures, is given by

$$e_{\text{Parkinson}}^2 = \frac{1}{N*4*\log(2)} \sum_{k=1,N} (h_k - l_k)^2$$

with $h = \log(\text{high})$ $l = \log(\text{low})$ $o = \log(\text{open})$ $c = \log(\text{close})$

[1]Bollerslev, T., General autoregressive conditional heteroscedasticity, *Journal of Econometrics*, **31**, 1986, pp. 307–327.

[2]Spurgin, Richard B., and Schneeweis, Thomas, *Efficient estimation of intraday volatility: A method-of-moment approach incorporating trading Range* (CISDM working paper); and Taleb, *Dynamic Hedging*.

Comparing the Parkinson's number with the periodically sampled volatility can reveal very important information to traders, especially exotic option traders trading knockouts or lookbacks, about the nature of mean reversion of the asset path as well as the distribution of stop losses. From the above formula, it is obvious that the theoretical relationship between Parkinson's number and the periodically sampled volatility is

$$\text{Parkinson's number}(\text{P}) = 1.67 * \text{Historical volatility}$$

If the Parkinson's number is more than 1.67 times the historical volatility (over the same continuous sample period), then the traders can infer that there is a clear bias in favor of a wider high-low range than is assumed by a random walk.

Given the high volatility environment today and a growing volume in the volatility products (variance swaps, vol swaps, short strangles, etc.), it would be interesting to see how the Parkinson's number compares with the historical volatility in various asset markets.

3.9.2 ROGERS SATCHELL ESTIMATOR

Rogers and Satchell (1991) derived an estimator that allows for nonzero drift:[3]

$$\sigma_{RS}^2 = \frac{1}{N} \sum_{k=1,N} (h_k - o_k)(h_k - c_k) + (l_k - o_k)(l_k - c_k)$$

Yang and Zhang[4] devised an estimator that combines the classical and Rogers–Satchell estimator, showing that it has the minimum variance and is both unbiased and independent of process drift and opening gaps. Their estimator is given by

$$\hat{\sigma}_{YZ}^2 = \hat{\sigma}_o^2 + k\hat{\sigma}_c^2 + (1-k)\hat{\sigma}_{RS}^2$$

where the constant k takes the form

$$k = \frac{0.34}{1 + \dfrac{m+1}{m-1}}$$

3.9.3 GARMAN–KLASS ESTIMATOR

Garman and Klass provide an estimator with superior efficiency, having minimum variance on the assumption that the process follows a geometric Brownian motion with zero drift:[5]

---

[3]Rogers, L. C. G., Satchell, S. E., Estimating variance from high, low and closing prices, *Annals of Applied Probability*, **1**, 1991, pp. 504–512.

[4]Yang, D., Zhang, Q., Drift independent volatility estimation based on high, low, open and close prices, *Journal of Business*, **73**, 2000, pp. 477–491.

[5]Garman, M., Klass, M., On the estimation of security price volatilities from historical data, *Journal of Business*, **53**, 1980, pp. 67–78.

$$\sigma_{GK}^2 = \frac{1}{N}\sum_{k=1,N} 0.511(u_k - d_k)^2 - 0.019(c_k(u_k + d_k) - 2u_k d_k) - 0.383c_k^2$$

with $u_k = \log(\text{high})_k - \log(\text{open})_k$, $d_k = \log(\text{low})_k$, $c_k = \log(\text{close})_k - \log(\text{open})_k$.

FURTHER READING

Augen, J., *The Volatility Edge in Options Trading: New Technical Strategies for Investing in Unstable Markets*, Pearson Education, New York, 2008.

Cherubini, U., Luciano, E., Vecchiato, W., *Copula Methods in Finance*, John Wiley & Sons, Hoboken, NJ, 2004.

Cumby, R., Figlewski, S., Hasbrouck, J., Forecasting volatilities and correlations with EGARCH models, *Journal of Derivatives*, **1**, 1993, pp. 51–63.

Danielsson, J., *Financial Risk Forecasting*, John Wiley & Sons, Hoboken, NJ, 2011.

Engel, R. F., Mezrich, J., Grappling with GARCH, *Risk*, September 1995, pp. 112–117.

Hull, John C., *Options, Futures and Other Derivatives*, 6th edition, Pearson/Prentice Hall, Englewood Cliffs, NJ, 2009.

Hull, J., *Risk Management and Financial Institutions*, 3rd edition, John Wiley & Sons, 2012.

Knight, J., Satchell S., *Forecasting Volatility in the Financial Markets*, 2nd edition, Butterworth-Heinemann Finance, 2002.

Poon, S.-H., *A Practical Guide to Forecasting Financial Market Volatility*, Wiley Finance, Hoboken, NJ, 2005.

Taleb, N., *Dynamic Hedging: Managing Vanilla and Exotic Options*, John Wiley & Sons, 1997.

Torben G. A., Bollerslev, T., Christoffersen, P. F., Diebold, F., Volatility forecasting, Working Paper, National Bureau of Economic Research, March 2005.

Tsay Ruey S., *Analysis of Financial Time Series*, 2nd edition, Wiley Series in Probability and Statistics, John Wiley & Sons, Hoboken, NJ, 2005.

CHAPTER FOUR

Diversification, Portfolios of Risky Assets, and the Efficient Frontier

Diversify your investments.

—John Templeton

Portfolio diversification is a widely embraced investment strategy that reduces your portfolio investment risk. Simply stated, by combining assets that are not perfectly correlated—that is, do not move in perfect lock-step together—the risks embedded in a portfolio are lowered and higher risk-adjusted returns can be achieved. The lower the correlation between assets, the greater the reduction in risk that can be derived. Modern Portfolio Theory was first developed with individual securities in mind but can also be applied to combinations of asset classes.

To understand the benefits of global diversification, it is useful to separate the risk of investments into two broad types, security-specific risks and market risks. Security-specific risks result from factors specific to the security, such as management skill at a corporation. Security-specific risks can be almost eliminated by gaining an exposure to a whole asset class. Market risk results from factors that impact on groups of securities or a whole asset class, such as interest rates or macroeconomic factors like the business cycle. By diversifying between asset classes, we can reduce market risk; and because of different economic factors between countries, global diversification can reduce these risks even further. The benefits of global diversification are illustrated in Figure 4.1, which considers a simulation that takes the 500 securities and their weights within the S&P 500. Each simulation randomly picks N stocks and then normalizes the weight to sum to 100% invested. It then calculates what the realized volatility would have been over the last year using daily returns data. We do this for N stocks to 250 stocks. We then repeat the simulation 1000 times so that for each portfolio of N stocks we have 1000 volatilities. We then take the average volatility of the 1000 portfolios of N stocks.

Handbook of Market Risk, First Edition. Christian Szylar.

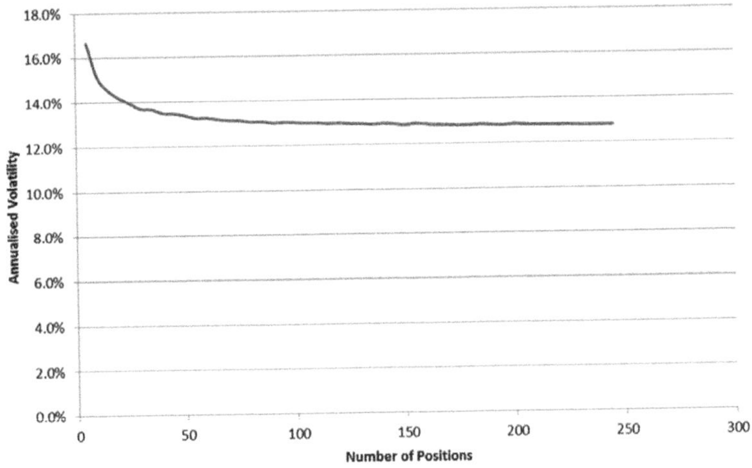

FIGURE 4.1 The benefit of diversification.

All investments involve some degree of risk. The reward for taking on more risk is the potential for achieving a greater return. However, risk also increases the chance that you could lose your nest egg. In general, financial instruments like equities and alternative investments have the greatest risk and highest potential returns among major asset classes. Bonds are less volatile than equities but offer more modest potential returns. Finally, cash and cash equivalents are the less risky options, but offer the lowest returns. Various asset classes tend to perform differently under the same market conditions. Take bonds and equities as an example: When bonds go up, equities tend to go down and vice versa. Long-term studies have shown a portfolio of a mix of asset classes with low. Correlation can help deliver returns in the long term. That's because the asset class that outperforms can counter the poor returns of the underperforming asset class. This allows the investor to achieve higher returns without taking on much more risk at different times.

Portfolio diversification is a widely embraced investment strategy that helps mitigate the unpredictability of markets for investors. It has the key benefits of reducing portfolio loss and volatility and is especially important during times of increased uncertainty. As we discuss later in this book, diversification benefit is more difficult to achieve during stressed periods because asset classes tend to become more correlated.

Diversification leads to the reduction of the total risk of the portfolio. Hence it can be regarded as the method of risk reduction. As already mentioned, there are many definitions of risk in financial literature; but in general, risk can be regarded as the divergence of the actual return of the asset (portfolio of assets) from the expected return. It is assumed that asset returns follow normal distribution; and even when this is not the case, their distributions can be converted into a normal one through some mathematical transformations. When assets are combined into portfolios, portfolio returns follow the normal distribution. Normal distribution is characterized by its first two moments, namely, mean (expected return) and standard deviation. We have already stated that dispersion of returns around the mean is measured by standard deviation or variance. Hence, those two measures are commonly accepted as the measures of asset (portfolio) risk. Risk can be reduced either by increasing the number of assets in the portfolio or including assets with low or negative correlation in the portfolio. To understand how portfolio risk is calculated, let us reinforce the statistical concept of variance and covariance.

4.1 Variance and Covariance

Consider the random variables X and Y with variance $V(X)$ and $V(Y)$. The variance of the random variable Z, which is a linear combination of X and Y (i.e., $Z = aX \pm bY$), is

$$\begin{aligned} V(Z) &= V(aX) + V(bY) \pm 2\mathrm{Cov}(aX, bY) \\ &= a^2 V(X) + b^2 V(Y) \pm 2ab\mathrm{Cov}(X, Y) \end{aligned}$$

where the term Cov(X,Y) is called the covariance between random variables X and Y. The formula for the covariance is

$$C_{AB} = \sum_{i=1}^{N} h_i [R_{Ai} - E(R_A)][R_{Bi} - E(R_B)]$$

where hi are the probabilities.

Covariance is the statistical measure of the relationship between two random variables. It shows the way (direction) in which securities in the portfolio are moving. Positive covariance means that securities move in the same direction, while the negative one implies movements in the opposite direction. Zero covariance shows that there is no linear relationship between securities; that is, that they move independently. The variance is a special case of covariance and is derived by assuming that $X = Y$ (i.e., covariance of a random variable with itself will be equal to its variance).

4.2 Two-Asset Portfolio: Expected Return and Risk

Consider an investor who has two assets, A and B, that are components of his/her portfolio. If the proportion of total investment in asset A is w_1 and in asset B is $1 - w_1$, then the return on a two-asset portfolio is given by

$$E(r_p) = w_1 E(r_1) + w_2 E(r_2)$$

Since

$$w_1 + w_2 = 1$$

$$w_2 = 1 - w_1$$

then

$$E(r_p) = w_1 E(r_1) + (1 - w_1) E(r_2)$$

In the same manner the variance of portfolio P is

$$V(P) = w_1^2 V(A) + (1 - w_1)^2 V(B) \pm 2w_1(1 - w_1)\text{Cov}(A, B)$$

If we introduce the denotations

$$V(P) = \sigma_p^2$$
$$V(A) = \sigma_1^2$$
$$V(B) = \sigma_2^2$$
$$\text{Cov}(A, B) = \sigma_{1,2}$$

then the variance on a two-asset portfolio can be written as

$$\sigma_p^2 = w_1^2 \sigma_1^2 + (1 - w_1)^2 \sigma_2^2 + 2w_1(1 - w_1)\sigma_{1,2}$$

Example: Suppose $\sigma_1^2 = 4$, $\sigma_2^2 = 9$ and $\sigma_{1,2} = -9$. Let us find the variance of the following portfolios:

Weight in Asset 1	Weight in Asset 2	Total
25%	75%	100%
50%	50%	100%
75%	25%	100%

$$\sigma_p^2 = 0.25^2 \sigma_1^2 + 0.75^2 \sigma_2^2 + 2 \times 0.25 \times 0.75 \sigma_{1,2} = 43.19$$

$$\sigma_p^2 = 0.5^2 \sigma_1^2 + 0.5^2 \sigma_2^2 + 2 \times 0.5 \times 0.5 \sigma_{1,2} = 19.8$$

$$\sigma_p^2 = 0.75^2 \sigma_1^2 + 0.25^2 \sigma_2^2 + 2 \times 0.75 \times 0.25 \sigma_{1,2} = 10.7$$

The second and third portfolio have produced variances that are smaller than the variances of the individual assets. This is the example of the *diversification effect.*

4.3 Correlation Coefficient

Let X and Y be random variables. The correlation coefficient of X and Y is denoted by ρ and has the following relationship with covariance of X and Y:

$$\rho \frac{\sigma_{X,Y}}{\sigma_X \sigma_Y}$$

Correlation coefficient is the covariance standardized by the product of the individual standard deviations of the two assets. Correlation coefficient is bounded between −1 and +1, and it shows the investor both the direction and the extent in which two securities move together. Correlation coefficient of +1 indicates perfect positive correlation; that is, two securities move in the same direction in the exactly same manner, while perfect negative correlation of −1 shows that two securities are moving in the exactly same manner but in the opposite direction. Correlation of zero implies no linear relationship between securities.

Let's have a look at two markets—for example, equities and bonds—and their day-to-day changes. The statistical dispersion of returns is: The more linear, the more correlated the two return developments are; and the more widespread, the more uncorrelated they are (Figure 4.2).

4.3.1 CORRELATION COEFFICIENT AND ITS IMPACT ON PORTFOLIO RISK

The lower the correlation between assets/asset classes, the greater the diversification benefit to a portfolio.

Future (ex-ante) correlation is also a key issue. For every portfolio investment decision, investors rely on a predicted correlation, as the example below illustrates.

Within a multi-asset portfolio, investors expect a diversification benefit because the correlation between asset classes like bonds, equities, commodities, and hedge funds is not perfect and will therefore provide stability (e.g., if the

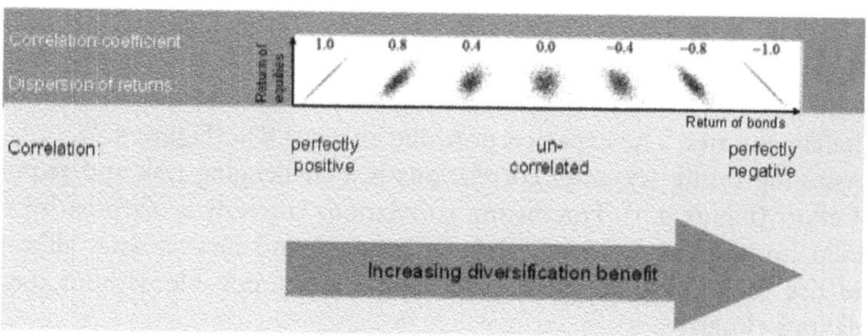

FIGURE 4.2 Dependency of return developments.

Assumptions	Weight	Risk (volatility)	Correlation	Correlation	Correlatio
Italian bonds	75%	3%			
			–0.5	0	0.5
Italian equities	25%	16%	⬇	⬇	⬇
Results:	**Expected portfolio risk**		3.80%	6.60%	8.50%

FIGURE 4.3 Portfolio risk and correlation different assumptions.

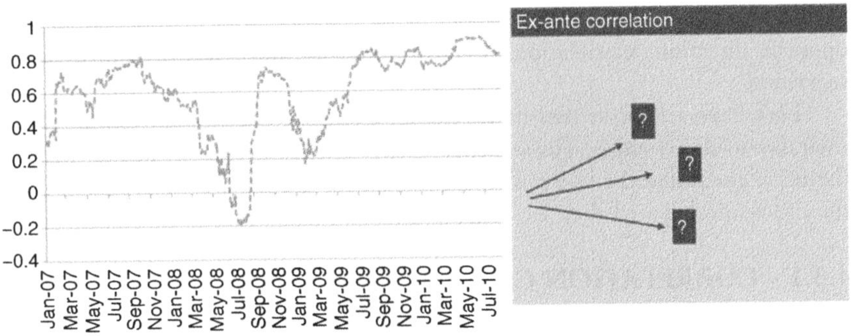

FIGURE 4.4 *Ex-ante* correlation.

economy overheats and interest rates rise, bonds (and partly equities) suffer, whereas commodities perform well).

Worst-case scenario: Extreme market turmoil putting all asset classes under pressure and making correlations between all asset classes increase.

If an investor relies on falsely predicted correlations that finally turn out to be higher, the portfolio risk may get out of control.

Example: Let's assume a portfolio of Italian bonds and Italian equities, and the portfolio manager predicts an ex-ante correlation of –0.5 between Italian bonds and Italian equities. The expected portfolio risk is 3.8% (Figure 4.3).

Assessing future (ex-ante) correlations is a challenging task and requires a lot of effort (Figure 4.4). Forecasting correlations correctly is essential for every portfolio investment decision, for both strategic and tactical asset allocation. Sound risk monitoring and risk management are impossible without tracking correlations closely!

The risk of a portfolio depends on the correlation of return of the securities that make up the portfolio.

Since

$$\sigma_p^2 = w_1^2\sigma_1^2 + w_2^2\sigma_2^2 + 2w_1w_2\sigma_{1,2}$$

and

$$\sigma_{1,2} = \rho_{1,2}\sigma_1\sigma_2$$

we can rewrite the formula for the risk on a two-asset portfolio as

$$\sigma_p^2 = w_1^2\sigma_1^2 + w_2^2\sigma_2^2 + 2w_1w_2\rho\sigma_1\sigma_2$$

If we assume that

$$\sigma_1 = \sigma_2 = \sigma$$

$$w_1 = w_2 = \frac{1}{2}$$

then

$$\sigma_p^2 = \frac{1}{2}\sigma^2(1+\rho)$$

4.3.1.1 Zero Correlation Case. Furthermore, if we assume that $\rho = 0$, we obtain

$$\sigma_p^2 = \frac{1}{2}\sigma^2$$

Combining the two securities produces a portfolio variance, which is half of the variance of the assets.

4.3.1.2 Perfect Negative Correlation Case. If we assume that $\rho = -1$, the variance of a portfolio becomes

$$\sigma_p^2 = 0$$

that is, all risk is eliminated, and the portfolio variance becomes zero.

4.3.1.3 Perfect Positive Correlation Case. If we assume that $\rho = 1$, we obtain

$$\sigma_p^2 = \sigma^2$$

that is, combining the assets does not reduce the risk.

Diversification Example: The average return and standard deviation of returns for 10 FTSE 100 companies in the period 2000–2005 quoted on the stock exchange are given below.

Company Name	Average Monthly Return(%)	Monthly Standard Deviation(%)
BHP BILLITON PLC	1.6	9.4
BP PLC	0.1	7.3
BRIT AMER TOBACC	1.7	6.3
DIAGEO PLC	0.8	4.6
GLAXOSMITHKLINE	0.0	5.2
HSBC HLDGS PLC	−0.1	6.7
RIO TINTO PLC	1.3	10.8
VODAFONE GROUP	−0.1	7.7
ASTRAZENECA PLC	0.4	7.1
BG GROUP PLC	1.3	6.3

The correlation coefficients for all pairs of asset returns are given in the matrix shown in Figure 4.5.

An equally weighted portfolio—that is, a portfolio where each stock represents one-tenth of the value of the portfolio—produced the following mean return and risk over the period:

Expected return	−0.70%
Risk (standard deviation)	4.23%

The risk of the portfolio is lower than the risk of any individual stock!

Important note: The return in a portfolio *is always* just a weighted average return—it is not reduced with the reduction of risk, it is only averaged out.

4.3.2 THE NUMBER OF ASSETS IN A PORTFOLIO AND ITS IMPACT ON PORTFOLIO RISK

When we have N assets in a portfolio, the formula for portfolio variance becomes

$$\sigma_p^2 = \sum_{i=1}^{n} w_i^2 \sigma_i^2 + \sum_{i=1}^{n} \sum_{j=1}^{n} w_i w_j \sigma_{i,j}, \qquad i \neq j$$

Consider an equally weighted portfolio, where the weight assigned to each asset is $1/N$. The formula for variance of the N-asset portfolio then becomes

$$\sigma_p^2 = \sum_{i=1}^{n} \left(\frac{1}{N}\right)^2 \sigma_i^2 + \sum_{i=1}^{n} \sum_{j=1}^{n} \left(\frac{1}{N}\right)^2 \sigma_{i,j}$$

	BHP BILLITON PLC	BP PLC	BRIT AMER TOBACC	DIAGEO PLC	GLAXOSMITHKLINE	HSBC HLDGS PLC	RIO TINTO PLC	VODAFONE GROUP	ASTRAZENECA PLC	BG GROUP PLC
BHP BILLITON PLC	1.0000									
BP PLC	0.5655	1.0000								
BRIT AMER TOBACC	0.2577	0.3204	1.0000							
DIAGEO PLC	0.1208	0.2129	0.3021	1.0000						
GLAXOSMITHKLINE	0.1078	0.1950	0.3022	0.4041	1.0000					
HSBC HLDGS PLC	0.3651	0.2959	0.2455	0.1770	0.0277	1.0000				
RIO TINTO PLC	0.7129	0.4218	0.2660	0.1287	0.0941	0.3540	1.0000			
VODAFONE GROUP	0.2208	0.1965	–0.0272	0.0039	0.0118	0.3175	0.2200	1.0000		
ASTRAZENECA PLC	0.1897	0.1924	0.2680	0.2595	0.5274	0.1384	0.1270	–0.0205	1.0000	
BG GROUP PLC	0.5105	0.5241	0.4362	0.2101	0.2575	0.1961	0.5372	0.0281	0.1956	1.0000

FIGURE 4.5 Correlation coefficients.

Factoring out $1/N$ from the first summation and $(N-1)/N$ from the second yields

$$\sigma_p^2 = \frac{1}{N}\sum_{i=1}^{n}\left[\frac{\sigma_i^2}{N}\right] + \frac{N-1}{N}\sum_{i=1}^{n}\sum_{j=1}^{n}\left[\frac{\sigma_{i,j}}{N(N-1)}\right]$$

When we have N assets in a portfolio, there are N variance terms and $N(N-1)$ covariance terms (there are N values of i and $N-1$ values of j since $i \neq j$). Therefore, the terms in the brackets in the above equation are averages:

$$\sigma_p^2 = \frac{1}{N}\bar{\sigma}_i^2 + \frac{N-1}{N}\bar{\sigma}_{i,j}$$

As the number of assets N increases and N approaches infinity, $1/N$ approaches zero. However, as N becomes large, $(N-1)/N$ approaches 1, so the covariance term approaches the average covariance. In conclusion, the risk of individual securities can be diversified away, but the contribution to the total risk caused by the covariance terms cannot be diversified away.

4.3.3 THE EFFECT OF DIVERSIFICATION ON RISK

What happens when more and more randomly selected stocks are combined into portfolios is shown in Figure 4.6. As the number of stocks increases, the risk of the portfolio decreases rapidly initially, then very slowly and then not at all.

In other words, random combination of securities in portfolios will reduce some of the risk but not all the risk. So we can say that the risk of each security is made up of two components, the diversifiable risk (known as unique, unsystematic or company-specific risk) and the nondiversifiable risk (known as common, systematic, or market risk). In a portfolio that is a random combination of assets, diversifiable risk can be eliminated but systematic risk cannot (it

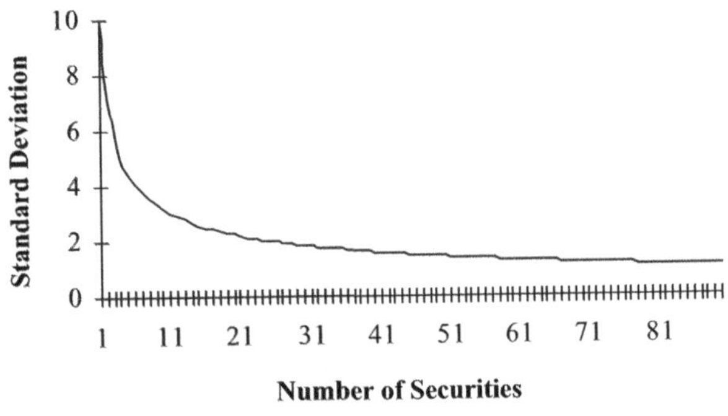

FIGURE 4.6 Diversification and risk.

can only be brought to the level of average market risk). Systematic risk is attributed to factors that affect all stocks. How many stocks is enough to diversify unsystematic risk? The evidence from the 1950s and 1960s suggests that 25–30 randomly selected securities will form a portfolio with small-company-specific stocks, while recent empirical evidence (Malkiel, 2003) suggests that that number nowadays is around 200 stocks.

4.4 The Efficient Frontier

A minimum variance set is the set of all portfolios that have the least volatility for each level of possible expected return.

An efficient set (frontier) is the part of the minimum variance frontier that offers the highest expected return for each level of standard deviation.

The concept of efficient frontiers and optimal portfolio selection was originated by Harry Markowitz in 1952.

The shape of the efficient frontier (constructed both for two-asset portfolios and portfolios with many assets) depends on the correlation coefficient between those assets, which will be demonstrated below.

Correlation and the Shape of Efficient Frontier of a Two-Asset Portfolio. We have established that the expected return and the variance of a two-asset portfolio are given by

$$E(r_p) = w_1 E(r_1) + (1 - w_1) E(r_2) \tag{4.1}$$

and

$$\sigma_p^2 = w_1^2 \sigma_1^2 + (1 - w_1)^2 \sigma_2^2 + 2w_1(1 - w_1)\rho_{1,2}\sigma_1\sigma_2 \tag{4.2}$$

Perfect Positive Correlation. If $\rho_{1,2} = 1$, then

$$\sigma_p^2 = w_1^2 \sigma_1^2 + (1 - w_1)^2 \sigma_2^2 + 2w_1(1 - w_1)\sigma_1\sigma_2 = (w_1\sigma_1 + (1 - w_1)\sigma_2)^2 \tag{4.3}$$

Therefore

$$\sigma_p = w_1\sigma_1 + (1 - w_1)\sigma_2$$

and

$$w_1 = \frac{\sigma_p - \sigma_2}{\sigma_1 - \sigma_2}$$

In this case the efficient frontier is a straight line.

Substituting w_1 into expected return equation, we obtain

$$E(r_p) = \frac{\sigma_p - \sigma_2}{\sigma_1 - \sigma_2} E(r_1) + \left(1 - \frac{\sigma_p - \sigma_2}{\sigma_1 - \sigma_2}\right) E(r_2)$$

$$= \frac{\sigma_p - \sigma_2}{\sigma_1 - \sigma_2} E(r_1) + E(r_2) - \frac{\sigma_p - \sigma_2}{\sigma_1 - \sigma_2} E(r_2)$$

$$E(r_p) = \left(E(r_2) - \frac{E(r_1) - E(r_2)}{\sigma_1 - \sigma_2}\sigma_2\right) + \left(\frac{E(r_1) - E(r_2)}{\sigma_1 - \sigma_2}\right)\sigma_p$$

which is a straight line connecting the two assets in expected return/standard deviation space.

Example: Consider the expected return, standard deviation, and variance on the following two assets:

	Equity	Bond
Expected return	12%	4%
Risk (standard deviation)	20%	9%–
Variance	4.00%	0.81%

Scenario 1: Correlation between bond and equity is equal to 1.

$$\text{Variance covariance matrix} = \begin{bmatrix} \sigma_1^2 & \rho\sigma_1\sigma_2 \\ \rho\sigma_1\sigma_2 & \sigma_2^2 \end{bmatrix} = \begin{bmatrix} 0.0400 & 0.0180 \\ 0.0180 & 0.0081 \end{bmatrix}$$

Equity Allocation	Bond Allocation	Portfolio Return	Portfolio Variance	Portfolio Standard Deviation
0%	100%	4.00%	0.81%	9.00%
10%	90%	4.80%	1.02%	10.10%
20%	80%	5.60%	1.25%	11.20%
30%	70%	6.40%	1.51%	12.30%
40%	60%	7.20%	1.80%	13.40%
50%	50%	8.00%	2.10%	14.50%
60%	40%	8.80%	2.43%	15.60%
70%	30%	9.60%	2.79%	16.70%
80%	20%	10.40%	3.17%	17.80%
90%	10%	11.20%	3.57%	18.90%
100%	0%	12.00%	4.00%	20.00%

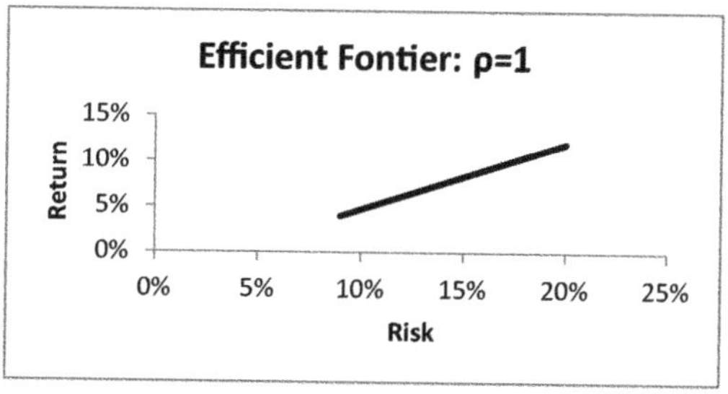

Zero Correlation. If $\rho_{1,2} = 0$, then

$$\sigma_p^2 = w_1^2\sigma_1^2 + (1-w_1)^2\sigma_2^2$$
$$\sigma_p = \left(w_1^2\sigma_1^2 + (1-w_1)^2\sigma_2^2\right)^{1/2} \tag{4.4}$$

Important note: Standard deviation from (4.4) is smaller than the one from (4.3) for all $w_1 \geq 0$. Therefore, the efficient frontier of the two uncorrelated assets will be on the left from the frontier derived when assets were perfectly positively correlated.

Example: Using the assets with the same risk/return characteristics as in the previous example, we can create scenario 2.

Scenario 2: Correlation between bond and equity is equal to 0.

$$\text{Variance covariance matrix} = \begin{bmatrix} \sigma_1^2 & \rho\sigma_1\sigma_2 \\ \rho\sigma_1\sigma_2 & \sigma_2^2 \end{bmatrix} = \begin{bmatrix} 0.0400 & 0 \\ 0 & 0.0081 \end{bmatrix}$$

Equity Allocation	Bond Allocation	Portfolio Return	Portfolio Variance	Portfolio Standard Deviation
0%	100%	4.00%	0.81%	9.00%
10%	90%	4.80%	0.70%	8.34%
20%	80%	5.60%	0.68%	8.24%
30%	70%	6.40%	0.76%	8.70%
40%	60%	7.20%	0.93%	9.65%
50%	50%	8.00%	1.20%	10.97%
60%	40%	8.80%	1.57%	12.53%
70%	30%	9.60%	2.03%	14.26%
80%	20%	10.40%	2.59%	16.10%
90%	10%	11.20%	3.25%	18.02%
100%	0%	12.00%	4.00%	20.00%

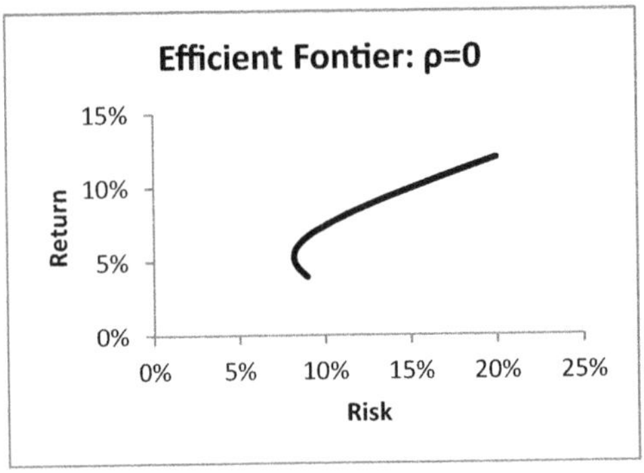

Perfect Negative Correlation. If $\rho_{1,2} = -1$, then

$$\begin{aligned} \sigma_p^2 &= w_1^2\sigma_1^2 + (1-w_1)^2\sigma_2^2 - 2w_1(1-w_1)\sigma_1\sigma_2 \\ &= (w_1\sigma_1 - (1-w_1)\sigma_2)^2 \qquad (4.5) \\ \sigma_p &= w_1\sigma_1 - (1-w_1)\sigma_2 \end{aligned}$$

When we have perfect negative correlation between assets, we can find the weight that should be assigned to each asset to produce a portfolio that will have zero standard deviation (variance); that is, standard deviation from Eq. (4.5) is lower than standard deviation obtained in a portfolio where assets have zero correlation (Eq. (4.4)).

In this case, efficient frontier consists of two lines connecting the zero variance portfolio with the two assets in the expected return/standard deviation space (see graph in the Figure 4.7).

Example: Using the assets with the same risk/return characteristics as in the previous example, we can create scenario 3.

Scenario 3: Correlation between bond and equity equal to −1.

$$\text{Variance covariance matrix} = \begin{bmatrix} \sigma_1^2 & \rho\sigma_1\sigma_2 \\ \rho\sigma_1\sigma_2 & \sigma_2^2 \end{bmatrix} = \begin{bmatrix} 0.0400 & -0.0180 \\ -0.0180 & 0.0081 \end{bmatrix}$$

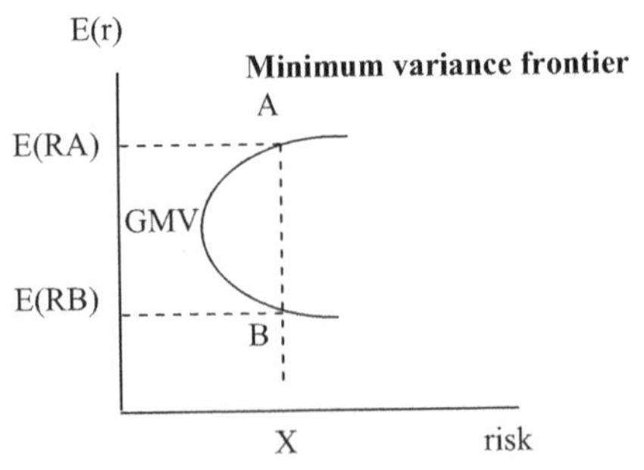

FIGURE 4.7 Minimum variance frontier.

Equity Allocation	Bond Allocation	Portfolio Return	Portfolio Variance	Portfolio Standard Deviation
0%	100%	4.00%	0.81%	9.00%
10%	90%	4.80%	0.37%	6.10%
20%	80%	5.60%	0.10%	3.20%
30%	70%	6.40%	0.00%	0.30%
40%	60%	7.20%	0.07%	2.60%
50%	50%	8.00%	0.30%	5.50%
60%	40%	8.80%	0.71%	8.40%
70%	30%	9.60%	1.28%	11.30%
80%	20%	10.40%	2.02%	14.20%
90%	10%	11.20%	2.92%	17.10%
100%	0%	12.00%	4.00%	20.00%

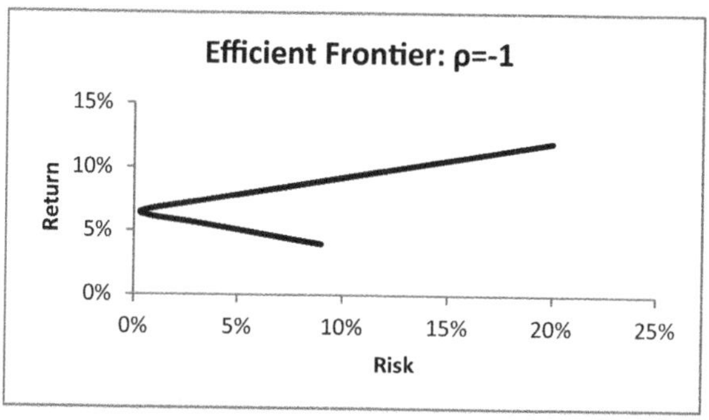

Minimum Variance Frontier and Efficient Frontier of* N*-Assets (without Short-Selling). Given the level of risk or standard deviation, investors prefer positions with higher expected return and given the expected return, they prefer the positions of lower risk. Taking this into account, we can determine the minimum variance set. It is the set that "given a particular level of expected return, the portfolio on the minimum variance set will have the lowest standard deviation, and therefore the lowest variance, achievable with the available population of stocks." This can be seen in Figure 4.7.

Note that all individual assets lie to the right inside the frontier in Figures 4.7 and 4.8. This tells that portfolios constituted of only a single asset are inefficient. The point where the standard deviation is at its lowest is the global minimum variance portfolio (GMV). Portfolios that lie from the GMV portfolio upwards provide investors with the best risk–return combinations and thus are the candidates for the optimal portfolio. These portfolios are called the *efficient set (frontier)*; and in order to be on the efficient frontier, the portfolios have to satisfy the following criterion: Given a particular level of standard deviation, the portfolios in the efficient set have the highest attainable expected rate of return, as singled out in Figure 4.8. In Figure 4.7, for a given level of risk, X, level of return of portfolio A is greater than the return on portfolio B, implying that A is on efficient frontier and B belongs to an inefficient set. Therefore, a typical,

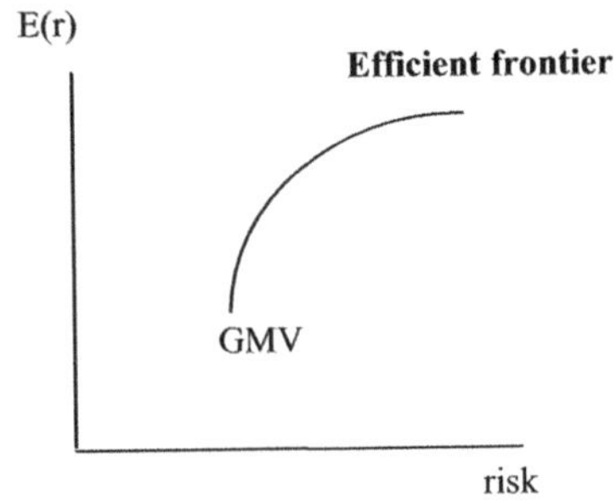

FIGURE 4.8 Efficient frontier and global minimum variance.

rational investor will choose portfolio A, which lies on the efficient set, over portfolio B, which lies on the inefficient set.

Equation of the Minimum Variance Frontier of N*-Assets, Vector of Weights of Frontier Portfolios, the Risk and Return of Global Minimum Variance Portfolio.* Let $w' = (w_1 \ldots w_n)'$ be the vector of n asset shares and let

$$\mathbf{r} = \begin{bmatrix} E(r_1) \\ E(r_2) \\ \vdots \\ E(r_n) \end{bmatrix}$$

be the vector of expected returns. The variance–covariance matrix Σ is given as

$$\Sigma = \begin{bmatrix} \sigma_1^2 & \sigma_{12} & \ldots & \sigma_{1n} \\ \sigma_{21} & \sigma_2^2 & \ldots & \sigma_{2n} \\ \cdot & \cdot & \cdot & \cdot \\ \sigma_{n1} & \sigma_{n2} & \cdot & \sigma_{nn} \end{bmatrix}$$

Suppose we want to construct a portfolio of n assets with expected return $E(r_p) = w'r = m_p$. Obviously there are many portfolios that will produce a return equal to m_p. Among the portfolios that may produce m_p, we want to identify the portfolio with the minimum possible variance. This portfolio is the solution to the following constrained quadratic programming problem:

$$\text{Minimize } \sigma_p^2 = \mathbf{w}'\Sigma\mathbf{w}$$

subject to

$$\mathbf{w}'\mathbf{r} = m_p \tag{4.6}$$

$$\mathbf{w}'\mathbf{1} = 1 \tag{4.7}$$

where $\mathbf{r}$ is the vector of expected asset returns, m_p is the required portfolio return, and $\mathbf{1}$ is a vector of ones. Equations (4.6) and (4.7) define the required rate of return and the budget constraint, respectively.

In order to find the vector of optimal weights for a portfolio that will have a minimum variance, mathematically we would have to use Lagrangean multiplier.

The exact position of efficient frontier in the risk–return space graph depends on so-called efficient set constants, which are in turn a function of expected returns, variances, and covariances between available stocks.

The efficient set constants are denoted as α, β, γ, and δ and they are given by

$$\alpha = \mathbf{r}'\Sigma^{-1}\mathbf{r}, \qquad \beta = \mathbf{r}'\Sigma^{-1}\mathbf{1} \tag{4.8a}$$

$$\gamma = \mathbf{1}'\Sigma^{-1}\mathbf{1}, \qquad \delta = (\alpha\gamma - \beta^2) \tag{4.8b}$$

Once we know the value of the constants, we can derive the vector of optimal weights of stocks that should be in the minimum variance portfolio. This is given by

$$\mathbf{w} = \frac{\alpha - \beta m_p}{\delta}\Sigma^{-1}\mathbf{1} + \frac{\gamma m_p - \beta}{\delta}\Sigma^{-1}\mathbf{r} \tag{4.9}$$

Note that the result of this calculation will be a vector of weights in the form of

$$\mathbf{w} = \begin{bmatrix} w_1 \\ w_2 \\ \vdots \\ w_n \end{bmatrix}$$

If in the equation for variance of a portfolio ($\sigma_p^2 = \mathbf{w}'\Sigma\mathbf{w}$) we replace w with Eq. (4.9), the variance of the rate of return on the portfolio then becomes

$$\begin{aligned}\sigma_p^2 = \mathbf{w}'\Sigma\mathbf{w} &= \frac{\alpha - \beta m_p}{\delta}\mathbf{w}'\Sigma\Sigma^{-1}\mathbf{1} + \frac{\gamma m_p - \beta}{\delta}\mathbf{w}'\Sigma\Sigma^{-1}\mathbf{r} \\ &= \frac{\alpha - \beta m_p}{\delta}\mathbf{w}'\mathbf{1} + \frac{\gamma m_p - \beta}{\delta}\mathbf{w}'\mathbf{r}\end{aligned}$$

From the constraints set at the beginning, we know that

$$\mathbf{w}'\mathbf{r} = m_p$$
$$\mathbf{w}'\mathbf{1} = 1$$

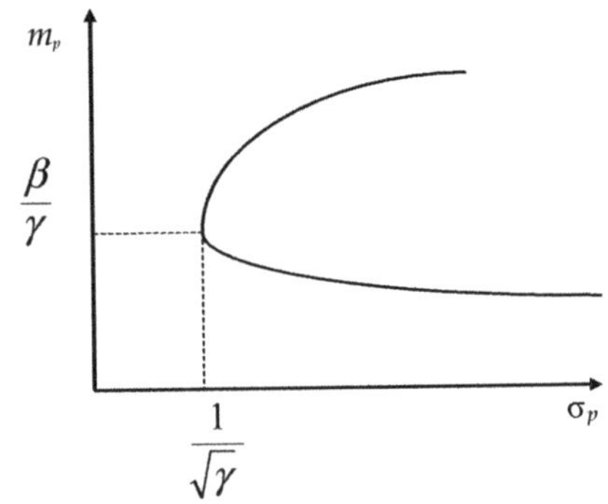

FIGURE 4.9 **Expected return and variance of the global minimum variance portfolio.**

so that the minimum variance portfolio for any level of return (m_p) chosen can be calculated as

$$\sigma_p^2 = \frac{\alpha}{\delta} - \frac{\beta}{\delta} m_p + \frac{\gamma}{\delta} m_p^2 - \frac{\beta}{\delta} m_p = \frac{\alpha}{\delta} - \frac{2\beta}{\delta} m_p + \frac{\gamma}{\delta} m_p^2 \tag{4.10}$$

Equation (4.10) gives us the minimum portfolio risk for any given level of return, that is, it determines the *minimum variance frontier* (set of portfolios). Portfolios that satisfy (4.10) are called *frontier portfolios.* As was noted in previous section, the set of all frontier portfolios for various level of returns make up the minimum variance frontier. Further, Eq. (4.10) suggests that in the (σ_p^2, m_p) space, the minimum variance frontier is a parabola vertex (high/low point of the graph) in $(1/\gamma, \beta/\gamma)$, while in the (σ_p, m_p) it is a hyperbola.

As can be seen from Figure 4.9, the expected return and variance of the global minimum variance portfolio are β/γ and $1/\gamma$, respectively. This can be proven mathematically, but such derivations are beyond the scope of this chapter.

Finally, note that the covariance between the rates of return on any two frontier portfolios p and q can be calculated as

$$\text{Cov}(r_p, r_q) = \mathbf{w}_\mathbf{p}' \Sigma \mathbf{w}_\mathbf{q}$$

The Concave Shape of the Efficient Frontier. The efficient set must be concave because it consists of the envelope curves of all the portfolios that lie from the GMV portfolio upward. The curves of separate portfolios in the efficient portfolio are concave, too. The reason for the concave shape is that the correlation coefficient between two assets (portfolios) is between –1 and +1, but it never takes the two extreme values. This is shown in Figure 4.10.

Minimum Variance Frontier and Efficient Frontier with Short-Selling of Risky Assets. Short-selling occurs because the short-seller expects the price of a security to fall and s/he can make a profit if s/he sells it when the price is still

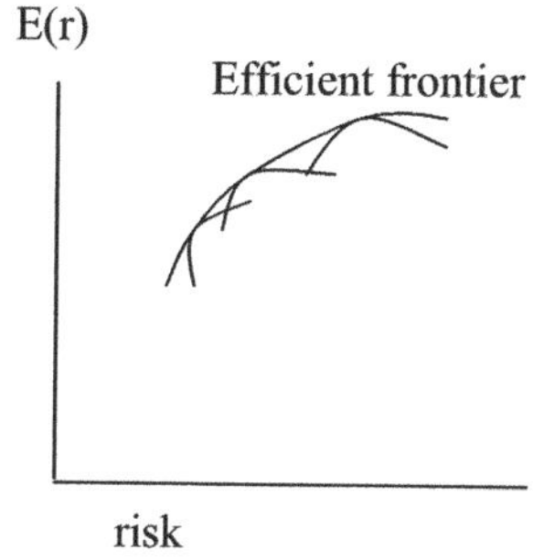

FIGURE 4.10 Concave shape of the efficient frontier.

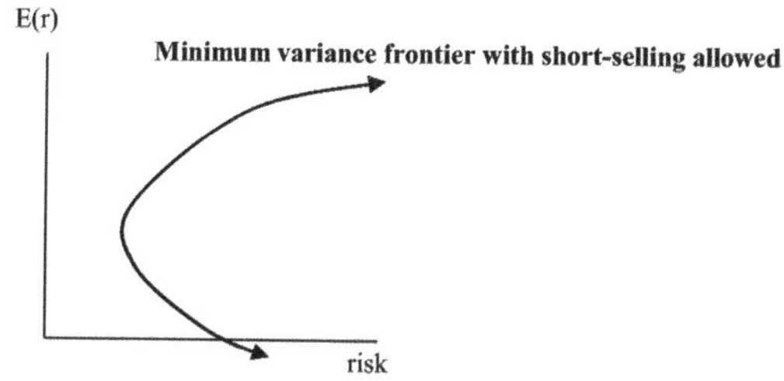

FIGURE 4.11 Minimum variance frontier with short-selling allowed.

high. Therefore, such an investor borrows the security from a broker and then sells it; and when the price falls, s/he buys the security back at the lower price and either returns it to the broker or gives him the proceeds from the short sale. Therefore, when short-selling is introduced, the goal of investment changes: We now want to maximize the return as well. Figure 4.11 shows the minimum variance set when short-selling is allowed.

Note that, in theory, short-selling enables portfolios to give infinite rates of return. This is because securities with low expected returns are sold and the proceeds are used to purchase securities with high returns. Needless to say, short-selling enables an investor to also increase standard deviation (risk) because short-selling may incur unlimited losses (hence the possibility of negative returns in Figure 4.5). Therefore, he or she will have to balance his risk and return according to his risk preferences (risk aversion). Limiting Figure 4.5 to the efficient frontier only, we obtain the

Figure 4.12 shows that the efficient frontier starts from the GMV portfolio and does not stop anywhere, but goes to infinity.

Without short-selling, an efficient frontier has a finite point where the portfolio with the maximum return is. It doesn't continue to infinity because the investor has no other funds to finance further investment. In other words, an efficient frontier when short-selling is not allowed is limited on both ends by GMV portfolio and maximum return portfolio.

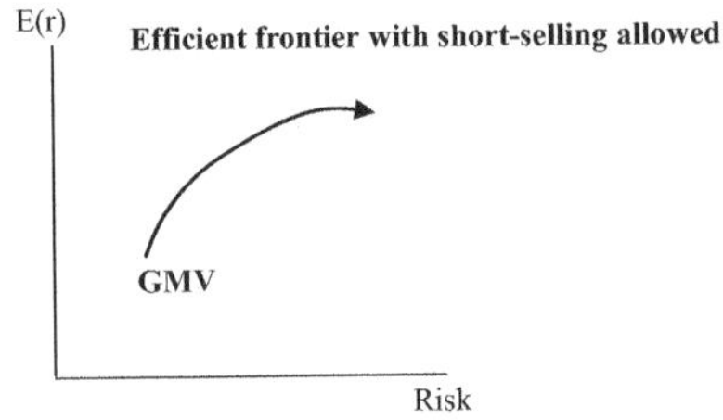

FIGURE 4.12 Efficient frontier with short-selling allowed.

The Choice of Optimal Portfolio and the Concept of Risk Aversion. Consider an investor who faces the following two choices:

Investment A: Receive £10 with certainty.

Investment B: Receive £100 with a 10% probability and £0 with a 90% probability.

Note that investment A is the expected value of the risky investment B (i.e., £10). Therefore, the choice the investor is facing is between the expected value of the risky investment with certainty or the risky investment itself.

An individual who prefers the risky investment is a risk seeker, one who is indifferent between a certain outcome and a risky investment is risk neutral, and one who prefers the certain outcome is a risk-averse investor.

The only rational investor behavior is a risk-averse investor. Even within the risk-averse group of investors, one can identify various degrees of risk aversion. Investors with different levels of risk aversion will require a different *risk premium* from an investment. Risk premium can be defined as a return that is required on a risky investment in excess of the risk free rate of return. It can be given as a function of a portfolio risk:

$$E(R_p) - r_f = 0.005 \times A \times \sigma_p^2$$

where r_f is the return on a risk-free asset and A is degree of risk aversion. Many studies find that investors' level of risk aversion is likely to be in the range of 2–4. 0.005 is a scaling factor, so that expected return and standard deviation can be entered as percentages and the way you trade off risk and return in reasonable in quantitative terms. This scaling factor has no real bearing on the analysis.

Utility Theory and Indifference Curves. Utility theory is derived from classic microeconomics and implies that investors (consumers) seek to maximize utility (i.e., satisfaction of level of happiness) subject to a constraint: Utility derived from investment in risky securities is a function of return and risk: $U = f[E(r), \sigma]$. Although return derived from risky assets, such as stocks and bonds, is a source of utility, the uncertainty (i.e., risk) surrounding the actual return is a source for *disutility* for risk-averse investors. Therefore, the impact of these two variables on utility is *inverse*. Such a tradeoff between risk and return for each individual investor is presented by a plot of indifference curves. Indifference curves show an investor's attitude toward risk. They are adopted from classic macroeconomic framework; and, in this context, each indifference curve (IC) represents one level of happiness (one level of tradeoff between risk and return) for each investor, so that the investor is indifferent to which point on that IC s/he wants to be at.

We have identified three types of investors according to their attitude toward the risk: risk-seeking, risk-neutral, and risk-averse. Their ICs will be characterized by different slopes. The slope is positive if the investor is risk-averse, negative if the investor is risk-seeking, and zero if the investor is risk-neutral. The shapes of ICs for the three types of investors are presented in the figure below:

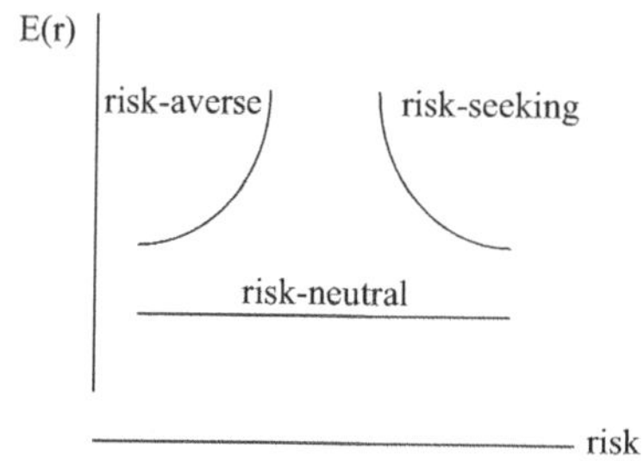

Using Indifference Curves to Identify Optimal Portfolios on the Efficient Set. Typical investors, as noted in earlier sections, are risk-averse and they face concave ICs. Those will be the only type of investors that we will consider in further analysis.

All investors are indifferent to which point they are at on one particular IC. They all try to be on the highest (furthest northwest) IC available. That highest available IC is the one that would be tangent to the efficient set. Consider an investor who faces three ICs, as in the graph below: We can see that IC_1 is unattainable because there are no portfolios available at that level; IC_3 is attainable, but the portfolios available are not efficient ones; therefore, an investor would choose efficient portfolios on the highest attainable IC—that is, portfolio O, which is a tangent of IC_2 on the efficient set. That will be the optimal portfolio for this particular investor. The graph refers to choice of an optimal portfolio when only risky assets are available to an investor.

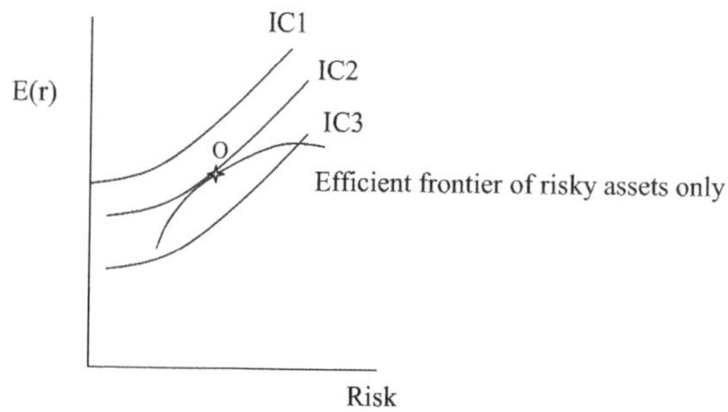

In other words, the point at which the slope of IC is equal to the slope of concave efficient frontier of risky assets is the point where an optimal portfolio is located.

4.5 Correlation Regime Shifts and Correlation Estimates

4.5.1 INCREASED CORRELATION

Everything tends to move together on the market since 2007. This increase in correlation is not without effect on the asset allocation and raises a lot of challenges from a diversification benefit perspective thus having uncorrelated returns from the market. Diversification minimizes risk of a group, or portfolio, of investments so when all markets start to behave on the same way it becomes more complex to provide diversification. Low correlation is desirable from an investment perspective, and diversification benefits materialize when a fall in one market is offset by a rise in another market. If the tendency is for all markets to fall simultaneously, however, the benefits of diversification will be overstated. It is in times of extreme market conditions that the benefits from diversification (and the effect of low correlations) are most needed. Sound risk monitoring and risk management are impossible without tracking correlations closely. The closer the number is to 1, the more the markets are moving in lockstep. As a general indicator, the correlation coefficient between different asset classes climbed to more than 0.8 in 2010, while this coefficient was around 0.3 at the start of the 1990s. The concepts of covariance and correlation are used to measure how the returns on assets relate to each other and the market in general and how they can be used to reduce the overall risk to the investor. Increase in correlation is a challenge to a portfolio manager as it makes more difficult to outperform and he may not be enough rewarded for taking risk. One of the main drivers of high correlation between either different asset classes (FX, equities, commodities, bonds,..) or pairwise correlation in a given benchmark used to be volatility. When volatility goes up, so does the correlation; and when the volatility goes down, then correlation goes down too. This pattern does not necessary exist today. For example, the VIX, which is a good gauge of future expected volatility, is extremely low (below levels of 2007); nevertheless, pairwise correlations in the United States as represented by the S&P500 is still high and still above its historical average. It seems that something other than the volatility is driving the correlation. We can even wonder if volatility is today the metric to follow-up. We argue that perhaps market stress is more reflected today in the level of correlation (pairwise correlation), (Figures 4.13 and 4.14). A healthy stock market is deemed one where fundamentals and economics dictate price changes, leading to divergences between industry sectors that each tend to react differently to the underlying macro story. High correlation mitigates such moves because all sectors tend to rise and fall together, becoming a real challenge for stock pickers (alpha).

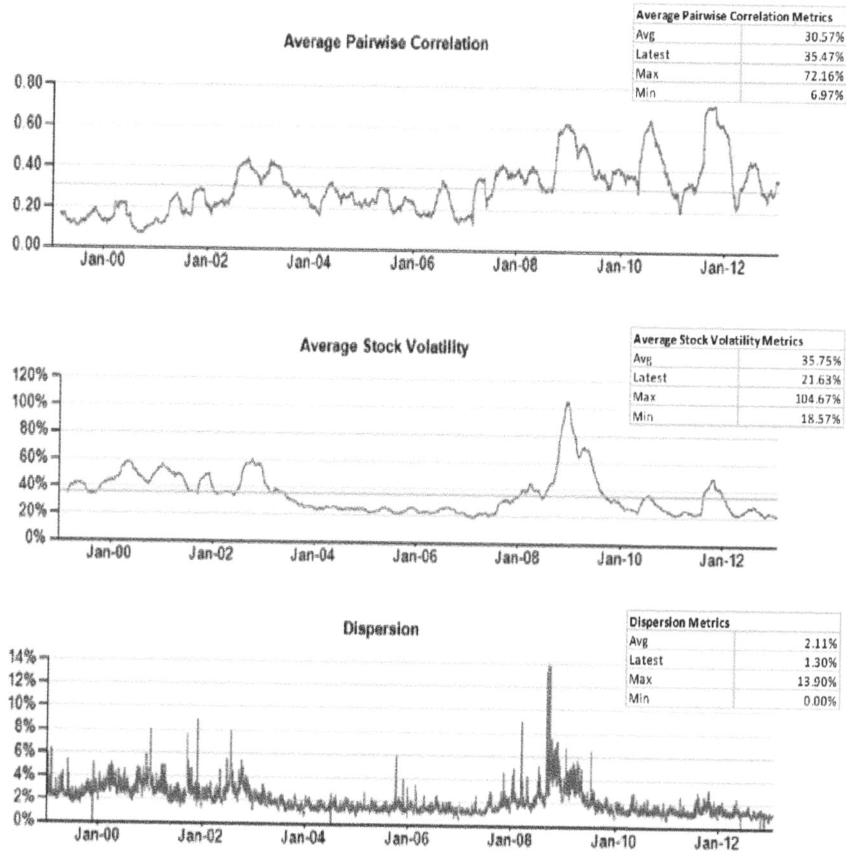

FIGURE 4.13 **Evolution of the pairwise correlation, stock's volatility, and dispersion in the S&P500 (60 days' rolling). Source: Marshall Wace LLP.**

High correlation reinforces pricing inefficiencies for active stock pickers and investors seeking to unlock opportunities. The question about increasing correlation has been studied in the past, but the current situation raises some new challenges in the sense that markets have drastically changed since 2007, leading to a new market paradigm. The question whether volatility will stay at a high level is an important question. We tend to argue that one has to become accustomed to this high level of correlation because the low level we had in the 1990s or early 2000s will not happen again. Several reasons can explain this phenomenon. The globalization of economy has certainly an impact on the level of correlation, and this process will continue to develop. The development of the technology and available information and resources reduces arbitrage opportunities. But it appears that one of the main drivers relies on the recent development of the ETF (Exchange Traded Funds) industry. As more and more investors buy and sell ETFs and indices, it helps maintain higher correlation between sectors (Figure 4.15). When you have instruments that mimic the market, it

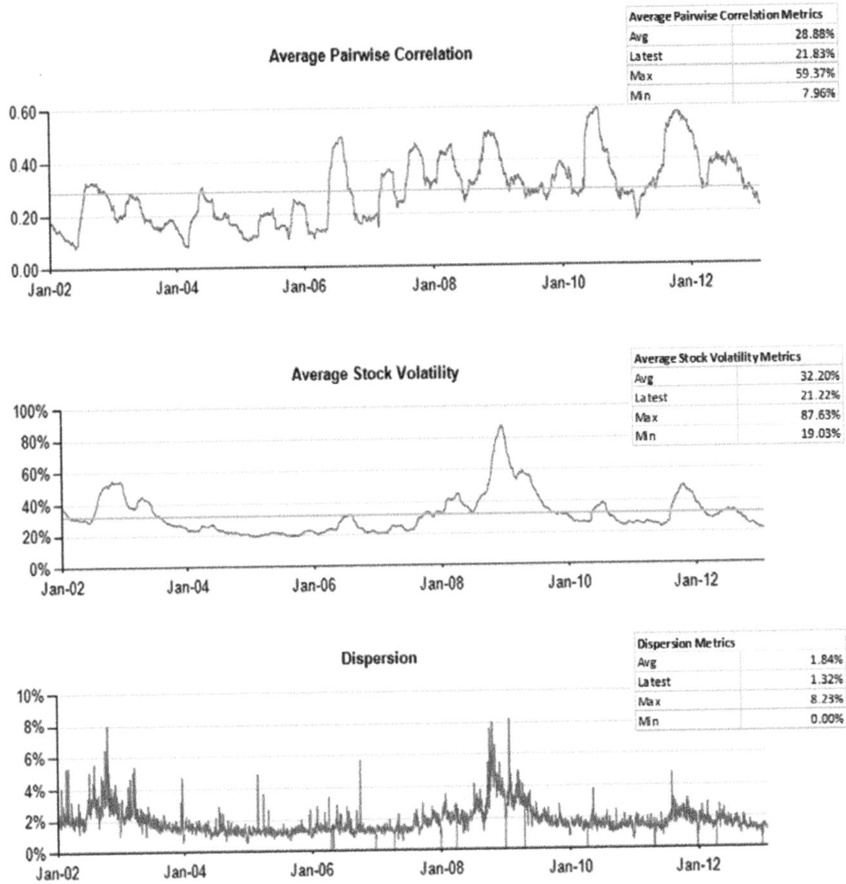

FIGURE 4.14 **Evolution of the pairwise correlation, stock's volatility, and dispersion in the STOXX Europe 600 (60 days' rolling). Source: Marshall Wace LLP.**

automatically increases correlation because you have fewer people making directional bets. Further studies will be necessary to really comprehend the effect of ETFs on this phenomenon.

Using a statistical risk model can also show some interesting information applying it to a benchmark. It can show how many statistical factors explain systematic risk in the benchmark using the top fifth of factors. Our assumption behind this analysis is that under normal market conditions several factors should explain risk or if risk appears to still be concentrated in a handful of factors. If so, it would mean that markets are still dominated by some macro concerns affecting all the segments of the markets. Figure 4.16 applies a statistical model for the S&P500 when we can clearly see when risk reaches high level of concentration in only a few factors.

Even by investing in foreign markets it becomes difficult, and it is more and more difficult to get diversification from investing in overseas markets. The

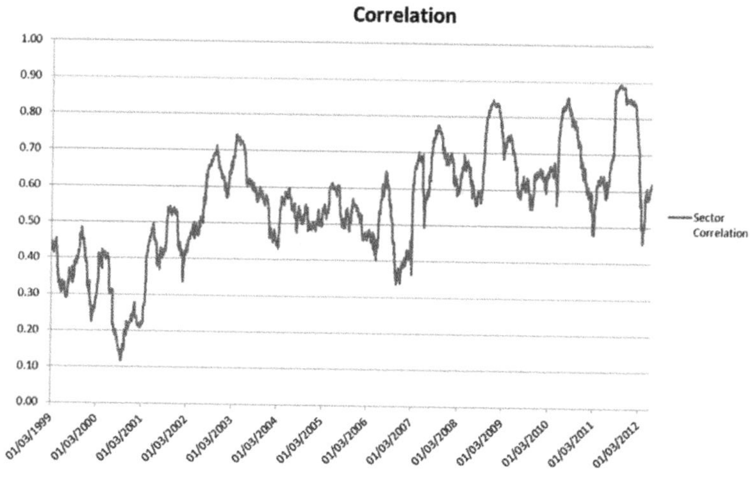

FIGURE 4.15 Sectors correlation evolution in the S&P500 since 1999.

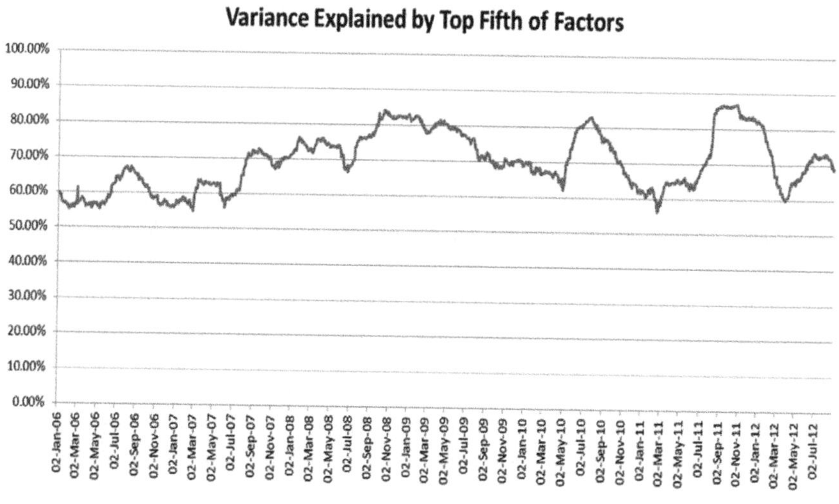

FIGURE 4.16 Variance explained by top fifth of factors using a statistical model. Source: Marshall Wace LLP.

causes of this correlation shift is a more globalized economy, development of trading technology, and especially the effects of growing ETF business. Correlation is also not limited to equities but also concerns the different asset classes (commodities, currencies, etc.), hence increasing also the difficulty of searching diversification benefits in other asset classes. For example, moves in the Dow Jones Industrial Average in 2010 matched copper prices by the most since at least 1988, resulting in a correlation coefficient of more than 0.9. The correlation of the Dollar Index, which tracks the U.S. currency against those of six trading partners, and Japan's Nikkei-225 Stock Average has been as much as minus 0.85 in 2010, the widest since 1988.

4.5.2 SEVERITY OF CORRELATION CHANGES

We also know that correlation increases in global financial market returns during bear markets. Correlations change during bull or bear markets, but we can anticipate now that even in bull markets we will still face higher correlations than what we used to have in former bull periods. So we tend to believe that the bull/bear distinction will play less of a role in the future in terms of distinguishing between correlation shifts. Nevertheless, what has been poorly analyzed if not done at all, is the understanding of the severity of how much correlation changes during short periods of time and even over longer periods. This subject has not been properly studied and monitored. We can have an average correlation coefficient of 0.5, but this average tells nothing about the volatility of correlation shifts. Standard deviation of correlation to a market is also very high, making average correlation less useful data to have and to use. The correlation among asset classes, markets, and sectors appears to be unstable, and unstable relationships complicate the asset allocation decision process.

The historical approach to use historical correlations (ex-post) is no longer the correct method. A lot of surveys clearly show that when predicting risk with historical correlation the realized figures thus obtained are subject to a huge range of errors. We have to understand how the shift and its severity in shift in correlation may affect the portfolio returns and how efficient management tools as a result of this analysis can help to have a pro-active management of correlation shifts and protect portfolios against those adverse shifts while still having some benefits from diversification—easy to say, more difficult to do. Forecasting correlation shifts and their severity in connection with a better estimate of future volatility can provide precious information to the portfolio manager. In the investment world of today we need a comprehensive and dynamic approach in the asset allocation decision which takes into consideration this unstable shift in correlation as well as shift in volatility. Forecasting correlations correctly (ex-ante) is a key aspect for every portfolio investment decision, for both strategic and tactical asset allocation. This work will be also useful for any derivative strategy if it appears worth to use. For example, in hedging strategies, if one uses an equity index future in order to hedge parts of our portfolio and ex-post correlation was 0.98, the hedge works decently well. The question whether this relationship persists going forward is covered by *ex ante* correlation.

Figure 4.17 shows correlation estimate error. For example, this means that if you have calculated a 21-day estimate of correlation of +0.2, then according to standard statistics the true value will lie between −0.02 and +0.42. The value of +0.42 is also the lower error bar on an estimate of +0.57. This means that if

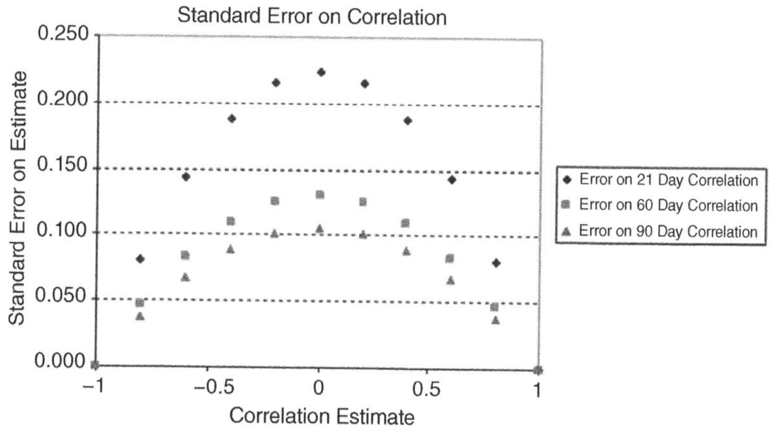

FIGURE 4.17 Correlation estimate error. Using 21-, 60-, and 90-day periods.

you see a value of +0.2 on one day, and +0.57 on the next, then (ignoring autocorrelation) this jump is entirely captured within the error terms of your estimate; that is, it would be hard to conclusively draw any significance from this jump in correlation.

Ex ante correlation is important because for every portfolio investment decision, investors rely on a predicted correlation. For alternative investments an investor expects to get uncorrelated returns and expects a diversification benefit when investing in hedge funds. Constructing a portfolio or managing a portfolio on falsely estimated correlations can have a direct consequence on the portfolio risk, being much more risky than anticipated by the portfolio manager and/or the investors. Understanding shift in correlations during bull and bear markets, as well as understanding the standard deviation of correlations, is a key point even though it is not easy.

The correlations in Figure 4.18 are based on daily returns correlations, taken from an example done in 2010.

Start with the markets correlations matrix for 1 year, 3 years, 5 years, and 10 years. There are less and less gray zones when you come to 1 year, and we would like to see more for diversification benefits.

The correlations between sectors also change and become more positively correlated, as suggested in Figure 4.19.

Figure 4.20 shows the correlation between sectors as part of the S&P 500; note the big change occurring between years 1 and 10.

How does one measure this shift in correlation? It is not easy to find the right way because, as mentioned, this subject has not been extensively studied. So for the time being, we can say that it is the standard deviation of correlation shifts. Figure 4.21 is just an example of what can be done when measuring shifts in correlation.

	MSCI AC Wo	S&P 500 IND	STXE 600 C I	NIKKEI 225	MSCI WORLI	S&P GSCI To	S&P GSCI Cr	USD-JPY X-R	USD-EUR X-I	H0A0 Index	USG5TR Ind	USG3TR Ind	USG1TR Ind	S&P GSCI Co	GOLD SPOT	VIX Index
MSCI AC World Local	1.00	0.91	0.87	0.40	0.96	0.67	0.65	0.40	-0.45	0.53	-0.54	-0.52	-0.41	0.56	0.22	-0.77
S&P 500 INDEX	0.91	1.00	0.67	0.16	0.91	0.60	0.59	0.40	-0.49	0.36	-0.58	-0.57	-0.49	0.45	0.23	-0.85
STXE 600 € Pr	0.87	0.67	1.00	0.29	0.80	0.59	0.56	0.33	-0.26	0.52	-0.38	-0.38	-0.29	0.55	0.19	-0.58
NIKKEI 225	0.40	0.16	0.29	1.00	0.35	0.24	0.23	0.23	-0.03	0.44	-0.16	-0.11	0.00	0.16	-0.10	-0.13
MSCI WORLD SMALL CAP	0.96	0.91	0.80	0.35	1.00	0.69	0.66	0.32	-0.49	0.52	-0.51	-0.49	-0.39	0.57	0.26	-0.76
S&P GSCI Tot Return Indx	0.67	0.60	0.59	0.24	0.69	1.00	0.97	0.20	-0.46	0.34	-0.36	-0.34	-0.27	0.66	0.38	-0.47
S&P GSCI Crude Oil T Ret	0.65	0.59	0.56	0.23	0.66	0.97	1.00	0.22	-0.43	0.31	-0.38	-0.36	-0.28	0.58	0.34	-0.47
USD-JPY X-RATE	0.40	0.40	0.33	0.23	0.32	0.20	0.22	1.00	0.06	0.17	-0.60	-0.64	-0.56	0.09	-0.14	-0.41
USD-EUR X-RATE	-0.45	-0.49	-0.26	-0.03	-0.49	-0.46	-0.43	0.06	1.00	-0.10	0.28	0.23	0.20	-0.38	-0.24	0.38
H0A0 Index	0.53	0.36	0.52	0.44	0.52	0.34	0.31	0.17	-0.10	1.00	-0.13	-0.13	-0.05	0.18	-0.01	-0.33
USG5TR Index	-0.54	-0.58	-0.38	-0.16	-0.51	-0.36	-0.38	-0.60	0.28	-0.13	1.00	0.92	0.74	-0.24	0.01	0.51
USG3TR Index	-0.52	-0.57	-0.38	-0.11	-0.49	-0.34	-0.36	-0.64	0.23	-0.13	0.92	1.00	0.90	-0.25	0.05	0.52
USG1TR Index	-0.41	-0.49	-0.29	0.00	-0.39	-0.27	-0.28	-0.56	0.20	-0.05	0.74	0.90	1.00	-0.20	0.06	0.45
S&P GSCI Copper Tot Ret	0.56	0.45	0.55	0.16	0.57	0.66	0.58	0.09	-0.38	0.18	-0.24	-0.25	-0.20	1.00	0.33	-0.34
GOLD SPOT $/OZ	0.22	0.23	0.19	-0.10	0.26	0.38	0.34	-0.14	-0.24	-0.01	0.01	0.05	0.06	0.33	1.00	-0.18
VIX Index	-0.77	-0.85	-0.58	-0.13	-0.76	-0.47	-0.47	-0.41	0.38	-0.33	0.51	0.52	0.45	-0.34	-0.18	1.00

Red	1.00	0.70
Blue	-1.00	-0.70
Grey	-0.20	0.20
One	1.00	

	MSCI AC Wo	S&P 500 IND	STXE 600 C I	NIKKEI 225	MSCI WORLI	S&P GSCI To	S&P GSCI Cr	USD-JPY X-R	USD-EUR X-I	H0A0 Index	USG5TR Ind	USG3TR Ind	USG1TR Ind	S&P GSCI Co	GOLD SPOT	VIX Index
MSCI AC World Local	1.00	0.89	0.85	0.45	0.95	0.51	0.48	0.53	-0.35	0.47	-0.42	-0.44	-0.43	0.50	0.09	-0.71
S&P 500 INDEX	0.89	1.00	0.61	0.13	0.89	0.40	0.39	0.55	-0.31	0.24	-0.44	-0.48	-0.48	0.34	0.04	-0.78
STXE 600 € Pr	0.85	0.61	1.00	0.40	0.76	0.49	0.45	0.42	-0.25	0.50	-0.32	-0.34	-0.31	0.56	0.07	-0.51
NIKKEI 225	0.45	0.13	0.40	1.00	0.36	0.22	0.19	0.18	-0.13	0.52	-0.10	-0.09	-0.07	0.25	0.06	-0.12
MSCI WORLD SMALL CAP	0.95	0.89	0.76	0.36	1.00	0.51	0.47	0.45	-0.42	0.43	-0.41	-0.42	-0.39	0.47	0.13	-0.71
S&P GSCI Tot Return Indx	0.51	0.40	0.49	0.22	0.51	1.00	0.97	0.20	-0.43	0.28	-0.29	-0.26	-0.19	0.63	0.38	-0.33
S&P GSCI Crude Oil T Ret	0.48	0.39	0.45	0.19	0.47	0.97	1.00	0.21	-0.37	0.23	-0.30	-0.26	-0.18	0.54	0.34	-0.31
USD-JPY X-RATE	0.53	0.55	0.42	0.18	0.45	0.20	0.21	1.00	0.10	0.13	-0.55	-0.58	-0.54	0.21	-0.13	-0.50
USD-EUR X-RATE	-0.35	-0.31	-0.25	-0.13	-0.42	-0.43	-0.37	0.10	1.00	-0.13	0.06	0.04	-0.01	-0.35	-0.42	0.23
H0A0 Index	0.47	0.24	0.50	0.52	0.43	0.28	0.23	0.13	-0.13	1.00	-0.10	-0.09	-0.10	0.31	0.04	-0.21
USG5TR Index	-0.42	-0.44	-0.32	-0.10	-0.41	-0.29	-0.30	-0.55	0.06	-0.10	1.00	0.91	0.72	-0.26	0.05	0.42
USG3TR Index	-0.44	-0.48	-0.34	-0.09	-0.42	-0.26	-0.26	-0.58	0.04	-0.09	0.91	1.00	0.90	-0.25	0.08	0.47
USG1TR Index	-0.43	-0.48	-0.31	-0.07	-0.39	-0.19	-0.18	-0.54	-0.01	-0.10	0.72	0.90	1.00	-0.21	0.12	0.48
S&P GSCI Copper Tot Ret	0.50	0.34	0.56	0.25	0.47	0.63	0.54	0.21	-0.35	0.31	-0.26	-0.25	-0.21	1.00	0.28	-0.30
GOLD SPOT $/OZ	0.09	0.04	0.07	0.06	0.13	0.38	0.34	-0.13	-0.42	0.04	0.05	0.08	0.12	0.28	1.00	-0.03
VIX Index	-0.71	-0.78	-0.51	-0.12	-0.71	-0.33	-0.31	-0.50	0.23	-0.21	0.42	0.47	0.48	-0.30	-0.03	1.00

Red	1.00	0.70
Blue	-1.00	-0.70
Grey	-0.20	0.20
One	1.00	

FIGURE 4.18 Asset correlations change.

	MSCI AC Wo	S&P 500 IND	STXE 600 C F	NIKKEI 225	MSCI WORLI	S&P GSCI To	S&P GSCI Cr	USD-JPY X-R	USD-EUR X-I	H0A0 Index	USG5TR Ind	USG3TR Ind	USG1TR Ind	S&P GSCI Co	GOLD SPOT :	VIX Index
MSCI AC World Local	1.00	0.89	0.85	0.44	0.94	0.45	0.43	0.48	-0.31	0.46	-0.38	-0.41	-0.40	0.44	0.13	-0.67
S&P 500 INDEX	0.89	1.00	0.59	0.12	0.87	0.35	0.34	0.49	-0.28	0.24	-0.40	-0.44	-0.44	0.29	0.07	-0.74
STXE 600 C Pr	0.85	0.59	1.00	0.39	0.75	0.43	0.39	0.38	-0.21	0.50	-0.29	-0.31	-0.29	0.50	0.11	-0.48
NIKKEI 225	0.44	0.12	0.39	1.00	0.38	0.19	0.16	0.16	-0.11	0.48	-0.09	-0.08	-0.06	0.21	0.08	-0.10
MSCI WORLD SMALL CAP	0.94	0.87	0.75	0.38	1.00	0.45	0.42	0.38	-0.40	0.43	-0.36	-0.38	-0.35	0.42	0.19	-0.66
S&P GSCI Tot Return Indx	0.45	0.35	0.43	0.19	0.45	1.00	0.96	0.15	-0.38	0.25	-0.24	-0.21	-0.14	0.56	0.40	-0.24
S&P GSCI Crude Oil T Ret	0.43	0.34	0.39	0.16	0.42	0.96	1.00	0.16	-0.33	0.20	-0.25	-0.21	-0.14	0.46	0.35	-0.23
USD-JPY X-RATE	0.48	0.49	0.38	0.16	0.38	0.15	0.16	1.00	0.17	0.12	-0.52	-0.56	-0.54	0.15	-0.13	-0.41
USD-EUR X-RATE	-0.31	-0.28	-0.21	-0.11	-0.40	-0.38	-0.33	0.17	1.00	-0.13	0.01	-0.01	-0.06	-0.30	-0.41	0.17
H0A0 Index	0.46	0.24	0.50	0.48	0.43	0.25	0.20	0.12	-0.13	1.00	-0.07	-0.07	-0.08	0.26	0.06	-0.19
USG5TR Index	-0.38	-0.40	-0.29	-0.09	-0.36	-0.24	-0.25	-0.52	0.01	-0.07	1.00	0.91	0.73	-0.28	0.04	0.34
USG3TR Index	-0.41	-0.44	-0.31	-0.08	-0.38	-0.21	-0.21	-0.56	-0.01	-0.07	0.91	1.00	0.98	-0.20	0.06	0.39
USG1TR Index	-0.40	-0.44	-0.29	-0.06	-0.35	-0.14	-0.14	-0.54	-0.06	-0.08	0.73	0.98	1.00	-0.16	0.09	0.41
S&P GSCI Copper Tot Ret	0.44	0.29	0.50	0.21	0.42	0.56	0.46	0.15	-0.30	0.26	-0.28	-0.20	-0.16	1.00	0.35	-0.24
GOLD SPOT $/OZ	0.13	0.07	0.11	0.08	0.19	0.40	0.35	-0.13	-0.41	0.06	0.04	0.06	0.09	0.35	1.00	-0.09
VIX Index	-0.67	-0.74	-0.48	-0.10	-0.66	-0.24	-0.23	-0.41	0.17	-0.19	0.34	0.39	0.41	-0.24	-0.09	1.00

Red	1.00	0.70
Blue	-1.00	-0.70
Grey	-0.20	0.20
One	1.00	

	MSCI AC Wo	S&P 500 IND	STXE 600 C F	NIKKEI 225	MSCI WORLI	S&P GSCI To	S&P GSCI Cr	USD-JPY X-R	USD-EUR X-I	H0A0 Index	USG5TR Ind	USG3TR Ind	USG1TR Ind	S&P GSCI Co	GOLD SPOT :	VIX Index
MSCI AC World Local	1.00	0.89	0.82	0.40	0.88	0.26	0.22	0.30	-0.06	0.37	-0.33	-0.37	-0.36	0.36	0.02	-0.68
S&P 500 INDEX	0.89	1.00	0.55	0.12	0.80	0.19	0.17	0.30	-0.05	0.19	-0.34	-0.38	-0.38	0.24	-0.01	-0.75
STXE 600 C Pr	0.82	0.55	1.00	0.32	0.66	0.24	0.19	0.25	0.02	0.39	-0.26	-0.29	-0.27	0.38	0.00	-0.44
NIKKEI 225	0.40	0.12	0.32	1.00	0.40	0.13	0.11	0.06	-0.07	0.36	-0.07	-0.08	-0.06	0.18	0.08	-0.10
MSCI WORLD SMALL CAP	0.88	0.80	0.66	0.40	1.00	0.31	0.27	0.17	-0.24	0.37	-0.29	-0.32	-0.29	0.37	0.14	-0.62
S&P GSCI Tot Return Indx	0.26	0.19	0.24	0.13	0.31	1.00	0.95	0.05	-0.23	0.15	-0.15	-0.13	-0.09	0.42	0.31	-0.15
S&P GSCI Crude Oil T Ret	0.22	0.17	0.19	0.11	0.27	0.95	1.00	0.05	-0.18	0.11	-0.15	-0.13	-0.08	0.31	0.24	-0.13
USD-JPY X-RATE	0.30	0.30	0.25	0.06	0.17	0.05	0.05	1.00	0.25	0.07	-0.34	-0.37	-0.35	0.07	-0.18	-0.26
USD-EUR X-RATE	-0.06	-0.05	0.02	-0.07	-0.24	-0.23	-0.18	0.25	1.00	-0.02	-0.11	-0.14	-0.17	-0.22	-0.41	0.03
H0A0 Index	0.37	0.19	0.39	0.36	0.37	0.15	0.11	0.07	-0.02	1.00	-0.02	-0.03	-0.03	0.22	0.05	-0.15
USG5TR Index	-0.33	-0.34	-0.26	-0.07	-0.29	-0.15	-0.15	-0.34	-0.11	-0.02	1.00	0.92	0.75	-0.14	0.08	0.26
USG3TR Index	-0.37	-0.38	-0.29	-0.08	-0.32	-0.13	-0.13	-0.37	-0.14	-0.03	0.92	1.00	0.91	-0.14	0.10	0.32
USG1TR Index	-0.36	-0.38	-0.27	-0.06	-0.29	-0.09	-0.08	-0.35	-0.17	-0.03	0.75	0.91	1.00	-0.11	0.12	0.34
S&P GSCI Copper Tot Ret	0.36	0.24	0.38	0.18	0.37	0.42	0.31	0.07	-0.22	0.22	-0.14	-0.14	-0.11	1.00	0.30	-0.20
GOLD SPOT $/OZ	0.02	-0.01	0.00	0.08	0.14	0.31	0.24	-0.18	-0.41	0.05	0.08	0.10	0.12	0.30	1.00	-0.02
VIX Index	-0.68	-0.75	-0.44	-0.10	-0.62	-0.15	-0.13	-0.26	0.03	-0.15	0.26	0.32	0.34	-0.20	-0.02	1.00

Red	1.00	0.70
Blue	-1.00	-0.70
Grey	-0.20	0.20
One	1.00	

FIGURE 4.18 *(Continued)*

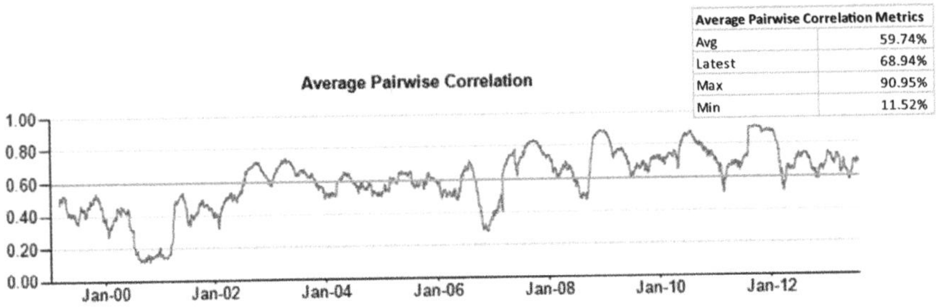

FIGURE 4.19 Sector correlation change.

4.6 Correlation Estimates

In this section we will give an overview of various different methods to estimate the conditional correlation between two random variables. We assume that the returns $R_{i,t}$ of an asset i at time t take the form

$$R_{i,t} = \sigma_{i,t}\varepsilon_{i,t}$$

where $\varepsilon_{i,t} \sim$ i.i.d.$N(0,1)$; that is, each disturbance $\varepsilon_{i,t}$ is independent and identically normally distributed. The mean and variance of $\varepsilon_{i,t}$ are respectively $E_t(\varepsilon_{i,t}) = 0$ and $Var_t(\varepsilon_{i,t}) = E_t(\varepsilon_{i,t}^2) = 1$.

The expected value and variance of R_t at time $t + 1$ can be easily evaluated as

$$\mu_{i,t+1} = E_t(\sigma_{i,t+1}\varepsilon_{i,t+1}) = 0$$
$$Var_t(R_{i,t+1}) = E_t([R_{i,t+1} - \mu_{i,t+1}]^2) = E_t(R_{i,t}^2) = \sigma_{i,t+1}^2$$

Then conditional correlation between the returns of two assets is defined as

$$\rho_{12,t+1} = \frac{E_t(R_{1,t+1}R_{2,t+1})}{\sigma_{1,t+1}\sigma_{2,t+1}}$$

which can also be rewritten as

$$\rho_{12,t+1} = \frac{E_t(R_{1,t+1}R_{2,t+1})}{\sqrt{E_t(R_{1,t+1}^2)E_t(R_{2,t+1}^2)}}$$

We now introduce a result that will be used later:

Sector	MATERIALS	ENERGY	CONS STAPLES	CONS DISCRET	INDUSTRIALS	UTILITIES	INFO TECH	TELECOM SERV	HEALTH CARE	FINANCIALS
MATERIALS	1	0.89	0.77	0.86	0.89	0.76	0.83	0.66	0.77	0.85
ENERGY	0.89	1	0.78	0.84	0.88	0.83	0.82	0.66	0.80	0.82
CONS STAPLES	0.77	0.78	1	0.80	0.81	0.78	0.78	0.73	0.81	0.73
CONS DISCRET	0.86	0.84	0.80	1	0.93	0.76	0.89	0.66	0.78	0.86
INDUSTRIALS	0.89	0.88	0.81	0.93	1	0.79	0.89	0.68	0.81	0.87
UTILITIES	0.76	0.83	0.78	0.76	0.79	1	0.76	0.68	0.77	0.71
INFO TECH	0.83	0.82	0.78	0.89	0.89	0.76	1	0.67	0.79	0.83
TELECOM SERV	0.66	0.66	0.73	0.66	0.68	0.68	0.67	1	0.67	0.62
HEALTH CARE	0.77	0.80	0.81	0.78	0.81	0.77	0.79	0.67	1	0.76
FINANCIALS	0.85	0.82	0.73	0.86	0.87	0.71	0.83	0.62	0.76	1

Red	1.00	0.70
Blue	-1.00	-0.70
Grey	-0.20	0.20
One	1.00	
3973	10	

Sector	MATERIALS	ENERGY	CONS STAPLES	CONS DISCRET	INDUSTRIALS	UTILITIES	INFO TECH	TELECOM SERV	HEALTH CARE	FINANCIALS
MATERIALS	1	0.74	0.64	0.77	0.83	0.58	0.62	0.59	0.62	0.69
ENERGY	0.74	1	0.59	0.59	0.65	0.65	0.47	0.50	0.60	0.56
CONS STAPLES	0.64	0.59	1	0.68	0.69	0.61	0.45	0.56	0.75	0.60
CONS DISCRET	0.77	0.59	0.68	1	0.88	0.56	0.76	0.68	0.66	0.79
INDUSTRIALS	0.83	0.65	0.69	0.88	1	0.60	0.75	0.66	0.69	0.79
UTILITIES	0.58	0.65	0.61	0.56	0.60	1	0.45	0.52	0.60	0.51
INFO TECH	0.62	0.47	0.45	0.76	0.75	0.45	1	0.63	0.51	0.62
TELECOM SERV	0.59	0.50	0.56	0.68	0.66	0.52	0.63	1	0.57	0.60
HEALTH CARE	0.62	0.60	0.75	0.66	0.69	0.60	0.51	0.57	1	0.61
FINANCIALS	0.69	0.56	0.60	0.79	0.79	0.51	0.62	0.60	0.61	1

Red	1.00	0.70
Blue	-1.00	-0.70
Grey	-0.20	0.20
One	1.00	
3973	10	

FIGURE 4.20 Sectors correlation in the S&P 500.

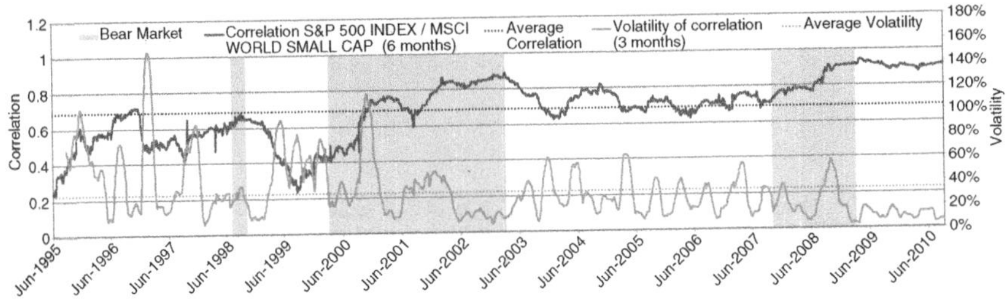

FIGURE 4.21 Measuring shifts in correlation.

$$
\begin{aligned}
E_t(\varepsilon_{1,t+1}\varepsilon_{2,t+1}) &= E_t\left(\frac{R_{1,t+1}}{\sigma_{1,t+1}}\frac{R_{2,t+1}}{\sigma_{2,t+1}}\right) \\
&= \frac{E_t(R_{1,t+1}R_{2,t+1})}{\sigma_{1,t+1}\sigma_{2,t+1}} \\
&= \frac{\sigma_{12,t+!}}{\sigma_{1,t+1}\sigma_{2,t+1}} \\
&= \rho_{12,t+1}
\end{aligned}
$$

Hence, the conditional correlation of raw returns is equivalent to the conditional covariance the standardized disturbances $\varepsilon_{i,t}$:

$$\rho_{12,t+1} = E_t(\varepsilon_{1,t+1}\varepsilon_{2,t+1}) = \mathrm{Cov}(\varepsilon_{1,t+!}\varepsilon_{2,t+1})$$

4.6.1 COPULAS

Copulas are used to model joint distribution of multiple underlyings. They permit a rich "correlation" structure between underlyings. They can be used for pricing, risk management, pairs trading, and so on, and are especially popular in credit derivatives.

Copulas provide a potential useful modeling tool to represent the dependence structure among variables and to generate joint distributions by combining given marginal distributions. Simulations play a relevant role in finance. They are used to replicate efficient frontiers or extremal values, determine price options, estimate joint risks, and so on. Using copulas, it is easy to construct and simulate from multivariate distributions based on almost any choice of marginals and any type of dependence structure. Interdependence of returns of two or more assets is usually calculated using the correlation coefficient. However, correlation only works well with normal distributions, while distributions in financial markets are mostly skewed. The copula, therefore, has been applied to areas of finance such as option pricing and portfolio value-at-risk to deal with the skewness.

In the case of the recent financial crisis and the collapse of credit derivatives, the Gaussian copula was a solution to the problem because the creators of these financial instruments were thinking that correlation would remain stable. Gaussian copula could have been useful to handle default correlation in such complex instruments.

Here are some examples of bivariate copula functions. They are readily extended to the multivariate case:

- Bivariate normal

$$C(u,v) = N_2\left(N_1^{-1}(u), N_1^{-1}(v), \rho\right), \qquad -1 \le \rho \le 1$$

where N_2 is the bivariate normal cumulative distribution function, and N_1^{-1} is the univariate normal cumulative distribution function.

- Frank

$$C(u,v) = \frac{1}{\alpha}\ln\left(1 + \frac{\left(e^{\alpha u}-1\right)\left(e^{\alpha v}-1\right)}{e^{\alpha}-1}\right), \qquad -\infty < \alpha < \infty$$

- Fréchet–Hoeffding upper bound

$$C(u,v) = \min(u,v)$$

- Gumbel–Hougaard

$$C(u,v) = \exp\left(-\left((-\ln u)^{\theta}\right) + \left(-\ln v)^{\theta}\right)^{1/\theta}\right), \qquad 1 \le \theta < \infty$$

4.6.2 MOVING AVERAGE

One of the simplest and most common estimators for the conditional correlation is the moving average. This is obtained from the definition of the conditional correlation in the previous section, by estimating the expectation vales in the formula using a rolling moving average. Indicating with n the size of the sample window, the moving average estimator is

$$\rho_{12,t+1} = \frac{\frac{1}{n}\sum_{\tau=0}^{n-1} R_{1,t-\tau}R_{2,t-\tau}}{\sqrt{\left(\frac{1}{n}\sum_{\tau=0}^{n-1} R_{1,t-\tau}^2\right)\left(\frac{1}{n}\sum_{\tau=0}^{n-1} R_{2,t-\tau}^2\right)}} = \frac{\sum_{\tau=0}^{n-1} R_{1,t-\tau}R_{2,t-\tau}}{\sqrt{\left(\sum_{\tau=0}^{n-1} R_{1,t-\tau}^2\right)\left(\sum_{\tau=0}^{n-1} R_{2,t-\tau}^2\right)}}$$

Another popular estimator is **exponential smoothing**, which is used in RiskMetrics with a declining weight of $\lambda = 0.94$. In this model the variances are estimated as

$$\sigma_{t+1}^2 = (1-\lambda)\sum_{\tau=0}^{\infty} \lambda^{\tau} R_{t-\tau}^2$$

Typically this infinite sum is computed using only 100 lags of squared returns, because this gives sufficient accuracy. The last formula can also be expressed in recursive form, which is computationally simpler to implement:

$$\sigma_{t+1}^2 = (1-\lambda)R_t^2 + \lambda\sigma_2^t$$

Similarly, the covariance is estimated as

$$\sigma_{12,t+1} = (1-\lambda)\sum_{\tau=0}^{\infty}\lambda^{\tau}R_{1,t-\tau}R_{2,t-\tau} = (1-\lambda)R_{1,t}R_{2,t} + \lambda\sigma_{12,t}$$

Using the relation $\rho_{12,t+1} = \sigma_{12,t+1}/(\sigma_{1,t+1}\sigma_{2,t+1})$ and substituting the previous expressions for the variances and covariance, we get the evaluation formula:

$$\rho_{12,t+1} = \frac{\sum_{\tau=0}^{\infty}\lambda^{\tau}R_{1,t-\tau}R_{2,t-\tau}}{\sqrt{\left(\sum_{\tau=0}^{\infty}\lambda^{\tau}R_{1,t-\tau}^2\right)\left(\sum_{\tau=0}^{\infty}\lambda^{\tau}R_{2,t-\tau}^2\right)}}$$

4.6.3 CORRELATION ESTIMATORS IN MATRIX NOTATION

In this section we introduce some matrix notation and express the moving average and exponential smoothing estimator in matrix form. Let's indicate with R_t a column vector of returns for a portfolio at time t. In the two-asset case, this is:

$$R_t = \begin{pmatrix} R_{1,t} \\ R_{2,t} \end{pmatrix}$$

With the notation R_t^T we indicated the transposed vector:

$$R_t^T = \begin{pmatrix} R_{1,t} & R_{2,t} \end{pmatrix}$$

We define the conditional covariance matrix of returns H_{t+1} as

$$H_{t+1} \equiv E_t\left(R_{t+1}R_{t+1}^T\right)$$

For a portfolio of two assets, this is equivalent to

$$\begin{aligned} E_t\left(R_{t+1}R_{t+1}^T\right) &= E_t\left(\begin{pmatrix} R_{1,t+1} \\ R_{2,t+1} \end{pmatrix}\begin{pmatrix} R_{1,t+1} & R_{2,t+1} \end{pmatrix}\right) \\ &= E_t\left(\begin{pmatrix} R_{1,t+1}^2 & R_{1,t+1}R_{2,t+1} \\ R_{1,t+1}R_{2,t+1} & R_{2,t+1}^2 \end{pmatrix}\right) \\ &= \begin{pmatrix} \sigma_{1,t+1}^2 & \sigma_{12,t+1} \\ \sigma_{12,t+1} & \sigma_{2,t+1}^2 \end{pmatrix} \end{aligned}$$

Using the previous result, we can express the moving average and exponential smoothing estimators in matrix form. For the moving average, we get

$$H_{t+1} = \frac{1}{n}\sum_{\tau=0}^{n-1} R_{t-\tau} R_{t-\tau}^{T}$$

In the two-asset case, this becomes

$$\begin{aligned} H_{t+1} &= \frac{1}{n}\sum_{\tau=0}^{n-1}\begin{pmatrix} R_{1,t}^2 & R_{1,t}R_{2,t} \\ R_{1,t}R_{2,t} & R_{2,t}^2 \end{pmatrix} \\ &= \begin{pmatrix} \frac{1}{n}\sum_{\tau=0}^{n-1} R_{1,t}^2 & \frac{1}{n}\sum_{\tau=0}^{n-1} R_{1,t}R_{2,t} \\ \frac{1}{n}\sum_{\tau=0}^{n-1} R_{1,t}R_{2,t} & \frac{1}{n}\sum_{\tau=0}^{n-1} R_{2,t}^2 \end{pmatrix} \\ &= \begin{pmatrix} \sigma_{1,t+1}^2 & \sigma_{12,t+1} \\ \sigma_{12,t+1} & \sigma_{2,t+1}^2 \end{pmatrix} \end{aligned}$$

Similarly, the exponential smoothing can be written in matrix notation as

$$H_{t+1} = (1-\lambda) R_t R_t^T + \lambda H_t$$

Again, expanding the notation for a portfolio of two assets, we get

$$\begin{aligned} H_{t+1} &= \begin{pmatrix} \sigma_{1,t+1}^2 & \sigma_{12,t+1} \\ \sigma_{12,t+1} & \sigma_{2,t+1}^2 \end{pmatrix} \\ &= (1-\lambda)\begin{pmatrix} R_{1,t}^2 & R_{1,t}R_{2,t} \\ R_{1,t}R_{2,t} & R_{2,t}^2 \end{pmatrix} + \lambda \begin{pmatrix} \sigma_{1,t}^2 & \sigma_{12,t} \\ \sigma_{12,t} & \sigma_{2,t}^2 \end{pmatrix} \end{aligned}$$

Finally, the conditional correlations can be estimated using the relation $\rho_{12,t+1} = \sigma_{12,t+1}/(\sigma_{1,t+1}\sigma_{2,t+1})$.

4.6.4 BOLLERSLEV'S CONSTANT CONDITIONAL CORRELATION MODEL

Bollerslev (1990) introduced a new class of multivariate GARCH estimators, called constant conditional correlation (CCC). In Bollerslev's model, the variances and covariances are allowed to change, while the correlations stay constant. In matrix form we have

$$H_t = D_t \Gamma D_t$$

where D_t is the stoachastic diagonal matrix with elements $\sigma_{1t}, \ldots \sigma_{Nt}$, Γ is the correlation matrix containing the constant correlations, and H_t is the time-varying conditional covariance matrix that we have introduced in the previous section.

Exemplifying in the case of three assets, the last equation becomes

$$H_t = \begin{pmatrix} \sigma_{1,t}^2 & \sigma_{12,t} & \sigma_{13,t} \\ \sigma_{12,t} & \sigma_{2,t}^2 & \sigma_{23,t} \\ \sigma_{13,t} & \sigma_{23,t} & \sigma_{3,t}^2 \end{pmatrix} = D_t \Gamma D_t$$

$$= \begin{pmatrix} \sigma_{1,t} & 0 & 0 \\ 0 & \sigma_{2,t} & 0 \\ 0 & 0 & \sigma_{3,t} \end{pmatrix} \begin{pmatrix} 1 & \rho_{12} & \rho_{13} \\ \rho_{12} & 1 & \rho_{23} \\ \rho_{13} & \rho_{23} & 1 \end{pmatrix} \begin{pmatrix} \sigma_{1,t} & 0 & 0 \\ 0 & \sigma_{2,t} & 0 \\ 0 & 0 & \sigma_{3,t} \end{pmatrix}$$

We have previously assumed that the returns $R_{i,t}$ take the form

$$R_{i,t} = \sigma_{i,t}\varepsilon_{i,t}$$

In matrix notation, this can be written as

$$R_t = D_t \varepsilon_t$$

which, expanding the notation in the three-asset case, becomes

$$\begin{pmatrix} R_{1,t} \\ R_{2,t} \\ R_{3,t} \end{pmatrix} = \begin{pmatrix} \sigma_{1,t} & 0 & 0 \\ 0 & \sigma_{2,t} & 0 \\ 0 & 0 & \sigma_{3,t} \end{pmatrix} \begin{pmatrix} \varepsilon_{1,t} \\ \varepsilon_{2,t} \\ \varepsilon_{3,t} \end{pmatrix}$$

Using the fact that $\varepsilon_t = D_t^{-1} R_t$ and $\text{Var}_{t-1}[R_{i,t}] = \sigma_{i,t}^2$, we can see that Γ is in fact a matrix containing the conditional correlations:

$$E_{t-1}(\varepsilon_t \varepsilon_t^T) = E_{t-1}(D_t^{-1} R_t R_t^T D_t^{-1}) = D_t^{-1} E_{t-1}(R_t R_t^T) D_t^{-1} = D_t^{-1} H_t D_t^{-1} = \Gamma$$

4.6.5 ENGLE'S DYNAMIC CONDITIONAL CORRELATION MODEL

A generalization of Bollerslev's approach has been proposed by Engle (2002), known as the Dynamic Conditional Correlation (DCC) model. The DCC model assumes that the matrix Γ is also time-varying:

$$H_t = D_t \Gamma_t D_t$$

Then, a small number of parameters are introduced to model the correlations, regardless of the total number of assets.

We have already seen that

$$\rho_{12,t} = E_{t-1}(\varepsilon_{1,t}\varepsilon_{2,t}) = Cov(\varepsilon_{1,t}\varepsilon_{2,t})$$

that is, the conditional correlation of the raw returns is equivalent to the conditional covariance between the standardized disturbances $\varepsilon_{i,t}$. This means that we can model the conditional covariance of the standardized disturbances $\varepsilon_{i,t}$, rather than directly modeling the conditional correlations.

In the *DCC integrated model,* exponential smoothing is used to model the conditional covariance of the standardised disturbances $\varepsilon_{i,t}$. This is achieved by introducing a new process:

$$q_{ij,t} = (1-\lambda)(\varepsilon_{i,t-1}\varepsilon_{j,t-1}) + \lambda q_{ij,t-1}$$

The previous formula can also be rewritten in matrix notation as

$$Q_t = (1-\lambda)(\varepsilon_{t-1}\varepsilon_{t-1}^T) + \lambda Q_{t-1}$$

Note that the parameter λ is the same for all the $q_{ij,t}$. In other words, we have only one additional parameter to estimate, regardless of the number of assets. Finally, the conditional correlation can be obtained by normalizing the $q_{ij,t}$ variables:

$$\rho_{ij,t} = \frac{q_{ij,t}}{\sqrt{q_{ii,t}q_{ij,t}}}$$

An alternative approach is given by the *DCC mean reverting* model. In this case, the $q_{ij,t}$ variables are modeled using a GARCH(1,1) process. Hence, the $q_{ij,t}$ represent a mean reverting to a long-term target $\bar{\rho}_{ij}$—that is, the *unconditional correlation* between the standardized disturbances $\varepsilon_{i,t}$ and $\varepsilon_{j,t}$:

$$q_{ij,t} = \bar{\rho}_{ij} + \alpha(\varepsilon_{i,t-1}\varepsilon_{j,t-1} - \bar{\rho}_{ij}) + \beta(q_{ij,t-1} - \bar{\rho}_{ij})$$

In matrix notation this becomes

$$Q_t = \bar{\rho}(1-\alpha-\beta) + \alpha(\varepsilon_{t-1}\varepsilon_{t-1}^T) + \beta Q_{t-1}$$

The DCC mean reverting model introduces only two parameters, α and β, regardless of the number of assets. As with the DCC integrated model, the conditional correlation can be obtained by normalizing the $q_{ij,t}$ variables:

$$\rho_{ij,t} = \frac{q_{ij,t}}{\sqrt{q_{ii,t}q_{ij,t}}}$$

4.6.6 ESTIMATING THE PARAMETERS OF THE DCC MODEL

To estimate the parameters of the DCC model, we can use a quasi-maximum likelihood approach. First, we shall remind the reader that we have assumed the vector of market returns R_t to be distributed as a multivariate normal of dimension N with null mean. The corresponding density function is then given by

$$f(R_t) = \frac{1}{(2\pi)^{N/2} |H_t|^{1/2}} \exp\left(-\frac{1}{2} R_t^T H_t^{-1} R_t\right)$$

The joint maximum likelihood L of the entire sample is then just the product of the $f(R_t)$ from time $t = 1$ to $t = T$:

$$L = \prod_{t=1}^{T} \frac{1}{(2\pi)^{N/2} |H_t|^{1/2}} \exp\left(-\frac{1}{2} R_t^T H_t^{-1} R_t\right)$$

Since the logarithm is a monotonic increasing function, maximizing L is equivalent to maximizing $\ln L$. Evaluating $\ln L$, we get

$$\begin{aligned}
\ln L &= \sum_{t=1}^{T} \ln\left[\frac{1}{(2\pi)^{\frac{N}{2}} |H_t|^{\frac{1}{2}}} \exp\left(-\frac{1}{2} R_t^T H_t^{-1} R_t\right)\right] \\
&= -\frac{1}{2}\sum_{t=1}^{T} \left(N \ln(2\pi) + \ln|H_t| + R_t^T H_t^{-1} R_t\right) \\
&= -\frac{1}{2}\sum_{t=1}^{T} \left(N \ln(2\pi) + \ln|D_t \Gamma_t D_t| + R_t^T D_t^{-1} \Gamma_t^{-1} D_t^{-1} R_t\right) \\
&= -\frac{1}{2}\sum_{t=1}^{T} \left(N \ln(2\pi) + 2\ln|D_t| + \ln|H_t| + \varepsilon_t^T \Gamma_t^{-1} \varepsilon_t\right) \\
&= -\frac{1}{2}\sum_{t=1}^{T} \left(N \ln(2\pi) + 2\ln|D_t| + R_t^T D_t^{-1} D_t^{-1} R_t - \varepsilon_t^T \varepsilon_t + \ln|\Gamma_t| + \varepsilon_t^T \Gamma_t^{-1} \varepsilon_t\right)
\end{aligned}$$

where we have used the fact that $\varepsilon_t^T \varepsilon_t R_t^T D_t^{-1} D_t^{-1} R_t$. We can rewrite the previous expression as the sum of two parts: One part is dependent on the parameters of the standard deviation matrix D (indicated by θ), and another part also depends on the additional parameters of Γ (indicated by ϕ):

$$\ln L = L_V(\theta) + L_C(\theta, \phi)$$

The volatility term is then given by

$$L_V = -\frac{1}{2}\sum_{t=1}^{T} \left(N \ln(2\pi) + 2\ln|D_t| + R_t^T |D_t|^2 R_t\right)$$

while the correlation term is

$$L_C(\theta, \phi) = -\frac{1}{2}\sum_{t=1}^{T} \left(\ln|\Gamma_t| + \varepsilon_t^T \Gamma_t^{-1} \varepsilon_t - \varepsilon_t^T \varepsilon_t\right)$$

The "trick" is to first estimate the parameters θ by maximizing $L_V(\theta)$ and then estimate ϕ by maximizing the second term $L_C(\theta,\phi)$. This approach will work under reasonably regularity conditions of the likelihood function.

In two dimensions, L_C can be expressed as

$$L_C = -\frac{1}{2}\sum_{t=1}^{T}\left[\ln\left|\begin{pmatrix} 1 & \rho_{12,t} \\ \rho_{12,t} & 1 \end{pmatrix}\right| + \frac{1}{1-\rho_{12,t}^2}\begin{pmatrix}\varepsilon_{1,t} & \varepsilon_{2,t}\end{pmatrix}\begin{pmatrix} 1 & -\rho_{12,t} \\ -\rho_{12,t} & 1 \end{pmatrix}\begin{pmatrix}\varepsilon_{1,t} \\ \varepsilon_{2,t}\end{pmatrix}\right.$$

$$\left. -\begin{pmatrix}\varepsilon_{1,t} & \varepsilon_{2,t}\end{pmatrix}\begin{pmatrix}\varepsilon_{1,t} \\ \varepsilon_{2,t}\end{pmatrix}\right]$$

$$= -\frac{1}{2}\sum_{t=1}^{T}\left[\ln\left(1-\rho_{12,t}^2\right) + \frac{\varepsilon_{1,t}^2 + \varepsilon_{2,t}^2 + 2\rho_{12,t}\varepsilon_{1,t}\varepsilon_{2,t}}{1-\rho_{12,t}^2} - \varepsilon_{1,t}^2 - \varepsilon_{2,t}^2\right]$$

The last two terms in the previous expression can be omitted, because they add a fixed contribution that does not depend on any of the parameters of the model.

4.6.7 IMPLEMENTING THE DCC MODEL

In this section we take a step-by-step approach to show how the DCC model can be implemented using an Excel spreadsheet. In summary, we would need to:

1. Estimate the variances of each asset using a GARCH model, by maximizing L_V.
2. Standardize each asset return using the standard deviations estimated at point 1.
3. Calculate the values of the $q_{ij,t}$, using the DCC Mean Reverting or Integrated model.
4. Evaluate the dynamic correlations $\rho_{12,t}$ from the $q_{ij,t}$.
5. Calculate L_C, that is the component of the joint likelihood which depends on the correlation parameters.
6. Estimate the parameters of the DCC model, so that L_C is maximized.

Figure 4.22 shows an excerpt of a two-asset return time series for the Dow Jones Industrial Average and NASDAQ-100 indices, respectively. We want to estimate the dynamic conditional correlations for these two indices using the DCC integrated model.

Here we will skip step 1 and assume that the conditional variances have been already estimated—for example, using a GARCH model. The results have been reported into the next two columns of the spreadsheet, as shown in Figure 4.23.

Then, we need to standardize the time series of asset return using the conditional variances. The standardized returns are just the disturbances $\varepsilon_{i,t}$, since

B	C	D
Date	DOW Returns	NASADQ Returns
02/03/1990	0.9354%	0.8856%
05/03/1990	–0.4072%	–0.1858%
06/03/1990	1.0232%	0.4870%
07/03/1990	–0.2697%	0.0463%
08/03/1990	0.9907%	0.9206%
09/03/1990	–0.4774%	0.0687%

FIGURE 4.22 Initial data.

DOW Conditional Variance	NASDAQ Conditional Variance
0.0000812	0.0001324
0.0000816	0.0001265
0.0000787	0.0001129
0.0000800	0.0001034
0.0000768	0.0000925

FIGURE 4.23 Conditional variances.

DOW Standardized Returns	NASADQ Standardized Returns	Product of Standardized Returns
1.0380	0.7698	0.7990
–0.4507	–0.1652	0.0745
1.1533	0.4584	0.5287
–0.3015	0.0455	–0.0137
1.1306	0.9574	1.0825

FIGURE 4.24 Standardized returns.

$\varepsilon_{i,t} = R_{i,t}/\sigma_{i,t}$. Hence, in the next two columns we calculate $\varepsilon_{1,t}$ and $\varepsilon_{2,t}$ using the previous formula. We also add a third column with the product $\varepsilon_{1,t}\varepsilon_{2,t}$, which will be used for the next computations. Figure 4.24 shows an excerpt of the three columns with the $\varepsilon_{1,t}\varepsilon_{2,t}$, and the product $\varepsilon_{1,t}\varepsilon_{2,t}$.

The next step consists of evaluation the $q_{ij,t}$. We have added three columns for $q_{11,t}$, $q_{22,t}$, and $q_{12,t}$, as shown in Figure 4.25. The initial value of $q_{11,t}$ and $q_{22,t}$

q_t DOW	q_t NASDAQ	q_t DOW-NASDAQ
1.0000000	1.0000000	0.7044025
1.0023293	0.9877556	0.7072466
0.9783134	0.9588928	0.6882306
0.9888883	0.9363916	0.6834362
0.9619031	0.9083145	0.6624862
0.9714124	0.9085659	0.6751083

FIGURE 4.25 *q* variables.

Dynamic Conditional Correlation	DCC Likelihood
0.7044025	–0.1974625
0.7107893	0.2259098
0.7105751	–0.4453162
0.7102244	0.2375532
0.7087499	–0.3147456

FIGURE 4.26 Estimation of the parameter of the DCC.

has been set to 1, while the initial value of $q_{12,t}$ can be estimated by computing the average of the products of the standardized returns (using in-sample or out-of-sample data). Also, the parameter λ has been initialized to the value of 0.94. This value must be inserted in a cell of the spreadsheet and referenced in the formulas, becuse later we will need to estimate the value of λ which maximizes the likelihood function.

In Figure 4.25, each of the values of $q_{11,t}$, $q_{22,t}$, and $q_{12,t}$ has been calculated using the formula of the DCC integrated model.

Then, we introduced two other columns for the dynamic conditional correlation and the likelihood function (Figure 4.26). The values of the dynamic conditional correlation have been computed from the $q_{ij,t}$ using the DCC integrated model, while the formula for the likelihood in the two-asset case was given at the end of the previous section.

The next step consists of calculating L_C, Which is obtained by summing all the values in the likelihood column. The result is shown in Figure 4.27 under the MLE row, while the previous row shows the initial value of the parameter λ.

Finally, we estimate the value of λ which maximizes the MLE. This can be done using Microsoft Excel Solver. The final result is shown in Figure 4.28.

Once the best value of λ has been obtained, all the $q_{ij,t}$ are automatically reevaluated using the new value of λ, and the dynamic conditional correlations are computed based on the new values of the $q_{ij,t}$.

λ	094
MLE	–1609.9495087

FIGURE 4.27 MLE initial estimation.

DCC Parameter Final Value	
λ	0.969949212
MLE	–1595.5509510

FIGURE 4.28 Estimation of the parameter of the DCC.

FURTHER READING

Baur, D., A flexible dynamic correlation model, in Dek Terrell, Thomas B. Fomby (eds.), *Economic Analysis of Financial and Time Series* (*Advances in Econometrics*, Vol. 20), Emerald Group Publishing, pp. 3–31.

Bollerslev, T., Modeling the coherence in short-run nominal exchange rates: a multivariate generalized ARCH model, *Review of Economics and Statistics*, **72**, 1990, pp. 498–505.

Cherubini, U., Luciano, E., Vecchiato, W., *Copula Methods in Finance*, John Wiley & Sons, Hoboken, NJ, 2004.

Cherubini U., Mulinacci S., Gobbi, F., Romagnoli S., *Dynamic Copula Methods in Finance*, Wiley Finance, Hoboken, NJ, 2011.

Cumby, R., Figlewski, S., Hasbrouck, J., Forecasting volatilities and correlations with EGARCH models, *Journal of Derivatives*, **1**, 1993, pp. 51–63.

Elton, E. J., Gruber, M. J., Brown, S. J., Goetzmann, W. N., *Modern Portfolio Theory and Investment Analysis*, 8th edition, John Wiley & Sons, Hoboken, NJ, 2010.

Engle. R. F., Dynamic conditional correlation: A simple class of generalized autoregressive conditional heteroskedasticity models, *Journal of Business and Economic Statistics*, **20**(3); 2002, pp. 339–350.

Engel, R., *Anticipating Correlations: A New Paradigm for Risk Management*, Economic Institute Lectures, Princeton University Press, Princeton, NJ, 2009.

Engel, R. F., Mezrich, J., Grappling with GARCH, *Risk*, September 1995, pp. 112–117.

Li, D., 1990 On default correlation: A copula function approach, RiskMetrics working paper, 2000.

Malkiel, B.G., The efficient market hypothesis and its critics, CEPS Working Paper No. 91, April 2003.

Markowitz, H., Portfolio selection, *Journal of Finance*, 7(1), March 1952, pp. 77–91.

Nielsen, R. B., *An Introduction to Copulas*, Springer Verlag, New York, 1999.

Trivedi P. K., Zimmer, D. M., *Copula Modeling: An Introduction for Practitioners*, Now Publishers, Hanover, MA, 2007.

Tsay R. S., *Analysis of Financial Time Series*, Wiley Series in Probability and Statistics, 2nd edition, John Wiley & Sons, Hoboken, NJ, 2005.

CHAPTER FIVE

The Capital Asset Pricing Model and the Arbitrage Pricing Theory

Every model is wrong, but some are useful.

—George Box

The original Capital Asset Pricing Model (CAPM) was derived by Sharpe, Lintner, and Mossin in 1964. We will consider this original model as well as extensions of it in lectures that follow. As with every other model, CAPM requires simplifying assumptions because of the complexity of the real world. There are a number of assumptions underlining the CAPM model, but only three of those are absolutely necessary for deriving the CAPM. The assumptions are as follows:

1. One-period investment horizon.
2. Rational, risk-averse investors.
3. Unlimited borrowing and lending is allowed at a risk-free rate that is the same for all investors.
4. There are no taxes.
5. There are no transaction costs and inflation.
6. All assets are infinitely divisible.
7. Free flow and instant availability of information.
8. There are many investors on the market.
9. All assets are marketable.
10. All investors have homogeneous expectations about expected returns, variances, and covariances of assets.

Handbook of Market Risk, First Edition. Christian Szylar.

Also, we have shown that in the presence of a risk-free asset and under the assumptions that all individuals (i) face the same universe of assets, (ii) have the same investment horizon, and (iii) have the same expectations about future returns, variances, and covariances, and efficient portfolios will be combinations of the tangent portfolio and the risk-free asset.

Hence, we can conclude that assumptions 1, 3, and 10 are the most relevant assumptions in deriving CAPM. However, it is obvious that the reality is distorted by making most of the assumptions outlined above.

5.1 Implications of the CAPM Assumptions

5.1.1 THE SAME LINEAR EFFICIENT FRONTIER FOR ALL INVESTORS

In the case of CAPM, the agreement on expected returns, variances, covariances (assumption 10), and the risk-free rate (assumptions 1 and 3) will make investors face the same linear efficient frontier and choose the same portfolio of risky assets, which is located on the linear efficient frontier and is tangent to the risky assets efficient frontier (Figure 5.1).

The degree of risk aversion of each individual investor simply determines the allocation of wealth between the risk-free asset and the risky portfolio, which in this case is common for all. In other words, all investors will have different indifference curves, allowing them to choose different optimal portfolios with different proportions of risk-free asset and risky portfolio.

5.1.2 EVERYONE HOLDS THE MARKET PORTFOLIO

When we introduce the risk-free asset, we show that all investors will hold the the same portfolio of risky assets—the market portfolio; that is, that *market portfolio is a tangent portfolio.* The market portfolio is the portfolio of risky assets that includes all globally available risky assets in the same proportion as in the market.

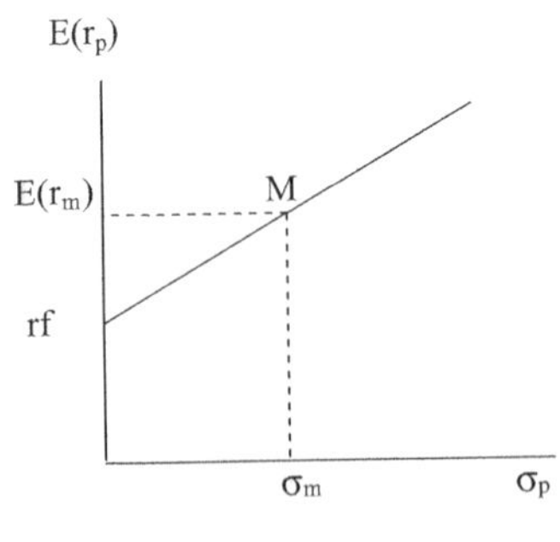

FIGURE 5.1 The same linear efficient frontier for all investors.

Consider an economy with three assets: equities, bonds, and a risk-free asset. Further, consider that the value of each asset in this economy is

Asset Class	Value
Equities	£100
Bonds	£30
Risk-free asset	£170

The total wealth in the economy is therefore £300.

The vector of risky asset values is

$$\mathbf{x}_M = \begin{bmatrix} 100 \\ 30 \end{bmatrix}$$

The example can be generalized to the case of an economy with *N* risky assets. The value of asset *j* is denoted by x_j. The vector of available assets is then

$$\mathbf{x}_M = \begin{pmatrix} x_1 \\ \vdots \\ x_N \end{pmatrix}$$

Let's assume that this is a closed economy inhabited by *k* individuals. Each individual has initial wealth of A_{i0}. The total wealth in the economy is given by $A_{m0} = \mathbf{x}'_M \mathbf{1}$, and it is owned by *k* individuals. Thus

$$\sum_{i=1}^{k} A_{i0} = A_{m0}$$

For the example above, with the two risky assets we have that

$$A_{m0} = (100 \quad 30)\begin{pmatrix} 1 \\ 1 \end{pmatrix} = 130$$

The proportion that each asset has in the market portfolio is defined as

$$\mathbf{w}_m = \frac{1}{A_{m0}} \mathbf{x}_m = \begin{bmatrix} 100/130 \\ 30/130 \end{bmatrix}$$

The example can be generalized to the case of an economy with *N* risky assets.

$$\mathbf{w}_m = \begin{pmatrix} w_{m1} \\ \vdots \\ w_{mN} \end{pmatrix}$$

where

$$w_{mj} = \frac{x_j}{A_{m0}}$$

is the share of asset j in the market portfolio. For example, if we assume that the proxy for the market portfolio is MSCI All Country World Index, then the weight of the Vodafone Group in that portfolio would be

$$w_{BA} = \frac{\text{Market value}_{\text{Vodafone}}}{\text{Total market value of MSCI All Country World}}$$

The return on the market portfolio is calculated as the return on a multi-asset portfolio:

$$r_m = \sum_{j=1}^{N} w_{mj} r_j$$

Taking the expectation of the above equation, we have

$$E(r_m) = \sum_{j=1}^{N} w_{mj} E(r_j)$$

If the variance–covariance matrix of risky assets in our example is

$$\Sigma = \begin{bmatrix} \sigma_E^2 & \sigma_{EB} \\ \sigma_{EB} & \sigma_B^2 \end{bmatrix} = \begin{bmatrix} 170.87 & 93.92 \\ 93.92 & 100.50 \end{bmatrix}$$

and the vector of expected returns (%) on the risky assets is given by

$$\begin{bmatrix} E(r_E) \\ E(r_B) \end{bmatrix} = \begin{bmatrix} 10.64 \\ 13.90 \end{bmatrix}$$

then the market portfolio expected return and standard deviation are given by

$$E(r_m) = [100/130 \quad 30/130] \begin{bmatrix} 10.64 \\ 13.90 \end{bmatrix} = 11.39$$

and

$$\sigma_m^2 = \mathbf{w}'_m \Sigma \mathbf{w}_m$$

Replacing the values from our example, we have

$$\sigma_m^2 = [100/130 \quad 30/130] \begin{bmatrix} 170.87 & 93.92 \\ 93.92 & 100.50 \end{bmatrix} \begin{bmatrix} 100/130 \\ 30/130 \end{bmatrix} = 139.80$$

Therefore, all investors will invest in the same combination of the risky assets, but the amount of borrowing or lending will depend on their risk/return preferences. This implication of CAPM is called the Separation Theorem.

5.2 The Separation Theorem

The separation theorem states that in the CAPM world, one can determine the optimal combination of risky assets for an investor without knowing his risk/return preferences. Separation theorem also implies that there cannot be a zero proportion of a risky asset in the optimal risky (tangent) portfolio. This is because of the market clearing assumption.

Let us consider what the market clearing assumption suggests. We know that all investors who maximize their utility function will hold the same portfolio of risky assets. Is it possible for that common tangency portfolio not to contain one of the available risky assets? The answer is no. Assume, for instance, that no investors hold equities. The weight in the common optimal risky portfolio is zero. Since the demand for equities is zero, the price of equity will be zero. That is, one would be given equities for free. If the expected price of equity one period hence is positive, then you can have a risk-free profit. Every rational investor will spot the opportunity and include equities in the portfolio. The price of equities as a result will go up to a point where it will not be desirable to hold more equities.

So, we can conclude that under market clearing, all assets will be included in the portfolio. In theory, a market portfolio includes all assets world-wide, but in practice it is restricted to ordinary shares only. Furthermore, the portfolio of ordinary shares is proxied by the market index.

According to separation theorem, in determining the overall optimal portfolio (risky + risk-free asset), the investor makes two separate decisions: (i) which portfolio of risky assets to hold, which is purely a technicality as the implication of CAPM assumptions is that everyone should hold all risky assets in exact same proportion that they have in the market portfolio (i.e., everyone holds market portfolio); and (ii) what should be the asset allocation between risky market portfolio and a risk-free asset; this purely depends on risk aversion level of individual investors.

Empirical Proof. The vector of optimal weights in the portfolio of risky assets (when risk-free lending and borrowing is allowed) is denoted as w is given by

$$\mathbf{w} = \frac{E(r_p) - r_f}{Z} \Sigma^{-1}(\mathbf{r} - \mathbf{1}r_f) \tag{5.1}$$

Note that the first term is based on portfolio risk premium (which is dependent on level of risk aversion) and slope of the efficient frontier Z (also dependent on level of risk aversion). Then, the equation for optimal weights can be rewritten as

$$\mathbf{w} = \frac{1}{A_i}\Sigma^{-1}(\mathbf{r} - \mathbf{1}r_F) \qquad (5.2)$$

where A_i is degree of risk aversion of different investors. In addition, think about the example where the total economy wealth is given by

Asset Class	Value
Equities	£100
Bonds	£30
Risk-free asset	£170

The total wealth in the economy is composed of two risky assets (equities and bonds) and a risk-free asset, and its value is therefore £170.

The variance–covariance matrix for equities and bonds is given as

$$\Sigma = \begin{bmatrix} \sigma_E^2 & \sigma_{EB} \\ \sigma_{EB} & \sigma_B^2 \end{bmatrix} = \begin{bmatrix} 170.87 & 93.92 \\ 93.92 & 100.50 \end{bmatrix}$$

and the vector of expected returns on the risky assets is given by

$$\begin{bmatrix} E(r_E) \\ E(r_B) \end{bmatrix} = \begin{bmatrix} 10.64 \\ 6.95 \end{bmatrix}$$

The value of the risk-free rate in this economy is 0.50%.

The issue to be examined here is in what proportions equities and bonds will be included in the optimal portfolio or risky assets that different investors hold. Let us assume three different investors, A, B, and C, which have degree of risk aversion of 0.05, 0.1, and 1, respectively. They have initial wealth of £100 each. Using Eq. (5.2), we shall show that the proportions that each investor places in equities and in bonds will be the same as in the market portfolio. The optimal asset allocation, determined according to investors' level of risk aversion using Eq. (5.2), is given by Figure 5.2.

Portfolio	Risk Aversion	W_E	W_B	R_F	Total
A	0.05	£65	£19	£16	£100
B	0.1	£32	£10	£58	£100
C	1	£3	£1	£96	£100
Total in the economy		£100	£30	£170	£300
Proportions invested		76.92%	23.08%		

FIGURE 5.2 Optimal portfolio.

All individuals, irrespective of their degree of risk aversion, hold the same portfolio of risky assets—that is, 77% of equity and 23% of bonds, the same as their proportions in the market portfolio.

5.3 Relationships Defined by the CAPM

There are two relationships that can be derived from CAPM:

1. The capital market line (CML), which determines the equilibrium relationship between the total risk and the expected return of the efficient portfolios.
2. The security market line (SML), which determines the equilibrium relationship between systematic risk and the expected return of both individual securities and portfolios.

Let us examine each relationship in turn.

5.3.1 THE CAPITAL MARKET LINE

The capital market line (CML) is a line used in the capital asset pricing model to illustrate the rates of return for efficient portfolios depending on the risk-free rate of return and the level of risk (standard deviation) for a particular portfolio.

CML is a straight line characterized by the intercept (r_f) and the slope. The slope of the CML is called the expected return/risk tradeoff for efficient portfolios—that is, the market price of risk for the efficient portfolios—and it is given by

$$\frac{E(r_{\mathrm{m}}) - r_{\mathrm{f}}}{\sigma_{\mathrm{m}}}$$

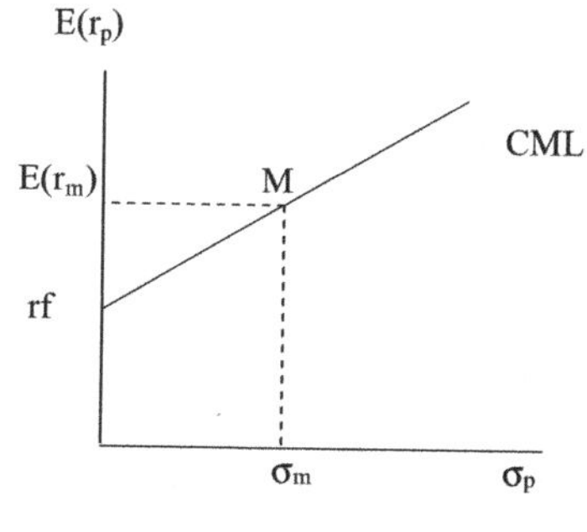

FIGURE 5.3 The capital market line.

Therefore the equation of the CML is

$$E(r_{\rm p}) = r_{\rm f} + \frac{E(r_{\rm m}) - r_{\rm f}}{\sigma_{\rm m}}\sigma_{\rm p} \tag{5.3}$$

Because CAPM assumes that investors are risk-averse, market risk premium will always be positive and CML will be an upward sloping line. However, in practice, historical observations have shown that CML can be downward sloping. If a standard deviation (total risk) of an efficient portfolio is known, CML enables an investor to identify the required rate of return on that portfolio.

However, investors are interested in determining the required return of individual assets as well. Hence, the second relationship from CAPM was derived—the security market line (SML).

As noted earlier, the SML determines the relationship between the expected return and systematic risk of individual assets. Let us then analyze how one measures the risk of individual asset in a market portfolio. In other words, we need to know how any individual security contributes to the market risk.

Measuring the Risk of an Individual Asset. Suppose that the market portfolio consists of two securities only, say, A and K. The variance of the market portfolio is

$$\sigma_{\rm m}^2 = w_{\rm A}^2\sigma_{\rm A}^2 + w_{\rm K}^2\sigma_{\rm K}^2 + 2w_{\rm A}w_{\rm K}\sigma_{\rm AK} \tag{5.4}$$

which can be rewritten as

$$\sigma_{\rm m}^2 = w_{\rm A}(w_{\rm A}\sigma_{\rm A}^2 + w_{\rm K}\sigma_{\rm AK}) + w_{\rm K}(w_{\rm K}\sigma_{\rm K}^2 + w_{\rm A}\sigma_{\rm AK}) \tag{5.5}$$

Note that from the property of covariance, the covariance between security A and the market portfolio is

$$\sigma_{\rm Am} = w_{\rm A}\sigma_{\rm A}^2 + w_{\rm K}\sigma_{\rm AK} \tag{5.6}$$

whereas the covariance between security K and the market portfolio

$$\sigma_{\rm Km} = w_{\rm K}\sigma_{\rm K}^2 + w_{\rm A}\sigma_{\rm AK} \tag{5.7}$$

Thus the variance of the market portfolio is a weighted average of the covariances of the two securities with it, where the weights are equal to the proportions of the securities in the market portfolio.

$$\sigma_{\rm m}^2 = w_{\rm A}\sigma_{\rm Am} + w_{\rm K}\sigma_{\rm Km} \tag{5.8}$$

Under the CAPM each investor holds the market portfolio and is concerned with its standard deviation, since that will influence the magnitude of his or her investment in the market portfolio. The contribution of each security to the standard deviation of the market portfolio is given by

$$\frac{\partial \sigma_m^2}{\partial w_i} = \sigma_{im}, \qquad \text{where i} = \text{A, K} \tag{5.9}$$

and depends on the size of the covariance of that security with the market portfolio. The relevant measure of risk of an individual security in the market portfolio is, therefore, its covariance with the market portfolio, σ_{im}. This means that securities with larger values of σ_{im} will be viewed by investors as contributing more to the risk of the market portfolio. It also means that securities with larger standard deviations should not be viewed as being riskier than those securities with smaller standard deviations.

From this analysis, it follows that securities with larger values for σ_{im} will have to provide proportionately larger expected returns, in order for investors to be interested in purchasing them. The relationship between market risk and return is expressed by means of the security market line.

5.3.2 THE SECURITY MARKET LINE

From the analysis above, it seems that the graphical depiction of the expected return/risk relationship for individual securities should be presented in the $E(r_i)/\sigma_{im}$ space. This is shown in Figure 5.4.

Similarly to the CML equation, the expected return of individual security, known as the SML equation, is

$$E(r_i) = r_f + \frac{E(r_m) - r_f}{\sigma_m^2}\sigma_{im}$$

Since

$$\beta_i = \frac{\sigma_{im}}{\sigma_m^2}$$

we can rewrite the SML equation as

$$E(r_i) = r_f + \beta_i(E(r_m) - r_f) \tag{5.10}$$

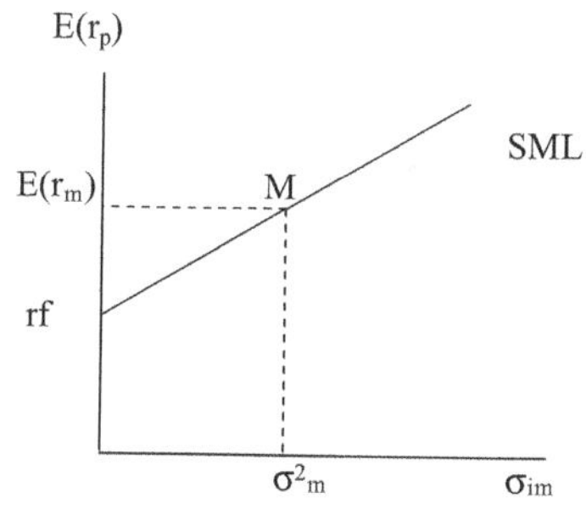

FIGURE 5.4 The security market line (1).

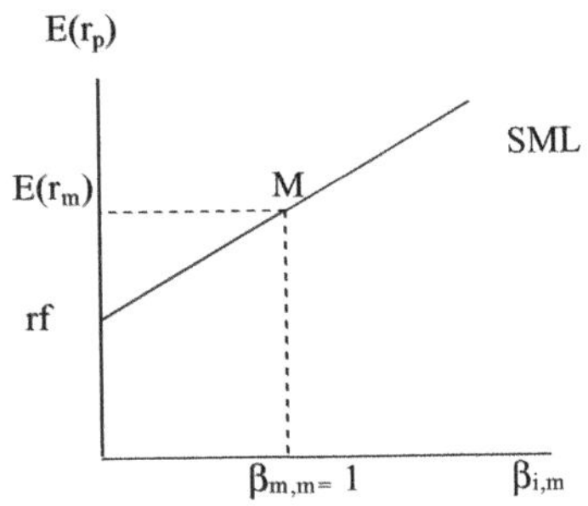

FIGURE 5.5 The security market line (2).

Stock	Beta	Change in the stock return	The stock is:
A	−0.5	−0.5%	Negatively correlated and *less* volatile than the market
B	0	0%	Not correlated with the market
C	0.5	0.5%	Positively correlated and *less* volatile than the market
D	1	1%	Perfectly positively correlated with the market
E	1.5	1.5%	Positively correlated and *more* volatile than the market

FIGURE 5.6 Estimation of beta.

Therefore, alternatively, SML line can be depicted in the $E(r_i)/\beta_{im}$ space, as in Figure 5.5.

SML shows a tradeoff between risks and returns for all assets. All securities and portfolios in the equilibrium, regardless of whether they are efficient of inefficient, plot on the SML. Therefore, efficient portfolios can be found on the CML and SML, while inefficient ones plot on the SML, but below the CML line. If securities are not plotting on the SML, they are considered to be overvalued or undervalued. This issue will be considered in one of the sections that follow.

5.4 Interpretation of Beta

Beta is a measure of the systematic risk which cannot be diversified away. Nevertheless, it has to be noted that in a long-short portfolio it can be *hedged* away. Beta of the market is equal to 1. Stocks that have beta greater than 1 are considered to be more volatile than the market and they are called aggressive stocks. On the other hand, stocks with betas lower than 1 are less volatile than the market and they are called defensive stocks. See the summary of beta interpretation in Figure 5.6.

Beta coefficient of a stock or a portfolio is estimated using historical time-series data in the following regression, where beta represents the slope of that regression:

$$R_i = \alpha_i + \beta_i Rm + \varepsilon_i \quad (5.11)$$

In Eq. (5.11) R_i is the return of asset i over a certain period, R_m is the rate of return on the market index, $\alpha_i$is the component of security i's return that is independent of the markets performance, and β_i is a constant beta that measures the sensitivity of asset returns to the market moves. Finally, ε_i is the random error term (also known as residual) representing the deviation of R_i from the return that is predicted by the model. This model is commonly referred to as the Market model.

The most common way used to estimate betas and intercepts of Eq. (5.11) is by using past data. In particular, historical market returns and security returns are needed as independent and dependent variables, respectively, in the regression. It is commonly accepted that 60 months (i.e., 5 years) of historical data is adequate to estimate beta coefficient. Once the regression is completed, in a spreadsheet such as Excel for example, the estimated parameters σ_{ei}^2, α_i and β_i are obtained and presented in the output table.

Separating the Risk in CAPM: Market versus Unique Risk.

Total risk = Market (systematic) risk + Unique (unsystematic) risk

This is quantified in the following equation for the total risk of an individual asset:

$$\sigma_i^2 = \beta_i^2 \sigma_m^2 + \sigma_{ei}^2 \quad (5.12)$$

where $\beta_i^2 \sigma_m^2$ is systematic risk and σ_{ei}^2 is unsystematic risk. For a portfolio, the equation is given by

$$\sigma_p^2 = \beta_p^2 \sigma_m^2 + \sigma_{ep}^2$$

where

$$\beta_p^2 = \sum w_i^2 \beta_i^2$$

and

$$\sigma_{ep}^2 = \sum w_i^2 \sigma_{ep}^2$$

Also, equivalently to the risk of individual security, the systematic risk of a portfolio is $\beta_p^2 \sigma_m^2$ and the unsystematic risk is σ_{ep}^2.

- According to the Market model: the larger the beta, the larger the market risk.
- CAPM: the larger the beta, the higher expected return of a security.

Therefore, there is a reward for bearing market risk but not for taking additional unique risk.

5.5 Determining the Level of Diversification of a Portfolio

There is one more number that describes regression and that would interest investment managers. That is, the number that shows the goodness of fit of the regression line—coefficient of determination or R^2. R-squared measures the proportion of movements in the dependent variable (security returns) that is explained by the independent variable (market returns). It takes values between 0 and 1. The larger it is, the better the changes in market returns explain the changes in security returns. The same analysis can be applied for portfolios. Therefore, the larger the R-squared, the stronger the relationship between a portfolio and the market is—that is, the larger the level of diversification of a portfolio. R-squared is equal to the squared value of the correlation coefficient between the dependent and the independent variable. It can be calculated as the market risk of a security (portfolio) divided by the total risk of a security (portfolio):

$$R^2 = \rho_{im}^2 \tag{5.13}$$

and

$$R^2 = \frac{\beta_{im}^2 \sigma_m^2}{\beta_{im}^2 \sigma_m^2 + \sigma_{ei}^2} = \frac{\text{Systematic risk}}{\text{Total risk}} \tag{5.14}$$

5.6 Investment Implications of the CAPM

We have shown that the CAPM postulates that when markets clear and individual investors select portfolios on the basis of their mean and standard deviation, then the market portfolio is the common risky portfolio held by all investors. The investment implication of the CAPM is that the investor should buy only the market portfolio and the risk-free asset. An investor should buy a small proportion of all available assets, the actual proportions being determined by the relative amounts that are issued in the market as a whole. If the stock market is taken as the set of available assets, then each person should purchase some shares in every stock, in proportion to the stocks' monetary share of the total of all stocks outstanding. It is not necessary to go to the trouble of analyzing individual issues and computing a Markowitz solution. The investor can simply buy the market portfolio.

In practice it is very difficult for an individual to invest in the entire market portfolio by buying all the available shares because of the costs involved. However, investing in the market through mutual funds, called index funds, that are designed to track the index closely is easy and relatively inexpensive. A believer of the CAPM would buy an index fund and invest some money in a risk-free asset such as a Treasury Bill.

So far we have discussed equilibrium in terms of rate of return. In this section we shall use the CAPM to describe equilibrium in terms of prices. The return on asset i is

$$E(r_i) = \frac{P_1 + D_1}{P_0} - 1 \tag{5.15}$$

The CAPM postulates that

$$E(r_i) = \frac{P_1 + D_1}{P_0} - 1 = r_F + \beta_i (E(r_m) - r_F) \tag{5.16}$$

from which we have that

$$P_0 = \frac{P_1 + D_1}{1 + r_F + \beta_i (E(r_m) - r_F)} = \frac{P_1 + D_1}{1 + E(r_i)} \tag{5.17}$$

This represents the fundamental pricing equation in finance. It says that the price of an asset is its discounted cash flow, where the discount factor is the equilibrium rate of return.

Now that we know that the relationship between prices and returns is inverse, we can show how one can use CAPM to determine whether securities are overvalued or undervalued.

SML and Overvalued/Undervalued Securities. Undervalued securities will plot above the SML because they offer greater expected return for a given level of risk, implying that their prices are low. Then, investors will recognize the arbitrage opportunity and they will start buying those securities. The increase in the demand will drive the prices of underpriced securities up, and drive their returns down, and the security will eventually be driven to the SML level.

Overvalued securities will plot below the SML, not offering enough return for a given level of risk. Investors' action will be exactly the opposite from the

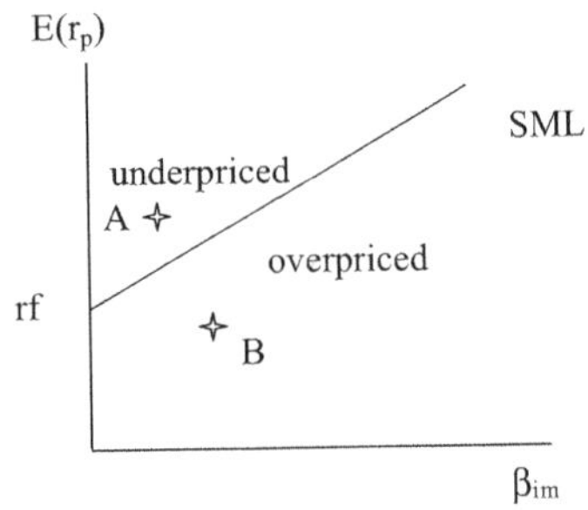

FIGURE 5.7 Undervalued and overvalued securities.

above case—that is, they will start selling overpriced securities, driving their prices down and returns up, until they are brought up to the equilibrium.

Let us present this graphically (Figure 5.7).

Linear Pricing. Consider two projects with expected values $E(F_1)$ and $E(F_2)$. According to the CAPM, the value of each project is

$$P_{01} = \frac{E(F_1)}{1 + r_F + \beta_1(r_m - r_F)}$$

$$P_{02} = \frac{E(F_2)}{1 + r_F + \beta_2(r_m - r_F)}$$

The value of a project with expected values of $E(F_1) + E(F_2)$ is

$$P_{01} + P_{02} = \frac{E(F_1) + E(F_2)}{1 + r_F + \beta_{1+2}(r_m - r_F)}$$

where β_{1+2} is the beta of the new asset, which is the weighted average of assets 1 and 2.

The reason for linearity in pricing can be traced back to the principle of arbitrage: If the price of the sum of two assets were not equal to the sum of the individual prices, it would be possible to make arbitrage profits. For example, if the combination asset (1 + 2) was priced lower than the sum of the individual assets 1 and 2 (selling at the higher individual price), one would be able to make a profit. By doing this in large quantities, we could make arbitrarily large profits. If the reverse situation occurs—that is, if the combination asset was priced higher than the sum of the two assets—we would buy the assets individually and sell the combination, again making arbitrage profits. Such arbitrage opportunities are ruled out if the pricing of assets is linear. This linearity of pricing is therefore a fundamental tenet of financial theory in the context of perfect markets.

5.7 Introduction to the Arbitrage Pricing Theory (APT)

Created by Stephen Ross, the APT model is one of the most famous asset valuation models. It is also one of the main competitors of the CAPM model.

A key underlying assumption of the APT model is that there is no arbitrage opportunity that lasts in time. Indeed, any asset A being as highly risky as asset B, but with a higher return, would see its demand rapidly increased until its return comes back to the return level of the asset B, therefore canceling any arbitrage opportunity.

An arbitrage opportunity is an investment that requires no net outflow of cash and does not carry any chance of loss, but it still has some potential to earn positive return. An arbitrage opportunity arises when two assets offer the same return but trade at different prices: An arbitrageur could buy the cheaper of the two assets and short-sell the more expensive one, earning arbitrage profits. Such arbitrage opportunities do not exist in the equilibrium.

APT, originally developed by Ross (1976), attempts to provide a model that explains asset pricing better than the original CAPM. APT is an equilibrium pricing model that that talks about what determines the equilibrium rates of return of capital assets, and it is based on the idea that an asset's returns can be predicted using the relationship between that asset returns and many common risk factors. Arbitrageurs use the APT model to profit by identifying the mispriced securities. A mispriced security will have an actual market price that differs from the theoretical price predicted by the APT model. In other words, the APT model implies that investors will hold *infinite positions* in an arbitrage opportunity, and this should create pressures on prices to go up where they are too low and fall where they are too high, so in equilibrium the market should satisfy the *no-arbitrage condition.* The absence of arbitrage implies the "law of one price": Two assets with identical investment characteristics must trade at the same price. *No arbitrage opportunities exist among well-diversified portfolios.*

An arbitrage opportunity is an investment that requires no net outflow of cash and does not carry any chance of loss, but it still has some potential to earn positive return. An arbitrage opportunity arises when two assets offer the same return but trade at different prices: An arbitrageur could buy the cheaper of the two assets and short-sell the more expensive one, earning arbitrage profits. Such arbitrage opportunities do not exist in the equilibrium.

The other underlying assumption of the APT model relies on the fact that one can model the expected return of any share with a linear function of various macroeconomic factors specific to the sector the share belongs to, weighted according its impact on that share by a specific beta coefficient.

These factors are multiple and can vary. They can be oil price or the U.S. GDP as well as key European interest rate or an exchange rate for a currency pair. All these factors can influence the value of the share concerned.

APT is a multifactor model that allows a number of potential variables (factors) to influence the expected return. The ideas behind APT are very different from those behind the CAPM. The CAPM is based on the behavior of optimizing mean-variance investors, all of whom have homogeneous expectations or beliefs, whereas in the APT the determinants of expected stock returns are the result of investors eliminating any risk-free arbitrage profits. In other words, Ross (1976) in APT calculated relations among expected rates of return that would rule out riskless profits.

The CAPM postulates a relationship between the risk and the expected return of an asset under the assumption that individual investors (a) prefer more wealth to less, (b) are risk-averse, and (c) are only concerned about the mean and the variance of terminal wealth. The Arbitrage Pricing Theory, on the other hand, postulates that pricing can be affected by influences beyond simply means and variances. An assumption of homogeneous expectations is also necessary in the APT. Further, APT makes two other assumptions: (i) There is a lack of arbitrage opportunities and (ii) assets returns are generated by a linear factor model. As far as lack of arbitrage opportunities is concerned (assumption (i)), APT is based on the law of one price. It means that two identical assets cannot have a different price. If there is a difference in price, arbitrage opportunities arise which are exploited until the prices are brought back to the equilibrium level. Therefore, to derive APT model, one needs to assume the existence of an arbitrage portfolio (characteristics: (1) no net investment; (2) betas are equal to zero and (3) it is well diversified). Assumption (ii) requires that the returns on any stock be linearly related to a set of factors, which can be formulated as

$$R_i = \alpha_i + \sum_{k=1}^{k} \beta_{ik} f_k + \varepsilon_i$$

The f_k are the factors, the β_{ik} are the factor loadings or measures of sensitivity of asset i to factor f_k and ε_i represents the residuals or unsystematic risks. The APT therefore assumes that there are k factors that are mainly responsible for the movements in the prices of all assets. Those factors have to have pervasive influence on the market; that is they have to be common to all assets. α_i is showing the expected return on asset i if all factors have the value of one or if all factor betas are equal to zero. The difference between the actual return (R_i) and the expected return α_i is due to the influence of k factors ($f_1, f_2, f_3, \ldots, f_k$). Since α_i at the beginning of the period already incorporates expectations, the k factors are largely unanticipated; that is, their influence on returns arises from unanticipated events or surprises. If all factors are zero and there are no surprises during the period, then the actual return will be equal to the expected return. If all the betas are zero, then the actual return (i.e., expected return) actually represents excess return. If a riskless asset is available, to avoid arbitrage, α_i must be equal to the risk-free rate.

The following assumptions in the APT are also made:

$$E(\varepsilon_i) = E(f_k) = E(\varepsilon_i \varepsilon_j) = E(\varepsilon_i f_k) = E(f_m f_k) = 0$$

$$E(\varepsilon_i^2) = \sigma^2$$

$$E(f_k^2) = 1$$

which means that since the factors are random, they have zero means and unit variances,[1] are uncorrelated with the unsystematic risks, and are not correlated with each other.

$$E(r_j) = r_f + b_{j1}\mathrm{RP}_1 + b_{j2}\mathrm{RP}_2 + \cdots + b_{jn}\mathrm{RP}_n$$

where $E(r_j)$ is the expected return of asset j, R_f is the return of the risk-free rate asset, RP_n is the value of the risk premium associated with the nth systematic factor influencing the value of the asset (these risk premiums are supposed to have a null average), and b_{jn} is the beta that represents the sensitivity of the asset to the factor RP_n.

As per the APT model, we obtain the expected return of any asset by adding the risk-free rate return with a serial of systematic factors weighted according to the asset's sensitivity to those factors.

For equity returns, commonly used explanatory factors are dividend yields, market values, price-to-book ratios, *P*/*E* ratios, and so on. However, APT doesn't specify how many factors there are, what the factors are, the size and the sign of the factor. This is perceived as the main drawback of the APT model, because it demands that investors identify the sources of risk themselves and that they can reasonably estimate factor sensitivities. Practitioners and academics also disagree on which of the risk factors are best to use, and the more factor betas you have to estimate, the more statistical noise you will have. Nevertheless, the linear factor model structure of the APT is used as the basis for many of the commercial risk systems employed by asset managers such as MSCI Barra. To do so, we have to follow three steps:

1. Identify the factors affecting the asset return.
2. Measure the impact of these factors on the asset (beta).
3. Estimate the risk premium associated with these factors.

The factors are not explicitly specified in Ross' theory because they are defined on a case-by-case basis and have to comply with a certain number of prerequisites:

- Their impact on the asset price must appear in unexpected movements.
- The influence of factors should be not diversifiable; that is, they should be more global than specific to a unique company.
- Some accurate and dated data have to be available on these factors.

[1] Let random variable x have mean μ and standard deviation σ. The random variable $y = \frac{x-\mu}{\sigma}$ has a mean equal to 0 and a standard deviation equal to 1.

- The relationship between these factors and the asset have to be proven on an economical basis.

Below is a nonexhaustive list of macro-factors that can influence on a recurrent basis the asset price:

- Variation of the GDP growth for a given country
- Variation of inflation for a given country or region such as the eurozone
- Variation of commodity prices (oil, metals, . . .)
- Variation of the yield curve for governmental obligations
- Variation of the spread for corporate obligations
- Etc.

We can then estimate and quantify the impact of these factors (beta) on the asset by using a linear regression of historical returns of the asset and the evolution of the selected factors.

The risk premium associated with each factor is equal to the difference between the factor return to the asset in the model and the return of the risk-free asset return.

One of the main applications of the APT model in practice is that it is used for building portfolios with specific characteristics. For example, consider an oil company that wants to build a pension fund portfolio that is immunized against oil price risk (shock). The APT model will allow a portfolio manager to choose a diversified portfolio of stocks that has low exposure to oil price movements and to unexpected inflation (it is well established that oil prices and inflation are highly correlated). Therefore, in this sense, one can view APT as a tailor-made model.

Another application of the APT model is to use it for sensitivity analysis of portfolio performance. For example, once we determine the factor loadings (factor betas), we can test how our portfolio will perform if there is a dramatic change in factor values—such as, How will our portfolio perform if there is steepening of the yield curve? How will it perform if there is a market downturn and the index falls by 15%? This and similar questions are typical for the APT analysis.

The CAPM and the APT are both models used for pricing assets in the financial markets. However, proponents of APT argue that APT is superior to the original CAPM because (a) the assumptions of APT are less restrictive and (b) APT is more amenable for empirical testing than the CAPM. These two arguments are in regard to the following:

The CAPM assumptions of quadratic utility functions and normal distribution of returns are not really necessary in APT. In APT, investors are not assumed to choose portfolios on the basis of expected returns and variances.

The APT does not require the existence of the market portfolio. One of the main criticisms of the CAPM is related to the fact that the market portfolio is unobservable.

The APT does not require assumption on the existence of the riskless lending and borrowing.

If the APT is the appropriate pricing model to use, and one uses CAPM instead, then stocks with different sensitivities to the factors but the same beta coefficient will be incorrectly classified as equally risky. The CAPM incorrectly implies that they have the same return.

The original CAPM is a one-period model, whereas the APT is a multiperiod model.

However, the APT does not specify which factors must be included in the model. In contrast, CAPM specifies the factor to be included in the model (returns on the market portfolio).

The CAPM is a special version of the APT, derived by assuming single factor APT where this one factor is market portfolio.

Both models assume that unique effects (errors) are independent—that is, $\mathrm{Cov}(e_i, e_j) = 0$—and it will be diversified away in the large portfolio.

Both models have the same problem: The CAPM is using the unobservable market portfolio, while the APT is using unknown factors.

Most of the above distinctions and similarities apply only when the original CAPM and the original APT are compared. However, nowadays we have the development of multibeta asset pricing models that use a different set of assumptions. Also the multiperiod CAPM has been derived.

FURTHER READING

Bodie, Z., Kane, A., Marcus, A., *Investments*, 8th edition, McGraw-Hill, New York, 2009, chapter 10.

Elton, E., Gruber, M., Brown, S., Goetzmann, W., in Bodie, Z., Kane, A., Marcus, A., *Investments*, 8th edition, McGraw-Hill, New York, 2009, chapter 16 (chapter on APT).

Ross, S. A., The arbitrage theory of capital asset pricing, *Journal of Economic Theory*, **13**, 1976, pp. 341–360.

Roll, R., Ross, S. A., An empirical investigation of the arbitrage pricing theory, *Journal of Finance*, **35**, 1980, pp. 1073–1103.

Roll, R., Ross, S. A., A critical reexamination of the empirical evidence on the arbitrage pricing theory: A reply, *Journal of Finance*, **39**, 1984, pp. 347–350.

Roll, R., Ross, S. A., The arbitrage pricing theory approach to strategic portfolio planning, *Financial Analysts Journal*, May–June 1984, pp. 14–26.

CHAPTER SIX

Market Risk and Fundamental Multifactors Model

It's impossible that the improbable will never happen.

—Emil Gumbel

This chapter is a reproduction of the risk model handbook published in June 2011 by Axioma™[1]. The Factors model is an important method for measuring market risk and therefore we believed it was convenient to introduce the readers to the technics and process when building and developing a fundamental equity model.

What is risk and what is the best way to measure it? There is no single answer to the question, What is the volatility of a given asset or portfolio? Economists, for example, typically associate risk with abstract notions of individual preference, whereas financial regulators may prefer a measure such as value-at-risk (VaR). Axioma defines risk as the standard deviation of an asset's return over time. This statistical definition is straightforward, broadly applicable, and intuitive. An asset whose return varies wildly over time is volatile and therefore risky; another whose return remains fairly constant is relatively predictable, and thus less risky.

Throughout the following discussion, $r_{i,t}$ will represent the return to an asset i, at time t:

$$r_{i,t} = \frac{p_{i,t} + d_{i,t} - p_{i,t-1}}{p_{i,t-1}} - r_{rf,t}$$

where $p_{i,t}$ is the asset's price at time t, $d_{i,t}$ is any dividend payout at time t, and $p_{i,t-1}$ is the price at the previous time period, adjusted for any corporate actions (e.g., stock splits). The time increment t used could be days, weeks, months, or any other period. $r_{rf,t}$ is the risk-free rate—the return to some minimal risk entity

[1]For further information about the suite of models offered by Axioma, we can visit their website: http://www.axioma.com/robust.htm

Handbook of Market Risk, First Edition. Christian Szylar.

(e.g., LIBOR rate). Returns net of the risk-free rate are termed excess returns and are usually used for the purposes of risk modeling. Henceforth, unless stated otherwise, return will be used to mean excess return. The risk of an asset over T time periods is thus given by

$$\sigma_i = \sqrt{\frac{1}{T}\sum_{t=1}^{T}(r_{i,t} - \overline{r_i})^2}$$

where $\overline{r_i}$ is the asset's mean return over time. Investors tend to think in terms of portfolios of assets rather than individual assets in isolation. A portfolio allows for diversication and risk reduction, as illustrated by a simple example: Consider a portfolio of two risky assets A and B, with weights w_A and w_B. The risk of this portfolio is

$$\sigma(w_A r_A + w_B r_B) = \sqrt{w_A^2\sigma_A^2 + w_B^2\sigma_B^2 + 2\rho_{AB}w_A w_B \sigma_A \sigma_B}$$

where $-1 \le \rho_{AB} \le 1$ is the correlation coecient between the two assets. It can be seen that

$$\sigma(w_A r_A + w_B r_B) \le w_A \sigma_A + w_B \sigma_B$$

with equality if $\rho_{AB} = 1$. When analyzing portfolio risk, it is therefore necessary to know not only the risk of each asset involved, but also the interplay or co-movement of each asset with every other.

This information is contained in a covariance matrix of asset returns:

$$Q = \begin{bmatrix} \sigma_1^2 & \rho_{12}\sigma_1\sigma_2 & \rho_{13}\sigma_1\sigma_3 & \cdots & \rho_{1n}\sigma_1\sigma_n \\ \rho_{21}\sigma_2\sigma_1 & \sigma_2^2 & \rho_{23}\sigma_2\sigma_3 & & \vdots \\ \rho_{31}\sigma_3\sigma_1 & \rho_{32}\sigma_3\sigma_2 & \sigma_3^2 & & \vdots \\ \vdots & & & \ddots & \vdots \\ \rho_{n1}\sigma_n\sigma_1 & \cdots & \cdots & \cdots & \sigma_n^2 \end{bmatrix}$$

Note that the matrix is symmetric and positive-semidefinite. The risk of a portfolio h, where

$$h = \begin{bmatrix} w_1 \\ w_2 \\ \vdots \\ w_n \end{bmatrix}$$

and w_i, $i = 1, \ldots, n$, are the weights of each asset, is simply

$$\sigma_h = \sqrt{h^T Q h}$$

6.1 Why a Multifactors Model?

Possessing an accurate estimate of the asset returns covariance matrix is the sine qua non of portfolio risk management. How does one calculate such a matrix in practice? The obvious solution is to build a history of asset returns and then calculate the variances and covariances directly. Computing sample statistics directly from historical data, however, is fraught with danger. Historical returns are typically noisy; even in the absence of actual data errors, false signals and spurious relationships abound. Two assets may appear closely related when their seemingly correlated behavior is in fact an artifact of data-mining.

Weak signals and noise aside, when a new asset enters the existing universe, there is no reliable way of calculating its relationships with the other assets, because it does not yet possess a returns history. One could construct various proxies, but such an approach is dubious at best.

Finally, data points totaling no less than the number of assets are required to accurately estimate all the variances and covariances directly. For any realistic number of assets, it is extremely unlikely that sufficient observations exist. Even with a universe of 100 assets, over $(1/2) \cdot 100 \cdot (100+1) > 5000$ relationships need to be estimated. For stock markets like the one in the United States (over 12,000 assets), this becomes completely infeasible.

Any one of the above problems is sufficient reason against constructing an asset returns covariance matrix directly. A better approach is to first impose some structure on the asset returns by identifying common factors within the market—that is, factors that drive asset returns. Returns can then be modeled as a function of a relatively small number of parameters, and estimating thousands—or tens, even hundreds of thousands—of asset variances and covariances can thus be simplified to calculating a much smaller handful of numbers.

Factors used in multifactor models can fall into several broad categories:

- Fundamental Factors
  - Industry and country factors reflect a company's line of business and country of domicile.
  - Style factors encapsulate the financial characteristics of an asset—a company's size, debt levels, liquidity, and so on. They are usually calculated from a mixture of market and fundamental (i.e., balance sheet) data.
  - Currency factors represent the interplay between local currencies of the various assets within the model.
  - Macroeconomic factors capture an asset's sensitivity to variables such as GNP growth, bond yields, inflation, and so on.
- Statistical Factors

Statistical factors are mathematical constructs responsible for the observed correlations in asset returns. They are not directly connected to any observable real-world phenomena, and they may change from one period to the next.

An asset's return is decomposed into a portion driven by these factors (common factor return) and a residual component (specific return), producing the following model at time t:

$$\begin{bmatrix} r_1 \\ r_2 \\ \vdots \\ r_n \end{bmatrix} = \begin{bmatrix} b_{11} & \cdots & b_{1m} \\ b_{21} & & b_{2m} \\ \vdots & \ddots & \vdots \\ b_{n1} & \cdots & u_n \end{bmatrix}$$

or, more succinctly, in matrix form:

$$r = Bf + u$$

where r is the vector of asset returns at time t, f the vector of factor returns, and u, the set of asset specific returns. B is the $n \times m$ exposure matrix. Its elements denote each asset's exposure to a particular factor.

Theoretical foundations for this model specification make up the Arbitrage Pricing Theory (APT), proposed by Ross (1976) as a generalization of the traditional Capital Asset Pricing Model to allow for multiple risk factors. The APT is therefore a logical starting point for building a factor risk model.

As an example, consider a simple model with four assets, a, b, c, and d, and three factors—two industry factors, IT and banking, and one style factor, size—which takes values of $\{-1, 0, 1\}$ to represent small, mid-cap, and large companies, respectively.[2] Assets a and b are IT companies, while c and d are banks. a and b are small-cap, c is mid-cap, and d is large-cap. The exposure matrix is thus

$$B = \begin{matrix} & \text{IT} & \text{bank} & \text{size} \\ a & 1 & 0 & -1 \\ b & 1 & 0 & -1 \\ c & 0 & 1 & 0 \\ d & 0 & 1 & 1 \end{matrix}$$

r and B are known, so the system of equations can be solved for f and u.

This process is repeated over time to build two time series—one of factor returns and another of asset specific returns. Given that there is a comparatively small number of factors, it is feasible to estimate a factor covariance matrix directly from the factor returns time series. Moreover, assuming that asset-specific returns are uncorrelated both amongst themselves and with factor returns, the $n \times n$ asset returns covariance matrix becomes

[2] In reality, style exposures usually take a continuum of values rather than simple scores as above.

$$\text{var}(r) = \text{var}(Bf + u)$$

$$\hat{Q} = B\Sigma B^T + \Delta^2$$

where Σ is the $m \times m$ factor covariance matrix and Δ^2 is the diagonal matrix of specific variances. In essence, the multifactor model is a dimension reduction tool, simplifying the problem of calculating an $n \times n$ asset returns covariance matrix into calculating the variances and covariances of a much smaller number of factors, and n specific variances.

The following sections will discuss in greater detail the various parts of a risk model and the stages in its construction. Interested readers may wish to consider Grinold and Kahn (1995) or Zangari (2003) for a full exposition on factor risk models and their applications.

6.2 The Returns Model

Recall the linear factor model of asset returns:

$$r = Bf + u$$

There are many possible solutions to this system of equations. If factor exposures B are known, f can be estimated using cross-sectional regression analysis. With macroeconomic factors, however, f is observed, and it is B instead that needs to be estimated, typically via time-series regression for each asset. In the case of statistical factors, neither B nor f is specified, so a rotational indeterminacy exists and both parameters are determined simultaneously, albeit only up to a nonsingular transformation.

For a more thorough discussion of multifactor models (and the APT), the curious reader is encouraged to consult Campbell et al. (1997).

6.2.1 THE LEAST-SQUARES REGRESSION SOLUTION

The ordinary least-squares (OLS) regression solution to the factor model of returns seeks to minimize the sum of squared residuals:

$$f_{ols} = arg \min_f \sum_{i=1}^{n} u_i^2$$

whose solution is straightforward:

$$\hat{f}_{ols} = (B^T B)^{-1} B^T r$$

6.2.1.1 Assumptions of the Least-Squares Solution. The field of regression theory is vast, so only the issues most relevant to risk modeling will be dealt with here. Further details can be found in any elementary econometrics textbook, such as Greene (2003).

1. B is an $n \times m$ matrix with full column rank $\rho(B) = m \leq n$. The OLS solution requires that $B^{T}B$ be invertible, which is satisfied only if the columns of B are linearly independent. Intuitively, this means the factors should all be distinct from one another.
2. Residuals are zero-mean and independent of the factor exposures. In order for the regression estimates to be unbiased (i.e., correct "on average"), $E[u] = 0$ and $E[B^{T} u] = 0$ are required.
3. Residuals are homoskedastic and have no autocorrelation. These constitute the Gauss–Markov conditions: $\text{var}(u_i) = \sigma^2$ and $\text{cov}(u_i, u_j) = 0$ for all u_i, $i = 1, \ldots, n$, $i \neq j$ (or more compactly, $E[uu^{T}] = \sigma^2 I_n$) and establishes the superiority of the least-squares solution over all other linear estimators. Unfortunately, large assets tend to exhibit lower volatility than smaller ones, and homoskedastic residual returns are rarely observed. Figure 6.1 shows the typical relationship between asset size and returns behavior.
4. Residuals are normally distributed: strengthening the previous assumption to $u \sim N(0, \Omega)$, where $\Omega = \sigma^2 \text{In}$ is not strictly required. Nevertheless, it is a convenient assumption for testing the estimators, to simplify constructing confidence intervals, evaluating hypothesis tests, and so forth.

6.2.1.2 Solving the Problem of Heteroskedasticity. Traditionally, one corrects for this phenomenon by scaling each asset's residual by the inverse of its

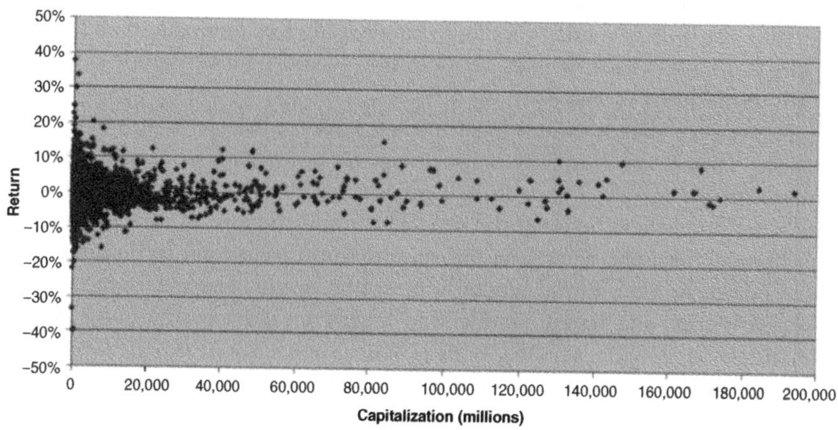

FIGURE 6.1 Daily returns vs. market capitalization of FTSE Global Index stocks, January 31, 2000.

residual variance, transforming the above into a weighted least-squares (WLS) problem:

$$W^{1/2}r = W^{1/2}Bf + W^{1/2}u$$

$$f_{wls} = arg\min_{f} \sum_{i=1}^{n} \frac{u_i^2}{\sigma_i^2}$$

where

$$W^{\frac{1}{2}} = \begin{bmatrix} \sigma_1^{-1} & & 0 \\ & \ddots & \\ 0 & & \sigma_n^{-1} \end{bmatrix}$$

The solution is easily shown to be

$$\hat{f}_{wls} = (B^T WB)^{-1} B^T W_r$$

The challenge lies in estimating the residual variances σ_i^2. One could calculate these directly from historical data, but such estimations are noisy and require sufficient history for each asset. As a proxy for the inverse residual variance, most Axioma models use the square-root of each asset's market capitalization.

Using 2006 data from the Axioma U.K. Risk Model, Figure 6.2b shows the typical relationship between the inverse residual variance and the square root of market capitalization.

Although the plot does not yield a straight line, there is certainly a stronger case than weighting by capitalization itself. Figure 6.2a demonstrates the following: With the bulk of market capitalization concentrated among a small number of mega-cap assets, clearly asset capitalization would be a very poor substitute for inverse residual variance.

Figure 6.2c shows natural logarithm of asset capitalization versus residual variance. This proxy, however, is too much of a "leveler," treating everything almost equally. Finally, Figure 6.2d looks at the fourth root of capitalization, which lies somewhere between the square root and the log.

Through trial and error, one may find the optimal weight to be some fractional power, or more exotic function, of capitalization. The square root proxy, however, is tried and tested, simple, and largely accepted by the industry as a standard.

There is also a practical reason for adopting a weighted regression. Using a weighting scheme such as square-root capitalization "tunes," the regression estimates in favor of larger assets. Large, liquid assets constitute the bulk of most institutional investors' universes, so there is a compelling case for modeling these assets accurately, sometimes even at the expense of smaller, less important assets.

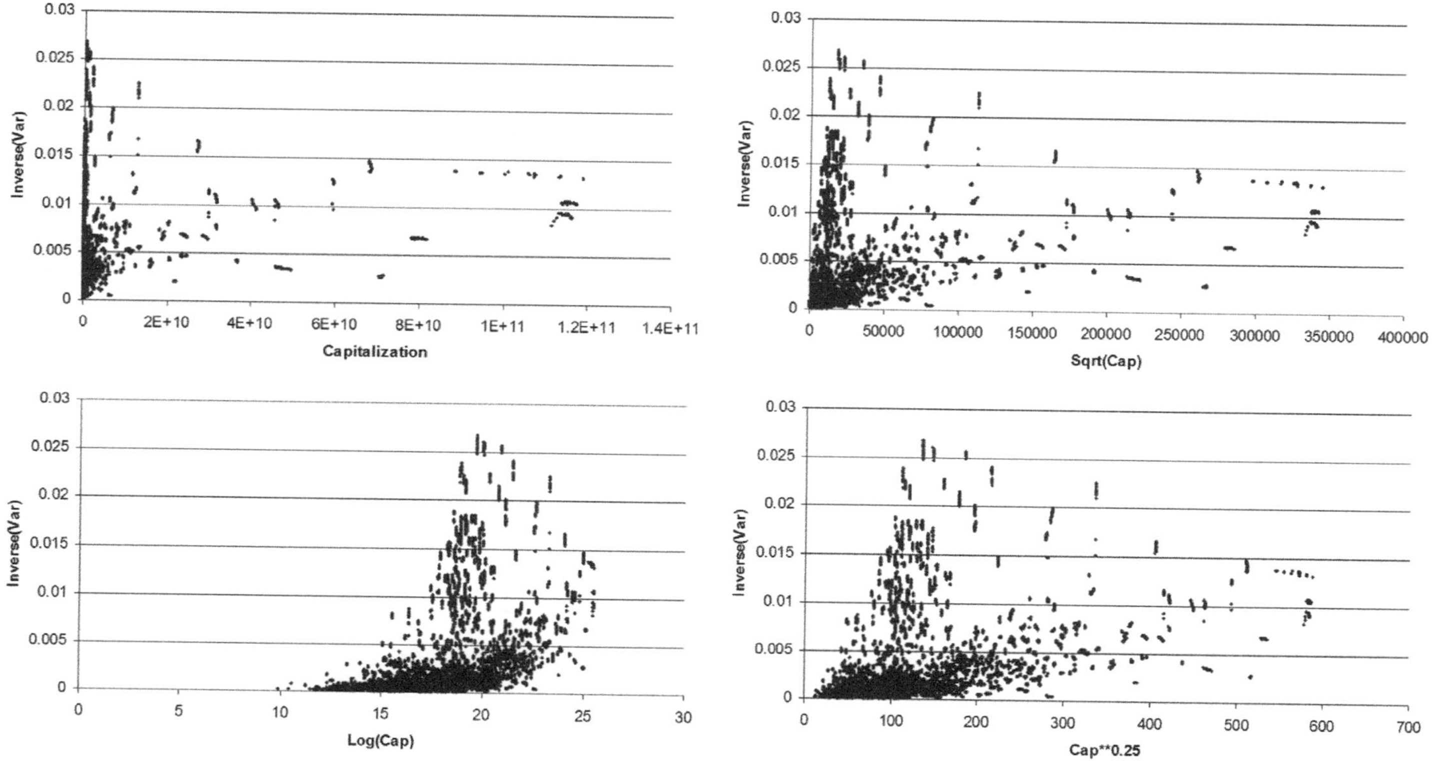

FIGURE 6.2 Relationship between various cap-based weighting schemes and inverse residual variance.

6.2.1.3 Outliers. Data frequently contain extreme values, or outliers, arising from outright errors in the data collection process, poor or unrepresentative sampling, or genuinely aberrant behavior. In particular, distributions of asset returns are known to exhibit "fat-tails"—large numbers of observations in the outer edges of the distribution, most likely attributable to economic shocks, poor liquidity, and so on.

Because least-squares attempts to minimize the sum of squared residuals, outlier returns produce large residuals that have a disproportionate effect on the solution, pulling it away from the "true" solution.

As an example, consider a vector of returns

$$r = [1.0 \quad 3.0 \quad 5.0 \quad 7.0 \quad 9.0 \quad 2.0 \quad 4.9 \quad 6.0 \quad 2.0 \quad 0.0]^T$$

an exposure matrix

$$B = \begin{bmatrix} 1 & 1 & 1 & 1 & 1 & 0 & 0 & 0 & 0 & 0 \\ 0 & 0 & 0 & 0 & 0 & 1 & 1 & 1 & 1 & 1 \end{bmatrix}^T$$

and weights

$$w = [2.0 \quad 1.0 \quad 3.0 \quad 4.0 \quad 6.0 \quad 1.0 \quad 8.0 \quad 1.0 \quad 3.0 \quad 5.0]^T$$

The weighted least-squares solution is

$$\hat{f}_{wls} = \begin{vmatrix} 6.375 \\ 2.556 \end{vmatrix}$$

Suppose the returns were altered ever so slightly, leaving exposures and weights unchanged:

$$\tilde{r} = [10000.0 \quad 3.0 \quad 5.0 \quad 7.0 \quad 9.0 \quad 2.0 \quad 4.0 \quad 6.0 \quad 2.0 \quad 0.0]^T$$

An intelligent observer will easily look at these new returns and identify the first observation (being significantly larger than the rest) as an aberration and discard it from the computation. Failing to exclude the outlier yields the solution

$$\tilde{f}_{wls} = \begin{bmatrix} 1256.250 \\ 2.556 \end{bmatrix}$$

which has obviously been substantially pulled away from the "true" solution. Note that the second element of the solution remains unchanged; this is due to the structure of B in the example—the first five assets have zero exposure to the second factor.

While this example is trivial in size and extreme in behavior, it illustrates a very real problem. Financial data are replete with outliers, legitimate and illegitimate, which obscure the genuine signals one is trying to trace. A simplistic solution may be to exclude or truncate all observations outside certain predetermined bounds. These bounds can be either static values (e.g., exclude returns above 200%) or statistical-based (e.g., exclude returns beyond 3 standard deviations from the mean).

Hard-coded figures are inadvisable because they take no account of changing market conditions over time and the resulting changes in the distribution of the returns: An extreme return during an uneventful period may be unremarkable during a market boom or bust. Actual use of the standard deviation as a measure is not robust either, because this itself is very sensitive to outliers.

Axioma models uses robust statistical methods to reduce the effect of outliers, described in the section below.

6.2.1.4 Robust Regression. A comprehensive treatment of robust regression is far beyond the scope of this discussion; rather, focus will be limited to the techniques that Axioma uses in its model construction.

The weapon of choice is a Huber M-estimator (where M stands for maximum-likelihood). Whereas the weighted least-squares regression seeks to minimize the sum of squared residuals

$$f_{wls} = arg\,\underset{f}{min} \sum_{i=1}^{n} w_i u_i^2$$

a robust regression estimator attempts to minimize the objective function

$$f_{\text{robust}} = \arg\min_{f} \sum_{i=1}^{n} \rho(u_i) = \arg\min_{f} \sum_{i=1}^{n} \rho(r_i - b_i^T f)$$

The function ρ fulfills the following criteria for all a, b:

$$\begin{aligned} &\rho(a) \geq 0 \\ &\rho(0) = 0 \\ &\rho(a) = \rho(-a) \\ &\rho(a) \geq \rho(b) f \quad \text{or} \quad |a| > |b| \end{aligned}$$

Denoting the derivative of ρ with respect to f as $\rho' = \varphi(a)$, the minimization program has the first-order conditions

$$\sum_{i=1}^{n} \varphi(r_i - b_i^T f) b_i^T = 0$$

Defining the weight function $w(a) = \varphi(a)/a$, and writing $w(u_i) = w_i$, the equation above becomes

$$\sum_{i=1}^{n} w_i (r_i - b_i^T f) b_i^T = 0$$

which can be solved via iteratively reweighted least-squares:

1. Using ordinary least-squares, solve the transformed system

$$\hat{r} = \hat{B}f + \hat{u}$$

   where $\hat{r} = W^{1/2} r$ and $\hat{B} = W^{1/2} B$, obtaining an initial estimate f^0.
2. For each iteration j, calculate residuals u_i^{j-1} and weights $w_i^{j-1} = w(u_i^{j-1})$.
3. Update the weighted least-squares estimator

$$f^j = (B^T W^{J-1} B)^{-1} B^T W^{J-1} r$$

Repeat steps 2 and 3 until successive estimates converge.

There are many different possibilities for the function ρ. Axioma models use the Huber function:

$$\rho(u_i) = \begin{cases} \frac{1}{2} u_i^2 & \text{if } |u_i| \le k \\ k|u_i| - \frac{1}{2} k^2 & \text{if } |u_i| > k \end{cases}$$

with $k = 1.345\sigma$ where σ is the standard deviation of the residual.

Returning to the simple example in the previous section, robust regression gives the solution

$$\hat{f}_{\text{robust}} = \begin{bmatrix} 7.901 \\ 2.556 \end{bmatrix}$$

and the final regression weights are

$$w = [0.00106 \quad 1.0 \quad 3.0 \quad 4.0 \quad 6.0 \quad 1.0 \quad 8.0 \quad 1.0 \quad 3.0 \quad 5.0]$$

The outlying return has been down-weighted by a factor of approximately 1000, thus bringing the solution back toward the original values.

6.2.2 STATISTICAL APPROACHES

Statistical factor models deduce the appropriate factor structure by analyzing the sample asset returns covariance matrix. There is no need to predefine factors and compute exposures, as required by fundamental factor models. The only inputs are a time series of asset returns and the number of desired factors. There are no concrete rules specifying the appropriate number of factors. One can, for example, use a Scree plot to assess the variance explained by each additional factor.

Factor analysis is used to estimate the factor exposures B and factor returns f. Principal components and maximum likelihood estimation are two popular methods of parameter estimation.

These, as well as others, are explained in detail in Johnson and Wichern (1998). Axioma risk models involving statistical factors typically employ a variation of principal components, described in detail below.

6.2.2.1 Principal Components. Principal components analysis (PCA) determines factors by eigendecomposition of the observed asset returns covariance matrix. Given an $n \times t$ matrix R of historical asset returns, we obtain

$$\hat{Q} = \frac{RR^T}{t} = UDU^T$$

Only the largest m eigenvalues and corresponding eigenvectors are kept, hence

$$\hat{Q} = U_m D_m U_M^T + \Delta^2$$

where Δ^2 is the $n \times n$ diagonal matrix of specific variances.

The exposure matrix B is taken to be $U_m D_m^{1/2}$. Factor and specific returns can then be computed by regressing, for each asset, historical returns against its exposures using ordinary or weighted least-squares:

$$F = (B^T WB)^{-1} B^T WR$$
$$\Gamma = R - BF$$

Unlike cross-sectional regression, the matrices (not vectors) F and Γ ($m \times t$ and $n \times t$, respectively) contain the entire time series of factor and specific returns and will subsequently be used to compute the factor covariance matrix and specific variances.

Additionally, one could try to perform the above estimation using only a subset of assets, both for computational efficiency and to avoid noisy historical data. Exposures and specific returns for assets outside this universe can be backed-out via ordinary least-squares. For each asset i, we have

$$r_{i,t} = \sum_{j=1}^{m} b_{i,j} f_{i,t} + u_{i,t}$$

$$b_i = (FF^T)^{-1} F_{r,i}$$

$$B = \begin{bmatrix} b_i^T \\ \vdots \\ b_n^T \end{bmatrix}$$

6.2.2.2 Asymptotic Principal Components. PCA requires that the number of assets n be smaller than the number of time periods t, in order for $\hat{Q}$ to be reliably estimated. In most capital markets, the number of assets far exceeds the number of time periods for which data are available, especially if returns are measured in weekly or longer intervals. If daily data were used to model the U.S. stock market, for example, one would require well over 10,000 data points—over 40 years of data! Even if such data were available, the resulting covariance matrix would be poorly estimated as noise and shocks from long in the past continue to inuence current estimates.

To address this inherent shortcoming of PCA, Axioma adopted the following: Instead of working with the $n \times n$ covariance metrix $\hat{Q} = (1/t)RR^T$, one can shift the analysis from n- to t-space and use the $t \times t$ covariance matrix $\tilde{Q} = (1/n)R^T\mathrm{R}$. The raw input data, R, remains unchanged. The process begins with eigendecomposition of the covariance matrix $\tilde{Q}$:

$$\tilde{Q} = \tilde{U}\tilde{D}\tilde{U}^T = \tilde{U}_m \tilde{D}_m \tilde{U}_m^T + \Phi$$

Because there is an infinity of solutions to $R = BF + \Gamma$, one can choose $F = \tilde{U}_m^T$. Choosing the eigenvectors (right singular vectors, if using singular value decomposition) is convenient because they provide orthogonal factors. Regressing asset returns against factor returns produces B:

$$B^T = (FF^T)^{-1} FR^T = FR^T$$

$$B = R\tilde{U}_m$$

At this stage, the factor returns and exposure estimates F and B are discarded, keeping only the specific return Γ, which are used to estimate a diagonal matrix of asset specific variances:

$$\Delta^2 = \frac{1}{t}\operatorname{diag}(\Gamma\Gamma^T)$$

The resulting specific risks are then used to scale each asset's returns. This is conceptually analogous to weighting assets by inverse residual variance in the earlier regression example, whereby the influence of more volatile assets is reduced:

$$R^* = \Delta^{-1} R$$

The scaled returns are then used to compute a new $t \times t$ covariance matrix, which will undergo the eigendecomposition routine again:

$$\tilde{Q}^* = \frac{1}{n} R^{*T} R^*$$

$$\tilde{Q}^* = U_m^* D_m^* U_m^{*T} + \tilde{\Phi}$$

The top m eigenvectors U_m^{*T} are chosen as the final estimates for the factor returns history. The final exposures B are calculated by regressing these against the uscaled asset returns R.

The above estimation can be carried out on a subset of assets to prevent noisy returns from contaminating the eigenstructure analysis. The procedure for doing so and recovering the exposures and specific returns for the remaining assets is similar to the procedure outlined for PCA.

Finally, it is easily seen that this methodology (and PCA) is equivalent to performing least-squares regression of asset returns against factor returns (or exposures) estimates. Therefore, regression statistics such as $\bar{R}^2$, standard error, or t-statistics are applicable, though such measures are likely to be rather high, because computing them is analogous to having look-ahead bias in a least-squares estimator.

6.2.2.3 Maximum-Likelihood Estimation.

Assuming factor and specific returns are jointly normally distributed and iid over time, factor exposures B and specific variances Δ^2 can be estimated as maximizers of the likelihood function

$$L(B, \Delta^2) = (2\pi)^{\frac{-nm}{2}} \det(BB^T + \Delta^2)^{\frac{n}{2}} e^{\frac{-1}{2}\mathrm{tr}\left[(BB^T + \Delta^2)^{-1}\hat{Q}\right]}$$

where $\hat{Q} = (1/t)RR^T$, the sample asset returns covariance matrix. Imposing the constraint that $B^T\Delta^2 B$ be diagonal ensures a unique solution. Consider the log-likelihood, which leads to a maximization of

$$\frac{-n}{2} \ln\left[\det(BB^T + \Delta^2) + \mathrm{tr}\left((BB^T + \Delta^2)^{-1}\hat{Q}\right)\right]$$

which can be solved by numerical methods, usually iteratively. Like PCA, factor returns can be recovered by time-series regression of asset returns against the factor exposures. The optimization problem is a formidable task: Even with a universe of 500 assets and 20 factors, 10,000 exposures + 500 specific variances = 10,500 parameters have to be determined simultaneously. Solving a single instance of such a problem may be trivial by today's computing standards; but because Axioma models are estimated on a daily basis, building a model history becomes prohibitively time-consuming. The question of which factor analysis methodology works best is difficult to answer, and evidence favoring any one particular technique is mixed at best. Axioma models prefer the asymptotic principal components approach because it requires far fewer assumptions on the data and is computationally less burdensome.

6.2.3 HYBRID SOLUTIONS

Fundamental and statistical factors represent complementary approaches to modeling return and forecasting risk. Fundamental factors capture distinct commonalities shared only by a narrow cross section of assets. Statistical factors may not possess enough "resolution" to differentiate between semiconductor manufacturers and consumer electronics makers, but fund managers will require and appreciate that level of differentiation. On the other hand, statistical factors can quickly reveal any broad factors missed by the fundamental model, particularly useful when market conditions differ widely from those on which the model specification was originally based (such as the turbulent period in July–August 2007).

Despite creating additional computational complexity, a "hybrid" factor model may capture the best of both worlds. A set of prespecified and intuitive factors account for most of the common variation in a portfolio, while a small number of statistical factors that pick up any remaining (possibly transient) effects in the recent returns history. Should a statistical factor turn out to be significant risk factor, a hybrid model will nevertheless fail to explain exactly what that factor represents, but the model user will at least have the comfort of knowing that all bets in his portfolio have been captured.

In practice, this is most easily implemented by keeping the fundamental factor model intact and looking for statistical factors within its specific returns. In theory, the reverse also works, but is likely to result in a disproportionately large fraction of return attributed to a single statistical factor, thereby diminishing the power of the fundamental factors when regressed against the statistical model's residuals. A comparison of fundamental versus statistical models, and combinations thereof, is presented in Connor (1995).

6.3 Estimation Universe

When estimating factor returns, one seldom uses the entire universe of asset returns from the market being modeled. The broad market may contain many illiquid assets as well as other potentially "problematic" assets such as investment trusts, depository receipts, and foreign listings, to name a few. Illiquid assets lack a stable, regular price, making their volatility diffcult to estimate reliably.

Composite assets such as investment trusts and ETFs are difficult to quantify in terms of their exposure to the market—if such an instrument invests in several different sectors or markets, how should one define its industry/country exposures? Similarly, is an ADR's return primarily driven by the U.S. market, or by the behavior of the underlying stock?

These are diffcult questions to answer and, depending on the market and the model, different assets need to be excluded from the estimation process. Ideally, the estimation universe should contain everything that is "important," relevant within the model universe. Most crucially, the estimation universe should include sufficient assets to keep the number of "thin" factors to a minimum. These are factors to which only a small handful of assets have nonzero exposure, and are among the worst evils one can encounter while modeling return, for reasons to be explained later.

The choice of estimation universe is therefore a subjective one, depending on the market being modeled and the model itself. One tried-and-tested means of devising an estimation universe is to use membership in an appropriate market index as the basis for inclusion. Benchmark providers typically employ sophisticated selection criteria involving price activity, liquidity, capitalization, free-float, and other business logic that would be cumbersome to replicate in-house. Legal implications notwithstanding, one could leverage off their research expertise.

6.4 Model Factors

6.4.1 MARKET FACTOR OR INTERCEPT

Sometimes we may wish to include a single factor that defines the particular broad market behavior. This could be one of the following:

Simple Intercept: Every asset has exposure to this factor, and the factor, return is simply the regression intercept term.

Market Beta: Each asset's exposure is calculated as its historical beta against a suitable market return (from a benchmark for instance), namely,

$$r_{i,t} = \beta_i r_{M,t} + \alpha_{i,t} \qquad \text{for each asset } i = 1, \ldots, n$$

where $r_{M,t}$ are the returns of the market benchmark index.

Macroeconomic Factor: Given an appropriate market return (again, perhaps from published benchmark figures), estimate each asset's exposure to this return via historic time-series regression.

6.4.2 INDUSTRY FACTORS

Returns of assets belonging to companies with similar lines of business often move together. In fact, industry factors are often the most important set of factors in a fundamental factor model, in terms of their explanatory power. Industry factors are formed from a set of mappings from each asset to one or more industries within the market. The mapping used can be a proprietary third-party scheme such as GICS or ICB, or a modification thereof, consolidating, splitting, or discarding industries where appropriate. Alternatively, one could create a new scheme altogether by investigating company fundamentals, or by statistical analysis of asset returns. Custom-tailored industry schemes may provide marginally more explanatory power but require intensive work to design. Wherever possible, Axioma prefers industry factor structures that correspond directly to classifications widely accepted among the investment community, particularly if an industry scheme is already a de-facto market standard.

Axioma generally defines industry exposures as 0/1 dummy variables. An asset has unit exposure to the industry corresponding to its company's main line of business, and zero to other industries. One could assign an asset multiple industry exposures|each exposure being a fraction representing the proportion of activity within that industry. For most markets, however, this level of detail is not easily available, and researching this information may require a significant amount of effort. Moreover, there is little or no evidence that multiple-industry schemes yield significantly more explanatory power than a simple dummy variable scheme. An important consideration in designing industry factors is avoiding thin industries within the model. A thin industry contains very few or no assets, or has most of its market capitalization concentrated in a small handful of assets.

6.4.2.1 Thin Industries. Thinness presents a very real problem for factor returns estimation. An industry factor return is predominantly a weighted average of asset returns within the industry. With sufficient assets, the specific return is averaged out, leaving something (hopefully) close to the true factor return. If there are very few stocks, however, a large element of specific return will likely remain, overestimating the industry factor return and inducing correlations in the specific returns. To see why, consider a simple model with two assets in industry k, equally weighted for the sake of simplicity:

$$r_1 = f_k + u_1$$
$$r_2 = f_k + u_2$$

This has solution $fk = (1/2)(r_1 + r_2)$ and residuals $u_1 = -u_2$, with perfect negative correlation between the two assets's specific returns. In general, if there are n mega-cap assets within an industry, all with similar weights, the average correlation across their specific returns will be of the order of $\rho = -1/(n - 1)$.

As stated previously, uncorrelated specific returns constitute a major assumption of the factor risk model. If this condition is violated, portfolio-specific risk may be overestimated, because the specific return correlations are not taken into account.

Because high concentrations of industry capitalization among a few assets is a common phenomenon in developed markets, the number of stocks in an industry is an inadequate measure of thinness. Many Axioma models rely on the "Herfindahl Index," an economic measure of the size of firms relative to their industry, frequently invoked in antitrust applications:

$$HI = \sum_j w_j^2$$

where w_j is stock j's weight within the industry. Then $1/HI$ represents the "effective" number of stocks within the industry. An industry with 100 assets but 99% of its capitalization in one asset has a Herfindhal index of 0.9801 and has an effective number of stocks equal to 1.0203. It is trivial to see that for an industry where every asset has equal weight, the effective and actual numbers of stocks are exactly equal.

The prevalence of concentrated industry capitalization is another reason why Axioma prefers square-root of capitalization weighting in the factor returns regression. Using capitalization weighting as is greatly reduces the effective number of assets in model industries.

6.4.2.2 Treatment of Thin Industries.

Thin industries can sometimes be avoided by merging similar industries within the same sector with closely correlated returns. This approach, however, is not always possible; as market structure evolves, a thin industry may become more populated as time goes by, or vice versa. Some Axioma models introduce a dummy asset within each thin industry, with market return and unit exposure to the industry, zero elsewhere. Its inclusion will therefore only directly affect the thin industry's factor return estimate. In order to reduce the impact of the other assets within the thin industry, this asset's regression weight is defined as

$$w_{\text{dummy},j} = \begin{cases} (\phi - 1)\dfrac{s_j^4 - \phi^4}{1 - \phi^4} \cdot \dfrac{w_j}{S_j} & \text{if } HI_j^{-1} < \phi \\ 0 & \text{if } HI_j^{-1} > \phi \end{cases}$$

where $s_j = HI_j^{-1}$ is the reciprocal of the Herfindahl index, w_j is the total regression weight of all assets in the industry, and ϕ is the effective number of assets below which an industry is deemed "thin." This functional form ensures that the dummy asset's weight decreases slowly as the effective number of assets increases from 1, but decays rapidly as the effective number approaches the limit ϕ. A great deal of experimentation has indicated that $\phi = 6$ is a reasonable threshold. Beyond this number, returns diversify sufficiently, but this will also depend on the particular market.

Clearly, the thinner the industry, the greater the weight of the dummy asset. This pulls the factor return estimate closer to the market return as the industry becomes thinner, reflecting a decreasing certainty over the true industry factor return in the face of sparse data.

Applying this correction to the earlier example, the new factor returns are

$$\tilde{f}_k = \frac{w_{\text{dummy}}}{w_k} r_M + \left(1 - \frac{w_{\text{dummy}}}{w_k}\right)\frac{1}{2}(r_1 + r_2)$$

with specific returns

$$\tilde{u}_1 = u_1 + \frac{w_{\text{dummy}}}{w_k}\left(\frac{1}{2}(r_1 + r_2) - \tilde{f}_k\right)$$

$$\tilde{u}_2 = -u_1 + \frac{w_{\text{dummy}}}{w_k}\left(\frac{1}{2}(r_1 + r_2) - \tilde{f}_k\right)$$

6.4.3 STYLE FACTORS

Whereas industry factors capture trends on the broad market level, style factors capture behavior on an asset level, net of the market. Style factor exposures are derived from market data such as return, trading volume, capitalization, and/or balance sheet (fundamental) data. For instance, to construct a style factor encapsulating the size of an asset's parent company relative to others in the market, one might consider a function of the company's market capitalization, total assets, and so on. In addition to size, common style measures include historic volatility, market sensitivity, liquidity, leverage, and value/growth.

Any measure that can be calculated and for which sufficient data exist can be considered as a style factor. Typically, when a model is first estimated, many candidate factors are created. These are then filtered down to an "optimal" set, based on some considerations:

- *Data Availability.* There must be sufficient depth and breadth of data to be able to calculate a variable reliably.
- *Reasonableness.* A style factor must be intuitive to investors, describing a sensible characteristic of an asset or company. The average shoe size of a company's employees may carry explanatory power, but is unlikely to appeal to users.
- *Empirical Performance.* A factor must be statistically significant, capable of explaining a non-negligible portion of returns variability.

6.4.3.1 Standardization of Style Factors. Because style factor definitions are expressed in a mixture of units, it is best to standardize them to ensure a level of consistency across the regression estimates. Failure to do so may result in scaling problems in the regression or possibly an ill-conditioned covariance matrix[3].

[3]Large spread of eigenvalues, causing numerical instability particularly when inverting.

To make a set of factor exposures b "unitless":

1. Using only the assets in the estimation universe portfolio $h\upsilon$, calculate the capitalization-weighted mean exposure:

$$\bar{b} = b^T h_\upsilon$$

2. Calculate the equal-weighted standard deviation of the exposure values in $h\upsilon$ about the capitalization-weighted mean (zero, per above step):

$$\sigma_b = \sqrt{\frac{1}{N-1}\sum_{i \in U}\left(b_i - \bar{b}\right)^2}$$

3. Subtract the weighted mean exposure from each asset's raw exposure and divide by the equal-weighted standard deviation:

$$\hat{b}_i = \frac{b_i - \bar{b}}{\sigma_b}$$

This ensures that the estimation universe has a capitalization-weigthed mean of zero and standard deviation of one; in other words, the "market" portfolio is factor neutral.

Outliers in the raw exposure data, however, can skew the standardizing statistics, so raw exposures are typically winsorized prior to standardization. Given an upper bound b_U and lower bound b_L, for a given raw style factor exposure, b_{raw}, set

$$\tilde{b}_i = \begin{cases} b_L, & b_{\text{raw}} < b_L \\ b_{\text{raw}}, & b_L < b_{\text{raw}} < b_U \\ b_U, & b_{\text{raw}} > b_U \end{cases}$$

Axioma models employ different methods to pick b_U and b_L:

Absolute Values. One may, for instance, have a prior belief that the data should lie within the interval [−5, 5], and set the bounds accordingly.

Standard Deviation. Compute the standard deviation of the entire set of exposures, and then pick a multiple k of the standard deviations and truncate all values above or below k standard deviations from the (possibly weighted) mean.

Robust Statistics. Rather than using the mean and standard deviation, employ the median and *median absolute deviation* (*MAD*):

$$\text{MAD}(b) = \text{median}\left(|b - \text{median}(b)|\right)$$

Then, pick a number of MADs above and below the median, and use the corresponding values to winsorize.

The first method relies upon having some idea of what "reasonable" values are; and it may be suitable for data that one is familiar with, such as market betas. For more complicated factor definitions, a dynamic approach may be more appropriate.

6.4.4 COUNTRY FACTORS

A risk model covering more than one market needs to distinguish between assets' countries of incorporation. Types of country exposure include:

- *Dummy Values.* Assets have unit exposure to its country of incorporation and zero otherwise.
- *Market Beta.* Asset i has β_i exposure to its home country and zero elsewhere. β_i is obtained from the time-series regression:

$$r_{i,t} = \beta_i r_{M,t} + \alpha_{i,t} \qquad \text{for each asset } i = 1, \ldots, n$$

  where $r_{M,t}$ are the returns of the local benchmark index.
- *Multiple Country Exposures.* Conceptually identical to multiple industry exposures, each exposure being a fraction (summing to 1) representing the proportion of the company's activity in, or revenue from, that country.

Dummy variables have the advantage of simplicity: A stock is either exposed to the market or it is not. Country betas are more computationally intensive and therefore may yield greater sensitivity and better fit, but care must also be taken when estimating betas from historical returns, which contain a great deal of noise.

As for industries, it is perfectly possible for country factors to exhibit thinness. We apply exactly the same form of correction that we detailed in the section on industry returns above.

6.4.5 CURRENCY FACTORS

Currency factors are rather different from other factors in that they do not participate in the returns regression. Rather, each asset has its return calculated using its local currency, ensuring that currency effects are (as far as is possible) eliminated from the factor regression. All noncurrency factor returns are then computed via the regression, while currency returns are calculated directly from exchange and risk-free rates. Currency factor exposures and returns are then appended to the noncurrency factor exposures and returns.

Suppose we have a set of m currencies, 1, 2, . . . , m. Then we define the following:

$P_{i,t}$ is the asset price at time t in currency i.

R_i is the asset return in local currency i from period $t-1$ to t.

r_i^f is the risk-free rate for currency i.

$X_{ij,t}$ is the amount of currency j which one unit of currency i fetches at time t.

r_{ij}^x is the return for an investor whose numeraire is currency j in buying currency i.

We therefore have

$$r_i = \frac{p_{i,t}}{p_{i,t-1}} - 1$$

$$r_{ij}^x = \frac{x_{ij,t}}{x_{ij,t-1}} - 1$$

$$p_{j,t} = p_{i,t} x_{ij,t}$$

We now define what we mean by a currency return. The asset's total return from a currency j perspective is expressed exactly as

$$r_j = \frac{p_{i,t} x_{ij,t}}{p_{i,t-1} x_{ij,t-1}}$$

This may be expressed more compactly as

$$r_j = (1 + r_i)(1 + r_{i,j}^x) - 1$$

If we consider log returns, the above may be written as

$$r_j \approx r_i + r_{ij}^x$$

This is exact for log returns, and it should provide a good approximation for returns over a short duration (e.g., daily returns). The above is written in terms of total returns. If we consider excess returns, we may write

$$r_j - r_j^f \approx r_i - r_i^f + r_{ij}^x + r_i^f - r_j^f$$

We have therefore expressed the excess return from the perspective of currency j as the sum of the local excess return (currency i) and that which we define to be the currency factor return, namely,

$$c_{ij} = r_{ij}^x + r_i^f - r_j^f$$

where c_{ij} represents the excess return to currency i expressed in terms of currency j. Note that when $i = j$, we obtain $c_{ij} = 0$.

6.4.6 THE PROBLEM OF MULTICOLLINEARITY

If a regression contains two or more of the following:

- A market intercept
- Country dummy exposures
- Industry dummy exposures

then it will fail to find a unique solution because the exposure matrix B is singular. To simply see why this is so, consider each asset's return. Ignoring style factors and specific return, it may be written as

$$r_i = 1 \, . f_M + 1 \, . f_{I_j} + 1 \, . f_{C_k}$$

where f_M is the market intercept return, f_{I_j} is the asset's industry return, and f_{C_k} is its country return. We may add an arbitrary amount to any one of these returns, provided that a similar negative amount is added to one of the other returns, and the overall fit will be unchanged. Thus there are an infinite number of solutions, all of which look equally good. This is the issue of multicollinearity or linear dependence between different sets of dummy factors.

A unique solution can be obtained if, for each set of dummy factors beyond the first, a constraint is imposed on the regression. In theory, almost anything will do. In practice, a common choice for researchers is to force one or more sets of factor returns to sum to zero. Assuming henceforth that we have a market intercept, dummy industries, and dummy countries, one could set the constraints

$$\lambda \sum_{j=1}^{P} w_{I_j} f_{I_j} = 0$$

$$\rho \sum_{j=1}^{Q} w_{C_j} f_{C_j} = 0$$

where w_{I_j} is the market capitalization of industry j, and w_{C_j} is the market capitalization of country j. The effect of this is to "force" the broad market return into the market intercept factor, while the country and industry factors represent the residual behavior of each net of the overall market. These constraints may be added to the regression as dummy assets and the regression performed in the normal fashion.

An alternative approach is to use a multistage regression. First regress the asset returns against the market factor,

$$r = X_M f_M + u$$

then regress the residual u against (for instance) the industry exposures X_I:

$$u = X_I f_I + v$$

then regress the residuals from this against the country exposures X_C:

$$v = X_C f_C + w$$

The factor returns can be then collected together, with the specific return being the final residual, w. This approach is useful when one wants a particular set of factors to extract as much power as possible from the returns, independent of the remaining factors, which will tend to be much weaker than if they were all included in one regression. In addition to a more cumbersome algorithm, however, analysis of the results becomes more complicated as different weights are used for the various regressions.

6.5 The Risk Model

Thus far the discussion has focused entirely on modeling returns, having said nothing whatsoever about the generation of risk forecasts. This is justified; if returns are modeled correctly and robustly, then deriving risk estimates is relatively straightforward. For the mathematically inclined, a more rigorous treatment of the subtleties can be found in Zangari (2003) and De Santis et al. (2003).

If the model has been sensibly constructed with no important factors missed, then the specific returns are uncorrelated with themselves and with the factors, and the factor risk model can then be derived as follows:

$$\mathrm{var}(r) = \mathrm{var}(Bf + u)$$

$$\hat{Q} = B\Sigma B^T + \Delta^2$$

The asset returns covariance matrix $\hat{Q}$ is a combination of a common factor returns covariance matrix Σ and a diagonal specific variance matrix Δ^2.

6.5.1 FACTOR COVARIANCE MATRIX

The factor covariance matrix is calculated directly from the time series of factor returns. Regression models estimate a set of factor and specific returns at each time period, eventually building up a returns history. Statistical models, on the other hand, generate the entire time series anew with each iteration

$$F = \begin{bmatrix} f_{1,1} & f_{1,2} & \cdots & f_{1,T} \\ f_{2,1} & f_{2,2} & \cdots & f_{2,T} \\ \vdots & \vdots & \ddots & \vdots \\ f_{m,1} & f_{m,2} & \cdots & f_{m,T} \end{bmatrix}$$

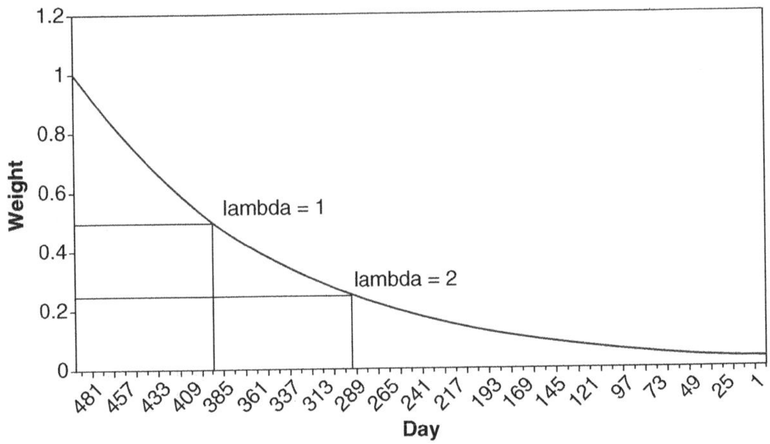

FIGURE 6.3 Typical exponential weighting scheme.

Recent events should exert more influence on the model than those in the distant past, but one cannot simply curtail the history of returns and use only the most recent observations. A sufficiently long history is required to estimate all the covariances reliably. Axioma models address this dilemma by weighting the returns matrix using an exponential weigthing scheme:

$$w_t = 2^{\frac{-(T-t)}{\lambda}}, \qquad t = 0, \ldots, T$$

where T is the most recent time period, λ is the half-time parameter, and t is the time period at which the weight is half that of the most recent observation.

Figure 6.3 shows how this looks for values of t from $t = 0$ (earliest) to $t = 500$ (most recent) for a half-life of 100 days. The weights have been scaled so that the maximum value (at $t = 500$) is one. As can be seen, at $t = 400$ (one half-life) the weight is 0.5, and at $t = 300$ (two half-lives) the weight is 0.25.

Thus, given a half-life, weights $W = \mathrm{diag}(w_1, w_2, \ldots, w_T)$ are computed, and the factor returns history is weighted to yield a new matrix of values:

$$\tilde{F} = FW^{\frac{1}{2}} = \begin{bmatrix} w_1^{\frac{1}{2}} f_{1,1} & w_2^{\frac{1}{2}} f_{1,2} & \cdots & w_T^{\frac{1}{2}} f_{1,T} \\ w_1^{\frac{1}{2}} f_{2,1} & w_2^{\frac{1}{2}} f_{2,2} & \cdots & w_T^{\frac{1}{2}} f_{2,T} \\ \vdots & \vdots & \ddots & \vdots \\ w_1^{\frac{1}{2}} f_{m,1} & w_2^{\frac{1}{2}} f_{m,2} & \cdots & w_T^{\frac{1}{2}} f_{m,T} \end{bmatrix}$$

and from this, the factor covariance matrix is simply calculated as

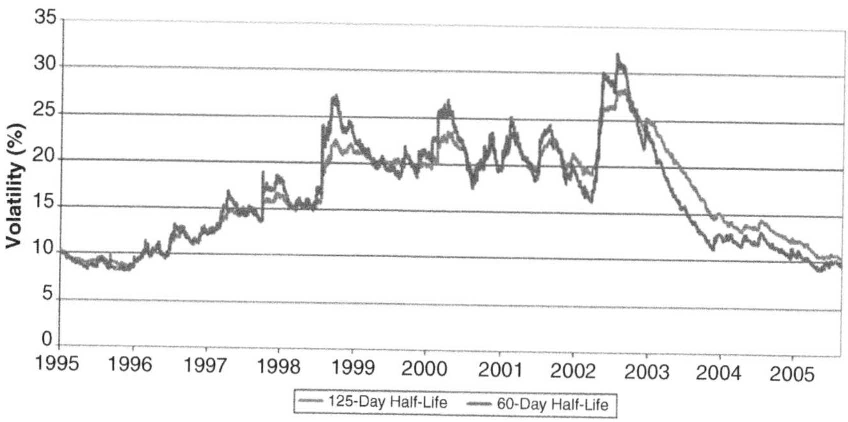

FIGURE 6.4 S&P 500 risk forecast using 60- and 125-day half-lives.

$$\Sigma = \text{var}\left(\tilde{F}\right) = \frac{FWF^T}{T-1}$$

Selecting an appropriate half-life is a major design question to which there is no definitive answer. This half-life indirectly affects the forecast horizon of the risk model. Too short a half-life may allow for a very responsive model but creates excessive turnover for asset managers; too long a half-life and the model will fail to respond sufficiently to changing market conditions. The half-life parameter therefore represents a balance between responsiveness and stability.

Figure 6.4 shows how the choice of half-life influences the computed volatility. The graph shows risk predictions for the S&P 500 Index using half-lives of 60 and 125 days. Interestingly, the longer half-life manages less well in "responding" to a change from high to low volatility (e.g., 2003–2004) than to a change from low to high. In the former case, smaller weights are being applied to relatively large numbers, so shocks from the past persist, whereas in the latter case, small weights are applied to small numbers.

Most Axioma risk models use multiple half-lives for greater flexibility—that is, a longer half-life for estimating the factor correlations and a shorter one for the variances. Apart from the observation that factor correlations are more stable over time than their volatilities, a relatively long half-life is necessary, given the large number of relationships to be estimated. The resulting correlations are then scaled by the corresponding variances to obtain the full covariance matrix. For even greater control over the model's forecast horizon, one could apply different half-lives for different factors (e.g., style versus industry factors). Quite often, however, the additional computation complexity adds little or no advantage.

6.5.2 AUTOCORRELATION IN THE FACTOR RETURNS

If factor returns were uncorrelated across time, the above procedure alone is sufficient for calculating a factor covariance matrix. Unfortunately, the assumption of serial independence is much less true for daily asset returns than for returns over longer horizons. Over short time frames, market mi- crostructure tends to induce lead-lag relationships that induce autocorrelation in the factor returns over time. Simply put, if an asset's price goes up one day, it is quite likely that it will go up the next day too. These "momentum" effects must be taken into consideration when aggregating risk numbers to longer horizons. For instance, one cannot simply derive a monthly risk forecast from daily numbers by the simple relationship[4]

$$\sigma_M = \sqrt{21}.\sigma_d$$

Without taking autocorrelation into account, such forecasts are likely to be under-or overestimated. Axioma adjusts its factor covariance matrix estimates using a technique developed by Newey and West (1987):

A factor's return over N days may be approximated as the sum of its daily returns:

$$f(t, t+N) = \sum_{i=t}^{t+N} f(i)$$

This approximation is exact using logarithmic returns. The forecasted covariance across two factors, f and g, from t to $t + N$, is then

$$\sigma_{f,g}(t:t+N) = N\sigma_f(t)\sigma_g(t)$$
$$\left[\rho_{f,g}(t) + \sum_{k=t}^{N-1}\left(1-\frac{k}{N}\right)(\varphi f, g(t, t+k) + \varphi g, f(t, t+k))\right]$$

where $\varphi f, g(t,t+k)$ and $\varphi g, f(t,t+k)$ represent the lagged correlations:

$$\varphi f, g(t, t+k) = \operatorname{corr}(f(t), g(t+k))$$
$$\varphi_{g,f}(t, t+k) = \operatorname{corr}(g(t), f(t+k))$$

In practice, one need not calculate lagged correlations for each lag up to N. By first analyzing serial correlation trends in the historical returns, it is reasonable to cut off the series at a point $h < N$, beyond which any correlations are insignificant.

A final note of caution: It is occasionally possible for the above to yield a covariance matrix that is not positive semi-definite. In the extremely unlikely event that it does occur, one final adjustment is made, beginning with an eigen-decomposition of the factor covariance matrix,

[4]Assuming that there are, on average, 21 trading days in a month.

$$\Sigma = UDU^T$$

where $D = \text{diag}(d_1, \ldots, d_k)$ are the eigenvalues of Σ. If Σ is nonpositive semidefinite, one or more eigenvalues will be negative. To force positive semidefiniteness, all negative eigenvalues are replaced by a positive, but very small, value. Denoting this adjusted eigenvalue matrix as $\tilde{D}$, the "corrected" factor covariance matrix is

$$\tilde{\Sigma} = U\tilde{D}U^T$$

FURTHER READING

Campbell, J. Y., Lo, A.W., MacKinlay, A., *The Econometrics of Financial Markets*. Princeton University Press, Princeton, NJ, 1997.

Connor, G., The three types of factor models: A comparison of their explanatory power, *Financial Analysts Journal*, **51**, 1995, pp. 42–46.

Connor, G., Korajczyk, R. A., Risk and return and an equilibrium APT, *Journal of Financial Economics*, **21**, 1988, pp. 255–289.

De Santis, G., Litterman, B., Vesval, A., Winkelmann, K., Covariance matrix estimation, in *Modern Investment Management: An Equilibrium Approach*, John Wiley & Sons, Hoboken, NJ, 2003, Chapter 16, pp. 224–248.

Engle, R. F., Granger, C. W. J., Co-integration and error correction: Representation, estimation, and testing. econometrica, *Econometrica*, **55**(2), 1987, pp. 251–276.

Fox, J., *Web Appendix, An R and S-PLUS Companion to Applied Regression*, Sage Publications, New York, 2002.

Greene, H., *Econometric Analysis*, 5th edition, Prentice-Hall, Upper Saddle River, NJ, 2003.

Grinold, R. C., Kahn, R. N., *Active Portfolio Management*, McGraw-Hill, New York,1995, pp. 37–66.

Johnson, R. A., Wichern, D. W., *Applied Multivariate Statistical Analysis*, 4th edition, Prentice-Hall, Englewood Cliffs, NJ, 1998.

Newey, W. K., West, K. D., A simple, positive semi-definite, heteroskedasticity and autocorrelation consistent covariance matrix, *Econometrica*, **55**(3), 1987, pp. 703–708.

Ross, S. A., The arbitrage theory of capital asset pricing, *Journal of Economic Theory*, **13**, 1976, pp. 341–360.

Zangari, P., Equity factor risk models, in *Modern Investment Management: An Equilibrium Approach*, John Wiley & Sons, Hoboken, NJ, 2003, Chapter 20, pp. 334–395.

CHAPTER SEVEN

Market Risk: A Historical Perspective from Market Events and Diverse Mathematics to the Value-at-Risk

If you don't make mistakes, you're not working on hard enough problems. And that's a big mistake.

—Frank Wilczer

The European UCITS Directives gives asset managers and investment trusts increased flexibility when it comes to selecting investment products, particularly with regard to derivatives, structured products, and hedge funds. This new freedom comes at a price: The implementation of UCITS has placed new regulatory requirements on risk management and risk measurement for funds that use derivatives to control risk and enhance their performance. This has far-reaching consequences for processes, systems, and controls. These challenges, however, are not at all fundamentally new to the financial markets as a whole. In UCITS space, many long-standing requirements for modern risk management at banks—such as internal value-at-risk (VaR) models—are arguably extended to asset managers.

The recent financial crisis has also put risk management functions under scrutiny and will constitute an important pillar for the re-construction of trust among investors.

If banks with Basel requirements for measuring their capital adequacy were the first to have strong risk management departments, it was not always the case for most asset managers (traditional and alternative managers). Before UCITS III came into force, there was no formal requirement of the EU Regulators to have a formal risk management process. Therefore it was up to each company to decide whether it is fundamental or not to invest in heavy risk management capabilities, which include people, IT, risk engines, and market data—hence

Handbook of Market Risk, First Edition. Christian Szylar.

requiring huge amount of money. Preference was given to the front office, we might say. Only very big, traditional asset managers were equipped with sufficiently competent quantity analysts and risk managers. Therefore when UCITS III came into force, this new regulation at the same time opened a new job market for those specializing in investment risks.

It was not easy for traditional asset managers and management companies domiciled sometimes in another country to find the right people and systems to cope with all of UCITS III requirements, should they want to benefit from all powers offered by this new regime. It therefore took some time before the asset managers or management companies in charge of the UCITS were properly equipped to sustain the investment in complex financial derivatives. The same learning curve happened with the funds' Board of Directors, who were not necessarily prepared and educated to review the risk figures submitted to them in the usual quarterly board reports and hence not able to interpret and utilize them in an efficient manner.

VaR, even if intuitively easy to understand, raised some important debates about how best to interpret global exposure expressed in this way. What does the fact that our fund has a global exposure of 13% VaR mean exactly? Is it acceptable? What does it mean exactly? Is this level aligned with acceptable VaR levels for such a fund? How should I know if the VaR is aligned with the investment mandate, as given to the investment managers? Finding answers to all these questions and making complete sense of them was not an easy process and took some time.

For all these reasons, it is interesting to see how risk management has grown over time and which events have made progress this field. As usual, we change our habits after an event that has had significant consequences. Business is unfortunately like this: As long as things go well, why should we change what we are doing?

7.1 A Brief History of Market Events

Risk-management systems in financial institutions have come under increasing scrutiny in light of the current financial crisis, resulting in calls for improvements to these systems and an increased role for regulators dealing with them. Even if it has deeper foundations, risk management, as it is practiced today, is essentially a post-1960s phenomenon.

Peter Bernstein wrote: "If everything is a matter of luck, risk management is a meaningless exercise. Invoking luck obscures truth, because it separates an event from its cause."

It is unfortunate but normal in a certain way that that the evolution of risk management has been influenced by some of the most important catastrophes or incidents that have happened in our history. Once they happened, we then tried to analyze their origins, their impact, and their severity. We tried to learn from catastrophes to avoid their occurrence again or, if they do occur again, to limit their impacts.

Below are the most significant milestones: the new ideas, books, and actions of individuals that have stimulated the discipline.

1900

The great Galveston hurricane and flood in Texas kills more than 5000 people and destroyed a city in less than 12 hours, materially changing the nature and scope of weather prediction in North America and the world.

1905–1912

Workers' compensation laws were first introduced in the United States based on their inception in Germany in 1881 by Chancellor Otto von Bismarck. These "social insurance" schemes proliferated worldwide, leading to government provision of pensions in most countries in the 1930s and afterwards. They signaled a shift from individual responsibility to corporate and governmental responsibility for retirement provisions.

1920

British Petroleum formed Tanker Insurance Company Ltd., one of the first captive insurance companies, beginning a movement that exploded in the 1970s and 1980s. Today there are almost 5000 such companies worldwide, reporting about $50 billion in annual premiums, $101 billion in capital and surplus, and $214 billion in investable assets. Captives illustrate the idea of prudent internal financing of risk, as compared to trying to shift it outside the organization.

1921

Frank Knight published *Risk, Uncertainty and Profit,* a book that became the keystone in the risk management library. Knight separated uncertainty, which is not measurable, from risk, which is. He celebrated the prevalence of "surprise" and he cautioned against over-reliance on extrapolating past frequencies into the future.

1921

A Treatise on Probability, by John Maynard Keynes, appeared. Keynes too scorned dependence on the "Law of Great Numbers," emphasizing the importance of relative perception and judgment when determining probabilities.

1926

John von Neumann presented his first paper on a theory of games and strategy at the University of Göttingen, suggesting that the goal of not losing is superior to that of winning. Later, in 1953, he and Oskar Morgenstern published *The Theory of Games and Economic Behavior.*

1933

The U.S. Congress passed the Glass–Steagall Act, prohibiting common ownership of banks, investment banks, and insurance companies. This Act, finally revoked in late 1999, arguably acted as a brake on the development of financial institutions and led the risk management discipline to be more fragmented in many ways rather than integrated.

1945

The U.S. Congress passed the McCarran–Ferguson Act, delegating the regulation of insurance to the various states, rather than to the Federal government, even as business was becoming more national and international. This was another needless brake on risk management, because it hamstrung the ability of the insurance industry to become more responsive to the broader risks of its commercial customers.

1952

The *Journal of Finance* published "Portfolio Selection" by Dr. Harry Markowitz, who later won the Nobel Prize in 1990. It explored aspects of return and variance in an investment portfolio, leading to many of the sophisticated measures of financial risk in use today.

1956

The *Harvard Business Review* published *Risk Management: A New Phase of Cost Control* by Russell Gallagher, then the insurance manager of Philco Corporation in Philadelphia. This city is the focal point for new "risk management" thinking from Dr. Wayne Snider, then of the University of Pennsylvania, who suggested to Dr. Herbert Denenberg in November 1955 that "the professional insurance manager should be a risk manager." Dr. Denenberg was another Penn professor who began exploring the idea of risk management using some early writings of Henri Fayol.

1962

In Toronto, Douglas Barlow, the insurance risk manager at Massey Ferguson, developed the idea of "cost-of-risk," comparing the sum of self-funded losses, insurance premiums, loss control costs, and administrative costs to revenues, assets, and equity. This moves insurance risk management thinking away from insurance, but it still fails to cover all forms of financial and political risk. That same year Rachel Carson's *The Silent Spring* challenged the public to seriously consider the degradation to our air, water, and ground from both inadvertent and deliberate pollution. Her work led directly to the creation of the Environmental Protection Agency (EPA) in the United States in 1970, the plethora of environmental regulations, and the global green movement so active today.

1966

The Insurance Institute of America developed a set of three examinations that led to the designation "Associate in Risk Management" (ARM) as the first such certification. While still heavily oriented toward corporate insurance management, its texts feature a broader risk management concept and are revised continuously, keeping the ARM curriculum up to date.

1972

Dr. Kenneth Arrow won the Nobel Prize in Economic Sciences, along with Sir John Hicks. Arrow imagines a perfect world in which every uncertainty is "insurable," a world in which the law of large numbers works without fail. He then points out that our knowledge is always incomplete—it "comes trailing clouds of vagueness"—and that we are best prepared for risk by accepting its potential as both a stimulant and a penalty.

1973

In 1971, a group of insurance company executives meet in Paris to create the International Association for the Study of Insurance Economics. Two years later, the Geneva Association, its more familiar name, held its first constitutive assembly and began linking risk management, insurance, and economics. Under its first, and current, Secretary General and Director, Orio Giarini, the Geneva Association provided intellectual stimulus for the developing discipline.

1973

That same year, Myron Scholes and Fischer Black published their paper on option valuation in the *Journal of Political Economy* and we began to learn seriously about derivatives.

1974

Gustav Hamilton, the risk manager for Sweden's Statsforetag, created a "risk management circle," graphically describing the interaction of all elements of the process, from assessment and control to financing and communication.

1975

In the United States, the American Society of Insurance Management changed its name to the Risk and Insurance Management Society (RIMS), acknowledging the shift toward risk management first suggested by Gallagher, Snider, and Denenberg in Philadelphia 20 years earlier. By the end of the century, RIMS has 3500 corporate members, some 7000+ deputy members and a wide range of educational programs and services aimed primarily at insurance risk managers in North America. It has links with sister associations in many other countries around the world through IFRIMA, the International Federation of Risk & Insurance Management Associations.

1976

With the support of RIMS, *Fortune* magazine published a special article entitled "The Risk Management Revolution." It suggests the coordination of formerly unconnected risk management functions within an organization and acceptance by the board of responsibility for preparing an organizational policy and oversight of the function. Twenty years lapse before many of the ideas in this paper gain general acceptance.

1980

The Society for Risk Analysis (SRA) formed in Washington, D.C. to represent advocates of public policy and of academic and environmental risk management. *Risk Analysis*, its quarterly journal, appeared the same year. By 1999 the SRA had over 2200 members worldwide and active subgroups in Europe and Japan. Through its efforts, the terms "risk assessment" and "risk management" are familiar in North American and European legislatures.

1983

William Ruckelshaus delivered his speech on "Science, risk and public policy" to the National Academy of Sciences, launching the risk management idea in public policy. Ruckelshaus was the first director of the EPA, from 1970 to 1973. He returned in 1983 to lead the EPA into a more principled framework for environmental policy. Risk management reaches the national political agenda.

1986

The Institute for Risk Management was set up in London. Several years later, under the guidance of Dr. Gordon Dickson, it began an international set of examinations leading to the designation "Fellow of the Institute of Risk Management," the first continuing education program looking at risk management in all its facets.

1987

"Black Monday," October 19, 1987 hit the U.S. stock market. Its shock waves were global, reminding all investors of the inherent risk and volatility in the market. That same year Dr. Vernon Grose, a physicist, student of systems methodology, and former member of the National Transportation Safety Board, published *Managing Risk: Systematic Loss Prevention for Executives*, a book that remains one of the best and clearest primers on risk assessment and management.

1990

The United Nations Secretariat authorized the start of IDNDR, the International Decade for Natural Disaster Reduction, a 10-year effort to study the nature and effects of natural disasters, particularly on the less-developed areas of the world, and to build a global mitigation effort. IDNDR concluded in 1999. Much of its work is detailed in *Natural Disaster Management*, a 319-page synopsis on the nature of hazards, social and community vulnerability, risk assessment, forecasting, emergency management, prevention, science, communication, politics, financial investment, partnerships, and the challenge for the twenty-first century.

1992

The Cadbury Committee issued its report in the United Kingdom, suggesting that governing boards are responsible for setting risk management policy, assuring that the organization understands all its risks, and accepting oversight for the entire process. Its successor committees (Hempel and Turnbull), along with similar work in Canada (Dey), the United Stated, South Africa, Germany (KonTraG), and France, established a new and broader mandate for organizational risk management.

The Committee of Sponsoring Organizations (COSO) was formed in 1985 to sponsor the National Commission on Fraudulent Financial Reporting, an independent private-sector initiative that studied the causal factors that can lead to fraudulent financial reporting. It also developed recommendations for public companies and their independent auditors, for the SEC (U.S. ***Securities and Exchange Commission***) and other regulators, and for educational institutions. *COSO Internal Control—Integrated Framework* was published in 1992 and amended in 1994. It will become the major reference for sound internal controls within organizations. The Institute of Internal Auditors uses COSO as the main standard to assess the quality of internal control.

The COSO framework defines internal control as a process, affected by an entity's board of directors, management, and other personnel, designed to provide "reasonable assurance" regarding the achievement of objectives in the following categories:

- Effectiveness and efficiency of operations
- Reliability of financial reporting
- Compliance with applicable laws and regulations

The COSO internal control framework consists of five interrelated components derived from the way management runs a business. According to COSO, these components provide an effective framework for describing and analyzing the internal control system implemented in an organization as required by financial regulations.[1] The five components are the following:

---

[1]Securities Exchange Act of 1934, Section 240 15d-15.

Control Environment: The control environment sets the tone of an organization, influencing the control consciousness of its people. It is the foundation for all other components of internal control, providing discipline and structure. Control environment factors include the integrity, ethical values, management's operating style, and delegation of authority systems, as well as the processes for managing and developing people in the organization.

Risk Assessment: Every entity faces a variety of risks from external and internal sources that must be assessed. A precondition to risk assessment is the establishment of objectives, and thus risk assessment is the identification and analysis of relevant risks to the achievement of assigned objectives. Risk assessment is a prerequisite for determining how the risks should be managed.

Control Activities: Control activities are the policies and procedures that help ensure that management directives are carried out. They help ensure that necessary actions are taken to address the risks that may hinder the achievement of the entity's objectives. Control activities occur throughout the organization, at all levels and in all functions. They include a range of activities as diverse as approvals, authorizations, verifications, reconciliations, reviews of operating performance, security of assets, and segregation of duties.

Information and Communication: Information systems play a key role in internal control systems because they produce reports, including operational, financial, and compliance-related information that make it possible to run and control the business. In a broader sense, effective communication must ensure information flows down, across, and up the organization. For example, formalized procedures exist for people to report suspected fraud. Effective communication should also be ensured with external parties, such as customers, suppliers, regulators, and shareholders about related policy positions.

Monitoring: Internal control systems need to be monitored—a process that assesses the quality of the system's performance over time. This is accomplished through ongoing monitoring activities or separate evaluations. Internal control deficiencies detected through these monitoring activities should be reported upstream, and corrective actions should be taken to ensure continuous improvement of the system.

1993

The title "chief risk officer" (CRO) was first used by James Lam, at GE Capital, to describe a function to manage "all aspects of risk," including risk management, back-office operations, and business and financial planning.

1995

A multidisciplinary task force of Standards Australia/Standards New Zealand published the first *Risk Management Standard,* AS/NZS 4360:1995, bringing together several of the different subdisciplines for the first time. This standard was followed by similar efforts in both Canada and Japan in 1997. While some observers thought the effort was premature, because of the constantly evolving nature of risk management, most hailed it as an important first step toward a common global frame of reference.

That same year Nick Leeson, in Singapore, found himself disastrously overextended and managed to topple Barings. This unfortunate event, a combination of greed, hubris, and inexcusable control failures, received world headlines and became the "poster child" for fresh interest in operational risk management.

1996

The Global Association of Risk Professionals, representing credit, currency, interest rate, and investment risk managers, is set up in New York and London. An organization attuned to the new Internet world, it first operate electronically, without official offices or staff. By 2002, it grew to be the world's largest risk management association, with over 5000 paid and 17,000 associate members.

In 1996, risk and risk management made the best seller lists in North America and Europe with the publication of Peter Bernstein's *Against the Gods: The Remarkable Story of Risk.* Now in paperback and translated into 11 different languages, this single book, more than any of the preceding papers, speeches, books, ideas, or governmental acts, popularized our understanding of risk and the attempts to manage it.

1998

The failure of long-term capital management, a famous hedge fund, is said to have nearly destroyed the world's financial system.

2000

The widely heralded Y2K bug failed to materialize, in large measure because of billions of dollars spent updating software systems. It is a noted success for risk management.

2001

The terrorism of September 11 and the collapse of Enron reminded the world that nothing is too big for collapse.

The same year, the Enron scandal resulted in the indictment and criminal conviction of the Big Five auditor Arthur Andersen on June 15, 2002. Although the conviction was overturned on May 31, 2005, by the Supreme Court of the United States, the firm ceased performing audits and is currently unwinding its business operations. These catastrophes reinvigorated risk management.

2004

The COSO *Enterprise Risk Management-Integrated Framework* was published in 2004 and defines ERM as a "... process, effected by an entity's Board of Directors, management, and other personnel, applied in strategy setting and across the enterprise, designed to identify potential events that may affect the entity, and manage risk to be within its risk appetite, to provide reasonable assurance regarding the achievement of entity objectives."

The COSO enterprise risk management framework has eight components and four categories of objectives. It was an expansion of the COSO published in 1992 and amended in 1994. The eight components highlighted are:

- Internal environment
- Objective setting
- Event identification
- Risk assessment
- Risk response
- Control activities
- Information and communication
- Monitoring

The four categories of objectives (additional components) highlighted are:

- *Strategy:* High-level goals, aligned with and supporting the organization's mission
- *Operations:* Effective and efficient use of resources
- *Financial Reporting:* Reliability of operational and financial reporting
- *Compliance:* Compliance with applicable laws and regulations

2007

Liquidity and the credit crunch. The credit crisis of 2007 started in the U.S. subprime mortgage industry. Far from being confined to the residential real estate market, the effects of the subprime collapse spread throughout the U.S. economy and into global markets. The impact has been especially rough on the financial services industry, as many investment banks had a short but extensive history of using mortgage-backed securities (or MBS) as a way to spread risk and free up additional capital. The failure of the MBS market shrunk the capital supply available to institutional investors, creating a snowball effect. The long-term consequences of this crisis are yet to be known. This event has largely influenced the revision of management practices as well as the way banks and portfolio managers are monitoring their liquidity risk. This has led, for example, to the ILAS (Individual Liquidity Adequacy Standards) requirement in the United Kingdom, as set by the Financial Services Authority.

2008

Lehman Brothers filed for Chapter 11 bankruptcy protection on September 15, 2008. The bankruptcy of Lehman Brothers is the largest bankruptcy filing in U.S. history, with Lehman holding over $600 billion in assets.

The same year (December 2008), Bernard Lawrence "Bernie" Madoff, former Chairman of the NASDAQ stock exchange, admitted being the operator of a Ponzi scheme. In March 2009, Madoff pleaded guilty to 11 felonies and admitted to turning his wealth management business into a massive Ponzi scheme that defrauded thousands of investors out of billions of dollars. The amount missing from client accounts, including fabricated gains, was almost $65 billion.

2009

On October 5, 2009, the Financial Services Authority published its final rules for a far-reaching overhaul of firms' liquidity risk management systems and controls. All BIPRU firms (including asset managers and brokers) are impacted by the rules and need to put liquidity risk management policies in place and undertake appropriate stress testing. The new rules under the Financial Services Authority BIPRU 12 are more detailed than the existing requirements of Chapter 11 of the *Senior Management Arrangements, Systems and Controls (SYSC) Sourcebook* that firms must comply with at present.[2]

Each time an event has happened, we have tried to avoid its occurrence by improving risk management tools and any other regulatory requirements. Each industry learns from its own mistakes. In financial risk management, the improvements were supported by mathematicians and statisticians who tried to capture the essence of risk through models. One of the models is the VaR, which also has its own specific history, covered in the next section.

7.2 Toward the Development of the Value-at-Risk

The rapid growth of the concept of value-at-risk (VaR) and its use during the 1990s can be astonishing to some. Traditional stories that have mainly focused on financial theory or prudential practices are not the best indicator of this phenomenon. Here we will explain this rapid development from the formalism of the VaR based on "Condorcet's principle," renowned in the fields of social, management, and engineering sciences. From a theoretical point of view, the important events from the last century are have led us to admit thresholds of conventional probability theory and to replace this principle with an expression allowing to us to voice a comparison.

[2]http://www.fsa.gov.uk/pages/Library/Policy/Policy/2009/09_16.shtml, accessed February 16, 2010.

VaR represents the exposure of a portfolio to market risk; diverse literatures insist on the distinction between metric and measure: the former is a function, while the latter corresponds to particular mathematical values. Although multiple metrics exist, we generally consider VaR as a threshold for confidence interval and timeframe. For example, we speak about a daily VaR at 99%. As such, VaR represents statistical confidence intervals, therein being a financial application of the works of Pearson and Neyman. In reality, statistical theories of scattering (spreads) have a much longer history, with roots coming from social sciences. It is, hence, an institutional history of these subjects that leads us to consider the works of political arithmetic linked to the development of diverse mathematical theories at the end of the eighteenth century, before commenting on the origin of actuarial and mathematical risk theory. From there, we will explore the transformation of the political economy into an economic science, along with the separation of finance, which distinguishes itself not only as an academic discipline but also as an area of practice.

7.2.1 DIVERSE MATHEMATICS

The history of economics and statistical mathematics suffered the disdain of economic and scientific historians. Even if this era has seemingly finished today, it seems incongruous to mention the "economic works" of D'Alembert or Laplace, who are "pure" mathematicians. Blaise Pascal was also instrumental in the salvation of equation principles. Diverse aspects of economic calculus were of interest to mathematicians of the eighteenth century; and they are now known, thanks to the works of de Bernard Bru, Pierre Crépel, and Jean-Nicolas Rieucau. We will successively examine the relation between the safety-first principle and Condorcet's principle, Condorcet's model, and the curious ideas of Tetens.

7.2.1.1 Safety-First Principle. In the writings of French authors, the idea of "moral certainty," which Rieucau (1998) tells us was already widespread in 1730, has been made popular by Buffon, who talks of a "zero moral probability." To solve the Petersburg Paradox, Buffon suggests we allocate the extremely small probabilities a value of zero. On the other hand, Condorcet prefers talking about "high insurance." To him, Buffon's position is interesting, yet too simple.

Condorcet's principle considers only variables for which the probability of a risk is insignificant as plausible choices. Once this probability has been identified, how would you put this principle into practice? Condorcet (1994) distinguishes three "events" by examining the necessary conditions for economic activity:

- "Gain back from one's activity a normal profit."
- "Avoid losing more than a certain threshold."
- "Avoid losing everything."

We can hence compare the risk of evaluating these probabilities, which unfortunately is not flawless. On one hand, Condorcet introduces three measures without instructing on how to order them; hesitancy is thus prevailing. On the other hand, the determination of thresholds is not based on any objective criteria. However, this proposition, usually called the "disaster threshold," has improved because conventional thresholds are now globally accepted.

7.2.1.2 Condorcet. The text in which Condorcet gives greater details on his theory of thresholds is part of the *Encyclopedie Méthodique*. He tries to promote every form of insurance (and especially agricultural insurance) by convincing the readers with an economic calculus method, applied to both the insurer and the insured. From an abstract point of view, this method is rather simple. Condorcet modeled the insurer being confronted with n identical operations, each resolving into either a failure or a successful outcome. From a practical point of view, if the probability of failure is p, the probability of m failures in n draws is: $C_n^m p^m (1-p)^{n-m}$, yet we do not have an explicit probability distribution. However, we can restate the aim of this formalization: To fix the insurance selling price in order to reduce the probability, the insurer will default to a negligible amount. Therefore, trying to determine the charging rate in order to prevent the company from the consequences of an accumulation of disasters is therefore a risk theory problem.

Unfortunately, Condorcet does not succeed entirely: He clearly demonstrates the importance of his theory, yet its analytical complexity makes it inadequate.

Condorcet's principle applied to enterprise management can be summarized as follows: The profit rate is fixed in order to make VaR compatible with an almost certain solvency. At the same time as Condorcet's works, a German philosopher called Johannes Nicolaï Tetens studied the same problem: risk theory in mathematics and the question of estimation.

7.2.1.3 Tetens. Usually, Tetens does not appear in the history of probability calculus. He is more closely related to philosophy and his interactions with Kant. Tetens belongs to the "German Combinatory School" that mainly based its mathematical theories on Carl Friedrich Hindenburg's theory on combinatory problems. This could explain Tetens' works, where he represents random variables by polynomials. The probabilistic theories of Tetens are thus algebra theorems interpreted by random variables.

The *Risico* of Tetens is neither the average error,[3] as thought by Borch (1969), nor the average linear risk,[4] as thought by Bohlmann (1911). At first, the measure presented by Tetens is the expectation of the differences in outcomes

[3]Average error would be defined as $\sum_{i=1}^{n} p_i |\overline{x} - x_i|$.

[4]The average linear risk would here be $\sum_{i \leq n_0} p_i x_i$.

of less than the mean.[5] He demonstrates this with the case of six-faced dice, numbered from 0 to 5. The expectation of a variable is hence defined as 5/2, where the outcomes, being less than the mean, are 0, 1, and 2, with variations of 5/2, 3/2, and 1/2. Because each outcome has the same probability, the risk indicator for such a hazard game would be $(5/2 + 3/2 + 1/2) \times 1/6 = 3/4$.

In the case of symmetric hazard games, such as the throw of a fair dice, the average error and the risk indicator are equal, but not the average linear risk, because there are no negative outcomes. If we subtract the mean from the random, then the three measures are equal. We can hence demonstrate the equality between Tetens' indicator with other measures. Although Tetens is remembered by actuarial professionals for his concept of risk (*Risico der Casse),* we should insist on the particular use of it. While Condorcet, Laplace, and Lacroix accept the necessity of a *charge* to cover the fees of the insurer and to guarantee its security, Tetens does not believe in such practices. The fair principle residing in the risky decisional process does not suffer in Tetens' works. If the *Risico* from Tetens does not help to calculate the fee charges, then what is its utility? At first glance, we could think that Tetens tried to theorize a suggestion by Abraham de Moivre. In the *Doctrine of Chances*, de Moivre stated (de Moivre, 1756):

> The risk to lose a certain sum, is the opposite of its expectation; its true measure is the product of its forward sum by the probability of its loss.

Tetens' works on this subject could easily be seen as a mathematical exercise aiming to generalize this notion of risk to more complex random variables than the Bernoulli variables used by de Moivre. The philosopher's interest in the *Risico* risk and the estimation risk brings us toward a different interpretation. The author tries to end a debate on the stammering of the insurance sector, which tries to determinate whether risk rises with the number of contracts. Common sense would tend to suggest that the risk of a loss would rise, while analyses, such as the law of large numbers, seem to state the opposite. The indicator built by Tetens allows us to answer in a concrete way: It allows us to proportion the growth of guarantees to the growth of the volume of contracts.

Although Tetens' works are quite exotic, they show us that the importance of risk already existed in the eighteenth century and that risk was defined as the probability of reaching a certain threshold. This concept is actually the VaR concept.

7.2.1.4 Actuarial Works. If the notion of risk is defined as the probability of exceeding a certain threshold, then this concept was widespread in the 1780s, yet this notion was only developed by the direct heirs of Condorcet, Laplace, and Lacroix. The English mathematicians had no interest in this theory.

---

[5]Tetens' risk is therefore $R = \sum_{i \leq n_0} p_i |\overline{x} - x_i|$.

We usually tend to believe that the history of classic actuarial mathematics is renowned thanks to the works of Lorraine Daston (Daston, 1988). However, her considerations on the "risk domestication" could prove confusing: Daston considers the expectation of the disaster a risk and not a potential analysis of variance. This risk definition does not hold much importance or interest in the insurance markets, except for the life insurance markets. Nonetheless, if we are defining risk as seen by Markowitz, then this interpretation is misleading, and we will have to look somewhere else. Bohlmann, at the beginning of the nineteenth century, gave clues as his works related to Laplace and Tetens. Yet, there is one person who caught attention, Richard Price, who worked on estimation and insurance. In the first part of a thesis that was submitted to the *Royal Society* (Bayes, 1764), Bayes then wrote *Observations on Reversionary Payments* in 1771, which constitutes the "bible" of actuary. In charge of actuarial calculus at Equitable between 1768 and 1775, Price was looking to protect his company against a series of abnormal disasters—hence against risk—as were Condorcet, Laplace, and Tetens. Despite it being mutual, Equitable refused to reallocate profits in the case of "extraordinary events" or in case "of a season of abnormal mortality." There was therefore a charge for taking on risk, which was left out of all the existing theories at that time. Price did not develop a theory on randomness; he never felt the urge to do it.

7.2.1.5 Laplace. This leads us to Laplace, who inherited not only the problematic but also the modeling of Condorcet. In his work *Théorie Analytique*, we found identical operations with a binary outcome (fail/success), and hence a binomial draw. Laplace's method consists of a normal approximation of binomial variables; the probability $P(X \leq m) = \sum_{k=0}^{m} C_n^k p^k (1-p)^{n-k}$ is therefore explained by the integral $(1/\sqrt{\pi})\int_{-\infty}^{(m-np)/\sqrt{2npq}} \exp(-v^2)\, dv$. This cannot possibly be a simplification; yet as long as the upper limit of the integral changes, we can use a table of the law of Laplace– de Moivre to obtain the values of the integral without any calculus.

Condorcet's model hence becomes usable, and it becomes plausible to quickly calculate the amount of charge necessary in relation to the required security level. Laplace's method is based on an analytical approximation and not on a convergence theorem in probability (central limit theorem). Instead of considering only binomial outcomes (fail/success), the author first utilizes the possibility of different variables and then multinomial draws. Finally, Laplace develops the law of future by events considering past events (Laplace, 1812), meaning that he also suggests a Bayesian estimation of frequencies instead of probabilities.

We should, however, insist on the link between the awareness of risk and handling of the question of statistical estimation. Laplace's series of demographical works (Laplace, 1781) allows him to define his "method," where the analytical approximation has been crucial in the integration of security decisions. In the hypotheses test—mathematics applied to statistical estimation—we reason on the observation of binary characteristics. These hypotheses question the probability of a real frequency being distant from its estimate over a sample. The analytical form of this problem is the study of a variable, for which the probability distribution is

$$\frac{C_p^q \int_0^1 x^q (1-x)^{p-q} x^{q'+1} (1-x)^{p'-q'} dx}{\int_0^1 x^q (1-x)^{p-q} dx}$$

This quantity allows us to study any binomial variable with the same approximation afterwards. It is therefore the mathematical analogy, between identical functional forms, and certainly not a conceptual analogy that drove Laplace to use the same tools.

To conclude on Laplace in the perspective of the VaR, we can note that he applies Condorcet's principle as a criterion for the management of diverse activities, and that he further develops the link with the question of estimation. The importance of the latter point led him to form conventional thresholds of probability. Laplace therefore enlightens us not only by the generality of his work, but also by its precision.

7.2.1.6 Lacroix. It would be useful in our quest to historicize the concept of VaR to recall the works of Lacroix. In 1821, he published a *Traité Élémentaire du Calcul de Probabilités*, where he aimed to popularize probability calculus in its various applications. He developed examples to explain the computation of the charge fee given the security threshold wanted. He discarded insured individuals' viewpoints, stating that only the threshold condition from the insurer's viewpoint of view was enough to decide the bonuses. Lacroix developed Condorcet's works on the insurer, in the simple case where the contracts have a binary outcome.

If we use the notations from Condorcet, the balance of the insurer is

$$n'b' - m'(a+b)$$

The highest loss is noted c. By posing

$$n'b' - m'(a+b) = c$$

we obtain b' as

$$\frac{c + m'(a+b)}{n'}.$$

This equality could not provide any explanation for Condorcet. Indeed, if the value of threshold c is chosen, the problem holds to its probability, as we need to deduce the smaller number of disasters m' in n' draws. As long as n' is of any consequence on the equation, we need to calculate high powers of elementary probability (binomial law), which takes time. Hence, Lacroix gives us an example: Say $n' = 200$ insured ships with an average disaster (sink) rate of 1 for every 100 cruises. If the insurer admits a chance of 1/100,000 of an extreme loss, then we obtain $m' = 10$. By choosing -7 $(a + b)$, as the value for an extreme loss, we find that

$$b' = \frac{-7(a+b)+10(a+b)}{200} = \frac{3(a+b)}{200} = 1.5\% \text{ of the insured capital}$$

As with Condorcet, it is by fixing the VaR that we obtain a rule for management. To find the probability of a "normal" gain, we only need to fix the threshold of the gain. We note it e, and we find that it corresponds to the maximum number of disasters m'', such that

$$n'b' - m''(a+b) = e$$

We therefore have

$$m' - m'' = \frac{e - c}{a + b}$$

When the threshold for a normal gain is set as 0.7 $(a + b)$, such as in Lacroix's work, we arrive at

$$m'' = 10 - \frac{0.7(a+b) - (-7)(a+b)}{a+b} = 2.3$$

We then proceed by interpolation, from the values of the binomial table, to find the probability: There is a 67% chance of having two disasters or less, an there is an 85% chance of having three or more disasters; hence "2.3 losses" gives us a probability around 75%. This means that in three-quarters of cases, the insurer gains a profit above 0.7 $(a + b)$ for a turnover of $3(a + b)$, or a rate of 23%.

Lacroix hence formalizes some of Condorcet's ideas by presenting a definitive theory on the risk of threshold.

7.2.1.7 Political Economy.

Edgeworth. The influence of Laplace on Edgeworth is evident and renowned. Edgeworth's [EDG 88] choice to illustrate the history of the concept of VaR could seem paradoxical, considering that his article does not mention risk. He observes that the "solvability and the profit of the banker depend of the probability that he will not be asked to reimburse at once more than nth of his capital." This is exactly the same definition of risk used by Condorcet and Laplace. Edgeworth presents banking activity as a "game" where we need to arbitrate between profit and solvability. He also demonstrates the determination of a minimal threshold for the liquid reserves compatible with an almost certain solvability, and insists on the consequences of the addition of random variables.

To achieve the determination of the reserve threshold, Edgeworth uses a simplified hypothesis: the independence of withdrawals. Under this hypothesis, the central limit theorem allows us to consider withdrawal statistics as outcomes of a random variable, and to obtain the minimal reserves threshold. He only now needs to estimate the location and scale parameters of its variable: the mean and the modulo.

Instead of the widespread use of the density function:

$$f(x) = \frac{1}{\sigma\sqrt{2\rho}} e^{-\frac{x^2}{2\sigma^2}}$$

(where the variance is σ^2), Edgeworth writes

$$y = \frac{1}{c\sqrt{\rho}} e^{-\frac{x^2}{c^2}}$$

After Laplace, Edgeworth reinstates the probabilistic convergence theories in economics. He can therefore far more easily obtain the probability that a variable exceeds a certain threshold. We are hence astonished by the fact that Edgeworth did not mention a notion of global risk.

Wicksell–Fisher. Wicksell developed Edgeworth's theory with a very simple statistical innovation: he uses the expected variance instead of the modulo (Wicksell, 1898).[6]

Paradoxically, the economic interpretation has gained a lot since the model is now of use for every firm (not only insurance companies). We can therefore calculate the probability that a given company will default on its engagements. Yet, Wicksell does not use the word of risk, like Edgeworth.

In the measure that Edgeworth's article does not seem to have been studied, we could be tempted to show the importance of Wicksell in the rules of management. But this was not enough to draw interest from researchers on the subject. The posterity of Wicksell's works would therefore have to wait, which was not the case with Fisher's works.

By reusing Edgeworth's idea of the solvability risk, Fisher instead applied the standard deviation to calculate the probability of insolvency risk. Standard deviation as a measure of dispersion is accepted, so we could be tempted to give credit to Fisher for the propagation of Edgeworth's thesis. Yet the Fisherian ideas on finance did not hold much importance or interest for one of two reasons: because they were confusing or because Fisher was ruined after the 1929 Wall Street crash.

[6]Here Wicksell uses the value of a quartile from a normal distribution. It is equal to 0.67 of the standard deviation.

7.2.1.8 1930s England.

In 1934, Hicks used his knowledge in statistics to develop a systemic approach to a decision (Hicks, 1934):

> The form of each frequency curve can be studied thanks to its moment functions—in the statistical term. Each curve can be defined by choosing a large enough number of moments, and by choosing only a certain restricted number of these, we obtain an approximation of this problem.

However, the description by moment function only allows for a density approximation. We still need to determine the decision, which Chambers will do. Chambers (1934) considers the investment problems. The random variables used in this matter establish the perspective of returns on investment. The main point for Chambers is that the mean dictates the average return, and the standard deviation represents the risk. He comments:

> If an individual can receive 2 per cent risk-free, he would be indifferent between these 2 per cent risk-free and 2.5 per cent with a standard deviation of 1, for all the values of the indifference curve.

We understand that indifference curves are increasing because we accept a growth of risk only for a higher remuneration. Indifference curves are, hence, convex. Chambers is completely aware of the estimative character of a model that only takes into account the first two moments. He therefore indicates that it is possible to use higher moments, which prove discriminating in special cases, but points out that he did not purse the analysis above the first two moments. As such, Hicks concludes that an analysis based on only the first two moments is too vague. Marschak (1938) is the first to explicitly justify the importance of the skew (third generating moment).

The dominant theme in the articles of Chambers, Hicks, and Marschak is the monetary market. The risk is taken into account as a deciding aspect in the arbitrage linking to the holdings of share or bonds. These long-term developments show that the thematic explored by Edgeworth and Wicksell has been lost to the profit of abstract works—such as Markowitz's works. We had to wait until the 1950s and the development of institutional finance to see a reappearance of a concept close to the VaR.

7.2.1.9 Financial Theory.

Arthur D. Roy. The relationship between economics and finance, both on a theoretical and institutional basis, are complex. Until recently, it has not been a "noble" subject to study, so much that finance builds itself as a subject from its exclusion by economists. Therein, Markowitz plays a particular role, because he is the first *excluded*, and his development led to the institutionalization of finance—a subject where the concept of risk is fundamental. This exclusion was made famous by Friedman during Markowitz's thesis presentation:

> Harry, I don't see any problems with your mathematics, yet I have a problem. This is not economics, and we cannot give you a Ph.D. of Economics for a thesis which is not economics. This is not mathematics, it is not economics, and it is not even management.

Indeed, the 1930s economic viewpoint was based on choosing a portfolio to understand the conditions of political economy. Here, questions clearly arise as to the best way to obtain an optimal portfolio. As a theoretical subject, finance strives to differentiate itself from macroeconomics. Roy (1961) condemned a too complex economic theory and an exacerbated wish of its application.

Roy insisted on the fact that financiers request rough-and-ready rules of thumb, instead of theories. The Englishman considered a maximization program for return with a "security" constraint. He imposed a very large probability (95%) that the return exceeds a given minimum. We find Condorcet's principle here, along with the idea of fixing a confidence threshold and a loss level, thus creating an admissible maximal VaR.

Roy's works have the merit of reinstating the importance of the VaR as a management principle, while determining the choice of probabilistic thresholds. Yet Roy also showed the fundamental ambiguity of the Markowitz analysis, which suggests its application (despite its uselessness).

7.2.1.10 The VaR Concept. The VaR concept seems to be recent and uncertain. It seems that in the late 1980s we saw the concepts of dollars-at-risk (DaR), capital-at-risk (CaR), income-at-risk (IaR), earnings-at-risk (EaR), and VaR come together. In the end, the term value was the most general and the most nominal as it evocates the *shareholder value.* After the publication of *RiskMetrics Technical Document* by J.P. Morgan in 1994, the term VaR was settled. Holton (2002) gave a broad view with references, in particular to Guldimann, who directed the RiskMetrics project at JP Morgan. He insisted on the fact that RiskMetrics offered a simplified version of VaR and that the essential part of the work accomplished by J.P. Morgan was the distribution of the concept.

The spontaneous creation of the expression VaR at the beginning of the 1990s tells us a lot about the concept of a community of practice—because VaR is more of a practice than a theory—and the grounding of the subject before the phenomenon. Nonetheless, we must take into account the important role of regulatory bodies.

As early as 1922, the New York Stock Exchange forced market participants to provision 10% of their investments. Thereafter, the prudential American regulation developed alongside the subject of risk. It has to be noted that for regulators the risk is great: The systemic risk of banking institutions defaulting could lead to the destruction of the financial system.

In the United States, even though there have been regulations since the 1920s, the importance of regulations began with the SEC (Security Exchange Commission) in 1908: for the first time, the system was clearly regulated in terms of VaR. The VaR at 95% for 40 days for banking institutions must be compatible with their reserves. It is this approach, again, that dominated the Basel principles in 1988 and became transposed in European Law.

In 1996, VaR was validated by the Basel Committee as *the* measure of aggregate risk, and for the first time regulators register a private concept of metrics. From this date on, regulators did not impose its metrics. They can just validate methodologies. Besides, it seems difficult to determine the complexity of financial transactions.

The aims for regulation are therefore to not only regulate the risk of credit institutions and market makers effectively, but also to allow the development and the circulation of *good practices.* Indeed, temptation exists for institutions to consider risk management as a cost and to then forget it. Perhaps risk management models will be the cause of innovation, as the models of evaluation of complex or structured products could have been.

The history of the concept of value-at-risk (VaR) covers more than just the history of financial theory. The formalization of the VaR began with the mathematicians of the 1780s, who looked to solve political arithmetic questions that considered the subjects of management and demographics. Actually, Condorcet, Laplace, and their successors invented a quantitative management and statistical mathematics. In the nineteenth century, the *Mathematical Theory of Risk* forces its way through actuarial circles, and economists such as Edgeworth suggest extending the prudential management model to the banking industry.

If this prudential management brought back the classical VaR metric, we also observed more abstract developments in the 1930s. The addition to this subject in the 1950s was more of a generalization of confidence intervals. During the 1950s, portfolio theorists developed basic mathematics for VaR measures. It is therefore not astonishing to see that VaR entered common knowledge in practices afterwards.

The only change in the 1980s–1990s is that from the management point of view to a comparison point of view: The VaR is not only of interest for the manager, it is also part of the information required by regulators, investors, and all market participants. VaR has its origins in portfolio theory and capital requirements. The latter can be traced to New York Stock Exchange capital requirements of the early twentieth century. During the 1970s, U.S. regulators prompted securities firms to develop procedures for aggregating data to support capital calculations discussed in their FOCUS reports.

By the 1980s, a need for institutions to develop more sophisticated VaR measures had arisen. Markets were becoming more volatile, and sources of market risk were proliferating. By that time, the resources necessary to calculate VaR were also becoming available. Processing power was inexpensive, and data vendors were starting to make large quantities of historical price data available. Financial institutions implemented sophisticated proprietary VaR measures during the 1980s, but these remained practical tools known primarily to professionals within those institutions.

During the early 1990s, concerns about the proliferation of derivative instruments and publicized losses spurred the field of financial risk management. J.P. Morgan publicized VaR to professionals at financial institutions and corporations with its RiskMetrics service. Ultimately, the value of proprietary VaR measures was recognized by the Basel Committee, which authorized their use by banks for performing regulatory capital calculations. An ensuing "VaR debate" raised issues related to the subjectivity of risk, which Markowitz had first identified in 1952.

Time will tell if widespread use of VaR contributes to the risks that VaR is intended to measure.

7.3 Definition of the Value-at-Risk

In simple terms, risk measures how volatile an asset's returns are. Value-at-risk (VaR) is a measure of how volatile a portfolio's assets are.

VaR has three important parameters: the time horizon, the confidence level, and the observation period.

The first one we are going to analyze is the time horizon (i.e., the length of time over which we plan to hold the assets in the portfolio—the "holding period"). The typical holding period is one day, although a period of 10 days is used. For UCITS funds, for example, the holding period is one month.

The second parameter is the confidence level at which we plan to make the estimate. This is a probability of loss associated with VaR measurement. Confidence levels generally range between 90% and 99%. 99% is the confidence level to use under UCITS unless the regulator is notified with detailed explanations of why using a different confidence level.

The third parameter is the observation period, which tells about the history of risk factors. It can be one month, one year, five years, or more. The observation period is a critical VaR setting because it has a significant impact on the end-result figure. Under UCITS the observation period is at least one business year (250 business days). It can be more than 250 days but cannot be less.

We also will have to define the currency that will be used to denominate the VaR.

VaR, with the parameters

- holding period x days and
- confidence level y%,

measures what the maximum loss over x days will be if we assume that the x-days period will not be one of the $(100 - y)$% x-days periods that are the worst under normal market conditions. We can also define VaR as a lower y% quantile of a profit/loss probability distribution—that is, the best outcome from a set of bad outcomes on a bad day.

VaR reflects the riskiness of the portfolio based on the portfolio's current composition.

VaR is a number that expresses the maximum expected loss for a given time horizon, a given confidence interval, and a given position or portfolio of instruments under normal market conditions, attributable to changes in the market price of financial instruments.

The advantages of VaR are numerous:

- it provides a measure of total risk.
- It is an easy number to understand and explain to clients.
- It is useful for monitoring and controlling risk within the portfolio.
- It can measure the risk of many types of financial securities (i.e., stocks, bonds, commodities, foreign exchange, off-balance-sheet derivatives such as futures, forwards, swaps, and options, etc.).
- As a tool, VaR is very useful for comparing a portfolio with a selected benchmark.

VaR measures how much could be lost with a probability defined at the very outset (*a priori*), and it gives a figure for this loss. VaR is then the loss that could be exceeded with a probability of only p% within a period t. In other words, there is $(1 - p)$% of chance of losing less than the VaR within the period t.

If $p = 5\%$ (which is generally used), we assume that only 5% of the next coming observed fluctuations are "abnormal" or "unusual."

A VaR of 5% and $1.6 million means that we estimated that there would be 5/100 chances that more than $1.6 million would be lost but it could be $3 million or $10 million. This is why we also need stress testing—to compensate for this limitation of VaR approach.

VaR and standard deviation are both related measures of a distribution of returns (Figure 7.1). Standard deviation is designed to measure the overall width of a distribution and therefore considers both positive and negative returns.

VaR, on the other hand, seek to measure just the size of the loss (left) tail. It is characterized by a percentage that represents the area under the curve not considered as VaR. Thus a 95% VaR means that 95% of the area under the curve is to the right, with 5% of the area to the left. These percentages are of course directly related to the probability that you will lose an amount equal to or greater than the calculated VaR.

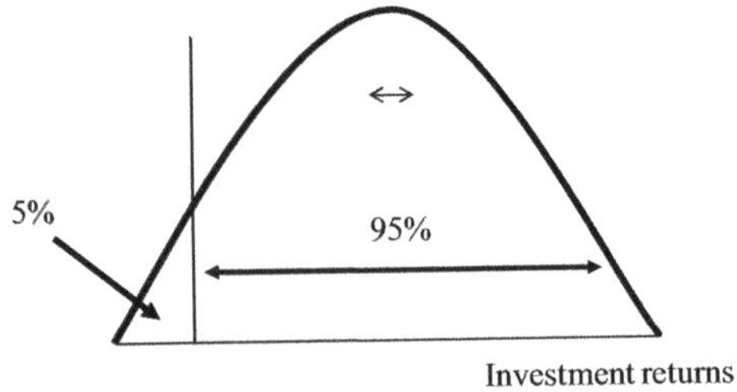

FIGURE 7.1 Distribution of returns where 1 sigma is one standard deviation.

7.4 VaR Calculation Models

Most of the regulators do not specify which VaR calculation models have to be used or under which circumstances a certain tone should be used. They limit themselves to stating that a VaR approach has to be applied for sophisticated funds.

A variety of models exist for estimating VaR. It is even possible that readers may find different ways to explain these various VaR models and the mathematical calculations accompanying each of them in other books. Each model has its own set of assumptions. One of the most common assumptions is that historical market data are the best estimators for future changes in market value. Common models include:

- *Variance–Covariance or Delta-Normal:* Assuming that risk factor returns are always normally distributed and that the change in portfolio value is linearly dependent on all risk factor returns.
- *Historical Simulation:* Assuming that asset returns in the future will have the same distribution as they had in the past (historical market data).
- *Monte Carlo Simulation:* Where future asset returns are more or less randomly simulated.

When selecting a risk engine to compute VaR for a portfolios, it is important to consider whether they allow the choice between the three VaR models as mentioned above. Using a risk engine that is only using the variance–covariance approach may limit its usage to simple assets and derivatives. If this model is applied to nonlinear assets, the results may completely underestimate the total risk of the portfolio. Monte Carlo simulation is much more sophisticated in terms of how the risk engine has been built.

7.4.1 VARIANCE–COVARIANCE

The variance–covariance, or delta-normal, model was popularized by JP Morgan Chase (formerly JP Morgan) in the early 1990s. In the following, we will take a simple case where the only risk factor for the portfolio is the value of the assets themselves.[7] The following two assumptions enable us to translate the VaR estimation problem into a linear algebraic problem:

- The portfolio is composed of assets whose deltas are linear. More exactly, the changes in the value of the portfolio are linearly dependent on all of the

[7]Readers may find some further references about books detailing VaR analysis in the bibliography. This sole subject could be a book in itself, and this current book intends to give a general description about risk management under the UCITS regime. For further information, see especially Jorion, P., Dowd, K., *Measuring Market Risk*, John Wiley & Sons, Hoboken, NJ, 2005.

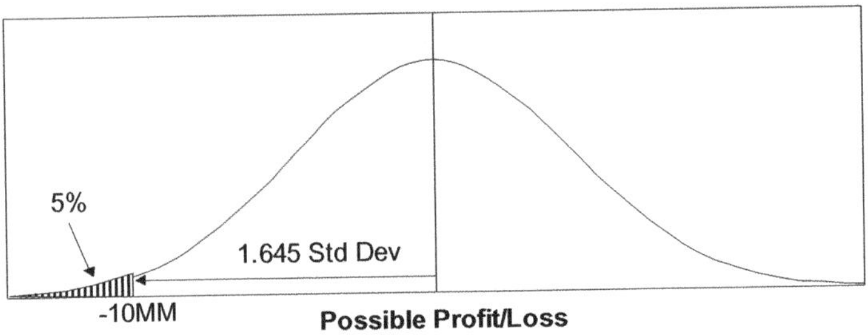

FIGURE 7.2 Normal distribution.

changes in the values of the assets. The portfolio return is therefore also linearly dependent on all of the asset returns.

- The asset returns are jointly normally distributed.

The implications in the above points is that the portfolio return is normally distributed because it always holds that a linear combination of jointly normally distributed variables is itself normally distributed.

Using the hypothesis of normal distribution of returns is very useful when calculating VaR. A lot of studies and researches over the years have tried to capture the most accurate distributions of certain stocks' returns, for example. The conclusion is that the normal distribution is a fair approximation of reality.

A distribution is said to be normal (Figure 7.2) if there is a high probability that an observation will be close to the mean and a low probability that an observation is a long way from the mean. The normal distribution has some known features and characteristics that are helpful when modeling market risk.

The term bell curve is used to describe the mathematical concept called normal distribution, sometimes referred to as Gaussian distribution. "Bell curve" refers to the shape that is created when a line is plotted using the data points for an item that meets the criteria of "normal distribution."The center contains the greatest number of a particular value and therefore would be the highest point on the arc of the line. This point is referred to as the mean, but in simple terms it is the highest number of occurences of an element. (statistical term, the mode). The important thing to note about a normal distribution is the curve is concentrated in the center and decreases on either side. This is significant in that the data have less of a tendency to produce unusually extreme values, called outliers, as compared to other distributions. Also the bell curve signifies that the data are symetrical, and thus we can create reasonable expectations as to the possibility that an outcome will lie within a range to the left or right of the center, once we can measure the amount of deviation contained in the data. These are measured in terms of standard deviations. A bell curve graph depends on two factors, the mean and the standard deviation. The mean identifies the position of the center, and the standard deviation determines the the height and width of the bell. For example, a large standard deviation creates a bell that is short and wide, while a small standard deviation creates a tall and narrow curve.

To understand the probability factors of a normal distribution, you need to understand the following "rules":

1. The total area under the curve is equal to 1 (100%).
2. About 68% of the area under the curve falls within 1 standard deviation.
3. About 95% of the area under the curve falls within 2 standard deviations.
4. About 99.7% of the area under the curve falls within 3 standard devations.

Items 2, 3, and 4 are sometimes referred to as the "empirical rule" or the 68–95–99.7 rule. In terms of probability, once we determine that the data are normally distributed (bell curved) and we calculate the mean and standard deviation, we are able to determine the probability that a single data point will fall within a given range of possibilities.

Example: Let's imagine a portfolio the called XYZ Fund. Its average yearly performance has been 0.52% with an annualized standard deviation of 2.56%.

XYZ Fund	
Average yearly performance	0.52%
Annualized standard deviation	2.56%
In 68% of cases	0.52% – 2.56% = –2.04%
	0.52% + 2.56% = –3.08%
In 95% of cases	0.52% – 2 times 2.56% = –4.60%
	0.52% + 2 times 2.56% = 5.64%

Normal distributions have many convenient properties, and random variates with unknown distributions are often assumed to be normal to allow for probability calculations. Although this can be a dangerous assumption, it is often a good approximation due to a surprising result known as the central limit theorem. This theorem states that the mean of any set of variates with any distribution having a finite mean and variance tends to the normal distribution. Many common attributes such as test scores, height, and so on, follow roughly normal distributions, with few members at the high and low ends and many in the middle.

The distribution is completely described by the mean and standard deviation. The normal distribution $N(\mu, \sigma)$ has mean μ and standard deviation σ. Mathematical formula for a normal distribution is

$$\frac{1}{\sqrt{2\pi\sigma^2}} e^{\frac{-(X-\mu)^2}{2\sigma^2}}$$

where μ is the mean, σ is the standard deviation, π is a constant 3.14159, and e is the base of natural logarithms = 2.718282.

7.4.1.1 The Standard Normal Distribution or *Z* Distribution. The standard normal distribution is a normal distributions with a mean of 0 and a standard deviation of 1. Normal distributions can be transformed to standard distributions by the formula

$$Z = X - \mu / \sigma$$

where X is a score from the original normal distribution, μ is the mean of the original normal distribution, and σ is the standard deviation of original normal distribution.

The standard normal distribution is sometimes called the Z distribution. A Z score always reflects the number of standard deviations above or below the mean a particular score is. For instance, if a person scored a 70 on a test with a mean of 50 and a standard deviation of 10, then he scored 2 standard deviations above the mean. Converting the test scores to Z scores, an X of 70 would be

$$Z = (70 - 50)/10 = 2$$

So, a Z score of 2 means that the original score was 2 standard deviations above the mean. Note that the Z distribution will only be a normal distribution if the original distribution (X) is normal.

7.4.1.2 Skew and Kurtosis. When returns fall *outside* of a normal distribution, the distribution exhibits skewness or kurtosis. Skewness is known as the third "moment" of a return distribution, and kurtosis is known as the fourth moment of the return distribution, with the mean and the variance being the first and second moments, respectively. (Variance is a statistic that is closely related to standard deviation; both measure the dispersion of an investment's historical returns.) Ideally, investors should consider all four moments or characteristics of an investment's return distribution.

Skewness: Skewness measures the degree of asymmetry of a distribution around its mean. Positive skewness indicates a distribution with an asymmetric tail extending toward more positive values. Negative skewness indicates a distribution with an asymmetric tail extending toward more negative values.

Kurtosis: Kurtosis measures the degree to which a distribution is more or less peaked than a normal distribution. Positive kurtosis indicates a relatively peaked distribution. Negative kurtosis indicates a relatively flat distribution. A normal distribution has a kurtosis of 3. Therefore, an investment characterized by high kurtosis will have "fat tails" (higher frequencies of outcomes) at the extreme negative and positive ends of the distribution curve. A distribution of returns exhibiting high kurtosis tends to overestimate the probability of achieving the mean return.

Skew is given by the following formula:

$$\text{Skew} = \sum \left(\frac{(R_{\text{Fund}} - \text{Avg}[R_{\text{Fund}}])}{\text{Stdev}[R_{\text{Fund}}]} \right)^3 * \frac{n}{(n-1)*(n-2)}$$

Excess kurtosis is given by the following formula:

$$\text{Excess kurtosis} = \sum\left(\frac{(R_{\text{Fund}} - \text{Avg}[R_{\text{Fund}}])}{\text{Stdev}[R_{\text{Fund}}]}\right)^4 * \frac{n(n+1)}{(n-1)(n-2)(n-3)} - \frac{3(n-1)^2}{(n-2)(n-3)} - 3$$

7.4.1.3 Standard Deviation and Correlation. Let us consider a well-diversified portfolio, which generates 10% annual returns.

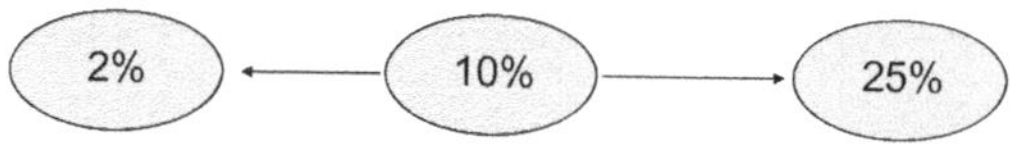

According to standard deviation lessons, the likelihood that next month will produce a return below or above mean is low. This also means that reaching extreme values is rare. On the contrary, the likelihood that the portfolio moves from 10 to 11 or from 10 to 9 is high.

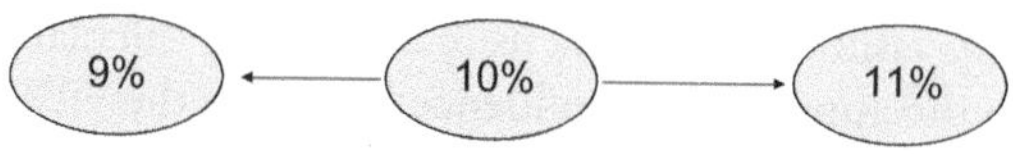

There is an increased likelihood a portfolio will move from 10 to 9 or 10 to 11% than 10 to 2%.

The more volatile an asset is, the higher its standard deviation is and the more at risk this asset is. Standard deviation is at then a fair measure of the risk linked with an asset.

We can therefore assimilate the risk linked with an investment with the dispersion or variability of its returns around its anticipated value. To measure this dispersion, we use standard deviation.

These concepts were already introduced, but we will repeat them here.

Standard deviation is the square root of the variance:

$$s(x) = \sqrt{v(x)}$$

The variance formula is

$$v(x) = \frac{\sum_{i=1}^{n}(x_i - \bar{x})^2}{n}$$

The covariance between two series of data is given by the formula

$$\text{cov}(X,Y) = \frac{1}{N}\sum_{i=1}^{i=n}(x_i - \bar{X})(y_i - \bar{Y})$$

The variance of a portfolio is given by the formula

$$s_p^2 = \sum_{i=1}^{N} X_i^2 s_i^2 + \sum_{i=1}^{N} \sum_{j=1}^{N} X_i Y_j C_{i,j}$$

where X_i is the quantity of asset I, s_i^2 is the standard deviation of asset i, Y_j is the quantity of asset j, and $C_{i,j}$ is the covariance between the variances of assets i and j.

Adding standard deviations (and VaR), we obtain

$$s_{\text{Total}}^2 = s_A^2 + s_B^2 + s_C^2 + 2r_{AB}s_A s_B + 2r_{AC}s_A s_C + 2r_{BC}s_B s_C$$

where s is the standard deviation and r is the correlation.

Normal distribution tables show the probability of a particular observation moving a certain distance from the mean. If we look along a normal distribution table, we see that at -1.645 standard deviations, the probability is 5%. This means that there is a 5% probability that an observation will be at least 1.645 standard deviations below the mean. This level is used in many VaR models.

The normality assumption allows us to *z*-scale the calculated portfolio standard deviation to the appropriate confidence level. For the 99% confidence level we use 2.33.

This method assumes that the returns on risk factors are normally distributed, the correlations between risk factors are constant, and the delta (or price sensitivity to changes in a risk factor) of each portfolio constituent is constant. Using the correlation method, the volatility of each risk factor is extracted from the historical observation period. Historical data on investment returns are therefore required. The potential effect of each component of the portfolio on the overall portfolio value is then worked out from the component's delta (with respect to a particular risk factor) and that risk factor's volatility.

Correlation. Measures of correlation between variables are important to fund managers who are interested in reducing their risk exposure through diversifying their portfolio. Correlation is a measure of the degree to which a value of one variable is related to the value of another. The correlation coefficient is a single number that compares the strengths and directions of the movements in two instruments values. The sign of the coefficient determines the relative directions that the instruments move in, while its value determines the strength of the relative movements. The value of the coefficient ranges from −1 to +1, depending on the nature of the relationship. So if, for example, the value of the correlation is 0.5, this means that one instrument moves in the same direction by half the amount of the other instrument. A value of zero means that the instruments are uncorrelated, and their movements are independent of each other. Correlation is a key element of many VaR models, including parametric models. It is particularly important in the measurement of the variance (hence volatility) of a portfolio.

If we take the simplest example, a portfolio containing just two assets, Eq. [7.1] gives the volatility of the portfolio based on the volatility of each instrument in the portfolio (*x* and *y*) and their correlation with one another:

$$V_{\text{port}} = \sqrt{x^2 + y^2 + 2xy \times \rho(xy)} \tag{7.1}$$

where *x* is the volatility of asset *x*, *y* is the volatility of asset *y*, and ρ is the correlation between assets *x* and *y*.

The correlation coefficient between two assets uses the covariance between the assets in its calculation. The standard formula for covariance is

$$\text{Cov} = \frac{\sum_{i=1}^{n}(x_i - \bar{x})(y_i - \bar{y})}{(n-1)}$$

where the sum of the distance of each value *x* and *y* from the mean is divided by the number of observations minus one. The covariance calculation enables us to calculate the correlation coefficient, shown as

$$r = \text{Cov}\frac{(1,2)}{s_1' s_2}$$

where *s* is the standard deviation of each asset.

The equation may be modified to cover more than two instruments as per the following example with 10 stocks. In practice, correlations are usually estimated on the basis of past historical observations. This is an important consideration in the construction and analysis of a portfolio, because the associated risks will depend to an extent on the correlation between its constituents.

It should be apparent that from a portfolio perspective a positive correlation increases risk. If the returns on two or more instruments in a portfolio are positively correlated, strong movements in either direction are likely to occur at the same time. The overall distribution of returns will be wider and flatter, because there will be higher joint probabilities associated with extreme values (both gains and losses).

A negative correlation indicates that the assets are likely to move in opposite directions, thus reducing risk.

It has been argued that in extreme situations, such as market crashes or largescale market corrections, correlations cease to have any relevance, because all assets will be moving in the same direction. However, under most market scenarios, using correlations to reduce the risk of a portfolio is considered satisfactory practice, and the VaR number for a diversified portfolio will be lower than that for an undiversified portfolio.

Correlation measures the degree to which the value of one datum is related to the value of another. Figure 7.3 shows how two series of data would behave in time if they are positively correlated.

FIGURE 7.3 Positive correlation over time.

- A correlation of −1 implies perfect negative linear association.
- When stock A is making returns below average, stock B is making returns above average and vice versa.
- A correlation of 1 implies perfect positive linear association.
- Where correlation of 1 exists, there is no benefit from diversification.
- A correlation of 0 implies no linear association.
- Benefits from diversification are not as strong as when correlation is equal to −1.

In this case the portfolio variance will be the same as for each stock taken individually. The combination of these two stocks brings nothing to the portfolio in terms of risk.

7.4.1.4 VaR Calculation Using Variance-Covariance. To calculate the VaR for a single asset, we would calculate the standard deviation of its returns, using either its historical volatility or *implied volatility*.[8]

If a 95% confidence level is required, meaning we wish to have 5% of the observations in the left-hand tail of the normal distribution, this means that the observations in that area are 1.645 standard deviations away from the mean. Consider the following statistical data for a government bond, calculated using one year's historical observations:

Nominal (millions):	£10
Price (millions):	£100
Average return:	7.35%
Standard deviation:	1.99%

The VaR at the 95% confidence level is 1.645×0.0199 or 0.032736. The portfolio has a market value of £10 million, so the VaR of the portfolio is

[8]The historical volatility is estimated according to the historical price, while the implicit volatility is estimated from the price of options.

0.032736 × 10,000,000 or £327,360. So this figure is the maximum loss the portfolio may sustain over one year for 95% of the time. We may extend this analysis to a two-stock portfolio. In a two-asset portfolio, we stated that there is a relationship that enables us to calculate the volatility of a two-asset portfolio; this expression is used to calculate the VaR and is shown as

$$\text{VaR}_{\text{port}} = \sqrt{w_1^2 s_1^2 + w_2^2 s_2^2 + 2w_1 w_2 s_1 s_2 r_{1,2}}$$

where w_1 is the weighting of the first asset, w_2 is the weighting of the second asset, s_1 is the standard deviation or *volatility* of the first asset, s_2 is the standard deviation or *volatility* of the second asset, and $r_{1,2}$ is the correlation coefficient between the two assets.

In a two-asset portfolio the undiversified VaR is the weighted average of the individual standard deviations; the diversified VaR, which takes into account the correlation between the assets, is the square root of the variance of the portfolio. In practice, banks will calculate both diversified and undiversified VaR.

The diversified VaR measure is used to set trading limits, while the larger undiversified VaR measure is used to gauge an idea of the bank's risk exposure in the event of a significant correction or market crash. This is because in a crash situation, liquidity dries up as market participants all attempt to sell off their assets. This means that the correlation between assets ceases to have any impact, because all assets move in the same direction. Under this scenario then, it is more logical to use an undiversified VaR measure.

The drawbacks of the variance–covariance method are that it assumes stable correlations and only measures linear risk. It also places excessive reliance on the normal distribution, and returns in the market are widely believed to have "fatter tails" than a true normal distribution. This phenomenon is known as *leptokutosis*—that is, the non-normal distribution of outcomes.

Example: Here we present a step-by-step guide for VaR computation for the covariance–variance approach for a portfolio consisting of 10 equities.

1. Get the price at the end of each month for the last 12 months.
2. Calculate the returns for each month using the simple formula S_i/S_{i-1}, where S_i is the stock price for the *i*th month.
3. Create a variance–covariance matrix for the shares without the weights of the portfolio.
4. Create a variance–covariance matrix with the weights of each share in the portfolio.
5. Sum all of the rows of the matrix to get the variance of the portfolio.
6. Take the square root of the variance in order to get the standard deviation of the portfolio.
7. Calculate the annualized standard deviation by multiplying the standard deviation by the square root of 12 (12 months).

Portfolio	100.00%
Anglo American PLC	15.00%
Xstrata Plc	10.00%
Vodafone	5.00%
BP PLC	20.00%
3i Group PLC	5.00%
Sainsbury	7.00%
AMEC PLC	13.00%
British Sky Brooadcasting Group PLC	15.00%
BAE Systems	5.00%
Rexam PLC	5.00%

FIGURE 7.4 Stocks in a portfolio.

8. Multiply it by 2.33 (the 99% quantile of the standard-normal distribution).

You have now obtained the VaR of your portfolio with a 99% confidence interval.

Figure 7.4 to 7.6 show a concrete application of the steps as mentioned above. For reasons of appearance, we have limited ourselves to monthly returns and not 250 days as per the UCITS VaR setting.

A stock portfolio is shown in Figure 7.4. Price at end of each month for the last 12 months is given in Figure 7.5.

The mean and standard deviation of the returns are then calculated using standard statistical formulae. This would then give the standard deviation of monthly price relatives, which are converted to an annual figure by multiplying it by the square root of the number of days in a year, usually taken to be 250.

7.4.2 HISTORICAL SIMULATION

The historical simulation method for calculating VaR is the simplest and avoids some of the pitfalls of the correlation method. Specifically, the three main assumptions behind correlation (normally distributed returns, constant correlations, constant deltas) are not needed in this case. The historical method only requires that we know the value of the position in the past (for example, an index price history). For a portfolio, we will need to rebuild its value passed from the price of assets and the current composition of the portfolio. After you identify significant risk factors for the portfolio, use historical data collected to deduct an amount of loss.

If a portfolio consists of several assets then in order to calculate the historical VaR to a day on this portfolio, one should be noted all the gains and the daily losses on the last 1000 days (for example). All these data must be classified in increasing order. If you want to get to 99% VaR, simply find the 10th (1000 * (100% - 99%)) value.

SBRY LN Equity	
Date	PX_LAST
28/11/2008	287
31/12/2008	328,5
30/01/2009	333
27/02/2009	315,25
31/03/2009	313
30/04/2009	330,5
29/05/2009	310,25
30/06/2009	313
31/07/2009	317,5
31/08/2009	325,7
30/09/2009	325
30/10/2009	329,9

AMEC LN Equity	
Date	PX_LAST
28/11/2008	525
31/12/2008	492,75
30/01/2009	565,5
27/02/2009	545
31/03/2009	533,5
30/04/2009	622
29/05/2009	674,5
30/06/2009	653
31/07/2009	705
31/08/2009	754
30/09/2009	755
30/10/2009	806,5

BSY LN Equity	
Date	PX_LAST
28/11/2008	439,5
31/12/2008	480
30/01/2009	497
27/02/2009	470,25
31/03/2009	433,5
30/04/2009	486,75
29/05/2009	442
30/06/2009	455
31/07/2009	546
31/08/2009	546
30/09/2009	571,5
30/10/2009	533

BA/LN Equity	
Date	PX_LAST
28/11/2008	354,25
31/12/2008	376,75
30/01/2009	402,25
27/02/2009	371,5
31/03/2009	334,5
30/04/2009	358,25
29/05/2009	341,75
30/06/2009	338,5
31/07/2009	307
31/08/2009	312,2
30/09/2009	349,2
30/10/2009	314,5

REX LN Equity	
Date	PX_LAST
28/11/2008	348
31/12/2008	351
30/01/2009	312
27/02/2009	262,25
31/03/2009	270
30/04/2009	316,5
29/05/2009	309,75
30/06/2009	284,5
31/07/2009	236
31/08/2009	267,5
30/09/2009	261
30/10/2009	277

FIGURE 7.5 Stock prices at the end of each month.

	Anglo American PLC		Xstrata Plc		Vodafone		BP PLC		3i Group PLC		Sainsbury		AMEC PLC		British Sky Brooadcasting Group PLC		BAE Systems		Rexam PLC	
	Price at end of…	Returns	Price at end of…	Returns	Price at end of…	Returns	Price at end of…	Returns	Price at end of…	Returns	Price at end of…	Returns	Price at end of…	Returns	Price at end of…	Returns	Price at end of…	Returns	Price at end of…	Returns
Nov–08	1534		930.5		127.2		526.75		411.75		287		525		439.5		354.25		348	
Dec–08	1546	0.0078	640	–0.3122	139	0.0928	526	–0.0014	272	–0.3394	328.5	0.1446	492.75	–0.0614	480	0.0922	376.75	0.0635	351	0.0086
Jan–09	1266	–0.1811	569.5	–0.1102	129.7	–0.0669	494.5	–0.0599	226.5	–0.1673	333	0.0137	565.5	0.1476	497	0.0354	402.25	0.0677	312	–0.1111
Feb–09	1001	–0.2093	695.5	0.2212	125.2	–0.0347	448.25	–0.0935	200	–0.1170	315.25	–0.0533	545	–0.0363	470.25	–0.0538	371.5	–0.0764	262.25	–0.1595
Mar–09	1186	0.1848	466.75	–0.3289	122.75	–0.0196	471.5	0.0519	271	0.3550	313	–0.0071	533.5	–0.0211	433.5	–0.0781	334.5	–0.0996	270	0.0296
Apr–09	1484	0.2513	607.5	0.3016	124.7	0.0159	482.5	0.0233	321	0.1845	330.5	0.0559	622	0.1659	486.75	0.1228	358.25	0.0710	316.5	0.1722
May–09	1777	0.1974	684	0.1259	116	–0.0698	511	0.0591	242	–0.2461	310.25	–0.0613	674.5	0.0844	442	–0.0919	341.75	–0.0461	309.75	–0.0213
Jun–09	1763.5	–0.0076	657.3	–0.0390	117.2	0.0103	477.8	–0.0650	242	0.0000	313	0.0089	653	–0.0319	455	0.0294	338.5	–0.0095	284.5	–0.0815
Jul–09	1930	0.0944	808.2	0.2296	122.7	0.0469	497.2	0.0406	273.75	0.1312	317.5	0.0144	705	0.0796	546	0.2000	307	–0.0931	236	–0.1705
Aug–09	2021	0.0472	826.5	0.0226	132.8	0.0823	532	0.0700	303.5	0.1087	325.7	0.0258	754	0.0695	546	0.0000	312.2	0.0169	267.5	0.1335
Sep–09	1993	–0.0139	922.5	0.1162	140.2	0.0557	553	0.0395	288.6	–0.0491	325	–0.0021	755	0.0013	571.5	0.0467	349.2	0.1185	261	–0.0243
Oct–09	2215	0.1114	882.5	–0.0434	134.55	–0.0403	572.3	0.0349	263.7	–0.0863	329.9	0.0151	806.5	0.0682	533	–0.0674	314.5	–0.0994	277	0.0613
Nov–09	2150.0	–0.0293	902.4	0.0225	145.2	0.0792	601.2	0.0505	245.7	–0.0683	333.3	0.0103	820.9	0.0179	505.4	–0.0518	329.3	0.0471	289.1	0.0437
Average of the returns	"=average(C5:C17)"	0.0378		0.0172		0.0127		0.0125		–0.0245		0.0137		0.0403		0.0153		–0.0033		–0.0099
Variance	"=var(C5:C17)"	0.0200		0.0401		0.0034		0.0030		0.0376		0.0027		0.0054		0.0082		0.0061		0.0116
Standard Deviation	"=sqrt(C19)"	0.1416		0.2001		0.0587		0.0550		0.1940		0.0521		0.0736		0.0903		0.0778		0.1076
Annualized Standard D	"=C20*sqrt(12)"	0.4905		0.6933		0.2035		0.1905		0.6719		0.1806		0.2550		0.3129		0.2695		0.3728

FIGURE 7.6 Variance–covariance matrix.

Variance-Covariance Matrix

	Anglo Americ	Xstrata Plc	Vodafone	BP PLC	3i Group PLC	Sainsbury	AMEC PLC	British Sky Brooadcasting	BAE Systems	Rexam PLC
Anglo American PLC	0.0183751	0.0016004	0.0001351	0.0051124	0.0114329	0.00067768	0.002886794	0.000745303	–0.002161866	0.00827488
Xstrata Plc	0.0016004	0.0367170	–0.0005996	–0.0000966	0.0033764	–0.00390954	0.0060733	0.004615458	0.000280971	–0.001798442
Vodafone	0.0001351	–0.0005996	0.0031621	0.0010201	0.0009235	0.001712036	–0.001284677	0.00221064	0.001838828	0.001724885
BP PLC	0.0051124	–0.0000966	0.0010201	0.0027734	0.0031530	0.000166052	0.000821391	–0.000253439	–0.000093	0.003203338
3i Group PLC	0.0114329	0.0033764	0.0009235	0.0031530	0.0344860	–0.001286624	0.002118572	0.002036021	–0.003887171	0.00533076
Sainsbury	0.0006777	–0.0039095	0.0017120	0.0001661	–0.0012866	0.002491343	–0.000287598	0.002392041	0.001664671	0.001857334
AMEC PLC	0.0028868	0.0060733	–0.0012847	0.0008214	0.0021186	–0.0002876	0.004969076	0.001493338	0.000727453	0.001919352
British Sky Brooadcastin	0.0007453	0.0046155	0.0022106	–0.0002534	0.0020360	0.0023920	0.0014933	0.007479392	0.002050525	–0.00132888
BAE Systems	–0.0021619	0.0002810	–0.0000934	–0.0000934	–0.0038872	0.0016647	0.0007275	0.0020505	0.005548632	0.0022564
Rexam PLC	0.0082749	–0.0017984	0.0017249	0.0032033	0.0053308	0.0018573	0.0019194	–0.0013289	0.0022564	0.010618889

Variance-Covariance Matrix with weights

	Anglo Americ	Xstrata Plc	Vodafone	BP PLC	3i Group PLC	Sainsbury	AMEC PLC	British Sky Brooadcasting	BAE Systems	Rexam PLC	Subtotals
Anglo American PLC	0.0004134	0.0000240	0.0000010	0.0001534	0.0000857	7.11564E–06	5.62925E–05	1.67693E–05	–1.6214E–05	6.20616E–05	0.0008036
Xstrata Plc	0.0000240	0.0003672	–0.0000030	–0.0000019	0.0000169	–2.73668E–05	7.89529E–05	6.92319E–05	1.40485E–06	–8.99221E–06	0.0005164
Vodafone	0.0000010	–0.0000030	0.0000079	0.0000102	0.0000023	3.2324E–06	–8.3504E–06	1.65798E–05	4.59707E–06	4.31221E–06	0.0000388
BP PLC	0.0001534	–0.0000019	0.0000102	0.0001109	0.0000315	4.41414E–05	2.13562E–05	–7.60317E–06	–9.34232E–07	3.20334E–05	0.0003931
3i Group PLC	0.0000857	0.0000169	0.0000023	0.0000315	0.0000862	0.000120701	1.37707E–05	1.52702E–05	–9.71793E–06	1.33269E–05	0.0003760
Sainsbury	0.0000071	–0.0000274	0.0000032	0.0000441	0.0001207	–6.30446E–06	–2.61714E–06	2.51164E–05	5.82635E–06	6.50067E–06	0.0001763
AMEC PLC	0.0000563	0.0000790	–0.0000084	0.0000214	0.0000138	–2.61714E–06	8.39774E–05	2.91201E–05	4.72845E–06	1.24758E–05	0.0002897
British Sky Brooadcastin	0.0000168	0.0000692	0.0000166	–0.0000076	0.0000153	2.51164E–05	2.91201E–05	0.000168286	1.53789E–05	–9.9666E–06	0.0003382
BAE Systems	–0.0000162	0.0000014	0.0000046	–0.0000009	–0.0000097	5.82635E–06	4.72845E–06	1.53789E–05	1.38716E–05	5.641E–06	0.0000246
Rexam PLC	0.0000621	–0.0000090	0.0000043	0.0000320	0.0000133	6.50067E–06	1.24758E–05	–9.9666E–06	5.641E–06	2.65472E–05	0.0001439
									Total (variance PF)		0.0031007
									Standard Deviation PF		0.055683517
									Annualized Standard Deviation PF		0.192893362

FIGURE 7.6 *(Continued)*

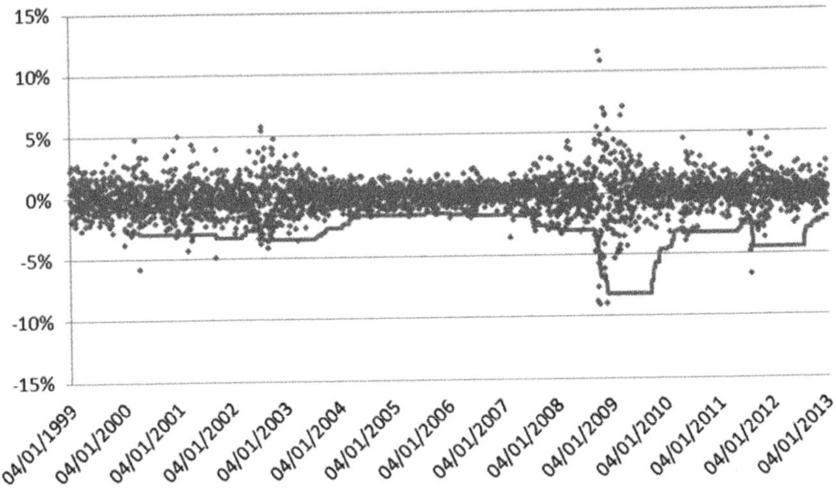

FIGURE 7.7 Historical VaR.

Example: We simply get the daily returns of the S&P 500 index since January 1, 2009 and we use a 99% confidence level.

Ticker:	SPX Index
Start date:	01/01/1999
End date:	22/01/2013
Period type:	D
Confidence:	99%
Number of periods:	250

On January 22, 2012 the historical VaR is, for example, −2%.

Let us use another simplified example to illustrate this.

Let us consider that we have 30 weekly past returns (in percentage): 2, 4, 7, 10, 24, 15, −3, −6, −10, −12, 6, 13, 3, 17, −5, 1, −11, −16, 1, 1, 3, −1, −7, −22, −30, −13, −9, −8, −1, 4 (Figure 7.8). By simply rearranging them from the smallest to the highest and considering that our goal is to compute a weekly VaR at 90% of confidence, by looking at the losses and isolating the 3 lowest returns (10% ∗ 30 = 3), we have identified our VaR, which is -16.

Pros and Cons of This Method. This method is a very expensive and time-consuming calculation technique. In addition, no prior assumptions about the shape of the distribution are needed.

On the other hand, this simplicity of implementation causes many limitations. And what can be considered as an advantage can quickly turn into a disadvantage. Indeed, the history must be sufficiently large compared to the horizon of the VaR and its trust level, but not enough to ensure that the law of

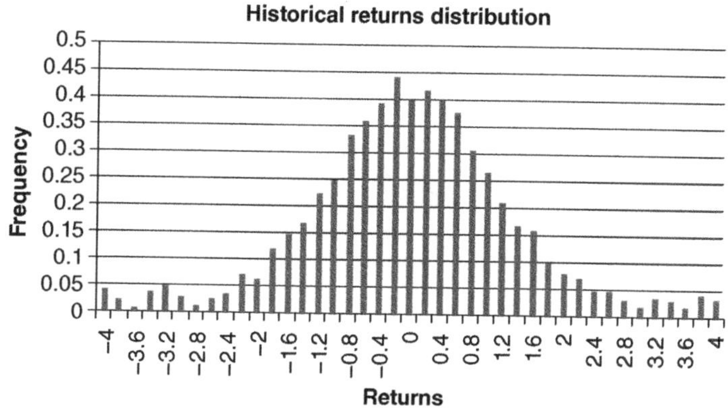

FIGURE 7.8 Historical returns distribution.

probability has not changed over the period. Another negative point, is that, this method is unsuitable for derivatives.

7.4.3 MONTE CARLO SIMULATION

As for historical computation, the Monte Carlo computation will not rely on defined returns distribution to estimate future returns; but instead of using past returns, they will be simulated.

The Monte Carlo approach (as long as the selected model is reliable and appropriate) is the most advanced method of VaR computation since the portfolio will be fully evaluated many numbers of times by using different values (randomly generated) for the main valuation factors of the instruments in the portfolio.

More than being a model as such, the Monte Carlo approach is more about an algorithmic approach that is here applied to the assessment of the VaR. Actually, the Monte Carlo concept can be used to evaluate many different types of measures by using a loop generating a high number of different random values aiming at evaluating a specific output.

Starting from an initial value of the portfolio, a high number of paths (usually several thousand) are simulated in order to generate the distribution of simulated returns that will be finally used to assess the VaR as done for the historical computation.

Figure 7.9 illustrates how the returns distribution is obtained from a high number of simulations.

Instead of using historical data to build an empirical P&L distribution, it may be more convenient to simulate the movements in underlying assets and risk factors from now until some future point in time (the "risk horizon" of the model). Taking their current values as starting points, thousands of possible values of the underlying assets and risk factors over the next h days are generated

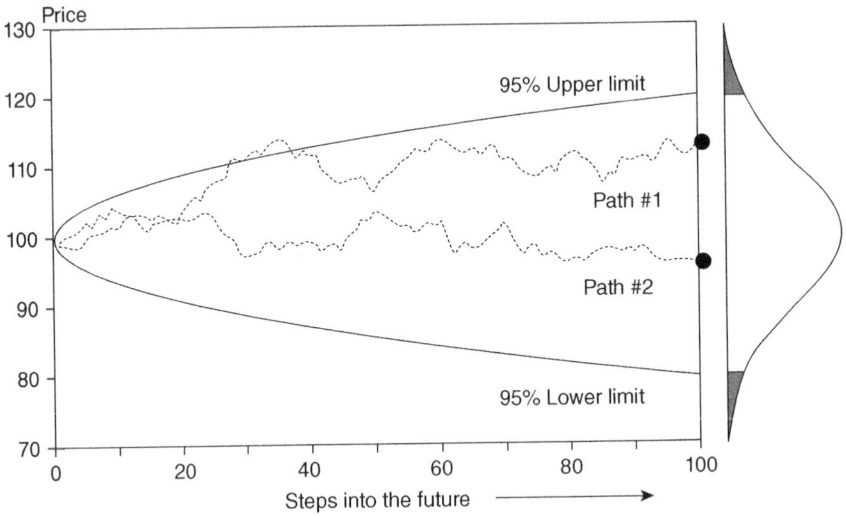

FIGURE 7.9 Monte Carlo returns simulation—"value-at-risk"[9].

using Monte Carlo methods. This very large set of scenarios is then used to obtain thousands of possible values for the portfolio in *h* days' time, and a histogram of the differences between these and the current portfolio value is obtained. As with the historical simulation method, the VaR measure is simply the lower percentile of this distribution.

The structured Monte Carlo simulation is used for market risk management. The extended elements and risk types are described in the next paragraphs.

Volatilities and the correlation of historical time series for interest rates, FX rates, prices and industry indices are used to generate correlated scenarios for future market development. We calculate the positions in the analysis portfolio in consecutive order on the basis of the scenarios. The result series thus generated represents a price distribution that indicates the risks by means of a confidence value.

This "Monte Carlo simulation" allows a more precise evaluation of market risks regarding non-linear instruments, such as options on shares, bonds, and futures. The variance of the option price distribution results in significant differences in VaR for long and short positions in comparison to the linear variance–covariance method.

The structured Monte Carlo simulation is characterized by the main features and evaluation principles given in Figure 7.10.

The evaluation system of the Monte Carlo simulation consists of the following steps:

[9]Jorion, Philippe, *Financial Risk Manager Handbook*, fourth edition, Wiley Finance, Hoboken, NJ, 2007, Part 3, Figure 12-1.

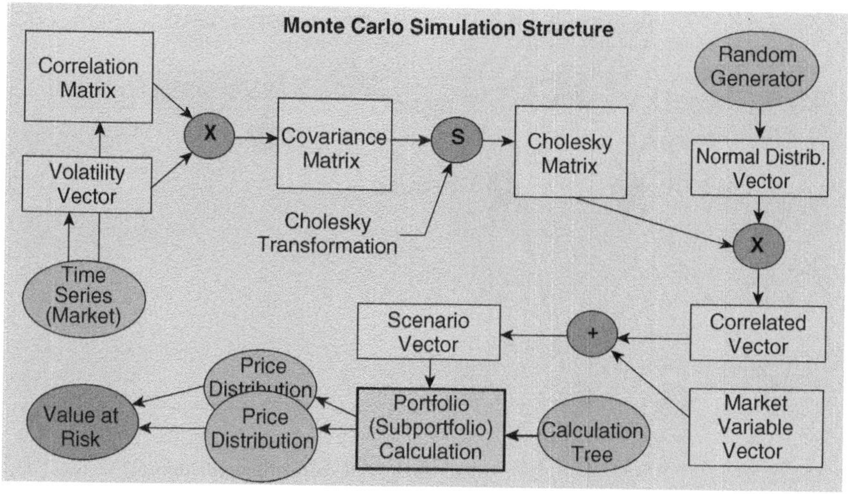

FIGURE 7.10 Structured Monte Carlo simulation.

1. The covariance matrix (*C*) results from the multiplication of the volatility vector (*V*) by the correlation matrix (*R*).
2. We create the Cholesky matrix (*A*) by means of the covariance matrix (*C*); this means $A \times A' = C$, where A' represents the transposed matrix (*A*).
3. The random generator generates normally (standard) distributed, independent random numbers (0.1) for each market variable—that is, expected value = 0 and standard deviation = 1. The generator generates a sufficient number (e.g., 10,000) of vectors (*D*), where the correlation between the series of random numbers for the market variables equals 0, and uses corrections to improve the quality of the random series.
4. Multiply each vector (*D*) by the Cholesky matrix, correlate the random series, and add the volatilities at the same time, thus obtaining the correlated vectors (*B*) as a result.
5. This module places the vectors (*B*) onto the vector of the market variables (interest rates, prices, indices, FX rates) and generates scenarios for each Monte Carlo run. A portfolio calculation is performed for each scenario, applying a tree-like evaluation structure that represents the portfolio price.
6. Steps 3–5 are repeated for all random vectors, which generates a resulting price series accordingly. This price series represents the portfolio distribution.
7. The prices being sorted, the risk can be assessed via confidence value (e.g., 5% of the market risk) on the basis of the portfolio distribution.
8. Most of risk engines enable a linear aggregation of price distributions in various portfolio simulations by storing the price series after each simulation and adding them for each simulation run. The resulting price series represents the aggregated portfolio distribution.

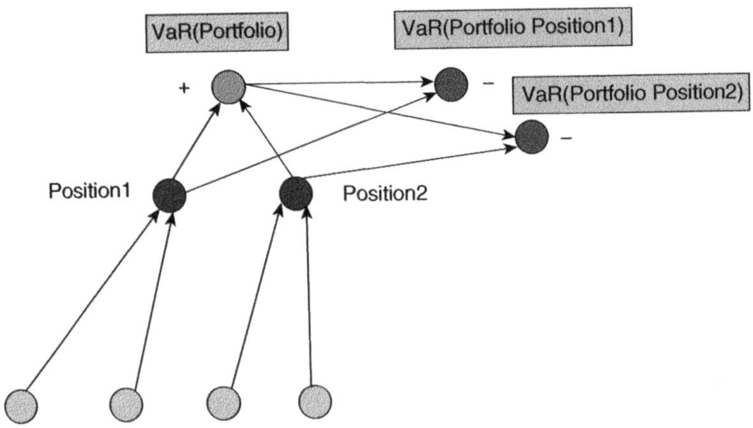

FIGURE 7.11 Incremental VaR calculation structure.

7.4.4 INCREMENTAL VaR

The (IVaR) of a position in relation to a portfolio can be understood as the risk magnitude the position adds to the portfolio. In other words, IVaR reflects how far the portfolio VaR would change if a particular position was sold. IVaR can be formally defined as the difference between the VaR of the entire portfolio and the VaR of the portfolio without the position (Figure 7.11).

The IVaR therefore represents the change of the portfolio VaR if an entire position was removed or if a new position was added. This is expressed symbolically by the following:

$$\text{IVaR} = \text{VaR}(\text{Portfolio}) - \text{VaR}(\text{Portfolio} - \text{position})$$

Additional calculation nodes in the portfolio evaluation tree can be used to compute the IVaR.

7.4.5 MARGINAL VaR

The marginal VaR (MVaR) indicates the potential effect of a purchase (buy transaction) or sale (sell transaction) of a relatively small percentage (e.g., 1%) of a position in relation to the portfolio risk. When restructuring a portfolio, for example, it is often necessary to use part of a position to reduce or increase the value instead of selling or purchasing the entire position. MVaR is a statistical parameter that provides information about the sensitivity of the VaR toward single position changes in the portfolio.

The MVaR symbolically reflects the change in the portfolio VaR in case of a minor change in the position (Figure 7.12):

$$\text{MVaR}_{t0,t} = \text{VaR}[\text{Portfolio} + 0.01 * \text{position}] - \text{VaR}(\text{Portfolio})$$

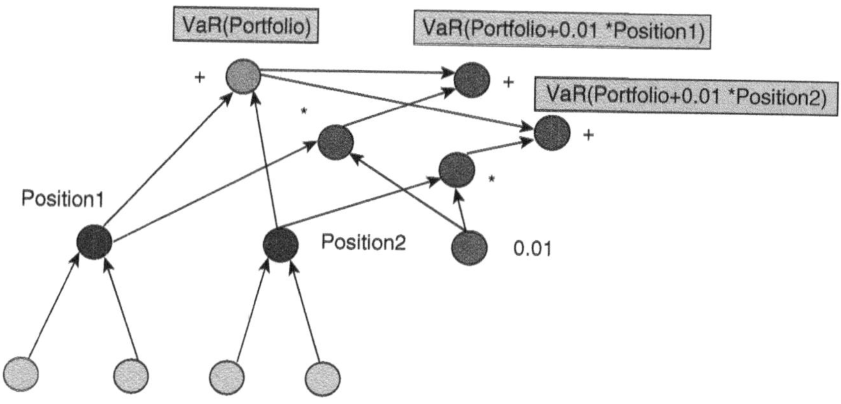

FIGURE 7.12 Marginal VaR calculation structure.

7.4.6 COMPONENT VaR

The following axioms must be fulfiled for the component VaR (CVaR) calculation of a position:

- The portfolio VaR should equal the sum of all CVaRs for all positions.
- If a position is removed from a portfolio, the CVaR should approximately reflect the change of the portfolio VaR.
- The CVaR should be negative for hedge positions—that is, positions used as hedge instruments.

One possibility by which the CVaR of a position can be calculated is to weight the IVaR of this position against the VaR weighting of the positions in relation to the portfolio VaR:

$$x = \text{VaR(Portfolio)/SUM(position}[i]\cdot\text{IVaR}, i = 0, \ldots, N)$$
$$\text{position}[i]\cdot\text{CVaR} = \text{position}[i]\cdot\text{IVaR} * x, i = 0, \ldots, N$$

After the portfolio division into subportfolios, each subportfolio CVaR should represent the sum of all position CVaRs.

7.4.7 EXPECTED SHORTFALL

The CVaR (expected shortfall, VaR-ES) is a subadditive risk that statistically indicates the extent of the average loss for all realizations to the left of the confidence level, thus offering a better presentation of risks in the case of flat risk distributions around the confidence level. Mathematically, one can assess the expected value (average) of all realizations that fulfill the condition of being below the confidence level (Figure 7.13).

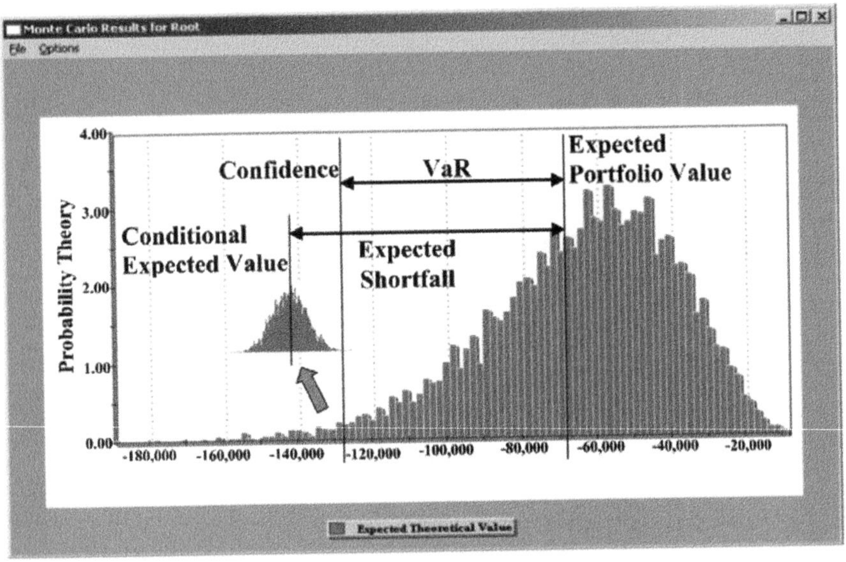

FIGURE 7.13 Expected shortfall calculation.

7.4.8 VaR MODELS SUMMARY

The variance–covariance model is the fastest; however, it relies heavily on several assumptions about the distribution of market data and linear approximation of the portfolio. It is probably the best method for quick estimates of VaR for a portfolio made of linear assets. We should be very careful when using this method for a nonlinear portfolio, however, especially in the case of high convexity in options or bonds.

The historical simulation method is useful when the amount of data is not very large and we do not have enough information about the profit and loss distribution. It is usually very time-consuming, but its main advantage is that it catches all recent market crashes. This feature is very important for risk measurement.

The Monte Carlo simulation method is very slow, but it is probably the most powerful method.

Figure 7.14 briefly describes each approach and its use.[10]

As we have seen, VaR is not a perfect measure and therefore it needs to be complemented by appropriate stress testing. This is appropriate for sophisticated funds and considers possible future events. It is important that the fund managers and the board of the UCITS understand the effects on a portfolio of sudden market changes such as price, volatility, and correlations that are outside the norm. Each fund's situation should then be analyzed in the event of sudden or

[10]Source RiskMetrics Group, *Managing risk—Lesson: Three Methodologies for Calculating VaR*, available at: http://www.riskmetrics.com/publications/techdoc.html.

Type	Description	Use
Parametric	Estimates VaR with an equation that specifies parameters (for example, volatility and correlation) as input	Accurate for traditional assets and linear derivatives, but less accurate for nonlinear derivatives
Monte Carlo	Estimates VaR by simulating random scenarios and revaluing instruments in the portfolio	Appropriate for all types of instruments, linear and nonlinear
Historical	Estimates VaR by reliving history; we take actual historical rates and revalue a portfolio for each change in the market	Appropriate for all types of instruments, linear and nonlinear

FIGURE 7.14 **Summary table of VaR models.**

unpredictable changes. Policies and procedures have to be reviewed after reacting to extreme situations, and senior management should be involved.

Whether evaluating a new model or assessing the accuracy of an existing model, a VaR back-testing policy should be adopted to validate them. Steps should be taken to identify the source of errors if some VaR estimates appear to be outside the confidence band expectations.

7.4.9 MAPPING OF COMPLEX INSTRUMENTS

"Mapping" complex financial derivatives consists of inserting the reference data corresponding to such an instrument into the risk calculation platform. The objective is to replicate its payoff function and at the same time preserve the correct level of exposure to the underlying risk factors.

A very complex structured derivative has to be decomposed in more elementary "pieces" before being mapped. Such pieces still correspond to financial instruments (cash, bonds, plain vanilla options, etc.) for which an evaluation function is known and a pricing process can be established.

It is very important to identify which ones are the relevant risk factors for a given instrument, since not all risk factors have a direct or indirect impact on portfolio value. Once the set of relevant risk factors has been identified, it is possible to compute the so-called "sensitivity measures," which indicate the magnitude of the variation in the price of the instrument due to an incremental movement of the relevant risk factor. Examples of sensitivities include the Greeks, duration, and convexity.

The risk (or volatility) of an instrument corresponds to the degree of dispersion of its price around an average value (the "mean"). This means that it is of paramount importance to have a way to price all the "sub-constituents" of the complex instrument and that the single volatilities can be "put together" in order to determine the risk of the overall instrument.

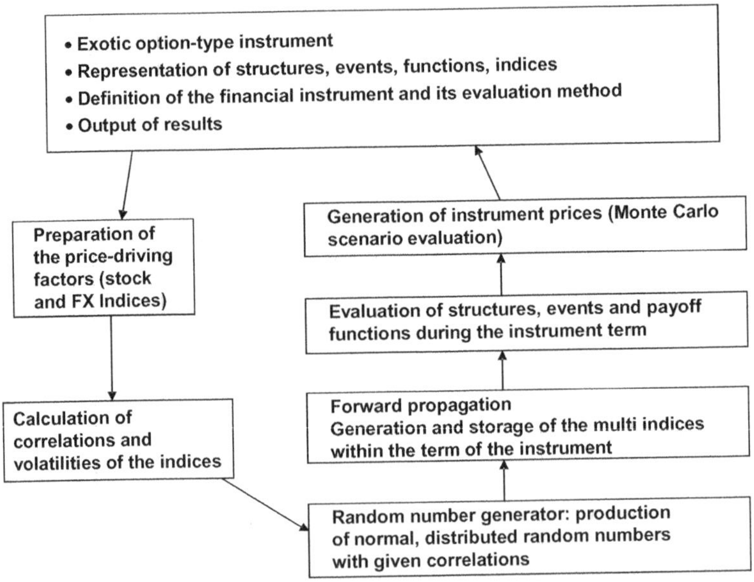

FIGURE 7.15 Process for mapping complex products.

Once the pricing functions have been identified, in order to compute the volatility of the instrument, it is necessary to add historical data corresponding to the underlying risk factors to the pricing function. If the historical data are not available (i.e., due to initial public offerings or lack of information), it is necessary to produce simulated paths of prices/returns satisfying a given distribution via a multifactor Monte Carlo simulation process.

For very complex structures that show a strongly nonlinear payoff function, use of the Monte Carlo approach is practically unavoidable.

7.4.10 CORNISH–FISHER VaR

The Cornish–Finsher VaR is expressed as

$$\mathrm{VaR}_{\mathrm{CF}} = \frac{\Phi^{*}\sigma}{\sqrt{252}} \tag{7.2}$$

where σ is the annualized model volatility estimate standard normal inverse cumulative distribution and Φ^* is a function—adjusted for skewness and kurtosis [see Eq. (7.3)]. The difference between this and the parametric VaR is the adjustment made to Φ for skewness and kurtosis as given by Eq. (7.3) In addition to this, the mean of the distribution is incorporated. The addition of the higher moments allows the Cornish–Fisher method to capture non-normal properties of the returns distribution; however it should be noted that the expansion is only valid for modest departures from "normality" [0].

$$\Phi^* = \Phi + \tfrac{1}{6}(\Phi^2 - 1)S + \tfrac{1}{24}(\Phi^3 - 3\Phi)K - \tfrac{1}{36}(2\Phi^3 - 5\Phi)S^2 \tag{7.3}$$

where Φ is the standard normal inverse cumulative distribution function (evaluated at a probability of 99%, this equates to 2.33), S is the sample skewness of the returns distribution, and K represents excess sample kurtosis of the returns distribution.

Validity of the Cornish–Fisher Adjustment. The Cornish–Fisher adjustment approximates the quantiles of a distribution using the higher moments, skewness, and kurtosis. This approximation is only valid for a given range of both skewness and kurtosis.

7.4.11 EXTREME VALUE THEORY (EVT)

The tail distribution of the historical simulation data is fitted to a generalized Pareto distribution, which has the following functional form [0]:

$$G_{\alpha,\beta}(x) = \begin{cases} 1 - \left(1 + \dfrac{\alpha x}{\beta}\right)^{-1/\alpha} \\ 1 - \exp\left(-\dfrac{x}{\beta}\right) \end{cases} \tag{7.4}$$

where α is the shape parameter and β is the scale parameter. Once α and β have been found, the VaR is computed as

$$\mathrm{VaR}_{\mathrm{EVT}} = u + \frac{\beta}{\alpha}\left(\left(\frac{n}{N}(1-q)\right)^{-\alpha} - 1\right) \tag{7.5}$$

where q is the percentile for the VaR (e.g., 0.99), n is the total number of observations in the simulated history distribution, and N is the number of losses in the simulated history distribution greater than the historical simulation VaR.

FURTHER READING

Basak, S., and Shapiro, A., Value-at-Risk-based risk management: Optimal policies and asset prices, *Review of Financial Studies*, **14**, 2001, pp. 371–405.

Bayes, T., An essay toward solving a problem in the doctrine of chances, in *Philosophical Transactions*, Royal Society, London, 1764.

Bohlmann, G., Poterin du Motel, H., Technique de l'assurance sur la vie, in J., Molk, *Encyclopédie des Sciences MathématiquesI*, volume 4, Paris, Reed Jacques Gabray, 1911.

Borch, K. H., A note on uncertainty and indifference curves, *Review of Economic Studies*, no. **1**, 1969.

Chambers, S. P., Fluctuations in capital and the demand for money, *Review of Economic Studies*, **2**, October 1934.

Condorcet, J. A. N., Assurances maritimes, in *Arithmétique Politique – Textes Rares ou Inédits*, Paris, INED, 1994.

Daston, L. J., *Classical Probability in the Enlightenment*, Princeton, N.J., Princeton University Press, 1988.

de Moivre, A., *The Doctrine of Chances*, third edition, London, W. Pearson, 1756.

Dowd, K., *Beyond Value at Risk: The New Science of Risk Management*, Wiley, Hoboken, NJ, 1998.

Hicks, G. A., History of Value-at-Risk: 1922–1998, Contingency Analysis, available at 1934: http://129.3.20.41/eps/mhet/papers/0207/0207001.pdf (accessed 08 March 2010), 2002.

Hicks, J. R., Application of mathematical methods to the theory of risk, *Econometrica*, **2**, March 1934.

Jorion, P., *Value at Risk: The New Benchmark for Controlling Market Risk*, Irwin, Ontario, Canada, 1997.

Jorion, P., How informative are value-at-risk disclosures?, *The Accounting Review*, 77, pp. 911–932, 2002.

Laplace, P. S., *Théorie Analytique des Probabilités*, Gauthier-Villars, Paris, 1812, pp.432.

Laplace, P. S., Mémoires sur les probabilités, *Mémoires de l'Académie Royale des Sciences*, 1781, pp. 227–232.

Marschak, J., Money and the theory of assets, *Econometrica*, **6**, October 1938.

Rieucau, J. N., Les enterprises ou les hommes s'exposent à une perte, dans la vue d'un profit – Condorcet et l'heritage de D'Alembert, *Revue Économique*, **49**(5), 1998, pp. 1365–1505.

Roy, A. D., Review of portfolio selection, *American Economic Review*, **51**, 1961.

Wicksell, K., *Interest and Prices*, English translation of *Geldzins und Güterpreise* (1898), trans. R.F. Kahn, Macmillan, London, 1936.

CHAPTER EIGHT

Financial Derivative Instruments

One of the differences between UCITS III/IV and prior regulations is its more liberal scope for the use of derivatives—listed or OTC derivatives. The following pages present the most popular financial derivatives being used in funds managed under UCITS. This list is not exhaustive but constitutes the most commonly employed financial instruments that also allow replication of alternative investment strategies. It also worth noting that as part of the next coming AIFM Directive, alternatives may also have to measure leverage using commitment approach. Thus the following pages may also be interesting in the perspective of managing alternative funds.

Listing all financial derivatives including very complex OTC instruments would be a hard task. We cannot list all exotic derivatives that can be used because the financial industry demonstrates a strong innovation capacity in that respect. We have limited ourselves to the most common derivatives that allow us to develop alternative strategies under UCITS (Table 8.1).

8.1 Introducing Financial Derivatives Instruments

8.1.1 SWAP

A swap is a form of derivative in which two parties agree to exchange streams of payment at fixed intervals according to terms specified by the contract. The payments are either at fixed rates of return or indexed rates of return relative to a notional value. The most common type of swap is an *interest rate swap*.

In an interest rate swap, one party agrees to pay a fixed rate of interest in return for receiving a floating rate from the other party. Swaps can be used to hedge existing portfolio positions (by exchanging the return of an asset for a less risky rate of return) or to speculate on the return spread between the return of two payment streams. Other types of swaps that are commonly used are:

Handbook of Market Risk, First Edition. Christian Szylar.

TABLE 8.1 **List of the Main Financial Derivatives**

Forward:	Currency forward
Difference:	Contracts for difference
Futures:	General
	Equity future
	Equity index futures
	Bond index futures
	Currency futures
	Interest rate futures
	Bond futures
Options:	Currency options
	Equity index options
	Bond index options
	Equity option
	Bond options
	Interest rate options
	Options on bond futures
	Options on interest rate futures
Swaps:	Currency swaps
	Interest rate swap
	Inflation swap
	Total return swap
	Asset swap
	Index swap
	Swaption
	Credit default swap (also considered as a credit derivative)
	Spread lock
	Other credit derivatives
	Collateralized debt obligation
Warrant:	Equity warrants
	Bond warrants
	Fixed index warrants
Convertible:	Convertible equity
	Convertible bonds

- *Currency Swaps.* Where the parties exchange cash flows denominated in different currencies.
- *Total Return Swaps.* Where one party exchanges a cash flow indexed to a non-money market asset, i.e., an equity index in exchange for an interest rate; and
- *Swaptions.* An option on a swap—typically giving the holder the right to enter into swap at a future point in time at a prespecified level of interest on both payment streams of the swap.

8.1.1.1 Total Return Swap (TRS). Total return swap is a contract in which one party receives interest payments on a reference asset plus any capital gains and losses over the payment period. The other party receives a specified fixed or floating cash flow unrelated to the credit-worthiness of the reference asset, especially where the payments are based on the same notional amount. The reference asset may be any asset, index, or basket of assets.

Total return swap, then, allows one party to derive the economic benefit of owning an asset without putting that asset on its balance sheet and allows the other party (which does retain that asset on its balance sheet) to buy protection against loss in its value.

The essential difference between a total return swap and a credit default swap (CDS) is that the latter provides protection not against loss in asset value but against specific credit events. In a sense, a total return swap is not a credit derivative at all in the sense that a CDS is. A total return swap is funding-cost arbitrage.

Total return swaps are most commonly used with equity indices, single stocks, bonds, and defined portfolios of loans and mortgages.

8.1.1.2 Credit-Default Swap (CDS). The ability to take outright short positions has an important implication for asset managers of credit in particular due to the emergence in the past few years of a specific class of credit derivative called a CDS. A CDS allows managers to:

- Take advantage of their analysts' ability to identify deteriorating credits and generate positive returns where previously their only option was not to own the issue and thereby not incur a loss.
- Protect the portfolio against volatility and potential spread widening by buying protection on index products.
- Use a variety of additional strategies, such as selling protection against one index and buying protection against another.

Table 8.2 lists the type of existing CDS coverage as available under iTraxx, the brand name for the family of credit defaut swap index products. A CDS is a swap designed to transfer the credit exposure of fixed income products between parties. It is the most widely used credit derivative. It is an agreement between a protection buyer and a protection seller, whereby the buyer pays a periodic fee in return for a contingent payment by the seller upon a credit event[1] (such as a certain default) happening in the reference entity. Most CDS contracts are physically settled, where during a credit event the protection seller must pay the par amount of the contract against the protection buyer's obligation to deliver a bond or loan of the name against which protection is being sold.

A CDS is often used like an insurance policy or hedge for the holder of debt; but because there is no requirement to actually hold any asset or suffer a

[1]Default payments are triggered by "credit events." Credit events are strictly defined by an *International Swaps and Derivatives Association* agreement (2003). The standard credit events for corporate names are: bankruptcy, obligation acceleration, obligation default, failure to pay, repudiation/moratorium, and restructuring.

TABLE 8.2 iTraxx Credit Default Swap Products

Family	Type	Index Name	Number of Entities	Description
Europe	Benchmark Indices	iTraxx Europe	125	Most actively traded names in the six months prior to the index roll
		iTraxx Europe HiVol	30	Highest spread (riskiest) names from iTraxx Eruope index
		iTraxx Europe	50	Sub-investment grade names
	Sector Indices	iTraxx Non-Financials	100	Nonfinancial names
		iTraxx Financials Senior	25	Senior subordination financial names
		iTraxx Financials	25	Junior subordination financial names
		iTraxx TMT	20	Telecommunications, media, and technology
		iTraxx Industrials	20	Industrial names
		iTraxx Energy	20	Energy industry names
		iTraxx Consumers	30	Manufacturers of consumer products
		iTraxx Autos	10	Automobile industry names
North America	Benchmark Indices	CDX North America Investment Grade	125	Most activity traded names in the six months prior to the index roll
		CDX North America High Yield	100	Highest spread (riskiest) names from iTraxx Europe index
		CDX North America Crossover	35	Sub-investment grade names
Asia	Benchmark Indices	iTraxx Asia es-Japan	70	50 Investment grades and 20 non-investment grade entities
		iTraxx Japan	50	Most liquid traded investment grade entities
		iTraxx Australia	25	Most liquid traded investment grade entities on the Australian Stock Exchange

loss, a CDS is not actually insurance. The typical term of a CDS contract is five years; although being an over-the-counter derivative, almost any maturity is possible.

Example: XYZ plc credit spreads are currently trading at 120 bps over the benchmark government bond for 5-year maturities and 195 bps over for 10-year maturities. A portfolio manager hedges a $10 million holding for 10-years paper by purchasing the following credit default swap, written on the 5-year bond. This edge protects for the first five years of the holding and, in the event of XYZ's credit spread widening, will increase in value and may be sold on or before expiry at a profit. The 10-year bond holding also earns 75 bps over the short-term paper for the portfolio manager.

Term: 5 years

Reference credit: XYZ plc 5-year bond

Credit event: The business day following occurrence of specified credit event

Default payment: Nominal value of bond × (100 – price of bond after credit event)

Swap premium: 3.35%

Assume that midway into the life of the swap there is a technical default on XYZ plc.

8.1.1.3 First to Default (FTD). The protection buyer is covered against the first default among a basket of issuers (typically the basket ranges between 5 and 10). FTD are also sometimes called basket default swaps. FTD offers investors enhanced returns on the credit risk of a basket of corporate institutions. Detailed below is a simple explanation of the mechanics of FTDs, highlighted with some recent examples. FTD notes are similar in structure to the credit linked notes. The key difference is that instead of taking the credit exposure of a single company, here the investor takes the credit exposure on the first company to default within a specified basket of companies (as defined by an underlying reference portfolio). In exchange for taking this credit risk, the investor receives regular coupon payments.

The holder of an FTD contract buys protection against the credit risk on a basket of several entities for a notional (N) and a certain timeframe until maturity. Investors buying such securities pay a premium on a regular basis until maturity of the contract or the first default on one of the reference entities. In exchange, the seller of the protection guarantees until maturity that the buyer will recover the notional of the contract if there is a default on the reference entity. In the case of a default, the buyer stops paying the premium, and the seller of the protection either delivers $(1 - R)*N$, where R is defined as the recovery rate (cash settlement), or receives a notional N of individual deliverable obligation from the buyer of the defaulted reference entity (physical settlement).

Pricing. Pricing models for basket-based products are continually evolving. The underlying pricing model for FTDs is based on the impact that time has on the implicit default probability. This model carries out Monte Carlo simulations against different risk scenarios to arrive at the most appropriate spread for the basket. The scenarios are represented by the number and timing of defaults.

In simple terms, the premium to buy protection using an FTD basket is a percentage of the sum of the five individual credit default swap spreads. Underpinning FTDs is the notion that since it is extremely unlikely that all five names in one basket will default, an investor can buy protection on five names with an FTD basket for less than using individual credit default swap trades.

As a result, the more closely correlated the names within the FTD, the smaller the percentage of the total sum. For example, a basket of five Korean credits, which are considered strongly correlated, may cost 40% of the sum of the spreads since if one defaults, then the others are likely to follow and so the protection is less effective than for an uncorrelated basket.

8.1.1.4 Collateralized Debt Obligation (CDO). The protection buyer is protected on a tranche of loss among a CDS portfolio (typically between 50 and 100 names). Each tranche can be more or less risky, and each one is subject to a rating. For example, a CDO might issue four classes of securities designated as

1. Senior debt
2. Mezzanine debt
3. Subordinate debt
4. Equity

Each class protects the ones senior to it from losses on the underlying portfolio. The sponsor of a CDO usually sets the size of the senior class so that it can attain triple-A ratings. Likewise, the sponsor generally designs the other classes so that they achieve successively lower ratings. In a way, the rating agencies are really the ones who determine the sizes of the classes for a given portfolio.

Historically, CDOs were created to provide more liquidity in the economy They allow banks and corporations to sell off debt, which frees up more capital to invest or loan. The creation of CDOs is one reason why the US economy has been so robust in the last five years but at the same time also one of the main reasons for the 2007 financial crisis. However, the downside of CDOs is that they allow the originators of the loans to avoid having to collect on them when they become due, since the loans are now owned by other investors. This may make them less disciplined in adhering to strict lending standards.

Another downside is that CDOs are so complex that often the buyers are not really sure what they are buying. They often rely on their trust in the bank selling the CDO without doing enough personal research to be sure the package is really worth the price they are paying.

The opaqueness and complexity of CDOs can cause a market panic if something happens to make sellers lose their trust in the product. This then makes the CDOs difficult to resell. This helped cause the 2007 banking liquidity crisis.

A CDO is a transaction that transfers the credit risk on a reference portfolio of assets. The reference portfolio in a synthetic CDO is made up of credit default swaps.

8.1.1.5 Credit Linked Note (CLN). A credit linked note is issued under the form of a bond. It is a funded credit derivative. As opposed to an unfunded credit derivative, such as a default swap, credit-linked notes imply an investment in the cash instrument. These are notes given by one issuer (usually a bank), which has a credit risk exposure to a second issuer (most of the time a corporation, which is known as the "reference issuer"). These notes pay an enhanced coupon, typically linked to LIBOR (London interbank offered rate), to the investor for taking on the added credit risk of the second reference issuer. If the note defaults, the investor stands to lose some or all of his or her coupon income and principal. In this case, the investor is the protection seller and the bank is the protection buyer.

8.1.1.6 Currency Swap. A currency swap is a foreign exchange agreement between two parties to exchange a given amount of one currency for another and, after a specified period of time, to give back the original amounts swapped.

Currency swaps can be negotiated for a variety of maturities up to at least 10 years. Unlike a back-to-back loan, a currency swap is not considered to be a loan by U.S. accounting laws and thus it is not reflected on a company's balance sheet. A swap is considered to be a foreign exchange transaction (short leg) plus an obligation to close the swap (far leg) being a forward contract.

Currency swaps are often combined with interest rate swaps. For example, one company would seek to swap a cash flow for their fixed-rate debt denominated in U.S. dollars for a floating-rate debt denominated in euros. This is especially common in Europe where companies "shop" for the cheapest debt regardless of its denomination and then seek to exchange it for the debt in the desired currency.

Example: Company A and company B, respectively a U.S. firm and a European firm, enter into a five-year currency swap for $50 million. Let's assume the exchange rate at the time is $1.25 per euro (i.e., the dollar is worth €0.80). First, the firms will exchange principals. So, company A pays $50 million, and company B pays €40 million.

Let's say the agreed-upon dollar-denominated interest rate is 8.25% and the euro-denominated interest rate is 3.5%, and both companies make payments annually, beginning one year from the exchange of the principal.

Hence, company A pays €40 million * 3.50% = €1,400,000 to company B, which will pay company A $50 million * 8.25% = $4,125,000.

If, at the one-year mark, the exchange rate is $1.40 per euro, company B's payment equals $1,960,000 and company A will pay the difference ($4,125,000 – $1,960,000 = $2,165,000).

Finally, at the end of the swap, the parties re-exchange the original principal amounts. These principal payments are unaffected by exchange rates at the time.

8.1.1.7 Swaption. A swaption is a financial instrument granting the owner an option to enter into an interest rate swap. A swaption gives the buyer the right but not the obligation to enter into a swap. There are two types of swaption contracts: "a payer swaption" or "a receiver swaption." A payer swaption gives the owner of the swaption the right to enter into a swap where he or she pays the fixed leg and receives the floating leg. A receiver swaption gives the owner of the swaption the right to enter into a swap where he/she will receive the fixed leg, and pay the floating leg.

The buyer and seller of the swaption agree on:

- The strike rate
- Length of the option period (which usually ends on the starting date of the swap if swaption is exercised)
- The term of the swap
- Notional amount
- Amortization
- Frequency of settlement

Unlike ordinary swaps, a swaption not only hedges the buyer against downside risk, it also lets the buyer take advantage of any upside benefits. Like any other option, if the swaption is not exercised by maturity, it expires and is worthless.

If the strike rate of the swap is more favorable than the prevailing market swap rate, then the swaption will be exercised as detailed in the swaption agreement.

It is designed to give the holder the benefit of the agreed-upon strike rate if the market rates are higher, with the flexibility to enter into the current market swap rate if they are lower.

The converse is true if the holder of the swaption receives the fixed rate under the swap agreement.

There are three styles of swaptions. Each style reflects a different timeframe in which the option can be exercised.

In *American swaption*, the owner is allowed to enter the swap on any day that falls within a range of two dates.

In *Bermudan swaption*, the owner is allowed to enter the swap on a sequence of dates.

In *European swaption*, the owner is allowed to enter the swap on one specified date.

8.1.1.8 Variance Swap. A variance swap is a financial derivative whose payoff is equal to the difference between the square of annualized realized volatility (that is, the actual annual variance), σ^2 realized, of returns on the underlying price over that period and a fixed quantity, σ^2 strike, sometimes known as the variance strike; that is, in the above notation, the payoff is σ^2 realized − σ^2 strike. Effectively, it is a forward contract on the actual variance.

The actual annual variance is calculated based on a prespecified set of sampling points over the period. It does not coincide with the classic statistical definition of variance, but follows the usual market convention of not subtracting the mean.

The variance swap may be hedged and hence priced using a portfolio of European call and put options with weights inversely proportional to the square of strike.

The advantage of variance swaps is that they provide pure exposure to the variability of the underlying price, as opposed to call and put options which carry directional risk (delta).

The payout of a variance swap is often capped. It is market practice to determine the number of contract units as VegaNotational/$2\sigma_{\text{strike}}$ to approximate the payoff of a swap.

Closely related contracts include volatility swap, correlation swap, and gamma swap.

8.1.1.9 Contract for Difference (CFD). A contract for difference (or CFD) is a contract between two parties, buyer and seller, stipulating that the seller will pay the buyer the difference between the current value of an asset and its value at contract time (if the difference is negative, then the buyer pays the seller). Such a contract is an equity derivative that allows investors to speculate on share price movements, without the need for ownership of the underlying shares.

CFDs allow investors to take long or short positions and, unlike futures contracts, have no fixed expiry date or contract size. Trades are conducted on a leveraged basis with margins typically ranging from 1% to 30% of the notional value for CFDs on leading equities.

CFDs are currently available in listed and/or OTC markets.

As with any leveraged product, maximum exposure is not limited to the initial investment; it is possible to lose more than you put in. These risks are typically mitigated through use of stop orders and other risk reduction strategies (for the most risk averse, guaranteed stop-loss orders are available at the cost of an additional one-point premium on the position and/or an inflated commission on the trade).

CFDs allow a trader to go short or long on any position with a variable margin (set by the brokerage) that allows them to trade on margins of up to 5% (and sometimes 1%). Lack of appreciation for the sort of exposure that can be experienced from taking full advantage of such financing is hence a crucial reason that many CFD traders lose. A solid money management strategy, however, can allow a trader to take full advantage of CFDs to their benefit. The CFD broker or principal will always be required to mirror the underlying market valuation and, as a result, when risk management is applied, CFDs can be a solid trading tool.

Therefore, anyone approaching CFDs should always analyze what they could lose, as opposed to simply focusing on what they could gain.

Long Trade Example: A long trade is a position that is opened with a buy in the expectation that the share price will rise.

Vodafone is currently trading at 140.5 pence. Investor A believes that Vodafone is going to rise and places a trade to buy 10,000 shares as a CFD at 140.5 pence. The total value of the contract would be £14,050, but he would only need to pay an initial 10% deposit (initial margin) of £1405.

A week later, investor A's prediction is correct and Vodafone rises to 145.0 pence, and he decides to closes his position. By selling 10,000 Vodafone CFDs at 145p, he will make a profit on the trade of:

Opening level: 140.5 pence
Closing level: 145.0 pence
Difference: 4.50 pence
Profit on trade: 4.5 × 10,000 = £450.00

8.1.2 THE FORWARD CONTRACT

A forward contract is a form of OTC that obliges one party to purchase a good from another party at a fixed future date for a price and currency specified in the terms of the contract. This is in contrast to a spot contract, which is an agreement to buy or sell an asset today. Forwards are frequently used to hedge positions against price fluctuations in the underlying security, or to speculate on the price movement of that security. Initiating a position in a forward does not require any financial outlay, so it allows for leveraged positions to be taken. Forward contracts are very similar to futures contracts, except they are not taken to market, exchanged, traded, or defined on standardized assets.

Example: Microsoft goes to JP Morgan Chase and asks for a quote on a currency forward for €12 million in three months. JP Morgan Chase quotes a rate of $0.925, which would enable Microsoft to sell euros and buy dollars at a rate of $0.925 in three months' time. Under this contract, Microsoft would know it could convert its €12 million to $11,100,000 (12,000,000 × 0.925 = 11,100,000). The contract would also stipulate whether it will settle in cash or will call for Microsoft to actually deliver the euros to the dealer and be paid $11,100,000.

Now let us say that three months later, the spot rate for euros is $0.920. Microsoft is quite pleased that it locked in a rate of $0.925, as with the new spot rate they would receive: 12,000,000 × 0.920 = $11,040,000. Microsoft made a profit of $60,000 by entering into the forward currency contract.

However, had rates risen in the three-month period, Microsoft would have a made a loss (e.g., at a spot rate of $1.00, Microsoft would have received $12,000,000, but would still have to deliver the euros and accept a rate of $0.925, and therefore make a potential loss of $900,000).

8.1.3 THE FUTURES CONTRACT

This contract is an agreement to buy or sell an asset at a certain time in the future for a certain price. Futures are traded in exchanges and the delivery price is always such that today's value of the contract is zero. Therefore in principle, we can always engage in futures without the need for initial capital: the speculator's heaven!

Although similar in nature, futures and forwards exhibit some fundamental differences in the organization and the contract characteristics. The most important differences are given in Table 8.3.

8.1.3.1 Currency Future. A currency future contract is a transferable futures contract that specifies the price at which a currency can be bought or sold at a future date.

Currency future contracts allow investors to hedge against foreign exchange risk. Since these contracts are marked-to-market daily, investors can—by closing out their position—exit from their obligation to buy or sell the currency prior to the contract's delivery date.

8.1.3.2 Interest Rate Future. This is a contract where the holder agrees to take delivery of a given amount of the related debt security at a later date (usually no more than three years). Futures may be in treasury bills and notes, certificates of deposit, commercial paper, or GNMA (***Government National Mortgage Association***) certificates, and so on. Interest rate futures are stated as a percentage of the value of the applicable debt security.

The value of interest rate futures contracts is directly tied to interest rates. For example, as interest rates decrease, the value of the contract increases. As the

TABLE 8.3 **Differences between Forward and Futures Contracts**

	Forwards	Futures
Primary market	Dealers	Organized exchange
Secondary market	None	Primary market
Contracts	Negotiated	Standardized
Delivery	Contracts expire	Rare delivery
Collateral	None	Initial margin, mark-the-market
Credit risk	Depends on parties	None [clearing house]
Market participants	Large firms	Wide variety

price or quote of the contract goes up, the purchaser of the contract gains, while the seller loses.

A change of one base point in interest rates causes a price change. Those who trade in interest rate futures do not usually take possession of the financial instrument. In essence, the contract is used either to hedge or to speculate on future interest rates and security prices. For example, a pension fund manager might use interest rate futures to hedge the bond portfolio position. Speculators find financial futures attractive because of their potentially large return on a small investment due to the low deposit requirement. Significant risks exist, however.

8.1.3.3 Bond Future. A bond future is a contractual obligation for the contract holder to purchase or sell a bond on a specified date at a predetermined price. A bond future can be bought in a futures exchange market, and the prices and dates are determined at the time the future is purchased.

Bond contracts are standardized, and they are overseen by a regulatory agency that ensures a certain level of equality and consistency. However, this form of derivative can be risky because it involves trading at a future date with only current information. The risk is potentially unlimited, because either the buyer or seller of the bond because the price of the underlying bond may change drastically between the initial agreement and the exercise date.

8.1.4 OPTIONS

An option is a derivative contract that conveys to its purchaser the right (but not the obligation) to buy or sell the underlying security at a prespecified price (strike price) over a period that is defined within the terms of the contract.

If the option is exercised, the writer of the contract is obliged to fulfill the terms and conditions of the contract through transfer of the underlying (or its cash equivalent, if so defined). If the option is not exercised, then it expires and is worthless. The only transfer of the underlying cash would have been the premium paid by the purchaser at the time that the contract was written.

Options exist as calls (the right to buy the underlying) and puts (the right to sell the underlying).

Calls and puts can be either purchased or written to achieve a desired exposure to the underlying security without the capital constraint of physically purchasing that security.

Similarly to future contracts, an option contract provides exposure to an underlying asset, but offers increased liquidity, the ability to take either long or short positions, the ability to take positions in baskets of stocks (i.e., indexes), and the ability to introduce leverage through only minimal outlay, which would not be available through trading the underlying itself. Unlike futures contracts, option contracts require an initial premium, for which they confer the right to pass up exercise if that remains within the purchaser's interests. An out-of-the money option would expire worthless (with the loss of the premium) while an in-the-money option would be exercised under contractual terms. There are no offsetting margin payments under option contracts.

Similarly to futures contracts, the underlying can be any of a wide variety of securities or even other contracts, such as futures or swaps. From a strategic perspective, fund managers may combine different option contracts to achieve a variety of low-risk exposures. For example, buying a call and a put with the same exercise price (known as a straddle) allows the fund to benefit (less premium outlay) by either a rise or fall in the price of the underlying. If the fund manager expects the underlying price to be volatile, then this (or a similar strategy) may be employed. Options, contrary to popular press, can offer timely, low-risk, and highly liquid solutions to previously unattainable portfolio rebalancing requirements.

8.1.4.1 Currency Option. A currency option is a contract that grants the holder the right, but not the obligation, to buy or sell currency at a specified exchange rate during a specified period of time. For this right, a premium is paid to the broker, which will vary depending on the number of contracts purchased. Currency options are one of the best ways for corporations or individuals to hedge against adverse movements in exchange rates.

Investors can hedge against foreign currency risk by purchasing a currency option put or call.

8.1.4.2 Equity Option. An equity option is an option in which the underlier is the common stock of a corporation, giving the holder the right to buy or sell its stock, at a specified price, by a specific date. It is also called a stock option.

The specific stock on which an option contract is based is commonly referred to as the underlying security. Options are categorized as derivative securities because their value is derived in part from the value and characteristics of the underlying security. A stock option contract's unit of trade is the number of shares of underlying stock that are represented by that option. Generally speaking, stock options have a unit of trade of 100 shares. This means that one option contract represents the right to buy or sell 100 shares of the underlying security.

8.1.4.3 Interest Rate Option. Interest rate options are European-style, cash-settled options on the yield of U.S. Treasury securities. Options on short, medium, and long-term rates are available to meet your needs. These options give you an opportunity to invest based upon your views of the direction of interest rates.

In general, when yield-based options are purchased, a call buyer and a put buyer have opposite expectations about interest rate movements. A call buyer anticipates that the interest rates will go up, increasing the value of the call position. A put buyer anticipates that rates will go down, increasing the value of the put position. A yield-based call option buyer will profit if, by expiration, the underlying interest rate rises above the strike price plus the premium paid for the call. Alternatively, a yield-based put options buyer will profit if, by expiration, if the interest rate has declined below the strike price less the premium paid. Of course, taxes and commissions must be taken into account in all transactions.

8.1.5 WARRANT

Warrants are a type of option issued by a corporation giving the holder of the option the right to buy shares in the corporation for a prespecified price. When exercised, the corporation is obliged to issue new shares of its stock and deliver these to the holder of the warrant in exchange for the strike price. The main conceptual difference between a standard exchange traded option and a warrant is that the exercise of a warrant results in the issuance of new stock, whereas the writer of an exchange-traded option delivers previously issued stock upon exercise. This can result in a drop in the price of the underlying stock when the warrant is exercised (known as the dilution effect). Typically, warrants possess a much longer life than do regular options.

A wide range of warrants and warrant types are available. The reasons you might invest in one type of warrant may be different from the reasons you might invest in another type of warrant.

Different Types of Warrants.

Equity Warrants. Equity warrants can be call and put warrants:

- Call warrants give you the right to buy the underlying securities.
- Put warrants give you the right to sell the underlying securities.

Basket Warrants. As with a regular equity index, warrants can be classified at, for example, an industry level. Thus, basked warrants mirror the performance of the industry.

Index Warrants. Index warrants use an index as the underlying asset. Your risk is dispersed—using index call and index put warrants—just like with regular equity indexes. It should be noted that they are priced using index points.

8.2 Market Risk and Global Exposure

Financial institutions needs to implement a matrix of controls to ensure that investors are sufficiently protected from adverse events related to the use of derivatives. Thus, there are layers of controls and limits, such as global exposure and leverage limits, counterparty limits, issuer limits and proper documentation, as set out in the risk management process document that aims to meet this overall objective. The definition of "global exposure" is a direct reference to the use of financial derivatives in the UCITS space but will also influence the alternative investment via the AIFMD directive.

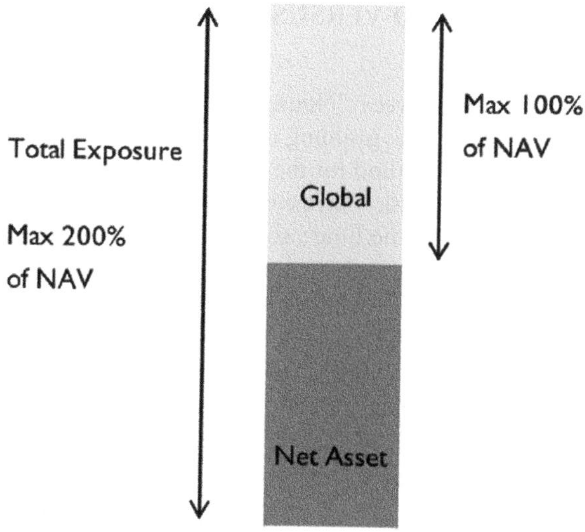

FIGURE 8.1 Total and global exposure for a UCITS fund.

8.2.1 GLOBAL EXPOSURE

UCITS *global exposure* is calculated by taking into account:

- The current value of the underlying assets
- The counterparty risk
- Future market movements
- The time available to liquidate the positions

The regulation also mentions the reference to total exposure. *Total exposure* should be assessed on the basis of both the default risk of the UCITS and the leverage produced by the use of derivatives (Figure 8.1).

Global exposure is understood to be the incremental exposure generated by using derivatives and *total exposure* is the combined net asset value (NAV) of the UCITS and its global exposure.

UCITS shall therefore ensure that the global exposure relating to derivatives does not exceed the total net value of the portfolio.

It is important to note that an UCITS may be considered as a nonsophisticated fund but may apply for the VaR approach when measuring its global exposure or market risk.

The question is how to distinguish between a sophisticated and nonsophisticated UCITS? What criteria can be used for such a distinction, and are they clear enough to avoid any doubts the regulator and ultimately the investors may have?

8.2.2 SOPHISTICATED VERSUS NONSOPHISTICATED UCITS

The fund's classification between "Nonsophisticated" and "Sophisticated" has been officially abandoned. Risk profiling is now the recommended approach for selecting the computation method for the global exposure measurement. This is probably more adapted to a Risk Management approach where the starting point is a proper understanding of the fund's strategy and related risks.

Based on ESMA guidelines, the main steps to consider when approaching the risk profile of a fund in order to select the global exposure computation method are the following[2]:

- It engages in complex investment strategies that represent more than a negligible part of the UCITS' investment policy,
- It has more than a negligible exposure to exotic derivatives, or
- The commitment approach doesn't adequately capture the market risk of the portfolio.

Even though the regulator is providing a defined path to assess the level of sophistication of the fund, a lot of the points to be considered are still leaving room for interpretation. Words like "complex," "negligible part," and "exotic" are not factual and need to be interpreted, defined and adapted to each fund and Management company taking into consideration both the concepts of risk appetite[3] and risk tolerance.[4] Probably, the most important point in analyzing and defining the fund's risk profile is the last bullet point mentioned here above. Unfortunately, it is also probably the least tangible aspect of the recommended approach since the perception of the market risk capture can dramatically differ from one actor to another.

A nonsophisticated UCITS must assess market risk by using the commitment approach, whereby the derivatives positions are converted into the equivalent positions of the underlying assets, provided that the buying and selling positions of the same underlying asset may be compensated.

In case of options, for instance, UCITS may apply the delta approach that is derived from the sensitivity of the change in the option's price to the marginal changes in the price of the underlying financial instruments. The conversion of forward, future, and swap positions should depend on the precise nature of the underlying contracts. In the case of simple contracts, the marked-to-market value of the underlying or the notional, as the case may be, of the contract will usually

---

[2]Committee of European Securities Regulator, 2010, CESR's *Guidelines on Risk Measurement and the Calculation of Global Exposure and Counterparty Risk for UCITS*, CESR/10-788, Box 1 point 4.

[3]The COSO framework defines risk appetite as "the amount of risk, on a broad level, an entity is willing to accept in pursuit of value."

[4]Risk tolerance is the acceptable level of variation relative to achievement of objectives.

be relevant. In general, a nonsophisticated UCITS will only use a limited number of simple derivative instruments for noncomplex hedging or investment strategies.

A sophisticated UCITS must apply a VaR approach regularly. The UCITS must apply stress tests in order to assess possible abnormal market movements. In applying the VaR approach, certain parameters must be used: typically 99% confidence level, a holding period of one month and "recent" volatilities—that is, less than one year from the calculation date. Other parameters may be used with prior approval of the supervisory authority.

Internal risk-measurement models proposed by a management company or an investment company are also acceptable on a case-by-case basis with prior approval by the supervisory authority.

In addition, the management company or the investment company must use stress tests. The supervisory authority must be convinced that the entity concerned has already developed and tested a VaR method in an appropriate manner and be happy with the extent to which these methods are duly documented.

The supervisory authority will review the UCITS risk management process to ensure that the rationale for self-classification is appropriate.

8.2.3 THE COMMITMENT APPROACH WITH EXAMPLES ON SOME FINANCIAL DERIVATIVES

To calculate global exposure, a nonsophisticated UCITS must apply the commitment approach. This approach converts the UCITS derivatives positions into the equivalent positions of the underlying assets. It therefore intends to ensure that the UCITS risks are monitored in terms of any future "commitments" to which it may be obligated. The commitment approach must also be used by all types of UCITS in determining issuer concentration risk limits.

A nonsophisticated UCITS must ensure that its global exposure calculated with the commitment approach does not exceed its total NAV. This represents a hard limit to simple leverage of 100% of NAV, as discussed before.

The commitment calculation for certain instruments may be adjusted by a probability factor that aims to reflect the probability of the derivatives commitment occurring. For options, warrants, and convertible bonds, the delta approach may be used. For sophisticated UCITSs that use credit derivatives, a probability-to-default percentage may be applied if the UCITS is in a position to calculate it. Where it is not possible to calculate a probability factor, the factor is assumed to be 1.

The calculation of global exposure is an absolute (positive) number that should be calculated after the application of netting rules. The methodology does not allow for the calculation of negative commitments.

The calculation frequency is at minimum bi-monthly when the commitment approach is selected. It is daily when the VaR method is utilized. It is important to note that under UCITS IV there will no longer be this distinction in terms of frequency because both will have to be measured on a daily basis.

Other methods, such as a sensitivity approach or add-on approach, may be used if adequate justification is given to the regulator. Such methods require approval before being officially used.

Examples of How to Compute the Commitment Approach.
Share Option. This is the market value of the underlying asset, adjusted by the option's delta:

$$\text{Number of contracts} \times \text{Number of shares} \times \text{Underlying price} \times \text{Delta}$$

Example 1: We hold a long call option on the Alcatel-Lucent share. The maturity date of the option is March 19, 2010. The strike price (or exercise price) is 2.60 EUR. The option is a European one, and therefore can only be exercised at the maturity date. The underlying asset price (the price of the Alcatel-Lucent share) is 2.54 EUR. Finally, the option's delta is 0.495071, and the number of contract is 0.10. Hence, the calculation of the commitment to be taken into account for the limitation of the global exposure is

$$0.10 \times 10 \times 2.54 \times 0.495071 = €1.21292395$$

Example 2—Options:

- Criteria: delta-adjusted underlying market value
- Market value to consider: option's delta*number of contracts face value/number of shares*underlying price
- Data: base currency EUR
- Option delta: 0.95
- 20 option contracts
- 1000 XYZ shares
- XYZ's share price €34.5

$$\text{Delta adjusted underlying market value} = 0.95 \times 20 \times 1000 \times 34.5 = €655{,}500$$

Bond Option: Market Value of the Underlying Asset, Adjusted by the Option's Delta.

$$\text{Number of contracts} \times \text{face value} \times \text{underlying price} \times \text{delta}$$

Example 1: We hold a long bond option, with maturity date of March 6, 2010. The underlying asset of the option is a bond on issued by the European Investment Bank that matures in July 2011. The face value of this bond is €100. The price of the bond is €107.489. The option's delta is 0.4567. Say we hold five contracts. Then, the calculation of the commitment to be taken into account to limit global exposure is

$$5 \times 100 \times 107.489 \times 0.4567 = €24{,}545.11315$$

Example 2 on Bond Option.

- Base currency USD
- Option delta: 1.05
- 35 option contracts
- Face value = 10,0000
- Underlying price in €108.65
- USD/EUR spot rate = 1.45

$$\text{Delta adjusted underlying market value} = \frac{1.05 \times 35 \times 10{,}000 \times 108.65}{100 \times 1.45} = \$275{,}371.55$$

Warrant: Market Value of the Underlying Asset, Adjusted by the Option's Delta.

$$\text{Number of contract} \times \text{Number of underlying} \times \text{Underlying price} \times \text{Delta}$$

Example: We hold a one call warrant issued by SocGen. The underlying (here cable and wireless share) is £142.30 and the number of underlying for the warrant is one. The delta of the warrant is 0.01447.

Therefore, the calculation of the commitment to be taken into account for the limitation of global exposure is

$$1 \times 1 \times 142.30 \times 0.01447 = £2.059801$$

Index Future: Market Value of the Contract or the Underlying Asset.

$$\text{Number of contracts} \times \text{Value of 1 point} \times \text{Index level}$$

Example 1: Say we have a future on the CAC 40 index. The future is CAC 40 10 future. The value of 1 point of the index future is €10, the index level is €3995, and the number of contracts we hold is say five.

Then, the calculation of the commitment to be taken into account for the limitation of global exposure is

$$5 \times 10 \times 3995 = €199{,}750$$

Example 2: FTSE 100 MAR 2008 Futures:

- 36 contracts purchased
- Index level 5884.5 points
- Contract size (value of one point):10

$$\text{Market value} = 36 \times 10 \times 5844.5 = £2{,}118{,}420$$

Bond Future: Market Value of the Contract or the Underlying Asset. This is the number of contracts × notional of the future contract × market value of the future or Number of contracts × notional × market price of the cheapest bond to be delivered, adjusted by the conversion factor.

Example 1: Say we have a long gilt future, maturing in January 2010. The market value of the future is £115.40. The contract value (or notional) of the future contract is 100,000, and say that we hold 10 futures.

Thus, the calculation of the commitment to be taken into account for the limitation of global exposure is

$$10 \times 1000 \times 115.40 = £1{,}154{,}000$$

Example 2: Bond Future.

Criteria: Market value of the contract or market value of the underlying bond.

> Criteria 1 = Number of contracts × notional of the future contract × market value of the future.
>
> Criteria 2 = Number of contracts × notional × market price of the CTD × CTD conversion factor.

Example 3:

- Base currency EUR
- Bond future BOBL 5Y DEC 07
- 180 contracts purchased
- Future notional 1000 units of underlying
- Market price of the future €108.965
- Underlying bond price €108.335 (CTD bond)
- CTD conversion ratio = 0.931197

$$\text{Criteria 1 market value} = 180 \times 1000 \times 108.695/100 = €195{,}651$$

$$\text{Criteria 2 market value} = 180 \times 1000 \times 108.335 \times 0.931197/100 = €181{,}586$$

Forward Exchange: Principal of the Contract. Say we have a forward exchange contract where we wish to exchange 1,000,000 USD into GBP with a forward date set at January 31, 2010. Then the principal of the contract will be $1,000,000.

Interest Rate Swap: Principal of the Contract. Say, for example, we have entered into an interest rate swap as the payer. We pay a fixed rate of 5.32% monthly to receive $1 million worth of Libor monthly on a notional $1 million for three years.

Hence, considering the commitment requirement, the commitment to be taken into account for the limitation of global exposure is $1,000,000.

Credit Default Swap. Protection buyer: sum of the premiums to be paid during the entire life of the contract protection seller: contract's notional value.

Example: A CDS spread of 593 base points for a five-year Brazilian debt means that the default insurance for a notional amount of $1,000,000 costs $59,300 per annum. This premium is paid quarterly (i.e., $14,825 per quarter).

Considering the calculation of the commitment to be taken into account for the limitation of global exposure, we have:

- Protection buyer: $5 \times 4 \times 14{,}825 = \$296{,}500$
- Protection seller: $1,000,000

Total Return Swap: Protection Buyer and Seller: Contract's Notional Value. Say two parties entered into a one-year total return swap, where Party A receives LIBOR and a fixed margin (2%) and Party B receives the total return of the S&P 500 on a principal amount of $1,000,000.

Then, the commitment approach will value the total return swap for both parties (protection seller and buyer) at $1,000,000.

Currency Swaps: Principal of the Contract. Suppose a UK-based company needs to acquire Swiss Francs (CHF). It would arrange with another company (usually based in Switzerland) to swap currencies (GBP and CHF) by establishing an interest rate, an agreed-upon amount and a common maturity date for the exchange. It wants to exchange, for example, 1,000,000 GBP into CHF.

Then, the commitment approach would be required to value the currency swap at £1,000,000 for the UK-based company.

Currency Forward Contract.

- Criteria: principal of the contract
- Total notional to consider

where n = total number of forward contracts.

Example:

- Base currency: USD
- First forward: forward contract bought €1,368,004.51 and sold $2,019,174.66.
- Second forward: forward contract bought $266,528.26 and sold £135,122.06.

$$\text{Total notional to be considered} = \$\text{-}2{,}019{,}174.66 + \$266{,}528.26 \text{ USD}$$
$$= \$\text{-}1{,}752{,}646$$

8.2.4 CALCULATION OF GLOBAL EXPOSURE USING VaR

With sophisticated funds using derivatives, global exposure is often confused with the term "leverage." Leverage has been variously defined and as such can be misunderstood. Although leverage is not an independent source of risk, leverage is important because of the impact it can adversely generate on market, credit, and liquidity risk. In the context of UCITS, simple leverage should be understood as being the UCITS' global exposure divided by the NAV.

As a general rule, an UCITS cannot have global exposure greater than its NAV, and so this means that there is a hard limit to an UCITS' simple leverage of 100% of the NAV. More specifically, the overall risk exposure of the UCITS may not be increased by more than 10% by means of temporary borrowing (cash flows mismatch), so that the UCITS' overall risk exposure may not exceed 210% of the NAV under any circumstances.

Total exposure, as defined above, may not therefore be greater than 200% of the NAV.

A sophisticated UCITS must use the VaR approach to assess its market risk. The use of such a technique is required in order to ensure that the leverage effect of using financial derivatives is not significant enough to cause disproportionate losses to the UCITS' overall value. Other methodologies may be acceptable and will be considered on a case-by-case basis.

The risk manager should be aware of limitations of the models used and should not put too much reliance on mathematical measures of leverage alone. Risk managers should use judgment based on business experience in calculating and assessing quantitative measures of leverage.

An important factor to consider is the degree to which the UCITS can modify its risk-based leverage, especially during periods of market stress. The risk manager should therefore assess the UCITS' ability to reduce its risk-based leverage by reducing the risk that is being accepted.

On the other hand, the supervisory authority should also recognize that financial derivatives can reduce the UCITS' overall VaR although the VaR of the financial derivative alone exceeds the VaR limit.

There are some limitations of the VaR methodology that require specific attention. Take, for instance, a deep out-of-the-money traded option in a portfolio. The resulting lack of liquidity of such an option will result in a stationary price that will be translated in a very low or nil VaR figure.

A sophisticated UCITS may also use additional methods of risk measurement, such as tracking at risk and tracking error volatility.

An UCITS must have a VaR model that builds in the following standards:

- The confidence level that must be used is 99%.
- The holding period must be one month.[5]
- The historical observation period should be recent volatilities—that is, less than one year.

Member states have mostly chosen the parameters suggested, but small variations can be indicated.

Absolute VaR Limitation. Those UCITS that are unable or for which it is not appropriate to determine a reference portfolio (example: an "absolute return"-type UCITS) must determine an absolute VaR on all of the portfolio's positions. The regulator expects that a UCITS, on the basis of the analysis of the investment policy and the given risk profile, fixes a maximum VaR; this management limit may not exceed the threshold of 20%.

Relative VaR seems to be a concept much more in line with the industry. Relative VaR can be defined as the the VaR of the UCITS divided by the VaR of a benchmark or a reference portfolio with no derivatives. This can be an index or a synthetic benchmark portfolio. The VaR of the UCITS shall not exceed twice the VaR of the comparable benchmark portfolio.

Example:

Fund Name	
Word Equity Fund	8.48%
Benchmark used for Relative VaR	
MSCI Barra Equities	7.67%
Relative VaR ratio	1,10

The relative ratio is below twice the VaR of the selected benchmark. The exposure is acceptable under UCITS relative VaR limit.

[5]Compliance Ireland Regulatory Service Limited speaks about a holding period of a maximum of one month.

8.3 Options

In this section we will emphasize the role that options play in the risk management framework within a broad portfolio. We will look at the different types of strategies for options, the pricing of options using the Black–Scholes formula, the derivation of the Greeks, and finally, how we can use Monte Carlo Simulations in order to calculate VaR for options.

8.3.1 DIFFERENT STRATEGIES USING OPTIONS

A call option gives you the right (but not the obligation) to buy the underlying asset at some time in the future, at a prespecified strike price (K). Similarly, a put option is the right to sell the underlying asset at maturity (T), at a predefined strike price (K).

Options are used for different reasons by different financial market participants:

- To hedge or
- To speculate.

We will look at the payoff of a call and put option first, and then we will show how we can combine these options in order to have some more advanced technical strategies.

Payoff of Call and Put Option. Let's take the example of a call option, with strike price $K = 80$ and current stock price $S = 80$. The payoff function of a European call option with strike price K at the maturity date T is

$$c(T) = \max[S(T) - K, 0]$$

The payoff function of this call option is shown in Figure 8.2.

Similarly, we can draw the payoff of a put option in the same way. Consider the put option with strike price 80, and the current stock price $S = 80$ as well.

Figure 8.3 shows the payoff function for a European put option. A European put option gives you the right (but not the obligation) to sell the underlying asset at some time in the future at a prespecifed strike price (K). In order to have the right to sell the underlying, you pay a put premium today.

8.3.2 BLACK SCHOLES FORMULA

Developed in 1973 by Fisher Black, Robert Merton, and Myron Scholes, the Black–Scholes model is regarded as the most accurate way to determine the price of options even if the formula exhibits some limitations. The mathematical model explains that the prices of traded assets follow a geometric Brownian motion that looks like a smile or smirk with constant drift and volatility. A graph of a Brownian motion is shown in Figure 8.4.

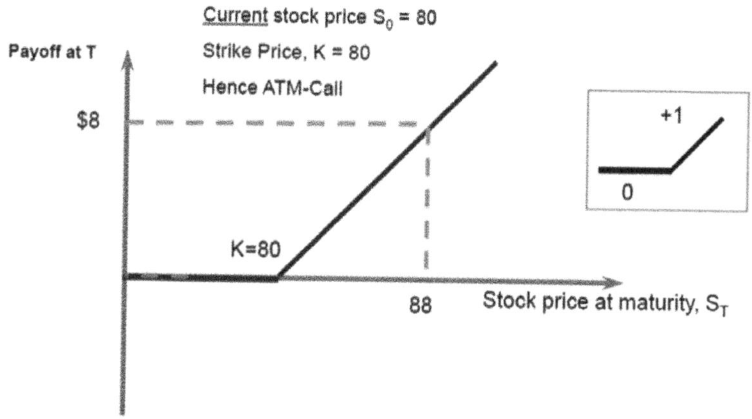

FIGURE 8.2 Payoff of a call option.

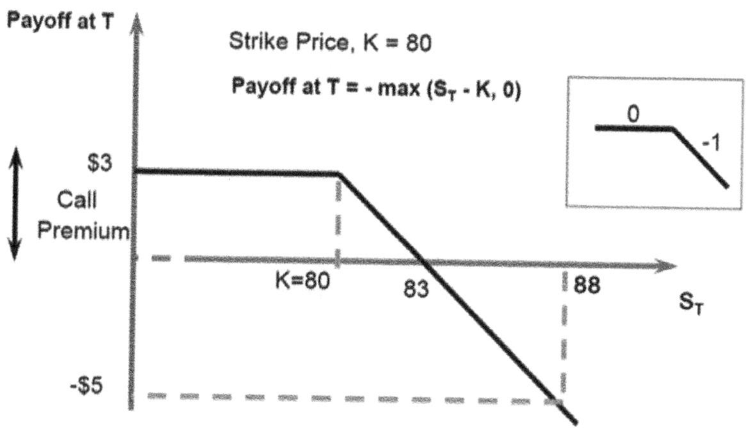

FIGURE 8.3 Payoff of a put option.

The Black–Scholes formula are based on a few assumptions, which are detailed below:

- The underlying stock does not pay any dividends during the life of the options.
- The options used here are European options, which can only be exercised at the end of the option's life, compared with American options, which can be exercised at any time.
- We need to consider that the markets are efficient, and there is no arbitrage opportunities.

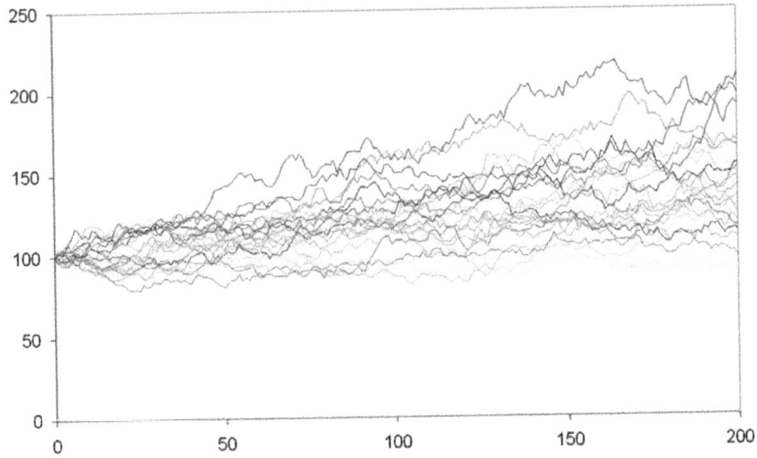

FIGURE 8.4 **Brownian motion of Stock price.**

The Black–Scholes formula calculates the price of European put and call options. The value of a call option for a nondividend paying underlying stock in terms of the Black–Scholes parameters is

$$C(S,t) = N(d_1)S - N(d_2)Ke^{-r(T-t)}$$

$$d_1 = \frac{\ln\left(\frac{S}{K}\right) + \left(r + \frac{\sigma^2}{2}\right)(T-t)}{\sigma\sqrt{T-t}}$$

$$d_2 = \frac{\ln\left(\frac{S}{K}\right) + \left(r - \frac{\sigma^2}{2}\right)(T-t)}{\sigma\sqrt{T-t}} = d_1 - \sigma\sqrt{T-t}$$

Similarly, the value of the put option using the Black–Scholes formula, which can also be derived using the put-call parity is

$$\begin{aligned} P(S,t) &= Ke^{-r(T-t)} - S + C(S,t) \\ &= N(-d_2)Ke^{-r(T-t)} - N(-d_1)S \end{aligned}$$

where $N(\cdot)$ is the cumulative distribution function of the standard normal distribution, $T - t$ is the time to maturity, S is the spot price of the underlying asset, K is the strike price, r is the risk free rate (annual rate, expressed in terms of continuous compounding), and σ is the volatility of returns of the underlying asset.

The formulas above allow us to calculate the value of a call and put premium at any point in time. The one parameter that needs to be estimated in the

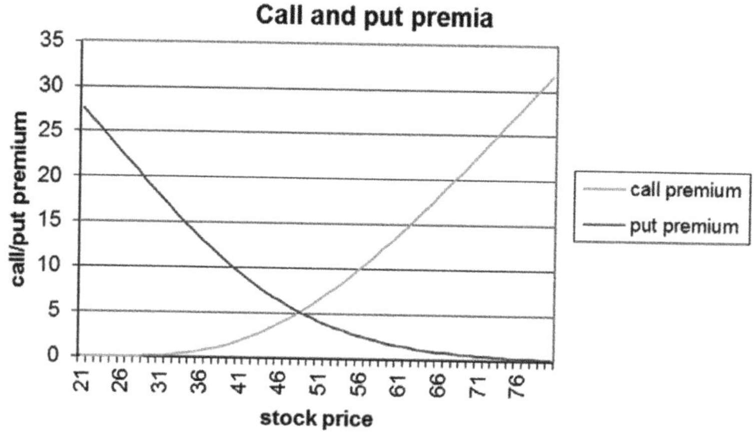

FIGURE 8.5 Call and put premia.

formula is the volatility of the underlying stock. There are numerous ways to calculate the volatility of the underlying, which have been detailed in a different chapter.

We can rewrite the Black–Scholes formula as

$$c(0) = e^{-rT}\left(S(0)e^{rT}N(d_1) - KN(d_2)\right)$$

The formula can be interpreted as follows. If the call option is exercised at the maturity date, then the holder gets the stock worth $S(T)$, but has to pay the strike price K. But this exchange only takes place if the options mature in the money (i.e., the stock price is currently trading above the strike price). Thus $S(0)e^{rT}N(d_1)$ represents the future value of the underlying asset condition on the end stock value being greater than the strike price K. The second term in the brackets $KN(d_2)$ is the value of the known payment K times the probability that the strike price will be paid $N(d_2)$. The terms inside the brackets are then discounted by the risk-free rate r, to bring payments into present value terms.

Figure 8.5 represents the call and put premia from a Black–Scholes formula for different stock prices, where both options have a strike price of 48.

8.3.3 THE GREEKS

An institution that writes an option to a client (sells an option) faces the problem of managing the risks due to the option. The risks in an option position are diverse, and they can be broadly represented by the Greeks.

8.3.3.1 Delta. The delta of an option, denoted Δ, is defined as the rate of change of the option prices, with respect to the change in price of the underlying asset. It is the slope of the curve that relates the option price to the underlying asset. Formally, Δ can be calculated as

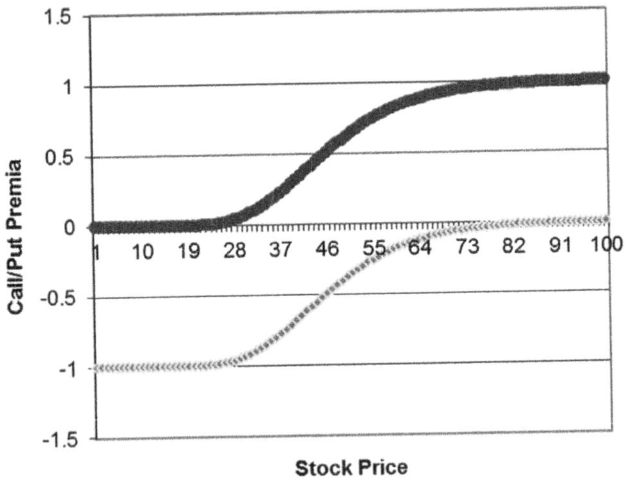

FIGURE 8.6 Call and put delta.

$$\Delta = \frac{\partial c}{\partial S}$$

where c is the price of the call option, and S the price of the underlying stock.

Figure 8.6 represents the delta for both a call and put option, and it shows how the delta changes with respect to the underlying stock price.

It is interesting to note that the delta of a European call option on a non-dividend-paying stock can be derived from the Black–Scholes formula. Hence

$$\Delta(call) = N(d_1)$$

where d_1 is defined in the Black–Scholes equation. The formula gives the delta of a long position in one call option. Using the call-put parity, we can show that the delta of a put option is

$$\Delta(put) = N(d_1) - 1$$

Here, the delta of a put option is negative, because a rise in the underlying stock prices decreases the probability of the put option being exercised and hence decreases the put premium.

8.3.3.2 Delta Hedging. As we have seen so far, we have defined the delta of both a call and put option. Consider the following example where a financial institution ABC has sold a call option to a pension fund and received $c = \$9.6$. Consider that this option has a delta equal to 0.4. The financial institution is worried that the stock price might rise over the next few days, which would

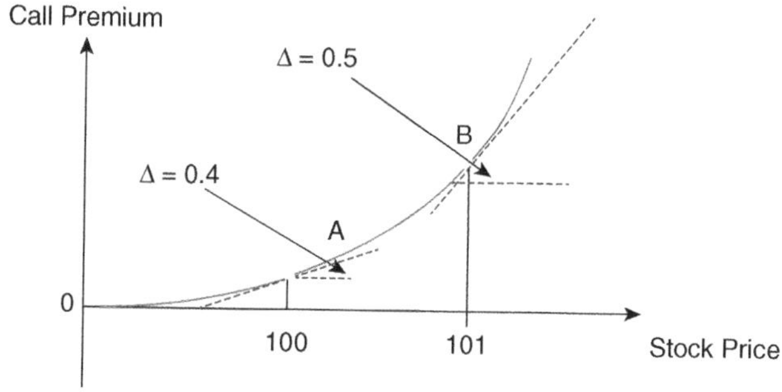

FIGURE 8.7 Delta hedging.

consist of a rise in the call premium, and the possibility of the option being exercised at maturity.

In order to hedge their position, they can buy the underlying shares with a ratio of 0.4 to 1 to the option. As they have sold the option, they then hedge their delta by buying the underlying stock. In this example, ABC buys 0.4 of one share.

Now suppose that the stock price S rises by $1 over the next day, then the call premium also rises to by 0.4 to c1 = $10. To close out the position, you would have to buy back an option at c1 = 10, which would make a net loss of 0.4$.

However, the loss on the call premium is hedged by the gain on the 0.4 shares. Here we have delta-hedged the portfolio, meaning the value of the portfolio remains unchanged over a small interval of time.

Delta hedging aims to keep the value of the financial institutions' position as close to unchanged as possible (Figure 8.7).

As a general rule of thumb, it can be shown that the following trades should be done in order to delta hedge:

For call option the rule is long–short, meaning that if the institution is long a call option, it should be short-selling delta stocks, and if the institution is short a call, it should be long delta stocks.

For put option, the rule is long–long or short–short:

- If long a put, then delta hedge by going long delta stocks.
- If short a put, then delta hedge by going short delta stocks.

The delta of a portfolio of options can be calculated from the deltas of the individual options in a portfolio. If a portfolio consists of a quantity w of options I, then the delta of the portfolio is given by

$$\Delta = \sum_{i=1}^{n} w_i \Delta_i$$

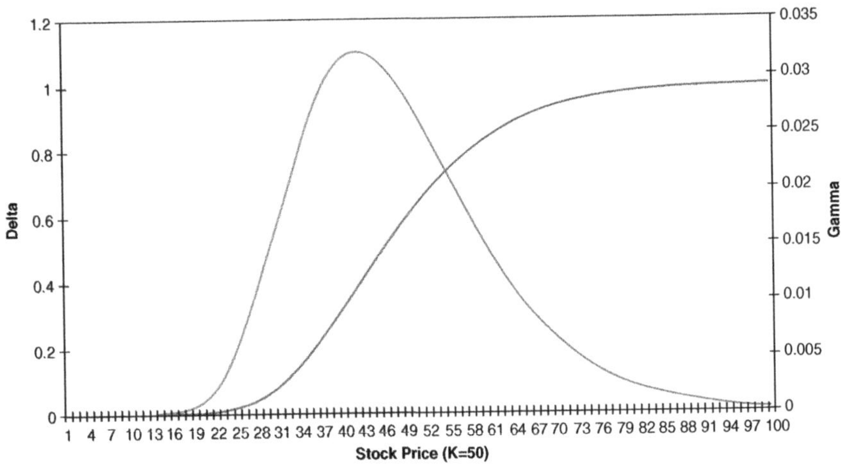

FIGURE 8.8 Delta and long call.

The formula can be used to calculate the position in the underlying asset necessary to make the delta of the portfolio zero. When this position has been taken, the portfolio is referred to as being delta neutral.

8.3.3.3 Gamma. The gamma of an option, denoted Γ, represents the rate of change of a portfolio's delta with respect to the price of the underlying asset. It is the second partial derivative of the portfolio with respect to the asset price and can be calculated as

$$\Gamma = \frac{\partial^2 f}{\partial S^2} = \frac{\partial \Delta}{\partial S}$$

Gamma is essentially the equivalent of a "convexity" in fixed income analysis. It is the sensitivity of the option price with regard to a large change in stock prices. If gamma is small, delta changes slowly, and if the absolute value of gamma is large, then the delta will be highly sensitive to the price of the underlying asset (Figure 8.8). Gamma measures the curvature of the relationship between the option price and the stock price.

Gamma is positive for both long call and long put and the gammas are equal for both options when they have the same strike price, same maturity, and same underlying. This can be shown using the call-put parity formula. Please note that the gamma of a stock is 0.

$$\Gamma_0 = \Gamma_p > 0$$

As we have seen before, a portfolio that is delta-hedged will be immune to small changes in the underlying stock prices (depending on dynamic hedging or static hedging as well). We can now use gamma to have a delta–gamma neutral portfolio, where the portfolio will not be affected by small or large change in the underlying price. In ortder to make a portfolio gamma neutral, we require a position in an instrument such as an option, which is not linearly dependent on the underlying asset.

Suppose that a delta-neutral portfolio has a gamma equal to Γ, and a traded option has a gamma equal to Γ_s. If the number of traded options added to the portfolio is w_S, then the gamma of the portfolio is

$$w_s\Gamma_s + \Gamma$$

Including a traded option in the portfolio will change the delta of a portfolio, so the position in the underlying asset then has to be changed to maintain delta-neutrality. Note that the portfolio is gamma neutral only for a short period of time. As time passes, gamma neutrality can be maintained only if the position in the traded option is adjusted.

For a European call or put option on a non-dividend-paying stock, the gamma is given by

$$\Gamma = \frac{N'(d_1)}{S_0\sigma\sqrt{T}}$$

where d_1 is defined from the Black–Scholes formula.

Figure 8.9 illustrates the gamma of a call and put option with same strike and same maturity.

8.3.3.4 Vega. The vega of an option, denoted υ, represents the rate of change of the value of the option, with respect to the volatility of the underlying asset. The following equation can be used to calculate the vega of an option. Vega represents the amount that an option price changes in reaction to a 1%

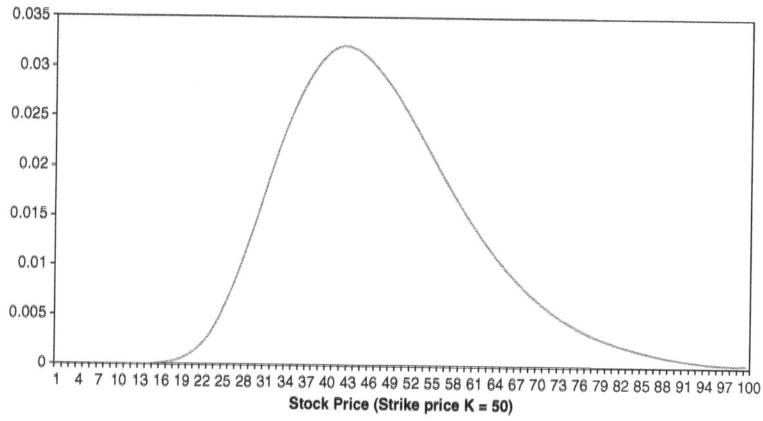

FIGURE 8.9 Gamma of call option.

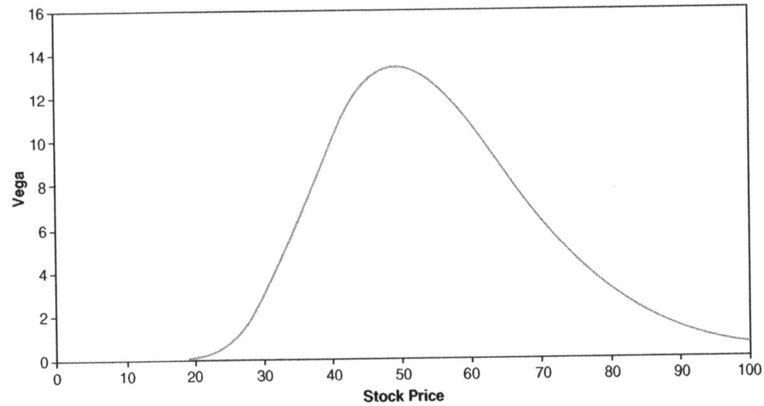

FIGURE 8.10 Vega (long call or put).

change in the volatility of the underlying asset. Volatility measures the amount of speed at which the prices of an underlying stock moves up or down.

$$\Lambda = \frac{\partial f}{\partial \sigma}$$

Let us consider an example. Consider a stock XYZ trading at $46, and a 3-month call option on the stock is selling for $2. Let's assume that the vega of the option is 0.15, and the underlying stock volatility is 25% per annum. If the underlying volatility increased by 1% to 26%, then the price of the option should rise to $2.15. However, if the volatility decreased by 2% down to 23% instead, the option price should drop to $1.70.

Figure 8.10 shows the vega of an option with respect to the stock price. It is quite similar to the gamma of an option. Note that the more time remaining to the expiration of the option, the higher the vega. This makes sense because the time value of the option makes up a larger portion of the premium for a longer-term option, and it is the time value that is sensitive to changes in volatility.

8.3.3.5 Theta. Finally, the theta of an option, denoted Θ, represents the options time decay. It measures the rate of change of the value of the option with respect to the passage of time with all else remaining constant. Theta is sometimes referred to as the time decay of an option. Generally expressed as a negative number, theta reflects the amount by which the options value will decrease with respect to time.

Let us consider an example. Consider a call option with a current price of $2 and a theta of -0.05. This means that the price of the option tomorrow with all else remaining constant will drop to $1.95.

8.3.4 OPTION VALUE AND RISK UNDER MONTE CARLO SIMULATION

Options exhibit a nonlinear pay-off profile.

There are two types of derivatives: linear derivatives and nonlinear derivatives. A linear derivative is one whose payoff function is a linear function. For example, a futures contract has a linear payoff in that every one-tick movement translates directly into a specific dollar value per contract. A nonlinear derivative is one whose payoff changes with time and space.

It is because of this skewed structure that options are said to have nonlinear payoffs; payoffs merely refer to the profits/gains on your investment. The same cannot be said of futures contract, because these contracts move linearly or proportionally with the spot price.

Parametric VaR is therefore not suitable for options type product. The risk in using a parametric VaR for a nonlinear instrument such as an option would result in underestimating its risk. For this reason it is highly recommended to apply a Monte Carlo simulation because it is believed to provide a more accurate estimation of risk exposure for option instruments. As already defined earlier in this book, Monte Carlo simulation refers to a process whereby a series of prices for an asset (or assets) is generated by a computer program; these prices are all theoretically possible given certain user-specified parameters (Figure 8.11). The

Inputs	
Start Date	01-Jun-11
Maturity Date	01-Jun-12
Days Remaining	366 days
Risk Free Rate	1.00%
Stock Volatility	25.00%
Current Price	88.000
Exercise Price	92.000
Dividend Yield	5.00%
Number of Simulations	1,000

Calculations	
Time to Maturity	1.003 yrs
d_1	(0.2126)
d_2	(0.4630)
Normalised d_1	0.4158148
Normalised d_2	0.3216986
Normalised $-d_1$	0.5841852
Normalised $-d_2$	0.6783014
$N'(d_1)$	0.3900267 coefficient

Outputs	
Option	Price
Call Option	5.5014
Put Option	12.8867
Simulated Call	5.6577
Simulated Put	13.0431
Iteration Count	1,000

Greeks		
Greeks for	Call	Put
Delta	0.4158	(0.5842)
Gamma	0.0177	0.0177
Theta	(2.6278)	(5.9018)
Vega	34.4164	34.4164
Rho	29.3813	(61.9504)

FIGURE 8.11 Black–Scholes European option pricing using a Monte Carlo simulation.

portfolio is then revalued at each of these possible prices, and this enables the user to calculate a VaR number for the portfolio.

8.3.5 EVALUATING OPTIONS AND TAYLOR EXPANSION

The changes in the value can be described by

$$df = \frac{\partial f}{\partial S} dS + \frac{1}{2}\frac{\partial^2 f}{\partial S^2} dS^2 + \frac{\partial f}{\partial r} dr + \frac{\partial f}{\partial r^*} dr^* + \frac{\partial f}{\partial \sigma} d\sigma + \frac{\partial f}{\partial \tau} d\tau + \cdots$$

Option pricing is about finding f. Option hedging uses the partial derivatives. Risk management combines those with the joint distribution of the risk factors. It is important to note that this approximation can fail for several reasons: large movements, highly nonlinear exposures, and cross-partial effects.

8.3.6 THE BINOMIAL AND TRINOMIAL OPTION PRICING MODELS

The binomial option pricing model was developed and first proposed in 1979, making it a fairly recent development in the field of options pricing because it is proposed after the Black–Scholes method of 1973 and the Monte Carlo methods which have been used in the option pricing field since the 1960s. The binomial option pricing method was created by John Cox and Stephen Ross. This group of three college economics professors pioneered this system as a means of being able to determine the price of an option at any point in its lifetime and, from there, determine the value of various options—most prominently, the American call option. Furthermore, many subsequent scholars have worked to try to tweak and perfect this pricing method. One basic extension is the trinomial tree, but further extensions create exotic looking models that aim to further enhance the accuracy of the pricing method by altering variables over time. The relative youth of this field of pricing means that its efficiency has not yet been maximized; therefore, it is an open and continuing problem with many economists trying to find the solution.

Cox, Ross, and Rubinstein created a pricing model that is often referenced as a binomial tree because of the way it looks. Most other option pricing methods like the Black–Scholes method have the user input a set of values and the algorithm spits out a number for the option price. With the binomial option pricing model, the user inputs a set of parameters and the output looks like a whole tree or lattice of values. Ultimately, the tree does funnel down into the value of the option today, but it is interesting to see the visual picture of the path an underlying value can take. The biggest advantage of the binomial tree is that it can be easily manipulated to price American options, something Black–Scholes is not built for. However, the binomial tree also has several drawbacks, primarily speed and accuracy in calculating these option prices. As with most calculations, there is a tradeoff between speed and accuracy, and this choice is made clear with binomial trees.

Perhaps the most radical idea proposed by Cox, Ross, and Rubinstein was the idea that over a given time period, it can be assumed that a stock can only take one of two actions: go up by a specified amount, or go down by a specified amount. It seems radical because stocks have all sorts of odd movements; they can go up or down by one percent, two percent, three percent, or even higher, and these amounts are by no means limited to whole number percentage increases. The most preposterous thought is that there is no way for a stock price to just remain constant over this time interval. If asked to draw a line on a graph that would most certainly contain the stock price at a given time, one would draw a vertical line, but Cox, Ross, and Rubinstein are saying that we can represent this with as little as two points. The reason this simplification works is that one is taking many of these time intervals to approximate the stock movement. When the tree is fully constructed, it is evident from the list of possible end values that the approximations of what the stock can do over the entirety of the applicable time frame are close to continuous. Also, the range of values can be thought of as a confidence interval for the range of values that the underlying can take on at time T. It cannot be said that there is 95% confidence because the calculation is based on the volatility, which is just an estimate to begin with. The better the guess at forward volatility for a stock, the more accurate the confidence interval of final values is. The reason it is not a perfect interval is that there could be a change that either sends the stock either shooting upward or dropping quickly. As long as the volatility estimate is correct, the stock cannot leave the range of values predicted by the binomial tree, but if something changes and the asset's volatility increases, its final value may not be predicted. However, this does not mean the model is bad. The possibility of an upward or downward spike is low, so it would hardly be factored into the option price anyways. In addition, the upward spike and downward spike potentials work to offset one another when calculating the value of an option, so this inaccuracy is reduced further. Ultimately, it is therefore safe to consider this set of possible end values produced by the binomial tree to be a good enough indicator of the possible end value of the stock. As stated earlier, the only way to truly capture a stock's price at a given time is to draw a vertical line. The binomial tree, however, makes a lot of points and aims to be close to that final price. So the end-nodes of the binomial tree are a good indicator of the final stock price's potential values despite allowing for only an upward or downward movement of a predetermined amount.

By making this simplification of the stocks movements, construction of the binomial tree becomes very easy. When the movement of a stock is simplified to either upward movements by a factor of u or downward movements by a factor of $d = 1/u$, the binomial tree has a recombining structure. What this means is that an upward movement followed by a downward movement results in the exact same final stock price as a downward movement followed by an upward movement. This recombining nature of the tree significantly reduces the number of values the stock can take on over a period of time. In reality, a stock can take on just about any value over a period of time. With the binomial tree, a finite number of nodes are created representing the values a stock can take on at any interval in this period of time. The recombining nature reduces the number of nodes that need to be calculated, greatly increasing the speed of calculations for the binomial tree. For example, if an investor wanted to construct a binomial tree with four time intervals, the end result would consist of five possible final outcomes for the stock price. If the tree did not recombine, and up, up, up, down were different from up, down, up, up, the investor's binomial tree would have 16 possible final outcomes for the stock. To calculate this fictitious tree that does not recombine, the investor would need to make a significantly higher number of calculations, which takes time. Speed is everything in the investments world, and the recombining nature of the binomial tree is one aspect that works in its favor to speed up the estimation process.

In order to create a binomial tree, there are four programming calculations that need to be made. The first two calculations involve creating a model for the paths the stock price can take over time T. The first calculation represents an upward movement in the stock and can be found by multiplying the previous stock price by u. The second calculation represents a downward movement in the stock price and is found by multiplying the previous stock price by d. First, take the initial stock price and multiply it by u, t times, where t is equal to the number of time intervals chosen. Then, from each of these values created, multiply by d for each remaining time interval. By producing the upward slope first, all subsequent values can be calculated off of this set of values by factoring in the downward movements to accompany these upward gains. The resulting tree will allow the user to see all possible paths the stock can take, but calculations are made simpler by doing them in this way. Now that the price tree has been created, it is time to evaluate the third calculation, the payoff formula. The tree ends with the final nodes showing the price of the stock at time T. The contract of an option instructs how to pay out at this time; therefore, the value of the option is known here at time T. Whatever the payoff function is, it can be entered in now; for a call option, the payoff is the maximum of the stock price minus the strike price, or zero. With this breakdown of payoffs, a pullback formula is used to come up with a value for the option now at time zero. What the pullback formula essentially does is take the two potential values the option can take from a given node and it both considers the probability of moving to either node, but also it factors out the riskless interest rate over that time interval. The formula for this pullback is as follows: The value of the option at time t is equal to the riskless interest rate times the quantity of the probability of an upward movement times the corresponding option value if an upward movement were to occur plus the probability of a downward movement times the corresponding option value if a downward movement were to occur. When applied to every node starting at time T and working back to the starting point, the last calculation yields the option's value.

The parameters and variables in this set of calculations are fairly straightforward and can be found or chosen easily. First, one must gather the stock information. The parameters needed from the site are: S_0 (the current stock price) and σ (the volatility of the stock). Next, one must find the riskless interest rate, r. The rest of the parameters are chosen by the user: K (strike price), T (time to expiry), t (the number of time intervals to be calculated). With these parameters, the variables become easy to calculate because it is just a matter of plugging in and solving. The parameters u and d were found by Cox, Ross, and Rubinstein to be $u = e^{\sigma\sqrt{\Delta t}}$ and $d = e^{-\sigma\sqrt{\Delta t}}$, where Δt equals the length of time in the time intervals chosen. This derivation makes a lot of sense logically. It makes sense that the size of the jump in stock price over a time interval should be based on both volatility and the length of the interval. A more volatile stock would be expected to have the potential for greater losses and gains than a less volatile stock over a constant time period, and this holds true in this calculation. Also, the same stock, meaning constant volatility, would obviously have an opportunity to move more over a long time period than a short one, and that is also considered in this equation. The fact that $u = 1/d$ means that the tree recombines, which is of great importance. The other variable that needs to be derived is p, the probability of an upward movement. This probability is most commonly derived from the Brownian motion that says a stock should follow a basic path of the riskless interest rate and then a random path associated with the random movements of a stock. By assuming that this stock is risk neutral and follows this inherent path, we can analyze the Brownian motion and solve the equation $S_0 e^{r\Delta t} = pS_u + (1 - p)S_d$ for p. When we do that, we find that $p = (e^{r\Delta t} - d)/(u - d)$. This value p is equal to the probability of an upward movement. $(1 - p)$ is the probability of a downward movement because there exist only two choices for the path the stock can take, and these must add up to one according to the laws of probability.

One important observation to make about the binomial distribution is that it converges to the Black–Scholes price for European options as the number of time intervals used in the calculations goes to infinity.

One such special feature of binomial trees is the ability to easily factor in dividends.

The American option is a problem that is very difficult for the Black–Scholes method to handle. The Black–Scholes looks at the possible end values of a stock without caring about the path it takes. American options, however, are greatly influenced by the path they take. The chance of a stock's highest value over an interval being exactly at expiry is very unlikely. More often, the stock will rise up and fall below the final price many times over the length of time. The effect of this is that the American option, which can be executed at any time up until expiry, is more valuable than the European option that can only be executed at expiry. The binomial tree has the advantage that it considers the path the option takes as it moves toward a final price. With the pullback formula, we can factor in the American option's advantage. Whenever the value of the option if executed is greater than the option value if allowed to continue to expiry, this becomes the value of the option at that node. As this starts from the back and works its way forward, this change in the pullback affects all subsequent nodes until we finally arrive back at the present time with the value of the American option. The same can be done with Bermudan options which have a limited number of execution points where the option can be executed and the holder can take the payout.

One proposed alternative to the binomial tree is the trinomial tree. The trinomial tree allows for a third option for a stocks movement: up, down, or middle (where the stock price stays constant over the time interval). The trinomial tree was first developed by Phelim Boyle in 1986. Since Boyle, others have attempted to formulate an improved version of the trinomial tree, most notably Kamrad and Ritchken. The trinomial tree constructed by Boyle can be compared to two binomial trees stacked on top of one another. The range of possible end values for the stock price is significantly wider than the range of values of the binomial tree. Boyle's approach to the problem seems to be to include a wider range of values, thus better representing the possible outcome of the stock price, giving a more accurate approximation of the option's value. Kamrad and Ritchken, however, produced a trinomial tree that more similarly resembles a binomial tree where every other step is missing. Rather than having a wide range of end values, the Kamrad and Ritchken approach looks at a smaller range of end nodes. Although their model may miss out on some far-from-average values that Boyle (1986) will pick up, they have a sort of confidence interval where the stock is most likely to be. By having a confidence interval of sorts, they can increase the number of end nodes in the expected range while reducing the overall number of calculations. This ultimately leads to a more accurate answer while increasing speed too, a huge advantage that makes this method very popular.

Kamrad and Ritchken (1991) found that a trinomial tree can be written with the following parameters:

$$p_u = \frac{1}{2\lambda^2} + \frac{1}{2}\left(\frac{\mu}{\lambda\sigma}\right)\sqrt{\Delta t}, \quad p_d = \frac{1}{2\lambda^2} - \frac{1}{2}\left(\frac{\mu}{\lambda\sigma}\right)\sqrt{\Delta t},$$

$$u = e^{\lambda\sigma\sqrt{\Delta t}}, d = e^{-\lambda\sigma\sqrt{\Delta t}}$$

and

$$p_m = 1 - \frac{1}{\lambda^2}$$

First, to look at u and d, it is very similar to the u and d for the Cox–Ross–Rubinstein method. The difference is this lambda that Kamrad and Ritchken have added. The lambda is essentially a calibrating parameter that can be tweaked as needed to optimize the speed and accuracy of the trinomial tree in pricing the option. One particularly interesting fact is that when lambda is set to be 1, this is just the Cox–Ross–Rubinstein binomial tree. The probability of a middle movement becomes zero and all other parameters can be simplified as the ones given by Cox, Ross, and Rubinstein. Another interesting lambda is the square root of two. When we set lambda to this, the trinomial tree is precisely a binomial tree where every other time interval is skipped in the calculations. This is most useful because it can be used to cut some corners and calculate the value of an option quicker. The problem with skipping every other step, however, is that some accuracy is lost, however, it is significantly closer than most methods of trying to speed up the tree calculation.

If we further analyze the lambda parameter, it becomes evident that there must be a way to maximize the accuracy and speed of convergence for a trinomial tree. Kamrad and Ritchken have also worked at finding the optimal lambda for speedy convergence to the Black–Scholes price. They found that a lambda of the square root of 3/2 produces the quickest convergence. What this implies is that if we use a lambda of the square root of 3/2 in our construction of a trinomial tree, then it is possible to approximate an option price in fewer steps, which means less time, than the binomial method. While Boyle is the one who should be credited with coming up with the idea of implementing a trinomial tree to price options, it is Kamrad and Ritchken who have fine tuned it to make it a superior model.

The question then becomes which model do we use and under what circumstances? The answer is not clear cut because both choices do a fairly good job of approximating option values. In the case of vanilla options, the binomial tree is often preferred because it is easier to program and implement; in addition, it converges just as fast as the trinomial tree. For exotic options, however, the trinomial tree is often preferred. The trinomial tree produces more end nodes in fewer calculations, enhancing the accuracy of the calculation. Like a bat trying to map out the walls of a cave by sending out as many screeches as possible to better visualize the surface, the trinomial places more points on the payoff pattern and thus gets a better readout on the abrupt changes in the payoffs.

There is really no limit to the number of branches one can put on these trees. There are examples of quadrinomial and pentinomial trees. Very little research has been done with these further extensions of multinomial trees; however, there is reason to believe that similar results can be found from them. Perhaps someday with more efficient methods and computers, these further advanced multinomial trees will find a way into options pricing, but for now the task is to perfect these methods.

One attempt to fine tune the binomial and trinomial trees is the implied volatility trees. It is evident in real life that the volatility of a stock is not constant and is changing; however, this does not mean that the change is unpredictable. Most volatilities follow a pattern called the volatility smile. Many economists are researching ways to work the volatility smile into the binomial tree. It is another potential advantage of the binomial tree as it has the path of the stock mapped out, unlike Black–Scholes. This volatility smile can be mapped onto the binomial or trinomial tree in a way that allows the updated volatility to just be factored in at each node. The problem with this method is that there are further calculations needed, and again the common theme of speed versus accuracy comes into play.

FURTHER READING

Albanese, C., and Giuseppe C., *Advanced Derivatives Pricing and Risk Management: Theory, Tools and Hands-on Programming Application*, Elsevier Academic Press, Amsterdam, 2006.

Berg, Imme van den, *Principles of Infinitesimal Stochastic and Financial Analysis*, World Scientific, River Edge, N.J., 2000.

Boyle, P., Option valuation using a three-jump process, *International Options Journal*, **3**, 1986, pp. 7–12.

Boyle, P., Boyle, F., *Derivatives: The Tools That Changed Finance*, Risk Books, London, 2001.

Daigler, Robert T., *Advanced Options Trading: The Analysis and Evaluation of Trading Strategies, Hedging Tactics, and Pricing Models*, Probus Publishing Company, Chicago, 1994.

Duffie, D., Debt management and interest rate risk, in Beaver, W., Parker, G. (eds.), *Risk Management: Challenges and Solutions*, McGraw-Hill, New York, 1995.

Fabozzi, F., *The Handbook of Financial Instruments*, Wiley Finance, Hoboken, NJ, 2002.

Flavell, R., *Swaps and Other Instruments*, Wiley, Chichester, 2002.

Hull John, *Options, Futures and Other Derivatives*, 7th edition, Pearson Education, Upper Saddle River, NJ, 2010.

Kamrad, B., P. Ritchken, Multinomial approximating models for options with k-state variables, *Management Science* **37**(12), 1991, pp. 1640–1652.

Stulz, R. M., *Risk Management and Derivatives*, Southwestern Publishing Company, Nashville, TN, 2003.

CHAPTER NINE

Fixed Income and Interest Rate Risk

Only buy something that you'd be perfectly happy to hold if the market shut down for 10 years.

—Warren Buffett

Interest rates are a key component in many market prices and represent an important economic barometer. Factors that influence the level of market interest rates include:

- Expected levels of inflation
- General economic conditions
- Monetary policy and the stance of the central bank
- Foreign exchange market activity
- Foreign investor demand for debt securities
- Financial and political stability

Fixed-income securities, which include bonds, treasury bills, and commercial papers, pay a fixed rate of interest. The value of the funds that purchase fixed-income securities will rise and fall as interest rates change. For example, when interest rates fall, the value of an existing bond will rise because the coupon rate on that bond is greater than the prevailing interest rates. Conversely, if interest rate rises, the value of an existing bond will fall.

The yield curve is a graphical representation of yields for a range of terms to maturity. Since current interest rates reflect expectations, the yield curve provides useful information about the market's expectations of future interest.

Interest rates determine the discount rate for all financial assets, so it is of crucial importance to asset values. Interest rates affect equities (via company debt or bank earnings, for example), convertibles, bonds, floating rate notes, inverse floating rate notes, interest rate, and bond futures—the list is more or less

Handbook of Market Risk, First Edition. Christian Szylar.

endless. Interest rates follow a normal or lognormal distribution; the impact of movements in rates on different assets depends on the asset structure. Certain convertible securities may also be subject to interest rate risk.

9.1 Bond Valuation

A vanilla bond pays a fixed rate of interest (coupon) annually or semi-annually, or very unsually quarterly. The fair price of such a bond is given by the discounted present value of the total cash flow stream, using a market-determined discount rate.

Yield to maturity (YTM) is the most frequently used measure of return from holding a bond. The YTM is equivalent to the internal rate of return on the bond, the rate that equates the value of the discounted cash flows on the bond to its current price. This is the same as the yield necessary to discount all the investment's cashflows to a net present value (NPV) equal to its current dirty price. For a given set of cashflows, the yield to maturity can vary slightly according to which bond bond basis convention is used. The YTM equation for a bond paying semi-annual coupons is

$$P = \sum_{t=1}^{2T} \frac{C/2}{\left(1 + \frac{1}{2}r\right)^t} + \frac{M}{\left(1 + \frac{1}{2}r\right)^{2T}} \tag{9.1}$$

where P is the fair price of bond, C is the coupon, M is the redemption payment (par), T is the number of years to maturity, and r is the required rate of return on the bond.

9.2 The Yield Curve

The yield curve, a graph that depicts the relationship between bond yields and maturities, is an important tool in fixed-income investing. Investors use the yield curve as a reference point for forecasting interest rates, pricing bonds, and creating strategies for boosting total returns. The yield curve has also become a reliable leading indicator of economic activity.

Yield refers to the annual return on an investment. The yield on a bond is based on both the purchase price of the bond and the interest, or coupon, payments received. Although a bond's coupon interest rate is usually fixed, the price of the bond fluctuates continuously in response to changes in interest rates, as well as the supply and demand, time to maturity, and credit quality of that particular bond. After bonds are issued, they generally trade at premiums or discounts to their face values until they mature and return to full face value. Because yield is a function of price, changes in price cause bond yields to move in the opposite direction.

There are two ways of looking at bond yields: current yield and yield to maturity.

Current yield is the annual return earned on the price paid for a bond. It is calculated by dividing the bond's annual coupon interest payments by its purchase price. For example, if an investor bought a bond with a coupon rate of 6% at par, and full face value of $1000, the interest payment over a year would be $60. That would produce a current yield of 6% ($60/$1000). When a bond is purchased at full face value, the current yield is the same as the coupon rate. However, if the same bond were purchased at less than face value, or at a discount price, of $900, the current yield would be higher at 6.6% ($60/$900). Likewise, if the same bond were purchased at more than face value or at a premium price of $1100, the current yield would be lower at 5.4% ($60/$1100).

Yield to maturity reflects the total return an investor receives by holding the bond until it matures. A bond's yield to maturity reflects all of the interest payments from the time of purchase until maturity, including interest on interest. Equally important, it also includes any appreciation or depreciation in the price of the bond. *Yield to call* is calculated the same way as yield to maturity, but assumes that a bond will be called, or repurchased by the issuer before its maturity date, and that the investor will be paid face value on the call date.

Because yield to maturity (or yield to call) reflects the total return on a bond from purchase to maturity (or the call date), it is generally more meaningful for investors than current yield. By examining yields to maturity, investors can compare bonds with varying characteristics, such as different maturities, coupon rates, or credit quality.

The yield curve is a line graph that plots the relationship between yields to maturity and time to maturity for bonds of the same asset class and credit quality. The plotted line begins with the *spot interest rate*, which is the rate for the shortest maturity, and extends out in time, typically to 30 years.

Figure 9.1 shows the yield curve for U.S. Treasuries on January 10, 2013. It shows that the yield at that time for the three-year Treasury bond was about 0.376% while the yield on the 30-year Treasury bond was about 3.084%.

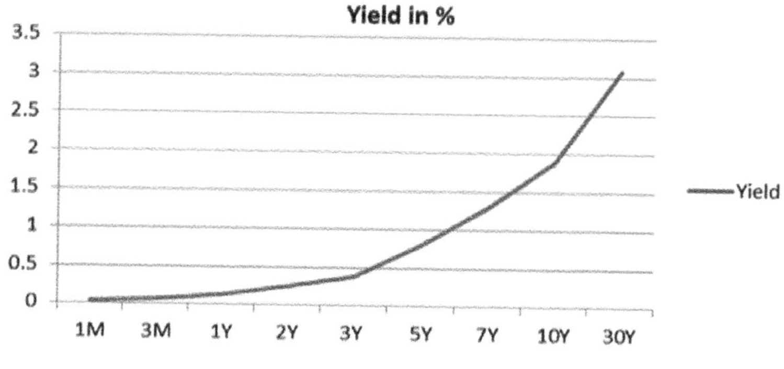

FIGURE 9.1 The U.S. Treasury yield curve.

A yield curve can be created for any specific segment of the bond market, from triple-A rated mortgage-backed securities to single-B rated corporate bonds. The Treasury bond yield curve is the most widely used, however, because Treasury bonds have no perceived credit risk, which would influence yield levels, and because the Treasury bond market includes securities of virtually every maturity, from 3 months to 30 years.

A yield curve depicts yield differences, or *yield spreads*, that are due solely to differences in maturity. It therefore conveys the overall relationship that prevails at a given time in the marketplace between bond interest rates and maturities. This relationship between yields and maturities is known as the *term structure of interest rates.*

As illustrated in Figure 9.1, the *normal* shape, or *slope*, of the yield curve is upward (from left to right), which means that bond yields usually rise as maturity extends. Occasionally, the yield curve slopes downward, or inverts, but it generally does not stay inverted for long.

What Determines the Shape of the Yield Curve? Most economists agree that two major factors affect the slope of the yield curve: investors' expectations for future interest rates and certain "risk premiums" that investors require to hold long-term bonds. Three widely followed theories have evolved that attempt to explain these factors in detail:

- **The Pure Expectations Theory** holds that the slope of the yield curve reflects only investors' expectations for future short-term interest rates. Much of the time, investors expect interest rates to rise in the future, which accounts for the usual upward slope of the yield curve.
- **The Liquidity Preference Theory**, an offshoot of the Pure Expectations Theory, asserts that long-term interest rates not only reflect investors' assumptions about future interest rates but also include a premium for holding long-term bonds, called the *term premium* or the *liquidity premium.* This premium compensates investors for the added risk of having their money tied up for a longer period, including the greater price uncertainty. Because of the term premium, long-term bond yields tend to be higher than short-term yields, and the yield curve slopes upward.
- **The Preferred Habitat Theory**, another variation on the Pure Expectations Theory, states that in addition to interest rate expectations, investors have distinct investment horizons and require a meaningful premium to buy bonds with maturities outside their "preferred" maturity, or habitat. Proponents of this theory believe that short-term investors are more prevalent in the fixed-income market and, therefore, longer-term rates tend to be higher than short-term rates.

Because the yield curve can reflect both investors' expectations for interest rates *and* the impact of risk premiums for longer-term bonds, interpreting the yield curve can be complicated. Economists and fixed-income portfolio managers put great effort into trying to understand exactly what forces are driving yields at any given time and at any given point on the yield curve.

Historically, the slope of the yield curve has been a good leading indicator of economic activity. Because the curve can summarize where investors think interest rates are headed in the future, it can indicate their expectations for the economy. A sharply upward sloping, or *steep*, yield curve has often preceded an economic upturn. The assumption behind a steep yield curve is that interest rates will begin to rise significantly in the future. Investors demand more yield as maturity extends if they expect rapid economic growth because of the associated risks of higher inflation and higher interest rates, which can both hurt bond returns. When inflation is rising, the Federal Reserve will often raise interest rates to fight inflation.

A *flat* yield curve frequently signals an economic slowdown. The curve typically flattens when the Federal Reserve raises interest rates to restrain a rapidly growing economy; short-term yields rise to reflect the rate hikes, while long-term rates fall as expectations of inflation moderate. A flat yield curve is unusual and typically indicates a transition to either an upward or downward slope (Figure 9.2).

An inverted yield curve, as the name implies, inverts the relationship described in the normal yield curve (Figure 9.3). Paradoxically, long-term yields

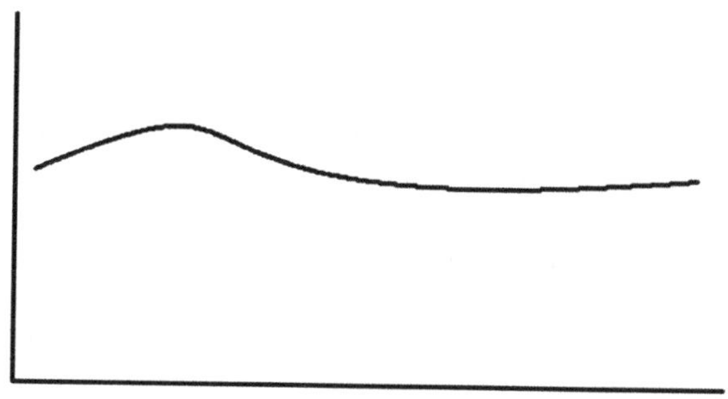

FIGURE 9.2 Flat yield curve.

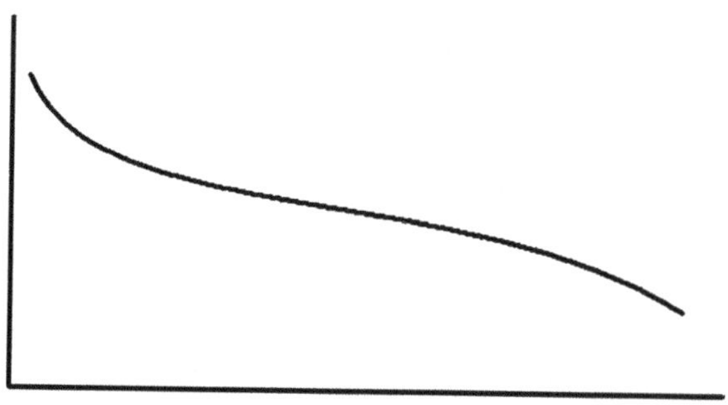

FIGURE 9.3 Inverted yield curve.

fall under short-term yields, indicating a negatively sloped curve. This trend indicates an expectation of a receding economy in the future, or a belief that the market will not exhibit any continuing inflation. Overall, low or negative expectations about future conditions might cause this kind of yield curve, as demand for short-term investments exceed long-term, driving up the interest rates on securities with a lower maturity date.

9.3 Risk of Holding a Bond

An investor in a fixed income security is exposed to a certain number of different risks. These risks are credit and default risk of the issuer, interest rate risk, inflation risk, liquidity risk and currency risk among the most significant ones.

Interest rate risk is most probably the most important risk because of the strong relationship between interests and bond prices. Duration and modified duration are the most frequent methods of measuring this risk. Convexity is the measure that is used to explain the variation away from the predicted return.

9.3.1 DURATION

Duration is the most commonly used measure of risk in bond investing. Duration incorporates a bond's yield, coupon, final maturity and call features into one number, expressed in years, that indicates how price-sensitive a bond or portfolio is to changes in interest rates.

Duration is usually defined as the weighted average time until the receipt of cash flows from an instrument, where the weights are the present values of cashflows. Initially developed by Macaulay in 1938 it is also often called "Macaulay's duration." The duration is given by the following the formula:

$$D = \frac{\sum_{t=1}^{n} \frac{tC_t}{(1+r)^t}}{P} \tag{9.2}$$

where D is duration, P is price of the bond, C_t is cash flow at time t, and r is yield to maturity.

9.3.2 MODIFIED DURATION

Modified duration is a slight variant of Macaulay duration. Duration is an important metric because it measures the interest rate elasticity of the bond price and is therefore a measure of interest rate risk. The lower the duration, the less responsive is the bond's value to interest rate moves. Modified duration measures the sensivity of the bond's price to changes in the yield curve. It is related to duration as per the following formula:

$$\text{MD} = \frac{D}{1+r} \tag{9.3}$$

where MD is modified duration and r is yield to maturity.

The concept of duration—and also modified duration and convexity—can be applied to any series of cashflows, and hence to a whole portfolio of investments rather than to a single bond. This will be referred to as "portfolio duration."

9.3.3 CONVEXITY

Duration is only the first-order measure of interest rate risk. For small yield the calculations are fairly accurate but for larger changes, they become less accurate. This can be improved by using a second-order measure being convexity. Convexity measures the curvature of the present value profile and describes how a bond's modified duration changes with respect to interest rates. Using convexity, it is possible to make a better approximation of the change in price due to a change in yield. This approximation is given by the following formula:

$$C = 10^8 \left(\frac{\Delta P_d'}{\Delta P_d} + \frac{\Delta P_d''}{P_d} \right) \tag{9.4}$$

where $\Delta P_d'$ is change in bond price if yield increases by 1 basis point (0.01) and $\Delta P_d''$ is change in bond price if yield decreases by 1 basis point.

High positive convexity is generally expected from an investor's perspective. If two similar bonds have equal price and yield but different convexities, the bond with higher convexity will perform better if the yield changes. In practice, therefore, the two bonds should not be priced the same. In the same way, when hedging a portfolio, an investor should try to ensure higher convexity in his long positions and lower convexity in his short positions.

9.3.4 FACTOR MODELS FOR FIXED INCOME

Movements in bond prices can be mapped on J Treasury factors and K credit spreads according to the following formula:

$$\Delta P_i = -\text{DVBP}_i \Delta y_i = -\text{DVBP}_i \Delta z_j - \text{DVBP}_i \Delta s_k - \text{DVBP}_i \Delta \varepsilon_i \tag{9.5}$$

The portfolio has n_i invested in each bond.

The portfolio change in value is the summarized by J and K general risk factors

$$\begin{aligned} \Delta V &= -\sum_{i=1}^{N} n_i \text{DVBP}_i \Delta y_i \\ \Delta V &= -\sum_{j=1}^{J} n_i \text{DVBP}_i \Delta z_j - \sum_{k=1}^{K} n_i \text{DVBP}_i \Delta s_k - \sum_{i=1}^{N} n_i \text{DVBP}_i \Delta \varepsilon_i \end{aligned} \tag{9.6}$$

A portfolio with thousands of securities can be summarized by just a few risk factors.

The radical change of the interest rate environment since the 2008 financial crisis led us to consider other models to capture interest rate risk. MSCI Barra has, for example, included the concepts of shift, twist, and butterfly effects into their model.[1]

9.3.5 HEDGE RATIO

Let's start to define some of concepts that will be used here.

A bond futures contract is an agreement on a recognised futures exchange to buy or sell a standard face value amount of a bond, at an agreed price, for settlement on a standard future delivery date. In some cases, the contract is nondeliverable. In most cases, the contract is based on a notional bond.

The conversion factor, for any particular bond deliverable into a futures contract, is a number by which the bond futures delivery settlement price is multiplied, to arrive at the delivery price for that bond.

The cheapest-to-deliver (CTD) bond is the one that is the most cost-effective for the futures seller to deliver to the buyer if required to do so.

Bond futures are used for a variety of purposes. Much of one day's trading in futures will be speculative—that is, a punt in the direction of the market. Another main use of futures is to hedge bond positions. In theory, when hedging a cash bond position with a bond futures contract, if cash and futures prices move together, then any loss from one position will be offset by a gain from the other. When prices move exactly in lock-step with each other, the hedge is considered perfect. In practice the price of even the cheapest-to-deliver bond (which one can view as being the bond being traded—implicitly—when one is trading the bond future) and the bond future will not move exactly in line with each other over a period of time. The difference between the cash price and the futures price is called the *basis*. The risk that the basis will change in an unpredictable way is known as *basis risk*.

Futures are a liquid and straightforward way of hedging a bond position. By hedging a bond position, the trader or fund manager is hoping to balance the loss on the cash position by the profit gained from the hedge. However, the hedge will not be exact for all bonds except the cheapest-to-deliver (CTD) bond, which we can assume is the futures contract underlying bond. The basis risk in a hedge position arises because the bond being hedged is not identical to the CTD bond. The basic principle is that if the trader is long (or net long, where the desk is running long and short positions in different bonds) in the cash market, an equivalent number of futures contracts will be sold to set up the hedge. If the cash position is short, the trader will buy futures. The hedging requirement can arise for different reasons. A market maker will wish to hedge positions arising out of client business, when they are unsure when the resulting

[1]MSCI Barra Research insight, Assessing interest rate risk beyond duration—shift, twist, butterfly, April 2010.

bond positions will be unwound. A fund manager may, for example, know that they need to (a) realize a cash sum at a specific time in the future to meet fund liabilities and (b) sell bonds at that time. The market maker will want to hedge against a drop in value of positions during the time the bonds are held. The fund manager will want to hedge against a rise in interest rates between now and the bond sale date, to protect the value of the portfolio.

When putting on the hedge position, the key is to trade the correct number of futures contracts. This is determined by using the *hedge ratio* of the bond and the future, which is a function of the volatilities of the two instruments. The amount of contracts to trade is calculated using the hedge ratio, which is given by

$$\text{Hedge ratio} = \frac{\text{Volatility of bond to be hedged}}{\text{Volatility of hedging instrument}} \tag{9.7}$$

Therefore one needs to use the volatility values of each instrument. We can see from the calculation that if the bond is more volatile than the hedging instrument, then a greater amount of the hedging instrument will be required. Let us now look in greater detail at the hedge ratio.

There are different methods available to calculate hedge ratios. The most common ones are the conversion factor method, which can be used for deliverable bonds (also known as the *price factor* method) and the modified duration method (also known as the basis point value method).

Where a hedge is put on against a bond that is in the futures delivery basket, it is common for the conversion factor to be used to calculate the hedge ratio. A conversion factor hedge ratio is more useful because it is transparent and remains constant, irrespective of any changes in the price of the cash bond or the futures contract. The number of futures contracts required to hedge a deliverable bond using the conversion factor hedge ratio is determined using the following equation:

$$\text{Number of contracts} = \frac{M_{\text{bond}} \times \text{CF}}{M_{\text{fut}}} \tag{9.8}$$

where M is the nominal value of the bond or futures contract.

The conversion factor method may only be used for bonds in the delivery basket. It is important to ensure that this method is only used for one bond. It is an erroneous procedure to use the ratio of conversion factors of two different bonds when calculating a hedge ratio. This will be considered again later.

Unlike the conversion factor method, the modified duration hedge ratio may be used for all bonds, both deliverable and nondeliverable. In calculating this hedge ratio the modified duration is multiplied by the dirty price of the cash bond to obtain the *basis point value* (BPV). The BPV represents the actual impact of a change in the yield on the price of a specific bond. The BPV allows the trader to calculate the hedge ratio to reflect the different price sensitivity of the chosen bond (compared to the CTD bond) to interest rate movements.

The hedge ratio calculated using BPVs must be constantly updated, because it will change if the price of the bond and/or the futures contract changes. This may necessitate periodic adjustments to the number of lots used in the hedge.

The number of futures contracts required to hedge a bond using the BPV method is calculated using the following:

$$\text{Number of contracts} = \frac{M_{\text{bond}}}{M_{\text{fut}}} \times \frac{\text{BPV}_{\text{bond}}}{\text{BPV}_{\text{fut}}} \tag{9.9}$$

where the BPV of a futures contract is defined with respect to the BPV of its CTD bond, as given by:

$$\text{BPV}_{\text{fut}} = \frac{\text{BPV}_{\text{CTDbond}}}{\text{CF}_{\text{CTDbond}}} \tag{9.10}$$

The simplest hedge procedure to undertake is one for a position consisting of only one bond, the cheapest-to-deliver bond. The relationship between the futures price and the price of the CTD given by Eq. (9.10) indicates that the price of the future will move for moves in the price of the CTD bond, so therefore we may set:

$$\Delta P_{\text{fut}} = \frac{\Delta P_{\text{Bond}}}{\text{CF}} \tag{9.11}$$

where CF is the CTD conversion factor.

The price of the futures contract, over time, does not move tick-for-tick with the CTD bond (although it may on an intra-day basis) but instead moves by the amount of the change divided by the conversion factor. It is apparent therefore that to hedge a position in the CTD bond we must hold the number of futures contracts equivalent to the value of bonds held multiplied by the conversion factor. Obviously if a conversion factor is less than one, the number of futures contracts will be less than the equivalent nominal value of the cash position; the opposite is true for bonds that have a conversion factor greater than one. However, the hedge is not as simple as dividing the nominal value of the bond position by the nominal value represented by one futures contract.

To measure the effectiveness of the hedge position, it is necessary to compare the performance of the futures position with that of the cash bond position, as well as to see how much the hedge instrument mirrored the performance of the cash instrument. A simple calculation is made to measure the effectiveness of the hedge, which is the percentage value of the hedge effectiveness:

$$\text{Hedge effectiveness} = -\left(\frac{\text{Fut } p/l}{\text{Bond } p/l}\right) \times 100 \tag{9.12}$$

Hedging a Bond Portfolio. The principles established above may be applied when hedging a portfolio containing a number of bonds. It is more realistic to consider a portfolio holding bonds that are not just outside the delivery basket, but are also not government bonds. In this case we need to calculate the number of futures contracts to put on as a hedge based on the volatility of each bond in the portfolio compared to the volatility of the CTD bond. Note that in practice, there is usually more than one futures contract that may be used as the hedge instrument. For example, in the sterling market it would be more sensible to use LIFFE's medium gilt contract, whose underlying bond has a notional maturity of four to seven years, if hedging a portfolio of short- to medium-dated bonds. However, for the purposes of illustration we will assume that only one contract, the long bond, is available.

To calculate the number of futures contracts required to hold as a hedge against any specific bond, we use:

$$\text{Hedge} = \frac{M_{\text{bond}}}{M_{\text{fut}}} \times \text{Vol}_{\text{bond/CTD}} \times \text{Vol}_{\text{CTD/fut}} \tag{9.13}$$

where M is the nominal value of the bond or future, $\text{Vol}_{\text{bond/CTD}}$ is the relative volatility of the bond being hedged compared to that of the CTD bond, and $\text{Vol}_{\text{CTD/fut}}$ is the relative volatility of the CTD bond compared to that of the future.

It is not necessarily straightforward to determine the relative volatility of a bond vis-à-vis the CTD bond. If the bond being hedged is a government bond, we can calculate the relative volatility using the two bonds' modified duration. This is because the yields of both may be safely assumed to be strongly positively correlated. If, however, the bond being hedged is a corporate bond and/or non-vanilla bond, we must obtain the relative volatility using regression analysis, because the yields between the two bonds may not be strongly positively correlated. This is apparent when one remembers that the yield spread of corporate bonds over government bonds is not constant, and will fluctuate with changes in government bond yields. To use regression analysis to determine relative volatilities, historical price data on the bond is required; the daily price moves in the target bond and the CTD bond are then analyzed to assess the slope of the regression line. In this section we will restrict the discussion to a portfolio of government bonds.

If we are hedging a portfolio of government bonds, we can use the following equation to determine relative volatility values, based on the modified duration of each of the bonds in the portfolio:

$$\text{Vol}_{\text{bond/CTD}} = \frac{\Delta P_{\text{bond}}}{\Delta P_{\text{CTD}}} \approx \frac{MD_{\text{bond}} \times P_{\text{bond}}}{MD_{\text{CTD}} \times P_{\text{CTD}}} \tag{9.14}$$

where MD is the modified duration of the bond being hedged or the CTD bond, as appropriate.

Once we have calculated the relative volatility of the bond being hedged, Eq. (9.5) [obtained from Eqs. (9.11) and (9.14)] tells us that the relative volatility of the CTD bond to that of the futures contract is approximately the same as its conversion factor. We are then in a position to calculate the futures hedge for each bond in a portfolio.

$$\text{Vol}_{\text{CTD/fut}} = \frac{\Delta P_{\text{CTD}}}{\Delta P_{\text{fut}}} \approx \text{CF}_{\text{CTD}} \tag{9.15}$$

9.3.6 DURATION HEDGING

Duration hedging assumes parallel moves in yields, using modified duration D^*

$$\Delta P = -(D^* P) \times \Delta y \tag{9.16}$$

Portfolio value changes are

$$\Delta V = Q\Delta S + N(M\Delta F) = (-QD_S^* S)\Delta y + N(-MD_F^* F)\Delta y$$

Optimal position is at

$$N^* = -\frac{QD_S^* S}{MD_F^* F} \tag{9.17}$$

Duration Hedging: Example

- Bond portfolio of \$10 million, with duration of 6.8 years, to be hedged for 3 months.
- The current futures price is 93-02 with a notional of \$100,000.
- The CTD is a 12%, 20-year bond, with duration of 9.2 years.
- The number of contracts to sell short for optimal protection is $N = (6.8 \times \$10{,}000{,}000)/(9.2 \times \$93{,}062.5) = 79.42$.

FURTHER READING

Duffie, D., Debt management and interest rate risk, in Beaver, W., Parker, G. (eds.), *Risk Management: Challenges and Solutions*, McGraw-Hill, New York, 1995.

Fabozzi, F., *Fixed Income Mathematics*, Probus, Chicago, 1993.

Fabozzi, F. J., *Duration, Convexity, and Other Bond Risk Measures*, Frank J. Fabozzi Associates, New Hope, PA, 1999.

Fabozzi, F. J., *Bond Markets, Analysis and Strategies*, 7th edition, Pearson, Prentice-Hall, Upper Saddle River, NJ, 2009.

Galitz, L., *Financial Engineering*, FT Pitman, London, 1995.

Kolb, R., *Futures, Options and Swaps*, Blackwell, Oxford, UK, 2000.

Reitano R., Non-parallel yield curve shifts and immunization, *Journal of Portfolio Management*, Spring, 1992, pp. 36–43.

CHAPTER TEN

Liquidity Risk

Liquidity is an elusive notion. Three basic definitions are commonly used: (1) the liquidity of financial instruments reflects the ease with which they can be exchanged for money without loss of value; (2) a related concept is market liquidity defined as the market's ability to trade a given volume of assets or securities without significantly affecting their prices; and (3) finally, monetary liquidity pertains to the quantity of fully liquid assets circulating in the economy. It is usually measured by a narrow or broad monetary aggregate or its ratio to nominal GDP. In this section we will focus on definitions 1 and 2. Liquidity risk in the context of banking will be covered in the chapter on Basel II/III (Chapter 13).

We have to distinguish between the risk to funding the firm, which is usually referred to as "funding liquidity risk," and the risk that a particular on- or off-balance sheet market or product is illiquid, which is referred to as "market liquidity risk." The management of "funding liquidity risk" is the risk that the firm will not be able to efficiently meet both expected and unexpected current and future cash flow and collateral needs without affecting daily operations or the financial condition of the firm." Market liquidity risk is defined as the risk that a firm cannot easily offset or eliminate a position without significantly affecting the market price because of inadequate market depth or market disruption. In this book, we will focus on the later.

In the context of asset management, liquidity risk must be seen from two different perspectives: assets (portfolio) and liability side (investor's behavior).

- Liquidity risk at the asset side arises when securities cannot be sold, liquidated, or closed at a limited cost in an adequately short timeframe.
- Liquidity risk at the liability side arises when the fund cannot meet redemption payments or is able to do so but with such an investment deviation that it could generate claims from the investors.

Handbook of Market Risk, First Edition. Christian Szylar.

In the context of UCITS, the regulator is expecting liquidity risk to be monitored as part of the risk manager tasks.[1] However, compared to what is done for counterparty risk and market risk, no recommendations in terms of implementation are provided but the expectations are challenging.

Because UCITS funds are open-ended, they are supposed to be able to pay redemptions at any time. Therefore, the regulator is putting a focus on that aspect by asking the risk managers to ensure that the portfolio risk profile is aligned with the redemption policy[2] and, where appropriate, that stress tests are conducted to assess the liquidity risk of the UCITS under exceptional circumstances.[3]

This lack of information and guidelines from the regulator probably makes liquidity risk management one of the main risk management challenges of the latest UCITS regulations.

How to approach liquidity risk in the context of investment funds?

Having securities in portfolio that are not liquid or which present low liquidity levels does not represent an issue as such. It only starts to be a concern as soon as investors start to leave the fund, because the fund manager will need to be able to face the cost of these redemptions which could trigger the sale of investments should cash levels appear to be not sufficient.

Also, because investment funds have to comply with a set of rules (a.o. UCITS law and investment policy), positions cannot be liquidated without considering the potential impact it could have on limits they have to respect. Furthermore, investors who are not leaving the fund should not be financing the cost of the redemptions of investors leaving the fund. Therefore, fairness for investors remaining invested is also a key point to consider while starting selling positions to face redemption payments.

A structured process needs then to be followed when analyzing liquidity risk within the investment industry (Figure 10.1).

The first step to consider when approaching liquidity risk for investment funds is to understand the expected and accepted level of liquidity risk exposure of investors. While this is not totally relevant for UCITS (broad range of investors); it could be different for less distributed funds. If the investors know from the launch of the fund that the selected investments are showing low liquidity levels and, thus, decide to invest in these instruments on purpose, then

---

[1]Committee of European Securities Regulator, 2010, CESR's Guidelines on Risk Measurement and the Calculation of Global Exposure and Counterparty Risk for UCITS, CESR/10-788, Box 1, explanatory text 1.

[2]Commission Directive 2010/43/EU of 1 July 2010 implementing Directive 2009/65/EC of the European Parliament and of the Council as regards organisational requirements, conflicts of interest, conduct of business, risk management, and content of the agreement between a depositary and a management company, Chapter IV, Section 2, art. 40.4.

[3]Commission Directive 2010/43/EU of 1 July 2010 implementing Directive 2009/65/EC of the European Parliament and of the Council as regards organisational requirements, conflicts of interest, conduct of business, risk management and content of the agreement between a depositary and a management company, Chapter IV, Section 2, art. 40.3.

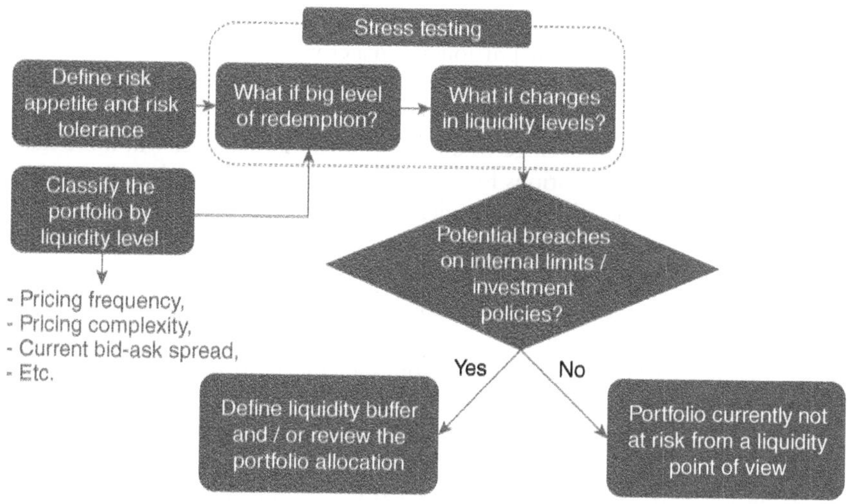

FIGURE 10.1 Liquidity risk for investment funds: decision tree. Source: PWC.

performing in deep liquidity analysis may appear to be not relevant since the output of that analysis will be aligned with investor's first expectations. However, in the context of a wide range of investors of different type (as it is for UCITS funds) knowing the current liquidity levels of invested instruments and going through a defined framework ensuring that the fund will be able to face redemption payments (even in stressed conditions) will, to a certain extent, limit the potential impact of liquidity events on the fund.

10.1 Traditional Methods and Techniques to Measure Liquidity Risk

As mentioned in the definitions, in the context of investment funds, liquidity risk must be seen and analyzed from two sides: assets (portfolio) and liabilities (investor behavior).

Part of the common indicators to measure liquidity risk of investments, the average traded volume, the bid–ask spread, and the liquidity VaR (LVaR) are probably the most well known.

10.1.1 AVERAGE TRADED VOLUME

Using the average traded volume to assess the capacity to sell a portion (or the total amount) of equities in a portfolio is probably one of the easiest ways to assess liquidity level of equities. The method is quite simple and the interpretation of the final results is easy.

As equities are traded on regulated markets, it is really easy to obtain the number of securities traded during the last days, weeks, or months. Therefore, the quantity held in portfolio can be compared to the average volume traded on the market. If the quantity the portfolio manager wants to sell on the market is really low compared to the average volume, we can then consider that it is really unlikely that trade will impact the market price. However, should that quantity be high compared to the average volume, the portfolio manager will more than likely be able to sell its positions for a longer period of time, and trading prices will probably be impacted by that trade.

As an illustration, let us consider the case where the trader would like to sell 100 shares (a) of company X. By gathering market information on these shares, he knows that during the last 20 days the average traded volume was of 10,000 shares (b). By comparing the quantity held in portfolio to the average quantity traded on the market, you can easily compute the ratio between (a) and (b) giving a ratio of 0.01 which, in simple words, means that the 100 shares of the portfolio could be liquidated within 1 day with a very low probability to see it impacting the price.

However, this computation implies that we are not considering that other market players could also decide to liquidate their positions at the same time. Therefore, haircuts are commonly applied on the average traded volume to compare portfolio positions to a portion of the average traded volume.[4]

The results of our previous computation would then have been (applying a percentage of 20%) 100/2000 = 0.05.

The computation results are easy to interpret because actually they represent the number of days required to liquidate the positions. Furthermore, it is really easy to implement since average traded volume can be easily obtained from the market data provider and some of them are providing interfaces and tools to facilitate the analysis.[5]

However, this indicator could in some cases be misleading, if we consider the situation where the high level of quantity traded is due to the fact that the related company is currently not behaving well and that high volumes are due to people disinvesting. This will lead to good levels for the selected liquidity risk indicators while, on the other hand, the trading price will probably be impacted at some point.

10.1.2 BID–ASK SPREAD

When talking about bonds, the previously described ratio will no longer be applicable. Bonds are generally traded over the counter, meaning that the information related to their traded quantity will not be as available as it is for equities. Therefore another indicator will need to be used.

It is quite common to see the bid–ask spread[6] used to assess liquidity of bonds. The wider the bid ask, the higher the liquidity risk because it would mean

[4]Ten, 20 or 30 percent of the average traded volume are commonly used.

[5]For example, LRSK function on Bloomberg stations.

[6]The difference in price between the highest price that a buyer is willing to pay for an asset and the lowest price for which a seller is willing to sell it.

that market makers and more globally buyers are considering that by buying that security they are taking a risk for not being able to sell it on the market for a good price.

Even though this approach seems to be relevant and adequate, it suffers from some drawbacks. Firstly, market information could appear as difficult to gather. Secondly, what does a wide bid–ask means exactly? Is 1% high or do we have to consider higher levels?

10.1.3 LIQUIDITY AND VaR

Risk is connected with deviation of the actual outcome from the expected one in the adverse direction for the agent. Nowadays, the VaR measure, which was initially developed for measuring market risk, is used also for control and regulation purposes, as well as in other areas. Market risk itself arises from the changes in level or volatility of market prices, and mid-prices are used for VaR evaluation. However, this approach causes questions, if it is assumed that portfolio of assets is liquidated, because the transaction will not be held at mid-price. The real price will depend on the ability of transaction's volume to influence existing spread and on the value of the spread itself, so that liquidity of the market begins to play the role. The reason for turning to the consideration of liquidity risk is VaR underestimation under usual framework in this situation, and the underestimation will lead to the increase of the market risk capital requirements, because they are connected with multiplication factor, determined by a number of VaR violations. Thus, if VaR is significantly underestimated, it will have consequences from the regulator side. The significance of underestimation will depend on the liquidity of liquidated portfolio.

There are number of studies that are devoted to incorporation of liquidity risk into VaR model. These studies are divided into two broad classes:

1. Some researchers develop the models of endogenous liquidity risk incorporation, when this type of risk is unique for the agent and presents the effect of liquidated quantity on the prices.
2. Other authors consider exogenous liquidity risk, which corresponds to the existing spread on the market. Moreover, some extensions were suggested in order to combine these two types of liquidity risk into one model.

VaR can be estimated with different methods and many modifications of these approaches exist, allowing it to overcome some drawbacks of the initial method. After the model is estimated, the natural question of interest is whether the chosen model is accurate. In order to respond to this question, a backtesting procedure has to be applied to results of estimation. In the literature different tests were suggested, which enable to verify the accuracy of the model according to certain points.

Liquidity risk is one of type financial risk and can be of great importance to financial institutions, as the history of LTCM has shown. In the most general way, the liquidity market can be defined as market, where market participants can quickly conduct transactions of big volume without significant influence on price. Liquidity risk itself can be divided into two groups: market liquidity risk and funding liquidity risk. The former appears when the real price of transaction differs from the market price, and the latter assumes that a company cannot meet its financial obligations (the ability to meet obligations strongly depends on the structure of assets and liabilities of the company, because when having short-term liabilities the company will have difficulties with their implementation if there are no high-liquid assets that can be easily transferred into cash). But we will focus here on the market liquidity risk.

Mid prices present the average values between bid and ask prices, and they are used for VaR calculation. However, this approach is not appropriate in reality, because the price of transaction differs from the mid price—the sale is implemented with respect to bid price, whereas the purchase is implemented with respect to ask price. Moreover, if the volume of position exceeds the normal market size, then bid and ask prices move in adverse direction for the trader, so that if the trader is liquidating large position, then bid price will be falling in some way after the traded quantity exceeds the normal market size. Thus, the market liquidity risk can be divided into exogenous liquidity risk, associated with observed bid–ask spread, and endogenous liquidity risk, connected with influence of liquidated quantity on the price of the asset. One way to deal with market liquidity risk is to set limits on positions in a portfolio, because it can enable us to escape sufficient losses when the necessity of portfolio liquidation appears. Bangia et al. (1999a) give a graphical representation of *exogenous* and *endogenous* liquidity that is reproduced in Figure 10.2. Below a certain size, transactions may be traded at the bid/ask price quoted in the market (*exogenous* liquidity), and above this size, the transaction will be done at a price below the initial bid or above the initial ask, depending on the sign of the trade (*endogenous* liquidity).

The market can be characterized as deep market or thin market according to the level of impact of sales on price (if the influence of traded quantity on price is not significant and the realized spread does not differ much from the observed one, then the market can be referred to category of deep markets; if the effect on price is large enough, then the market is thin). As an example of deep markets, the markets of high-liquid securities (such as Treasury bonds, main currencies) can be considered; the depth itself reflects the activity of participants of the market, namely, volume of trading. Another two characteristics of liquidity of the market are tightness and resiliency. Tightness shows how far the price of transaction deviates from the mid price, and resiliency reflects the time necessary for the price to recover after the transaction was conducted.

Because in certain models that will be considered below, spread is used in order to account for liquidity component in VaR, it will be useful to look at the concept of spread in more details.

Jorion (2001) points out that spread reflects three types of costs: order processing costs (these costs are associated, for example, with state of technology, cost of trading), asymmetric information costs (they are referred to orders coming from informed traders), and inventory-carrying costs (present the costs of maintaining open positions). Models associated with spread can be used for

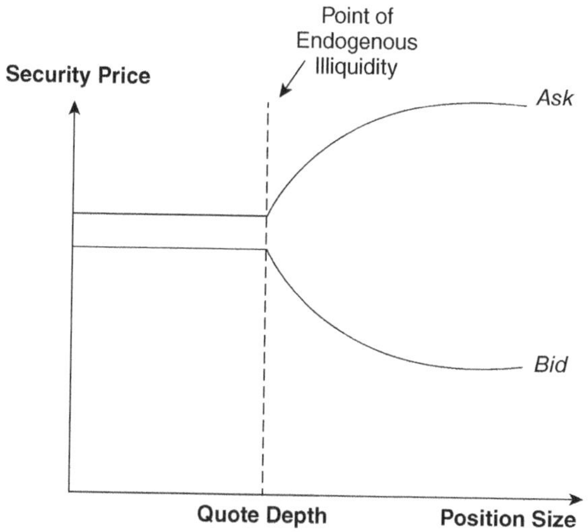

FIGURE 10.2 Effect of position size on liquidation value. **Source:** Bangia et al. (1999b).

incorporating exogenous and endogenous liquidity risk in VaR framework. Now we turn to the review of studies that were conducted in order to find the methods of including liquidity risk in the VaR model.

10.2 Liquidity at Risk

These studies can be divided into two broad classes. First, there are models that consider the problem of accounting for the endogenous liquidity risk by searching for optimal liquidation strategies of position. It is important because immediate liquidation of position results in high costs, but in the case of slow liquidation the position is exposed to price risk, so there is a tradeoff between execution costs and price risk and the problem of finding optimal trading strategy appears. The latter can be done by minimizing transaction cost or maximizing expected revenue from trading, then, based on received optimal strategy, liquidity-adjusted value at risk can be derived. The second class of models is devoted to modeling exogenous liquidity risk through studying the distribution of spread. In addition, certain modifications allow us to include endogenous liquidity risk in this class of models. But before we start with models presenting approaches of the first group, we should be mention the ad hoc way of adjusting VaR to liquidity risk.

One of the most simple ways of introducing liquidity risk in VaR model is to adjust the time horizon of VaR according to inherent liquidity of portfolio. This ad hoc approach does not enable us to reach the goal it is aimed at. In spite of adjusting the time horizon to the inherent liquidity of portfolio, the calculation of value at risk assumes that the liquidation of all positions occurs at the end of the holding period and does not occur orderly during the period. Shamroukh (2000) suggests the model, where the liquidation of portfolio occurs orderly throughout the holding period; thus the liquidation-adjusted value at risk is obtained. The author begins with the model for one asset and one risk factor. The main idea is to calculate the mean and variance of the portfolio value defined when the liquidation is over, but an important point here is that the portfolio is liquidated by parts during the holding period. The initial position is assumed to be uniformly liquidated over the period T (at time T the liquidation is completed). The liquidation schedule is characterized by the sequence of trade dates and volumes of trading. The logarithm of ratio of risk factor's levels is assumed to be normally distributed, and the portfolio value at time T can be computed as the sum of products of sold number of units of asset and the price of sale. After certain transformations, the variance of the portfolio value is received, and as a result the liquidation-adjusted value at risk can be found (it is computed as the usual value at risk, but because the liquidation is taken throughout the holding period, the variance differs from the ordinary case; thus, the obtained value at risk also differs from standard RiskMetrics VaR). The difference between two measures represents the liquidation factor, and it depends on the number of trading dates. If number of trading dates tends to infinity, then the liquidation factor tends to 1/3. The author also extends this model to the case of portfolio of multiple assets that are influenced by multiple risk factors. More complex derivations lead to the same result in the relation between liquidation-adjusted value at risk and the usual one. Then the author introduced exogenous and endogenous liquidity costs by constructing the liquidation price of the asset (endogenous liquidity cost presents the sensitivity of liquidation price to trade size). This liquidation price is used in the calculation of portfolio value at time T; thus, liquidation-adjusted and liquidity-cost adjusted value at risk (LA-VaR) is obtained. The holding period can then be considered as an endogenous variable and found as output of the model. The liquidation schedule defines the level of VaR, and the author offers to consider the minimal of these values as LA-VaR: for some given trading frequency, the number of trading dates that minimizes derived VaR can be found. Then, by definition, liquidation period T is computed as the product of trading frequency and optimal number of trading dates.

10.2.1 INCORPORATION OF ENDOGENOUS LIQUIDITY RISK INTO THE VaR MODEL

One of the basic studies devoted to finding optimal liquidation strategy and defining liquidity-adjusted VaR on its basis is the study of Almgren and Chriss (1999), who introduced the notion of liquidity-adjusted VaR in the framework of choosing the optimal strategy of portfolio liquidation. The authors considered a trading model where the initial portfolio consists of block of X units of security (extension for portfolios exist in this model, but we will turn to it later) and has to be liquidated by the fixed time T in the future (further we will talk in terms of shares, but also futures contracts and units of currency are considered as securities in the model). The whole time interval is divided into N small intervals of length τ in which the liquidation of shares takes place, so that at time T the number of holding shares in portfolio is zero. The trading trajectory $x = (x_0,$

$x_1, \ldots x_N$) represents number of shares that will be held at discrete times $t_k = k\tau$, $k = 0, \ldots, N$. In addition, the trade list is also defined; it represents the number of shares ($n_1, \ldots, n_N$) that are sold during small intervals; and, consequently, each number equals the difference between adjacent points of trading trajectory. Another variable that is constructed is average rate of trading; it is defined as the ratio of quantity traded in the time interval to the length of time interval itself: $\upsilon_k = n_k/\tau$.

The price of the stock is assumed to follow a discrete arithmetic random walk:

$$S_k = S_{k-1} + \sigma\tau^{1/2}\xi_k - \tau g\left(\frac{n_k}{\tau}\right), \qquad k = 1, \ldots, N, \qquad (10.1)$$

where σ is the stock's volatility, ξ_k-independent random variables (with zero mean and unit standard deviation), and $g(\upsilon)$ is a function of the average rate of trading. This function is the permanent market impact function.

The authors consider the influence of sale of shares on the stock's price through functions of permanent and temporary market impact. Permanent market impact is the impact of trades on the market price, the main feature of which is that, once occurred, it lasts until the portfolio is liquidated. The function of permanent market impact can be linear in the average rate of trading: $g(\upsilon) = \gamma\upsilon$, so that it depicts the decrease in the stock's price per unit time due to selling of shares at the average rate of trading. Thus, in order to include the resulting effect of selling a certain number of shares in one time interval on the stock's price, the sold number of shares has to be multiplied by the coefficient of proportionality γ.

In contrast to permanent market impact, temporary market impact exists only in the period when liquidation of the certain block of shares takes place: Selling of nk shares in the interval between t_{k-1} and t_k influences the price only in this time interval and does not influence the price in consequent time intervals. Hisata and Yamai (2000) note, that in order temporary market impact disappears in the next period, the price of stock has to increase by the value of temporary market impact in order only permanent market impact remains to the beginning of next period. Temporary market impact function also can be assumed to be linear function of average rate of trading, having additional term that represents fixed costs of selling (as an example of fixed costs authors cite half of bid–ask spread and fees): $h(\upsilon) = \epsilon.\ \mathrm{sgn}(n_k) + \eta\upsilon$, where ϵ-fixed costs of selling, sgn-sign function. This expression corresponds to decline in price per share; if n shares are sold, then full effect of temporary market impact will equal (in correspondence with definition of average rate of trading) $nh(n/\tau) = \varepsilon|n| + \eta/\tau n^2$ so that total costs are quadratic in number of shares sold. Accounting for temporary impact of trades on the price, the latter can be written in the next way (in general case):

$$\widetilde{S}_k = S_{k-1} - h(\upsilon_k) \qquad (10.2)$$

Using Eqs. (10.1) and (10.2), the authors deduce the trading revenue (so-called capture of the trading trajectory) that presents the sum of products of number of sold shares and the price of sale, expression for which was obtained before:

$$\sum_{k=1}^{N} n_k \bar{S}_k = XS_0 + \sum_{K=1}^{N} \sigma\tau^{1/2}\xi_k - \tau g\left(\frac{n_k}{\tau}\right)x_k - \sum_{k=1}^{N} n_k h\left(\frac{n_k}{\tau}\right) \tag{10.3}$$

Thus, the difference between the initial value of portfolio (XS_0) and its liquidation value ($\sum n_k \widetilde{S}_k$) can be found, this difference represents the total cost of trading (it is also considered as measure of transaction costs) and is called implementation shortfall. According to the assumptions of the model, it is a random variable (if $\xi_k \sim N(0, 1)$, then implementation shortfall is also normally distributed). Mathematical expectation and variance of total cost of trading can be calculated, these two moments depend on the trading trajectory x and are marked as $E(x)$, $V(x)$ respectively. For example, if all shares are sold in the first time interval, then variance is zero and mathematical expectation of total cost of trading increases with increase in number of time intervals.

Because mathematical expectation and variance depend on the chosen trading trajectory, the question of optimal trading trajectory appears. For the given value of variance, the trader will choose the trading strategy that minimizes expected cost (this problem of constrained minimization is solved with the help of Lagrange multiplier λ, which reflects the risk-aversion of the agent). Consequently, in the coordinate ($V(x)$, $E(x)$) the efficient frontier of optimal trading strategies can be built. In order to choose the trading strategy from those composing the efficient frontier, one can use the utility function approach or look at value at risk.

In the first case, the coefficient of risk aversion, which is determined by the utility function, is used instead of Lagrange multiplier, while the minimization problem remains the same. In the second case, the authors apply the concept of value at risk to the total cost of trading, so that value at risk is defined as level of transaction costs that will not be exceeded with probability p:

$$\mathrm{VaR}_p(x) = \lambda_\upsilon \sqrt{V(x)} + E(x) \tag{10.4}$$

where λ_υ is the quantile of standard normal distribution corresponding to the certain level of significance. As we can see, value at risk depends on the trading strategy x. Trading strategy x is called efficient if it allows to get the minimum possible value at risk for the given level of significance $(1 - p)$. Authors call this minimum possible value at risk L-VaR. It means that liquidity-adjusted value at risk is defined as value at risk for the optimal strategy x, and optimality of the latter is related to minimization of value at risk for given level of significance and given holding period T.

The authors also extend the model for portfolio of assets. The idea is the same as in the case of one asset, but now stock prices follow a multidimensional arithmetic Brownian random walk, instead of coefficients of proportionality in permanent and temporary market impact functions matrices beginning to depict the influence of trading on prices. As in the previous case, mathematical expectation and variance of total costs of liquidation can be computed, and then the optimal trading strategy can be found.

Hisata and Yamai (2000) continue the research of Almgren and Chriss and consider the problem of finding optimal execution strategy, but in the case of endogenous holding period with the assumption of sales at constant speed. The authors use practically the same model of price movement: Permanent and temporary market impact functions are included in the model of price movement (however, the sales price at time k is determined by deduction of temporary market impact function from the price of that period, whereas Almgren and Chriss deduct this function from the price of the previous period). On the basis of a given model of price movement, transaction costs are found as the difference between the initial value of the position and the liquidation value. Then mathematical expectation and variance of transaction costs are derived. On their basis the function, which has to be minimized in order to obtain the optimal execution strategy, is built. It represents the sum of mathematical expectation of transaction costs and the product of multiplication of standard deviation of transaction costs, cost of capital r, and certain percentile of standard normal distribution (the latter is determined by investor's risk aversion). While the first term of the sum presents the average change in the value of position, the second term reflects the influence of market risk. Minimization of the described function under condition of sales at constant speed with respect to number of sales enables us to find the optimal number of sales and, consequently, the optimal holding period. Then liquidity-adjusted VaR can be defined: It is defined as relative VaR and equals the product of percentile of standard normal distribution for given confidence level and standard deviation of transaction costs which occur in case of optimal trading strategy. The authors suggest also different extensions of the model such as continuous time model, stochastic market impact model, and extension for portfolio of assets in the continuous time framework.

Berkowitz (2000) suggested to account for liquidity risk in the usual VaR framework by considering the influence of the amount of sold assets on prices; and on the basis of these prices, they suggested to estimate portfolio value. The value of a portfolio is supposed to be determined by positions in assets and pricing function which defines the effect of risk factors on the portfolio value. But, as is known, changes in asset price are connected with the changes in volume of the position in this asset, so that the downward demand curve for the asset is observed (author uses the concept of elasticity of demand). The negative slope can be explained on the basis of the theory of asymmetric information: Selling large amounts of asset can be considered as a signal that informed agents try to deliver from it due to their private knowledge. Thus, the effect of selling asset at its price is included in the process of the price movement in the next way: The influence is linear and the total effect presents the negative value of the amount of asset sold multiplied by some parameter (in the capacity of assets shares are considered below, the estimation of the parameter will be described later). The manager of portfolio of shares faces the problem of maximizing expected revenue from trading over the whole holding period subject to the condition that the sum of traded shares has to be equal to a given number of shares. The price of the following period equals the price of the previous period adjusted to the market-wide change in price of the share and the above-described term presenting the influence of the amount of sold shares on the price. The optimal number of trading shares is found from the maximization problem (the solution for optimal number of trading shares obtained by Bertsimas and Lo 1 is used). Then, the solution is plugged into the equation that defines the process of price movement, and consequently the portfolio value can be obtained. The latter appears to consist of two terms: One term is responsible for market risk component and corresponds to the price of the previous period and the market-wide change in price; another term reflects the reaction of price to the amount of asset sold, as well as the effect of influence of liquidating position on the price. The mathematical expectation and variance of the portfolio value can be found (the market-wide change in price and number of shares sold are assumed to be independent, this leads to an additional term in the expression for variance). The parameter in the equation for price movement is obtained as the estimation from regression, where the dependent variable is difference in prices between two periods. Thus, the calculation of value at risk is based on the rebuilding of portfolio values that account for a decrease of price from optimal investor's sales. The author also points out that the distribution of portfolio values can be estimated by numerical methods.

Jarrow and Subramanian (2001) paid attention not only to the market impact of sales on the price of asset, but also to the existence of execution lag, so that the sale is not executed immediately after the order arrives. These two points are considered as features of liquidity, and the case of absence of execution lag and market impact is the case of absence of liquidity risk. In the model the price of stock follows geometric Brownian motion, the impact of sales on price is included with the help of a price discount function that owns certain properties (one of properties is that the function is nonincreasing in sales), and the existence of execution lag is defined by a nondecreasing function of sales (the latter means that the larger the sale is, the more time it will take to execute this order). The aim of the trader, who has some number of shares, is to find such strategy of liquidation that will maximize the expected revenue from sale. The authors found out that if the trader is price taker (the case of no liquidity risk), then the optimal trading strategy for him is block liquidation of assets. Depending on whether the drift in the price process is positive or negative, the block liquidation has to be taken, respectively, at the terminal date or immediately. In the case of liquidity risk, the optimal execution strategy will be the same as in the previous case only if the condition of economies of scale in trading holds. This condition provides that the cumulative price discount in the case of selling all shares in two parts is less than or equal to the price discount in the case of selling all shares at one time. The liquidity discount is computed then as difference between market price of the share and its liquidation value. The calculation of liquidity-adjusted value at risk, based on this model, requires knowledge of average and standard deviation of price discount for the number of shares sold and of the execution period, but there are no available data that can be used for estimation of necessary parameters.

All of the described models dealt with endogenous liquidity risk; however, it is not so easy to apply these methods in practice, due to lack of necessary data and difficulties in determining some parameters of the models (for example, coefficient of proportionality of temporary market impact function). On the contrary, the model that is described below can be evaluated on the basis of available data.

10.2.2 INCORPORATION OF EXOGENOUS LIQUIDITY RISK INTO THE VaR MODEL

Bangia et al. (1999a) proposed the model for incorporation of exogenous liquidity risk into the VaR model. The authors make a strong distinction between exogenous liquidity risk, which is similar to all market participants, cannot be influenced by the actions of one player and presents the market characteristics, and endogenous liquidity risk, which is special for each player according to the volume of trading position, because after the volume exceeds the level of quote depth, the influence of traded size on bid and ask prices occurs. The main idea of including the exogenous liquidity risk in the VaR model is that in the case of not perfectly liquid markets the liquidation of position is not executed at mid price, but this price has to be adjusted for the value of existed spread. Thus, because in order to compute usual VaR the worst price of asset for some confidence level is considered, then in order to account for the effect of spread on the price of a transaction in the VaR calculation, the worst value of spread for a certain confidence level has to be considered. Below the model itself is described.

One-day asset return is defined as the logarithm of the ratio of two adjacent prices and is assumed to be normally distributed with mathematical expectation $E(r_t)$ and variance σ_t^2:

$$r_t = \ln\left(\frac{P_t}{P_{t-1}}\right) \sim N(E(r_t), \sigma_t^2) \qquad (10.5)$$

For a given confidence level (the authors use a confidence level of 99%, the corresponding quantile equals 2.33), the worst return can be found and, consequently, the worst price of the asset:

$$P_w = P_{t^{e^{E(r_t)-2.33\sigma t}}} \qquad (10.6)$$

The authors consider a one-day horizon; the expected daily return is taken to be equal to zero, and then the parametric VaR can be written in the following way:

$$\text{P-VaR} = P_t(1 - e^{-2.33\sigma_t}) \qquad (10.7)$$

In the empirical analysis the authors computed variance using the exponential weighted moving average, as clustering effects are observed for time series of asset returns, when periods of large and small returns volatility are clustered and distinct from each other. It means that variance changes over time, and an exponentially weighted moving average enables this change to take place.

As the next step, the authors turn to spread behavior in order to include its effect in the VaR framework. As in the previous case, we were interested in the worst price (for a given confidence level), so now we are interested in the worst movement of spread. The exogenous cost of liquidity (COL) is determined in the following way:

$$\text{COL} = \frac{1}{2}[P_t(\bar{S} + a\tilde{\sigma})] \tag{10.8}$$

where $\bar{S}$ is the average relative spread ($S = (\text{Ask} - \text{Bid})/\text{Mid}$), Pt is the mid price of the asset, $\tilde{\sigma}$ is the volatility of the relative spread, and a is a scaling factor that has to provide the confidence level of 99%. With the latter parameter, certain problems are connected: This parameter has to be evaluated empirically, because the distribution of spread is far from normal and there are no tables from which the values of parameter can be taken. The estimated interval for values of a is [2;4.5], and the exact number depends on the instrument and market. The procedure of a estimation is based on the idea that the worst possible relative spread for some given confidence level can be computed using historical simulation method and using deviation from the mean relative spread: $\bar{S} + a\tilde{\sigma}$. The series of worst possible relative spreads estimated from the historical simulation method is known; on the contrary, until the a factor is unknown, the worst possible relative spreads cannot be estimated from the second method. Because one measure—worst possible relative spread—is obtained on the basis of two different methods, and the parameter, which is used in one of the methods, is not known, it can be estimated from the regression equation of known worst possible relative spreads from the first method (historical simulation method) on the worst possible relative spreads from the second method. Then, estimated a factor can be used for obtaining the exogenous cost of liquidity.

After the exogenous cost of liquidity, presenting the measure of exogenous liquidity risk, was derived, the assumption concerning the movement of prices and spreads is made: In an adverse market environment, extreme events in spreads and prices happen simultaneously. It means that if price has changed to its worst level for some given confidence level, then the spread changed for its worst value too. This enables us to write down the worst price of transaction in the next way:

$$P' = P_{t^{e^{-2.33\sigma_t}}} - \frac{1}{2}[P_t(\bar{S} + a\tilde{\sigma})] \tag{10.9}$$

On the basis of Eq. (10.9), the liquidity-adjusted VaR can be found:

$$\text{LAdj} - \text{VaR} = P_t(1 - e^{-2.33\sigma_t}) + \frac{1}{2}[\text{Pt}(\bar{S} + a\tilde{\sigma})] \tag{10.10}$$

Empirical studies show that distribution of returns is not normal and has fat tails. In order to deal with this fact, the authors introduce a parameter that will control for fat tails of returns distribution:

$$\text{P-VaR} = P_t(1 - e^{-2.33\theta\sigma_t}) \tag{10.11}$$

If the distribution is normal, $\theta = 1$; θ increases with the increase in deviation of distribution from normality.

All these derivations were done for single a asset. However, it is possible to extend the model to the portfolio level. The authors suggest to compute the second term in the formula for LAdj – VaR [Eq. (10.10)] by finding the spread for the portfolio. The latter can be calculated on the basis of a portfolio bid and ask series, which can be obtained as the weighted sum of a series of bids and asks of a portfolio's assets. Thus, in the case of a portfolio, LAdj – VaR is also calculated as the sum of two terms: the usual VaR and a component reflecting the exogenous liquidity risk. It should be mentioned here that another possible way of extending the model to the portfolio level is to redefine prices in correspondence with an existing spread and then use these new prices for VaR calculation. The model of Francois-Heude and Van Wynendaele (2001), which will be described here later, can be viewed as a certain point of redefining the prices (the way of adjusting the mid price to the spread, proposed in their model, can be useful for the problem of extending current approach to portfolio level).

In the paper the authors present also empirical results of model's estimation: They estimate the model for one asset case (data for currency exchange rates were used) using an EWMA scheme for volatility calculation, estimation was conducted also for different portfolios. The liquidity component is more significant for less liquid markets and matters in determining the number of VaR violations and, consequently, the multiplication factor.

10.2.3 EXOGENOUS AND ENDOGENOUS LIQUIDITY RISK IN VaR MODEL

Le Saout (2002) applies the model of Bangia et al. (1999a) to French stock market and extends the model in order to account for endogenous risk. The author substitutes the bid–ask spread that is used for value at risk calculation by weighted average spread (WAS). WAS is connected with the market, where sale and purchase of large blocks of assets are allowed to be performed in one transaction and its price has to be in the interval, defined by WAS for block of standard size. The WAS presents the difference between weighted bids and asks: Bids and asks are weighted according to the quantities pointed in the buy and sell orders (orders are added up in order to reach standard size of the block), and these weighted sums are divided then by the quantity, corresponding to the block's standard size. Thus, a transaction with a number of shares in the block equal to or more than standard size will be taken at some price from the described interval. It means that now the second term in the formula for LAdj – VaR incorporates also the influence of traded size on the price of stock and also accounts for endogenous risk. Empirical estimation of the part of LAdj – VaR, related to liquidity risk, changed in the case of incorporation of endogenous liquidity risk in comparison with the case when only exogenous risk was included in LAdj – VaR. The component responsible for liquidity risk has increased after calculations were held with WAS.

The idea of using WAS as the mean of including endogenous liquidity risk in the VaR framework is met also in the work of Francois-Heude and Van Wynendaele (2001). The authors criticize the model of Bangia et al. (1999a) and suggest certain modifications that allow us to escape the main disadvantages of this model, one of which is the problem of endogenous liquidity risk.

The authors emphasize the four main disadvantages of the model of interest: The necessity to estimate a parameter, since spread distribution is not normal; assumption that in an adverse market environment, extreme changes in prices and spreads happen simultaneously; lack of component of endogenous liquidity risk in the model; and ignorance of dynamic aspect of liquidity. In order to overcome first two problems, the new way of incorporating exogenous liquidity risk in value at risk is suggested:

$$\text{L-VaR}_t = \text{MidBL}_t - \left(\text{MidBL}_t \cdot \left(1 - \frac{\bar{S}_{pBL}}{2} \right) \cdot e^{-\alpha\sigma} \right) \tag{10.12}$$

where MidBL_t is mid price at the best limit at time t, $\bar{S}_{pBL}$ is average relative spread. Thus, this way of introducing exogenous liquidity risk does not require consideration of distribution of spread and does not assume extreme changes in prices and spreads to happen simultaneously. In the proposed framework the mid price is adjusted to the existence of spread, so that the redefined price is used for searching the worst price (for some confidence level) and VaR. In order to account for the dynamic aspect of liquidity, authors introduce the new term in the expression for L-VaR_t, which controls for difference between relative quoted spread and average relative spread:

$$\begin{aligned} \text{L-VaR}_t = {} & \text{MidBL}_t - \left(\text{MidBL}_t \cdot \left(1 - \frac{\bar{S}_{pBL}}{2} \right) \cdot e^{-\alpha\sigma} \right) + \text{MidBL}_t \\ & \cdot \left(\frac{\text{MidBL}_t - B\text{BL}_t}{\text{MidBL}_t} - \frac{\bar{S}_{pBL}}{2} \right) \end{aligned} \tag{10.13}$$

The sign of this difference (the third term of expression) will increase or decrease L-VaR_t, and the difference itself can be viewed as volatility of liquidity level. And the last modification concerns inclusion of endogenous liquidity risk in the model: Relative quoted spread and average relative spread have to be adjusted to the traded quantity. Proposed model was applied to the intraday data (holding period was taken to be 15 minutes).

Of course, the incorporation of exogenous liquidity risk in the VaR model—and more precisely, in the model of Bangia et al. (1999a) and its results—will depend on the method of calculation of liquidity-adjusted value at risk: historical simulation, variance–covariance approach, and Monte Carlo method.

10.3 Other Liquidity Risk Metrics

As seen earlier, the commonly used indicators are suffering from some drawbacks. Therefore, we need to go a step further should we want to properly assess the liquidity risk of the portfolio. We decided then to explore less-known liquidity indicators.

Percentage of Outstanding Shares: As for bonds, and the average traded volumes are not available, and the notional of the bond held in the portfolio can be compared to the total outstanding size giving information on the percentage of the total issue represented by the portfolio holdings. A high percentage suggests a low liquidity.

Stressed Bid–Ask: Volatility between the different bid–ask provided by the different contributors for one security. A high level suggests a low liquidity.

Number of Market-Pricing Providers: Having a high number of markets-pricing providers suggests a high liquidity.

Kyle's Lambda: This indicator based on Albert Kyle's research[7] can be used in a simple form. It represents the ratio between the stressed bid–ask spread and the volume exchanged. This indicator helps accounting for bid-ask spreads related to significantly different traded volumes.

Credit ratings—LOT[8]*:* Lesmond, Ogden, and Trzcinka analyzed the link between liquidity and credit ratings. This indicator was calculated based on an analysis (by LOT) of 4000 bonds, indicating a liquidity score for each credit rating.

Stale Prices: Having prices of investments that are remaining unchanged for a consecutive period of time is also an indicator of potential liquidity issue.

Having a broader set of indicators can be considered as a good start to perform relevant liquidity risk analysis. However, it does not solve the key issues that risk managers are facing when assessing their portfolio liquidity that can be summarized as follows:

[7]Kyle, A., Continuous auctions and insider trading, *Econometrica*, **53**(6), November 1985, pp. 1315–1335.

[8]Lesmond D., Ogden J., Trzcinka C., A new estimate of transaction costs, *Review of Financial Studies*, **12**, 1999, pp. 1113–1141.

- How can we interpret the results of each indicator?
- How can we aggregate the liquidity levels within a balanced portfolio?
- How can we communicate computation results in an efficient way?

These questions probably summarize the main practioners questions regarding liquidity when indicators have been identified and selected.

One way of solving them is the use of relative measures to qualify instruments liquidity levels. By being compared to a broad and representative set of results, each liquidity measure will then be considered as being high or low. They will probably better support analysis and decisions because the value of any of the indicators that have been described above will probably be difficult to interpret on an absolute basis. Furthermore, in order to have the broadest view of the liquidity level of an investment, we will need to use not only one indicator but a set of indicators that will then be aggregated to give a composite liquidity score.

Creating a relative liquidity measure by comparing securities results (each indicator's value or a score aggregating the results of a selection of indicators) to a representative benchmark will allow the creation of a liquidity score based on a limited scale (e.g., liquidity scale going from 1 to 5). That kind of approach will more than likely ease the communication as having a simple indicator (e.g., 1, 2, 3, 4, 5, with 5 being highly liquid); giving a quick idea of the liquidity of the instrument traded is easier to communicate than a bid–ask spread of 133 bps. Finally, a Liquidity score based on a defined and common scale will also allow the aggregation of results by simply weighting the final scores of each instrument and summing them.

So, investments liquidity levels will probably be more interpretable and easier to manage when defined on a relative basis compared to an absolute basis.

10.4 Methods to Measure Liquidity Risk on the Liability Side

As described earlier, the regulator expects a strong focus on the liability side bacause redemption payments may trigger the sale of a portion of the securities held in a portfolio should the cash levels be too low. Determining the potential level of redemptions based on the information available and estimating the impact of different levels of stress will definitely be a strong tool for managing liquidity risk for investment funds. Furthermore, this is also a clear and defined expectation of the regulator in the context of UCITS IV.[9]

[9]Commission Directive 2010/43/EU of 1 July 2010 implementing Directive 2009/65/EC of the European Parliament and of the Council as regards organizational requirements, conflicts of interest, conduct of business, risk management, and content of the agreement between a depositary and a management company, Chapter IV, Section 2, art. 40.3.

This can be a difficult challenge because a lot of investments done in investment funds are done through nominee accounts leading to a serious lack of transparency on investors. Therefore the country of origin and any other information that could potentially help the risk manager to do a deep analysis on potential redemptions will probably be difficult to gather.

Should that statement lead to the conclusion that nothing can be performed to determine the potential trends in future redemptions? We do not think so.

Actually, risk managers and investment managers are not too concerned about the effect that fund investors could have on a separate basis because what will impact them is a net redemption. Therefore, past trends in subscriptions and redemptions could constitute a reliable basis to determine potential future trends in redemptions as well as defining plausible[10] and relevant stress tests.

A simple approach could be computing the average past levels of redemptions identifying the maximum levels of redemptions that happened in the past as well as the standard deviation of past subscriptions and redemptions. These two indicators will give an idea of the normal trend (average) of redemption as well as the level of deviation that could be expected. That approach could potentially be sufficient regarding the regulator's expectation. However, the information remains quite limited because results are expressed in number of shares and the link with the liquidity of the portfolio could be quite difficult to do.

More advanced methodologies could then be used to provide risk managers and board members with information that is easier to materialize and offers a clear link with the liquidity at portfolio level.

Typically, as we are looking at past trends, a time series model can then be used to model future trends based on past trends. We apply a time series analysis framework like the Box–Jenkins approach[11] to model past time series and then use the level of random errors of the times series model to define potential future stress scenarios plausible based on the analyzed past periods (Figures 10.3 and 10.4).

Because the number of days before the fund runs out of cash will also give a prospective view to the asset manager of how many days he would potentially have before being required to sell a portion of the funds' investments, that final step in the approach will link redemption trends with portfolio liquidity (Figures 10.5 and 10.6). To illustrate that concept, should a fund determine that the number of days to survive is less than 2 or 3 days, as long as portfolio investments are highly liquid, this will probably not be a concern for the asset manager. On the other hand, should the investment's liquidity levels appear as

[10]This is, unlikely to occur but not impossible. Committee of European Securities Regulator, 2010, *CESR's Guidelines on Risk Measurement and the Calculation of Global Exposure and Counterparty Risk for UCITS*, CESR/10-788, Explanatory text 62.

[11]Bourdonnais, Régis, Terraza, Michel, 2010, *Analyse des séries temporelles—Applications à l'économie et à la gestion*, 3rd edition, Dunod, Paris, Chapter 3, Figure 7.2.

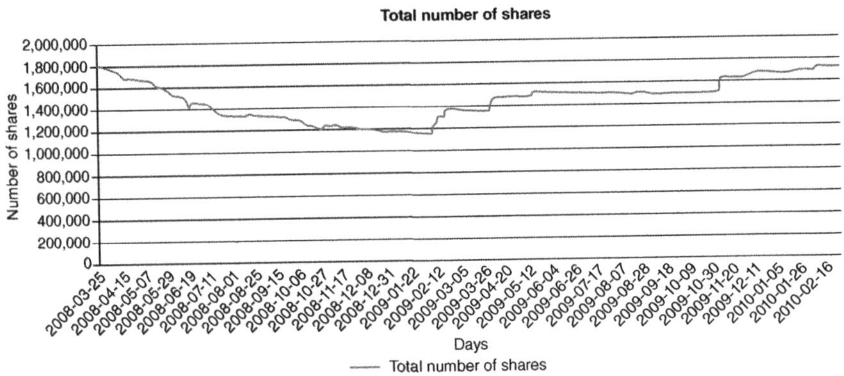

FIGURE 10.3 Past trends of numbers of shares.

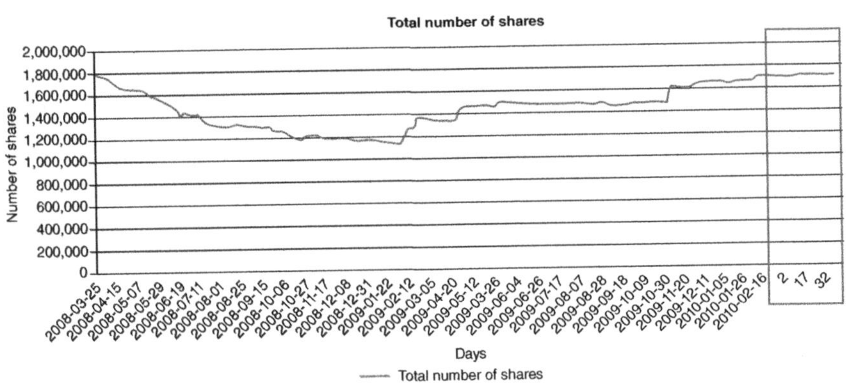

FIGURE 10.4 Expected trend (average) for the next 30 days.

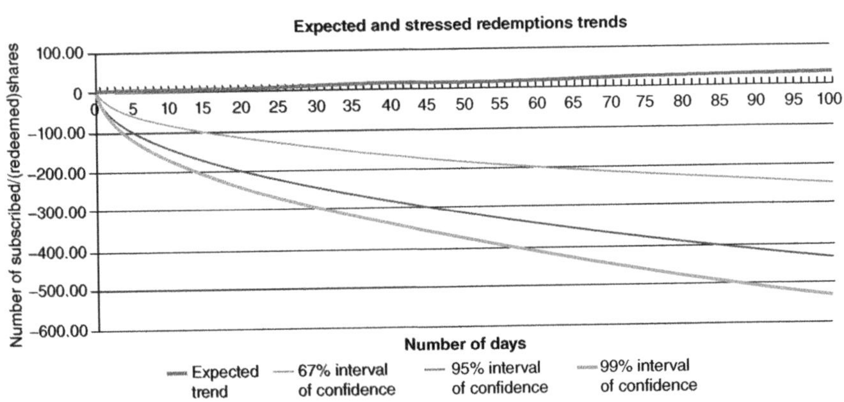

FIGURE 10.5 Redemption scenarios using different levels of stress.

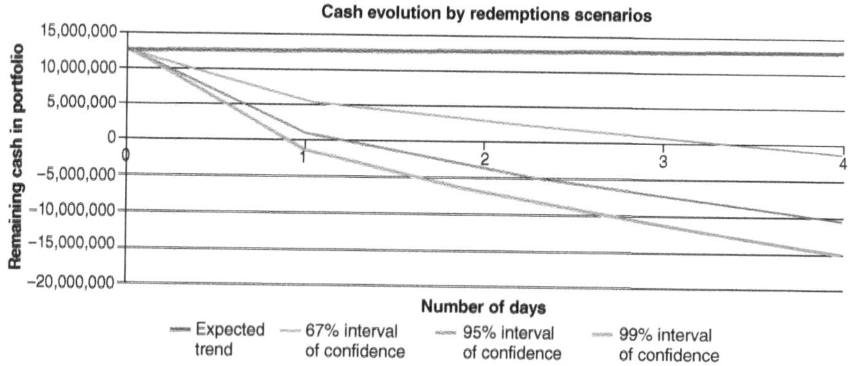

FIGURE 10.6 Linking redemption scenario to cash: Number of fund's surviving days to redemption payments using cash available.

being low, additional analysis and discussions will be required to determine how this would be managed and what cushions[12] should be determined to limit the potential impact of redemptions on portfolio management.

Limiting Redemptions. UCITS funds are, by definition, open-ended. Therefore the opportunities for these funds to limit redemptions, there by reducing their potential impact on portfolio management, are not numerous.

One could think about putting a certain level of fees on redemption trying to limit the level and frequency of redemptions where actual limits on redemptions will only be accepted on a case-by-case basis by the regulator (the same types of acceptance on limitations willapply to NAV temporary suspension and side pockets).

FURTHER READING

Almgren, R., Chriss, N., Optimal execution of portfolio transactions, working paper, University of Chicago, Department of Mathematics, 1999.

Bangia, A., Diebold, F., Schuermann, T., Liquidity on the outside, *Risk* **12**(6), 1999a, pp. 68–73.

Bangia, A., Diebold, F., Schuermann, T., Stroughair, J., Modeling liquidity risk with implications for traditional market risk measurement and management, Working Paper, The Wharton School, University of Pennsylvania, 1999b.

Berkowitz, J., Incorporating liquidity risk into value-at-risk models, working paper, University of Houston, September 2000.

[12]For example, increasing cash levels, rebalancing of average portfolio liquidity levels by investing in more liquid instruments, and so on.

Erwan, L. S., Incorporating liquidity risk in var models, Working Paper, University of Rene, 2001.

Francois-Heude, A., Van Wynendaele, P., Integrating liquidity risk in a parametric intraday VaR framework, working paper, 2001.

Giot, P., Time transformations, intraday data, and volatility models. *Journal of Computational Finance*, **4**(2), 2000, pp. 21–62.

Giot, P., Market risk models for intraday data. *The European of Journal of Finance*, **11**(4), 2005, pp.309–324.

Haberle, R., Persson, P., Incorporating market liquidity constraints in var', *Banque & Marches*, (44), 2000, pp. 14–19.

Hisata, Y., Yamai, Y., Research toward the practical application of liquidity risk evaluation methods, *Monetary and Economic Studies*, December 2000.

Jarrow, R., Subramanian, A., The liquidity discount, *Mathematical Finance*, 2001, pp. 447–474.

Jorion, P., *Value at Risk: The New Benchmark for Managing Financial Risk*, second edition, McGraw-Hill, 2001.

Le Saout, E., Intégration du risque de liquidité dans les modèles de valeur en risque, *Bankers Markets & Investors*, **61**, November–December 2002, pp. 15–25.

Shamroukh, N., Modelling liquidity risk in VAR models, working paper, Algorithmics UK, 2000.

CHAPTER ELEVEN

Alternatives Investment: Targeting Alpha, Idiosyncratic Risk

The active management is designed to outperform the market of reference (called "benchmark") of the managed portfolio. The manager, using various analytical tools, will select in a discretionary way products, securities, or sectors more likely to grow faster than the market. The excess return gained above the benchmark is usually called alpha.

Within the active management, there are different styles that can be classified according to the level of risk, geographic or sectoral portfolio distribution, the type of products used, or the investment time horizon.

These funds can also be handled in a "traditional" or "alternative" manner, using fundamental or quantitative criteria. Generally, many transactions are carried out in such a background and therefore the costs management becomes relatively high.

Conversely, the passive management or index is designed to faithfully replicate the performance of a market of reference (for example, an index such as the Dow Jones or the CAC 40). The method used is generally to replicate in miniature the benchmark index; for example, a CAC 40 Fund will consist of 40 values of the index, weighted according to the size of their capitalization.

This type of management requires significantly less search work for the manager, because it is often partially automated. In addition, fees are generally lower due to fewer transactions for its management.

11.1 Passive Investing

There are three main methods of replication of indices used in passive management:

Handbook of Market Risk, First Edition. Christian Szylar.

1. *Pure Replication.* This method, which was mentioned above, is the most widely used and involves buying all the components of an index and weighing them according to the size of their capitalization. You should readjust the weight of every action dynamically to adapt to the changes in the securities comprising the index. The disadvantage of this method is the number of transactions necessary for the dynamic adjustment of the portfolio.
2. *Synthetic Replication.* This method uses derivatives on index, mainly of futures (futures contracts) or the asset-swap (swap concluded OTC contract). This technique can reduce management fees not physically holding the securities.
3. *Statistical Replication (Approximated).* This type of replication is to get as close as possible to the performance of the index (tracking error the lowest possible) while minimizing the costs. One of the most frequently used methods is the stratification method, which consists in selecting only the largest capitalizations of an index, by varying their weighting in the portfolio to match the movements of the index. This method is moderately accurate, and it is difficult to optimize to the maximum the portfolio *tracking error.*

There is also another product, the ETF (Exchange Traded Funds or Tracker). The ETF is listed on the stock exchange as a single share, and it replicates a benchmark and offers daily liquidity. Regulators were recently concerned about synthetic ETFs, which led to further clarifications from the authorities.

The designation of "traditional management" includes the type of management called "benchmarking"—that is, investing in a type of defined financial asset and comparing the performance of the fund to a reference such as an index.

The orientation of the reference market will therefore play a leading role in such funds, whether administered in a "passive" way (indexing) or in an "active" way (through strategies of *stock picking*, for example).

Traditional funds can be invested in stocks, bonds, or currency titles and can identify four major fund families of this type of management:

1. *Equity Funds.* Invested in equities, as their name implies, these funds can be specialized based on the market capitalizations (the "small caps") or geographical areas (emerging Europe, Asia-Pacific) and sectors (new technologies, health, etc.). Their benchmark is thus usually a reference index (for example, CAC 40 for a fund invested in French equities).
2. *Bond Funds.* These funds mainly invested in corporate bonds and may offer different levels of risk/return according to the proportion of their investments in junk or senior obligation "junk." It can also be specialized with respect to certain geographic areas or reference currency.
3. *Money Market Funds.* These funds are largely invested in government bonds. They therefore offer a close performance of the minimum rate of a country and are used primarily by businesses and individuals to place their cash in the short term. Their benchmark is usually the reference of a country or currency rate—for example, EURIBOR or EONIA for the euro area.

4. *Diversified Funds.* The funds are invested in different asset classes listed above. Their risk/return will therefore vary according to their allocation to the various asset classes.

Tracking error reveals how closely the returns on the investment have followed the benchmark index returns. If the fund's tracking error is large, its returns have fluctuated considerably in relation to the returns of the benchmark index.

Correspondingly, a low tracking error reveals that the historical returns have not differed much from the benchmark returns.

$$\text{Tracking error} = \sqrt{\frac{\sum_{p=1}^{N}(R_p - R_b)^2}{N-1}}$$

where R_p is the return of fund, R_b is the return on benchmark index, and N is the number of days (return period).

11.2 Active Management

The alternative, unlike traditional management, is decorrelated from capital markets and has a goal of "absolute," and not relative to a benchmark performance. To say it differently, alternative management is targeting alpha.

It is designed to exploit the inefficiency of markets to improve the performance of its portfolio, through arbitrage strategies but also to a range of financial products more important than traditional management. An alternative investment fund (AIF) may use all types of derivatives to leverage, and they can also use short-selling techniques. In contrast, traditional funds cannot go physically short but synthetically. So, investing in alternative investment may be more risky in theory even if originally the short book can act as a hedge, hence limiting the total portfolio's risk. Because of the short book hedging the long book, it is not unusual that some alternative funds may exhibit a lower risk (expressed in either VaR or volatility) than a pure long-only fund.

As defined by the SEC, "hedge fund" is a general, nonlegal term used to describe private, unregistered investment pools that traditionally have been limited to sophisticated, wealthy investors. Hedge funds are not mutual funds and, as such, are not subject to the numerous regulations that apply to mutual funds for the protection of investors—including regulations requiring a certain degree of liquidity, regulations requiring that mutual fund shares be redeemable at any time, regulations protecting against conflicts of interest, regulations to assure fairness in the pricing of fund shares, disclosure regulations, regulations limiting the use of leverage, and more."

These funds are based mostly off-shore (Delaware, Cayman Islands, etc.) to work around regulations imposed on traditional management vehicles. In Europe, London, Geneva, Luxembourg, and Dublin are usually the places where alternatives are managed and domiciled.

The alternative may also be indirect—that is, that a fund can develop strategies for investment in other funds. These *hedge funds* are called "fund of funds" and practice alternative multi-management.

11.3 Main Alternative Strategies

The alternative has undergone significant developments since the creation of the first *hedge fund*—namely, *long/short equity*—at the end of the 1940s by Alfred Winslow Jones. Over the years, new management techniques have emerged through the creation of new media investments and the emergence of many markets across the globe.

The following is a nonexhaustive list of the main alternative strategies.

Long/Short Equity. The long/short managers attempt to identify both the most undervalued and the most overvalued companies. They go long the undervalued and short the overvalued companies' equity. The use of short-selling in general serves two main purposes. First, it can represent a view on an overvalued asset. Second, it can be used to hedge the market risk of the long position. The advantage of holding both long and short positions is that the portfolio should make money in most market environments.

Short selling involves the sale of a security not owned by the seller, a technique used to take advantage of an anticipated price decline. The short sellers use all available techniques for shorting securities, including outright securities shorting, uncovered put options, and occasionally futures shorting. A short seller must generally pledge to the lender other securities or cash as collateral for the shorted security in an amount at least equal to the market price of the borrowed securities.

Equity Market Neutral. The strategy seeks to be beta neutral and to only generate return from the relative outperformance of the long versus the short positions, regardless of how the market moves. The neutral position can refer to beta, sector, country, currency, industry, market capitalization, style neutral, or any combination of these factors.

Convertible Arbitrage. The Convertible Arbitrage strategy, as the name implies, is associated with convertible securities. The managers attempt to profit from three different sources: coupon return and short rebate, gamma trading, and mispricing. A convertible security is a fixed income instrument that can later be converted into a fixed number of shares. Holding a convertible is therefore equivalent to holding a bond position and a call option on the specified amount of underlying stocks. Until maturity, the bond holder will receive a coupon payment and thus will have a stable income source from the interest payment of the convertible bond, unless he decides to convert before maturity. The coupon payments, however, are usually low compared to normal bond coupons, and the managers therefore often use leverage. Additionally, a manager can receive an income from shorting the underlying stock and, much like the short-selling strategy, receive an immediate income from the sale which can be reinvested. Depending upon the negotiated short rebate, a convertible bond manager can often generate a higher return on the reinvestment than the short lending fee.

Global Macro. The Global Macro strategy is one of the oldest and most successful of all hedge fund strategies, but the strategy is in fact a departure from the literal meaning of the term "hedge fund" because most of the global macro hedge funds do not hedge their investments. Instead, the managers make very large directional bets that reflect their forecasts of market directions, as influenced by major economic trends and/or particular events. The managers trade interest rates, equity securities, currencies, and commodities and use leverage and derivatives extensively to hold large market exposures and to boost returns.

CTA/Managed Futures. A commodity trading advisor (CTA) or managed futures strategy uses the future markets for trades including commodities, interest rates, equity indices, and occasionally currency futures. The individual managers may specialize within a certain range of different futures. The strategy can further be broken down to two main substrategies: systematic and discretionary.

Managers who follow a systematic strategy use a proprietary trading model with a particular trading technique, such as trend-following, counter-trend, or spread trading. Systematic managers normally have a well-diversified portfolio across different markets, where they methodically abandon their losing trades while allowing their winning trades to run.

The discretionary managed futures strategy is very similar to the global macro strategy. The main differences are that discretionary managed futures managers exclusively make bets with futures. The managers make directional long-term positions based on fundamental forecasts and/or short-term bets based on specific information.

Event-Driven Strategies. Event-driven managers attempt to capitalize on company news events, such as earnings releases, spin-offs, carve-outs, mergers, Chapter 11 filings, restructurings, bankruptcy reorganizations, recapitalizations, and share buybacks. The portfolio of some event-driven managers may shift in majority weighting between risk arbitrage and distressed securities, while others may take a broader view. Instruments include long and short common and preferred stocks, as well as debt securities and options. Leverage may be used by some managers.

11.4 Specific Hedge Fund Metrics

Investors allocating to hedge funds are usually expecting to get some spicy returns from their investment and also expect to get uncorrelated returns with the markets. Hedge funds are perceived as having diversification benefits. Unfortunately, a lot of investors were disappointed because during the 2008 financial crisis hedge funds did not all deliver in terms of performance and more importantly they exhibited a high level of correlations with markets. It is then not surprising that the first metrics that investors are looking at closely is the level of alpha that the manager has generated. The main reason to put money into hedge funds is risk-adjusted performance. If you are certain of a bull market, there is no need to put money in hedge funds. Beta from index funds is all that an investor requires—assuming they can stomach the risk, which I certainly can't. Isolating and measuring alpha can also be difficult. Past betas and alphas are unstable and do not necessarily carry predictive information on the future. There is no real agreement in the industry about how to characterize and calculate alpha. Alpha is a measure of value added performance.

11.4.1 MARKET FACTOR VERSUS MULTIFACTOR REGRESSION

In simple terms, alpha is the abnormal rate of return on a security or portfolio in excess of what would be predicted by an equilibrium model like the capital asset pricing model (CAPM). It is called Jensen's alpha (using annualized numbers):

$$\propto_{\text{Jensen}} = (\text{AR}_{\text{Fund}} - \text{AR}_{\text{RFR}}) - [\beta_{\text{Fund}} * (\text{AR}_{\text{BM}} - \text{AR}_{\text{RFR}})]$$

Depending on the composition of the fund, using the fund's net market exposure (long exposure minus short exposure) is a valid proxy for the beta of the fund (one benefit being that large changes in portfolio composition are reflected instantly rather than based off a regression window).

Another method of calculating alpha is to use multifactors regression and the residual (unexplained by factors) is considered to be alpha.

The standard model in the hedge funds survey is the Fung and Hsieh (2004) seven factors model, which considerably explains time series variation in hedge funds return. It takes the form of a multifactor model where

$$r_i = \alpha + \beta_{i1} f_1 + \beta_{i2} f_2 + \beta_{i3} f_3 + \beta_{i4} f_4 + \cdots + \beta_{in} f_n + \varepsilon_i$$

where $f_1, f_2, f_3, f_4, \ldots, f_n$ are factors used in the model (fundamental factors) and β_{in} represents sensitivity of stocks *i*'s return to the factors.

In the Fung and Hsieh model it takes the form of

$$\begin{aligned} R_{it} = \alpha &+ \beta_1(\text{SP} - R_f) + \beta_2(\text{RL} - \text{SP}) + \beta_3(\text{TY} - R_f) + \beta_4(\text{BAA} - \text{TY}) \\ &+ \beta_5(\text{PTFSBD} - R_f) + \beta_6(\text{PTFSFX} - R_f) \\ &+ \beta_7(\text{PRFSCOM} - R_f) + \varepsilon \end{aligned}$$

Risk factors are defined as the excess return of the S&P 500 index (SP – R_f), the return of the Russell 2000 index minus the return of the S&P500 index (RL – SP), the excess return of the 10-year treasuries (TY – R_f), the return of Moody's BAA corporate bonds minus 10-year treasuries (BAA – TY), the excess returns of lookback straddles on bonds (PTFSBD – R_f), currencies (PTFSFX – R_f), and commodities (PTFSCOM – R_f).

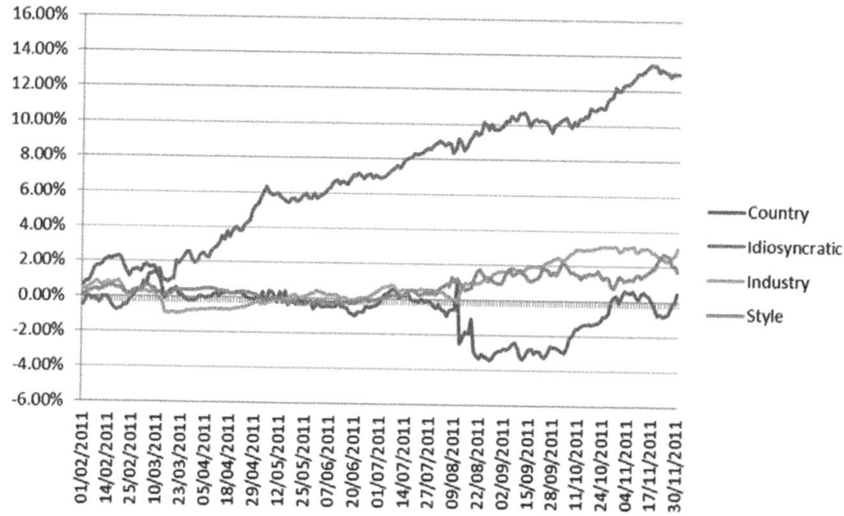

FIGURE 11.1 **Idiosyncratic return using the Axioma model.**

We can also use, for example, Axioma fundamental model or any other fundamental model to obtain alpha after regression of all the factors as Figure 11.1 shows.

11.4.2 THE SHARPE RATIO

$$\text{Sharpe} = \frac{AR_{\text{Fund}} - AR_{\text{RFR}}}{\text{Vol}_{\text{Fund}}}$$

where AR_{RFR} is the absolute return of the risk free rate.

The Sharpe ratio is calculated by subtracting the risk-free rate from the rate of return for a portfolio and dividing the result by the standard deviation of the portfolio returns.

The Sharpe ratio tells us whether a portfolio's returns are due to smart investment decisions or a result of excess risk. This measurement is very useful because although one portfolio or fund can reap higher returns than its peers, it is only a good investment if those higher returns do not come with too much additional risk. The greater a portfolio's Sharpe ratio, the better its risk-adjusted performance has been. A negative Sharpe ratio indicates that a riskless asset would perform better than the security being analyzed.

11.4.3 THE INFORMATION RATIO

The information ratio (also known as appraisal ratio) is basically a riskadjustment of alpha. It measures the alpha per unit of active risk—that is, tracking error.

This ratio allows to check that the risk taken by the manager in deviating from the benchmark is sufficiently rewarded. It is widely used as an indicator for evaluating manager skill. It is calculated using the following formula:

$$IR = \frac{AR_{Fund} - AR_{BM}}{Vol_{Alpha}}$$

11.4.4 *R*-SQUARE (R^2)

R^2 is the proportion of variance in fund returns that is related to variance of the benchmark returns: it is a measure of portfolio diversification (variance = the square of standard deviation).

The closer R^2 is to 1, the more portfolio variance is explained by benchmark variance. Its mathematical formulation is

$$R^2 = \left(\frac{\text{Avg}(R_{\text{Fund}} * R_{\text{Adj\_BM}}) - \text{Avg}(R_{\text{Adj\_BM}}) * \text{Avg}(R_{\text{Fund}})}{\text{Stdev}[R_{Fund}] * Stdev[R_{Adj\_BM}]} \right)^2$$

11.4.5 DOWNSIDE RISK

Maximum Drawdown (D_{Max}): Represents the maximum loss an investor would have suffered in the fund by buying at the highest point and selling at the lowest.

Largest Individual Drawdown: The largest individual uninterrupted loss in a return series.

Drawdown Recovery Time: Time taken to recover from maximum drawdown to the original level.

The above list is not exhaustive, and a lot of specific hedge funds' metrics exist to track their performance and risk they take over time.

Table 11.1 shows an example of a long/short equity fund for the period April 2011–December 2012.

Figure 11.2 charts the cumulative portfolio return, the benchmark return, and what we have called the adjusted benchmark return. It is convenient to measure the portfolio return with the adjusted benchmark return, considering that an hedge fund may not have 100% exposure to the market so this is why it has to be adjusted to the net market exposure of the portfolio.

Figure 11.3 is a nonexhaustive list of key performance risk adjusted metrics we can derive from the analysis of the cumulative returns. Those metrics are usually reviewed by hedge fund investors before deciding any allocation.

Figure 11.4 shows how the portfolio and the adjusted benchmark compares when we use the efficient frontier approach. And we can deduce that the hedge fund portfolio gives a better risk/reward than the adjusted benchmark. The hedge fund portfolio exhibits a much lower volatility and offers a better return.

TABLE 11.1 Time Series

Date	Net Market Exposure (NME)	Benchmark MSCI AC World Daily TR Net Local Index	Adjusted Benchmark
11-Apr-11	57.00%	−0.31%	−0.18%
12-Apr-11	53.00%	−1.16%	−0.66%
13-Apr-11	50.00%	0.37%	0.20%
14-Apr-11	49.00%	−0.24%	−0.12%
15-Apr-11	45.00%	0.14%	0.07%
18-Apr-11	40.00%	−1.24%	−0.56%
19-Apr-11	43.00%	0.28%	0.11%
20-Apr-11	39.00%	1.59%	0.68%
21-Apr-11	38.00%	0.51%	0.20%
22-Apr-11	43.00%	0.01%	0.00%
25-Apr-11	40.00%	−0.12%	−0.05%
26-Apr-11	37.00%	0.46%	0.18%
27-Apr-11	39.00%	0.36%	0.13%
28-Apr-11	35.00%	0.34%	0.13%
29-Apr-11	40.00%	0.15%	0.05%
02-May-11	41.00%	0.11%	0.05%
03-May-11	42.00%	−0.53%	−0.22%
04-May-11	45.00%	−0.86%	−0.36%
05-May-11	46.00%	−0.63%	−0.28%
06-May-11	43.00%	0.41%	0.19%
09-May-11	44.00%	0.06%	0.03%
10-May-11	40.00%	0.66%	0.29%
11-May-11	36.00%	−0.47%	−0.19%
12-May-11	40.00%	−0.22%	−0.08%
13-May-11	43.00%	−0.47%	−0.19%
16-May-11	47.00%	−0.52%	−0.22%
17-May-11	43.00%	−0.28%	−0.13%
18-May-11	44.00%	0.79%	0.34%
19-May-11	44.00%	0.23%	0.10%
20-May-11	42.00%	−0.50%	−0.22%
23-May-11	40.00%	−1.40%	−0.59%
24-May-11	37.00%	0.11%	0.04%
25-May-11	34.00%	0.23%	0.08%
26-May-11	34.00%	0.42%	0.14%
27-May-11	35.00%	0.48%	0.16%
30-May-11	36.00%	−0.04%	−0.01%
31-May-11	34.00%	1.14%	0.41%
01-Jun-11	36.00%	−1.32%	−0.45%
02-Jun-11	33.00%	−0.63%	−0.23%
03-Jun-11	34.00%	−0.63%	−0.21%
06-Jun-11	35.00%	−0.79%	−0.27%
07-Jun-11	37.00%	0.02%	0.01%
08-Jun-11	42.00%	−0.59%	−0.22%
09-Jun-11	43.00%	0.52%	0.22%

(Continued)

TABLE 11.1 ***(Continued)***

Date	Net Market Exposure (NME)	Benchmark MSCI AC World Daily TR Net Local Index	Adjusted Benchmark
10-Jun-11	41.00%	−1.14%	−0.49%
13-Jun-11	46.00%	−0.12%	−0.05%
14-Jun-11	47.00%	1.08%	0.50%
15-Jun-11	48.00%	−1.17%	−0.55%
16-Jun-11	47.00%	−0.51%	−0.25%
17-Jun-11	42.00%	0.08%	0.04%
20-Jun-11	46.00%	0.00%	0.00%
21-Jun-11	48.00%	1.39%	0.64%
22-Jun-11	49.00%	−0.20%	−0.10%
23-Jun-11	54.00%	−0.75%	−0.37%
24-Jun-11	58.00%	−0.29%	−0.16%
27-Jun-11	60.00%	0.34%	0.19%
28-Jun-11	64.00%	0.94%	0.56%
29-Jun-11	68.00%	1.14%	0.73%
30-Jun-11	65.00%	1.07%	0.72%
01-Jul-11	60.00%	0.95%	0.62%
04-Jul-11	57.00%	0.36%	0.21%
05-Jul-11	59.00%	−0.11%	−0.06%
06-Jul-11	54.00%	−0.08%	−0.05%
07-Jul-11	55.00%	0.63%	0.34%
08-Jul-11	55.00%	−0.58%	−0.32%
11-Jul-11	55.00%	−1.62%	−0.89%
12-Jul-11	57.00%	−0.80%	−0.44%
13-Jul-11	60.00%	0.55%	0.31%
14-Jul-11	63.00%	−0.65%	−0.39%
15-Jul-11	65.00%	0.20%	0.13%
18-Jul-11	60.00%	−0.96%	−0.62%
19-Jul-11	65.00%	0.96%	0.58%
20-Jul-11	69.00%	0.54%	0.35%
21-Jul-11	66.00%	0.97%	0.67%
22-Jul-11	70.00%	0.43%	0.28%
25-Jul-11	65.00%	−0.58%	−0.40%
26-Jul-11	63.00%	−0.15%	−0.10%
27-Jul-11	62.00%	−1.45%	−0.91%
28-Jul-11	67.00%	−0.36%	−0.22%
29-Jul-11	66.00%	−0.71%	−0.48%
01-Aug-11	61.00%	−0.30%	−0.20%
02-Aug-11	62.00%	−2.04%	−1.24%
03-Aug-11	59.00%	−0.77%	−0.48%
04-Aug-11	64.00%	−3.50%	−2.07%
05-Aug-11	59.00%	−1.45%	−0.93%
08-Aug-11	56.00%	−4.94%	−2.92%
09-Aug-11	52.00%	2.22%	1.24%
10-Aug-11	55.00%	−2.56%	−1.33%
11-Aug-11	54.00%	2.97%	1.64%

TABLE 11.1 ***(Continued)***

Date	Net Market Exposure (NME)	Benchmark MSCI AC World Daily TR Net Local Index	Adjusted Benchmark
12-Aug-11	55.00%	1.08%	0.58%
15-Aug-11	59.00%	1.68%	0.93%
16-Aug-11	56.00%	−0.48%	−0.28%
17-Aug-11	55.00%	0.17%	0.09%
18-Aug-11	54.00%	−3.77%	−2.07%
19-Aug-11	55.00%	−1.82%	−0.98%
22-Aug-11	51.00%	0.11%	0.06%
23-Aug-11	49.00%	2.23%	1.14%
24-Aug-11	49.00%	0.79%	0.39%
25-Aug-11	48.00%	−0.86%	−0.42%
26-Aug-11	47.00%	0.65%	0.31%
29-Aug-11	50.00%	2.11%	0.99%
30-Aug-11	53.00%	0.65%	0.32%
31-Aug-11	54.00%	1.23%	0.65%
01-Sep-11	49.00%	−0.30%	−0.16%
02-Sep-11	47.00%	−2.17%	−1.06%
05-Sep-11	52.00%	−1.68%	−0.79%
06-Sep-11	51.00%	−0.43%	−0.22%
07-Sep-11	48.00%	2.72%	1.39%
08-Sep-11	53.00%	−0.25%	−0.12%
09-Sep-11	55.00%	−2.23%	−1.18%
12-Sep-11	58.00%	−0.96%	−0.53%
13-Sep-11	56.00%	0.79%	0.46%
14-Sep-11	58.00%	0.83%	0.46%
15-Sep-11	57.00%	1.69%	0.98%
16-Sep-11	60.00%	0.71%	0.41%
19-Sep-11	56.00%	−1.24%	−0.75%
20-Sep-11	61.00%	0.29%	0.16%
21-Sep-11	58.00%	−1.68%	−1.02%
22-Sep-11	54.00%	−3.61%	−2.10%
23-Sep-11	52.00%	0.01%	0.01%
26-Sep-11	53.00%	1.10%	0.57%
27-Sep-11	49.00%	2.40%	1.27%
28-Sep-11	49.00%	−1.17%	−0.57%
29-Sep-11	51.00%	0.70%	0.34%
30-Sep-11	46.00%	−1.66%	−0.85%
03-Oct-11	46.00%	−2.41%	−1.11%
04-Oct-11	45.00%	−0.11%	−0.05%
05-Oct-11	46.00%	1.63%	0.73%
06-Oct-11	45.00%	2.42%	1.11%
07-Oct-11	47.00%	−0.01%	−0.01%
10-Oct-11	52.00%	2.20%	1.03%
11-Oct-11	48.00%	0.47%	0.25%
12-Oct-11	45.00%	1.04%	0.50%

(Continued)

TABLE 11.1 (*Continued*)

Date	Net Market Exposure (NME)	Benchmark MSCI AC World Daily TR Net Local Index	Adjusted Benchmark
13-Oct-11	44.00%	−0.23%	−0.10%
14-Oct-11	43.00%	1.00%	0.44%
17-Oct-11	44.00%	−0.91%	−0.39%
18-Oct-11	43.00%	0.48%	0.21%
19-Oct-11	47.00%	−0.44%	−0.19%
20-Oct-11	43.00%	−0.55%	−0.26%
21-Oct-11	39.00%	1.62%	0.70%
24-Oct-11	37.00%	1.57%	0.61%
25-Oct-11	39.00%	−1.15%	−0.42%
26-Oct-11	35.00%	0.61%	0.24%
27-Oct-11	30.00%	3.22%	1.13%
28-Oct-11	30.00%	0.22%	0.07%
31-Oct-11	26.00%	−2.18%	−0.65%
01-Nov-11	28.00%	−2.53%	−0.66%
02-Nov-11	27.00%	0.95%	0.27%
03-Nov-11	22.00%	1.30%	0.35%
04-Nov-11	24.00%	−0.07%	−0.02%
07-Nov-11	27.00%	0.22%	0.05%
08-Nov-11	24.00%	0.63%	0.17%
09-Nov-11	29.00%	−2.19%	−0.52%
10-Nov-11	28.00%	−0.32%	−0.09%
11-Nov-11	31.00%	1.69%	0.47%
14-Nov-11	31.00%	−0.41%	−0.13%
15-Nov-11	28.00%	−0.06%	−0.02%
16-Nov-11	30.00%	−0.95%	−0.27%
17-Nov-11	35.00%	−1.26%	−0.38%
18-Nov-11	36.00%	−0.59%	−0.20%
21-Nov-11	35.00%	−1.91%	−0.69%
22-Nov-11	34.00%	−0.33%	−0.12%
23-Nov-11	30.00%	−1.76%	−0.60%
24-Nov-11	32.00%	−0.17%	−0.05%
25-Nov-11	34.00%	−0.14%	−0.04%
28-Nov-11	29.00%	2.79%	0.95%
29-Nov-11	34.00%	0.54%	0.16%
30-Nov-11	37.00%	3.17%	1.08%
01-Dec-11	41.00%	0.39%	0.14%
02-Dec-11	41.00%	0.34%	0.14%
05-Dec-11	45.00%	0.79%	0.33%
06-Dec-11	40.00%	−0.35%	−0.16%
07-Dec-11	44.00%	0.26%	0.11%
08-Dec-11	42.00%	−1.62%	−0.71%
09-Dec-11	42.00%	0.77%	0.32%
12-Dec-11	45.00%	−1.16%	−0.49%
13-Dec-11	49.00%	−0.54%	−0.24%
14-Dec-11	46.00%	−1.25%	−0.61%

TABLE 11.1 (*Continued*)

Date	Net Market Exposure (NME)	Benchmark MSCI AC World Daily TR Net Local Index	Adjusted Benchmark
15-Dec-11	43.00%	0.01%	0.00%
16-Dec-11	38.00%	0.18%	0.08%
19-Dec-11	34.00%	–0.94%	–0.36%
20-Dec-11	30.00%	1.98%	0.67%
21-Dec-11	26.00%	0.35%	0.10%
22-Dec-11	22.00%	0.69%	0.18%
23-Dec-11	26.00%	0.80%	0.18%
26-Dec-11	31.00%	0.04%	0.01%
27-Dec-11	31.00%	–0.04%	–0.01%
28-Dec-11	28.00%	–0.98%	–0.30%
29-Dec-11	33.00%	0.78%	0.22%
30-Dec-11	34.00%	0.06%	0.02%
02-Jan-12	34.00%	0.27%	0.09%
03-Jan-12	36.00%	1.50%	0.51%
04-Jan-12	39.00%	0.02%	0.01%
05-Jan-12	37.00%	–0.22%	–0.08%
06-Jan-12	39.00%	–0.29%	–0.11%
09-Jan-12	43.00%	0.04%	0.01%
10-Jan-12	45.00%	1.10%	0.47%
11-Jan-12	45.00%	–0.01%	0.00%
12-Jan-12	44.00%	0.11%	0.05%
13-Jan-12	44.00%	–0.23%	–0.10%
16-Jan-12	40.00%	–0.04%	–0.02%
17-Jan-12	45.00%	0.76%	0.30%
18-Jan-12	49.00%	0.71%	0.32%
19-Jan-12	44.00%	0.72%	0.35%
20-Jan-12	49.00%	0.19%	0.08%
23-Jan-12	48.00%	0.24%	0.12%
24-Jan-12	51.00%	–0.19%	–0.09%
25-Jan-12	51.00%	0.53%	0.27%
26-Jan-12	49.00%	0.11%	0.06%
27-Jan-12	45.00%	–0.29%	–0.14%
30-Jan-12	40.00%	–0.59%	–0.26%
31-Jan-12	40.00%	0.21%	0.08%
01-Feb-12	36.00%	1.01%	0.40%
02-Feb-12	36.00%	0.35%	0.12%
03-Feb-12	41.00%	1.07%	0.39%
06-Feb-12	41.00%	0.05%	0.02%
07-Feb-12	38.00%	0.10%	0.04%
08-Feb-12	39.00%	0.36%	0.14%
09-Feb-12	35.00%	0.20%	0.08%
10-Feb-12	31.00%	–0.87%	–0.31%
13-Feb-12	34.00%	0.67%	0.21%
14-Feb-12	33.00%	–0.11%	–0.04%

(*Continued*)

TABLE 11.1 *(Continued)*

Date	Net Market Exposure (NME)	Benchmark MSCI AC World Daily TR Net Local Index	Adjusted Benchmark
15-Feb-12	34.00%	0.25%	0.08%
16-Feb-12	38.00%	0.40%	0.14%
17-Feb-12	39.00%	0.50%	0.19%
20-Feb-12	41.00%	0.40%	0.16%
21-Feb-12	43.00%	−0.03%	−0.01%
22-Feb-12	48.00%	−0.16%	−0.07%
23-Feb-12	48.00%	0.14%	0.07%
24-Feb-12	52.00%	0.28%	0.13%
27-Feb-12	57.00%	−0.18%	−0.09%
28-Feb-12	57.00%	0.39%	0.22%
29-Feb-12	55.00%	−0.20%	−0.11%
01-Mar-12	53.00%	0.44%	0.24%
02-Mar-12	58.00%	−0.03%	−0.02%
05-Mar-12	54.00%	−0.56%	−0.32%
06-Mar-12	58.00%	−1.78%	−0.96%
07-Mar-12	54.00%	0.40%	0.23%
08-Mar-12	50.00%	1.22%	0.66%
09-Mar-12	55.00%	0.51%	0.25%
12-Mar-12	56.00%	−0.11%	−0.06%
13-Mar-12	55.00%	1.42%	0.80%
14-Mar-12	58.00%	0.20%	0.11%
15-Mar-12	54.00%	0.41%	0.24%
16-Mar-12	51.00%	0.15%	0.08%
19-Mar-12	54.00%	0.14%	0.07%
20-Mar-12	58.00%	−0.53%	−0.29%
21-Mar-12	54.00%	−0.24%	−0.14%
22-Mar-12	55.00%	−0.62%	−0.34%
23-Mar-12	51.00%	0.12%	0.06%
26-Mar-12	52.00%	0.90%	0.46%
27-Mar-12	57.00%	0.08%	0.04%
28-Mar-12	54.00%	−0.53%	−0.30%
29-Mar-12	59.00%	−0.61%	−0.33%
30-Mar-12	61.00%	0.42%	0.25%
02-Apr-12	57.00%	0.82%	0.50%
03-Apr-12	53.00%	−0.43%	−0.25%
04-Apr-12	48.00%	−1.41%	−0.75%
05-Apr-12	48.00%	−0.07%	−0.03%
06-Apr-12	51.00%	−0.08%	−0.04%
09-Apr-12	51.00%	−0.76%	−0.39%
10-Apr-12	47.00%	−1.51%	−0.77%
11-Apr-12	49.00%	0.40%	0.19%
12-Apr-12	50.00%	1.15%	0.56%
13-Apr-12	49.00%	−0.87%	−0.43%
16-Apr-12	46.00%	−0.13%	−0.06%
17-Apr-12	44.00%	1.18%	0.54%

TABLE 11.1 ***(Continued)***

Date	Net Market Exposure (NME)	Benchmark MSCI AC World Daily TR Net Local Index	Adjusted Benchmark
18-Apr-12	42.00%	−0.11%	−0.05%
19-Apr-12	37.00%	−0.36%	−0.15%
20-Apr-12	40.00%	0.12%	0.05%
23-Apr-12	37.00%	−1.19%	−0.48%
24-Apr-12	35.00%	0.39%	0.14%
25-Apr-12	36.00%	1.01%	0.35%
26-Apr-12	40.00%	0.42%	0.15%
27-Apr-12	39.00%	0.26%	0.11%
30-Apr-12	43.00%	−0.20%	−0.08%
01-May-12	44.00%	0.26%	0.11%
02-May-12	46.00%	−0.16%	−0.07%
03-May-12	41.00%	−0.49%	−0.23%
04-May-12	46.00%	−1.32%	−0.54%
07-May-12	45.00%	−0.31%	−0.14%
08-May-12	49.00%	−0.67%	−0.30%
09-May-12	51.00%	−0.64%	−0.32%
10-May-12	55.00%	0.29%	0.15%
11-May-12	52.00%	−0.24%	−0.13%
14-May-12	56.00%	−1.24%	−0.64%
15-May-12	55.00%	−0.61%	−0.34%
16-May-12	52.00%	−0.72%	−0.40%
17-May-12	49.00%	−0.93%	−0.49%
18-May-12	50.00%	−1.11%	−0.54%
21-May-12	53.00%	1.07%	0.53%
22-May-12	58.00%	0.73%	0.39%
23-May-12	59.00%	−0.79%	−0.46%
24-May-12	63.00%	0.34%	0.20%
25-May-12	65.00%	−0.08%	−0.05%
28-May-12	63.00%	0.08%	0.05%
29-May-12	65.00%	1.01%	0.64%
30-May-12	65.00%	−1.27%	−0.83%
31-May-12	62.00%	−0.13%	−0.08%
01-Jun-12	61.00%	−1.93%	−1.20%
04-Jun-12	66.00%	−0.51%	−0.31%
05-Jun-12	67.00%	0.63%	0.41%
06-Jun-12	65.00%	2.01%	1.35%
07-Jun-12	65.00%	0.50%	0.32%
08-Jun-12	60.00%	0.06%	0.04%
11-Jun-12	58.00%	−0.39%	−0.23%
12-Jun-12	56.00%	0.66%	0.38%
13-Jun-12	59.00%	−0.27%	−0.15%
14-Jun-12	54.00%	0.36%	0.21%
15-Jun-12	53.00%	0.85%	0.46%
18-Jun-12	54.00%	0.42%	0.22%

(Continued)

TABLE 11.1 ***(Continued)***

Date	Net Market Exposure (NME)	Benchmark MSCI AC World Daily TR Net Local Index	Adjusted Benchmark
19-Jun-12	51.00%	0.98%	0.53%
20-Jun-12	47.00%	0.23%	0.12%
21-Jun-12	49.00%	−1.49%	−0.70%
22-Jun-12	54.00%	−0.01%	−0.01%
25-Jun-12	49.00%	−1.38%	−0.74%
26-Jun-12	45.00%	0.14%	0.07%
27-Jun-12	47.00%	0.96%	0.43%
28-Jun-12	46.00%	−0.13%	−0.06%
29-Jun-12	44.00%	2.35%	1.08%
02-Jul-12	44.00%	0.44%	0.19%
03-Jul-12	40.00%	0.93%	0.41%
04-Jul-12	45.00%	0.09%	0.04%
05-Jul-12	45.00%	−0.34%	−0.15%
06-Jul-12	46.00%	−0.87%	−0.39%
09-Jul-12	44.00%	−0.48%	−0.22%
10-Jul-12	40.00%	−0.38%	−0.17%
11-Jul-12	45.00%	−0.05%	−0.02%
12-Jul-12	48.00%	−0.79%	−0.36%
13-Jul-12	46.00%	1.19%	0.57%
16-Jul-12	51.00%	−0.09%	−0.04%
17-Jul-12	56.00%	0.41%	0.21%
18-Jul-12	56.00%	0.50%	0.28%
19-Jul-12	57.00%	0.63%	0.35%
20-Jul-12	58.00%	−1.03%	−0.59%
23-Jul-12	61.00%	−1.42%	−0.83%
24-Jul-12	61.00%	−0.66%	−0.41%
25-Jul-12	63.00%	−0.13%	−0.08%
26-Jul-12	60.00%	1.54%	0.97%
27-Jul-12	60.00%	1.78%	1.07%
30-Jul-12	59.00%	0.45%	0.27%
31-Jul-12	60.00%	−0.28%	−0.17%
01-Aug-12	62.00%	−0.08%	−0.05%
02-Aug-12	57.00%	−0.77%	−0.48%
03-Aug-12	59.00%	1.51%	0.86%
06-Aug-12	59.00%	0.59%	0.35%
07-Aug-12	60.00%	0.60%	0.36%
08-Aug-12	63.00%	0.09%	0.06%
09-Aug-12	58.00%	0.30%	0.19%
10-Aug-12	58.00%	−0.03%	−0.02%
13-Aug-12	61.00%	−0.19%	−0.11%
14-Aug-12	58.00%	0.24%	0.15%
15-Aug-12	55.00%	0.00%	0.00%
16-Aug-12	52.00%	0.69%	0.38%
17-Aug-12	52.00%	0.30%	0.15%
20-Aug-12	54.00%	−0.13%	−0.07%
21-Aug-12	58.00%	0.06%	0.03%

TABLE 11.1 ***(Continued)***

Date	Net Market Exposure (NME)	Benchmark MSCI AC World Daily TR Net Local Index	Adjusted Benchmark
22-Aug-12	59.00%	−0.37%	−0.21%
23-Aug-12	55.00%	−0.43%	−0.25%
24-Aug-12	59.00%	0.14%	0.07%
27-Aug-12	54.00%	0.01%	0.01%
28-Aug-12	49.00%	−0.28%	−0.15%
29-Aug-12	50.00%	0.01%	0.00%
30-Aug-12	51.00%	−0.79%	−0.39%
31-Aug-12	49.00%	0.27%	0.14%
03-Sep-12	52.00%	0.24%	0.12%
04-Sep-12	56.00%	−0.44%	−0.23%
05-Sep-12	58.00%	−0.19%	−0.11%
06-Sep-12	54.00%	1.74%	1.01%
07-Sep-12	58.00%	0.78%	0.42%
10-Sep-12	61.00%	−0.32%	−0.19%
11-Sep-12	57.00%	0.20%	0.12%
12-Sep-12	60.00%	0.39%	0.22%
13-Sep-12	58.00%	0.85%	0.51%
14-Sep-12	60.00%	1.14%	0.66%
17-Sep-12	55.00%	−0.26%	−0.15%
18-Sep-12	54.00%	−0.28%	−0.16%
19-Sep-12	59.00%	0.28%	0.15%
20-Sep-12	55.00%	−0.39%	−0.23%
21-Sep-12	57.00%	0.19%	0.11%
24-Sep-12	56.00%	−0.29%	−0.16%
25-Sep-12	61.00%	−0.47%	−0.26%
26-Sep-12	56.00%	−0.92%	−0.56%
27-Sep-12	56.00%	0.68%	0.38%
28-Sep-12	61.00%	−0.50%	−0.28%
01-Oct-12	62.00%	0.50%	0.30%
02-Oct-12	67.00%	0.08%	0.05%
03-Oct-12	65.00%	0.11%	0.08%
04-Oct-12	66.00%	0.48%	0.31%
05-Oct-12	62.00%	0.34%	0.23%
08-Oct-12	64.00%	−0.46%	−0.29%
09-Oct-12	59.00%	−0.75%	−0.48%
10-Oct-12	63.00%	−0.61%	−0.36%
11-Oct-12	65.00%	0.22%	0.14%
12-Oct-12	64.00%	−0.24%	−0.16%
15-Oct-12	59.00%	0.55%	0.35%
16-Oct-12	55.00%	1.08%	0.64%
17-Oct-12	59.00%	0.54%	0.29%
18-Oct-12	56.00%	0.11%	0.07%
19-Oct-12	60.00%	−1.01%	−0.56%
22-Oct-12	64.00%	−0.06%	−0.04%
23-Oct-12	69.00%	−1.27%	−0.82%

(Continued)

TABLE 11.1 ***(Continued)***

Date	Net Market Exposure (NME)	Benchmark MSCI AC World Daily TR Net Local Index	Adjusted Benchmark
24-Oct-12	69.00%	–0.18%	–0.12%
25-Oct-12	68.00%	0.29%	0.20%
26-Oct-12	71.00%	–0.26%	–0.18%
29-Oct-12	66.00%	–0.09%	–0.07%
30-Oct-12	61.00%	0.20%	0.13%
31-Oct-12	62.00%	0.03%	0.02%
01-Nov-12	66.00%	0.84%	0.52%
02-Nov-12	71.00%	–0.21%	–0.14%
05-Nov-12	75.00%	–0.11%	–0.08%
06-Nov-12	73.00%	0.56%	0.42%
07-Nov-12	68.00%	–1.43%	–1.05%
08-Nov-12	71.00%	–0.91%	–0.62%
09-Nov-12	67.00%	–0.02%	–0.01%
12-Nov-12	67.00%	–0.13%	–0.09%
13-Nov-12	68.00%	–0.23%	–0.16%
14-Nov-12	73.00%	–0.89%	–0.61%
15-Nov-12	70.00%	–0.30%	–0.22%
16-Nov-12	65.00%	0.09%	0.06%
19-Nov-12	70.00%	1.73%	1.12%
20-Nov-12	68.00%	0.14%	0.10%
21-Nov-12	68.00%	0.29%	0.20%
22-Nov-12	70.00%	0.39%	0.26%
23-Nov-12	70.00%	0.92%	0.64%
26-Nov-12	69.00%	–0.20%	–0.14%
27-Nov-12	69.00%	–0.15%	–0.11%
28-Nov-12	69.00%	0.28%	0.19%
29-Nov-12	74.00%	0.78%	0.54%
30-Nov-12	78.00%	0.11%	0.08%
03-Dec-12	75.00%	–0.18%	–0.14%
04-Dec-12	72.00%	–0.11%	–0.08%
05-Dec-12	69.00%	0.30%	0.22%
06-Dec-12	66.00%	0.34%	0.23%
07-Dec-12	70.00%	0.25%	0.17%
10-Dec-12	69.00%	0.10%	0.07%
11-Dec-12	71.00%	0.48%	0.33%
12-Dec-12	74.00%	0.22%	0.16%
13-Dec-12	75.00%	–0.29%	–0.22%
14-Dec-12	72.00%	–0.14%	–0.10%
17-Dec-12	72.00%	0.52%	0.37%
18-Dec-12	71.00%	0.82%	0.59%
19-Dec-12	75.00%	0.11%	0.08%
20-Dec-12	75.00%	0.24%	0.18%
21-Dec-12	79.00%	–0.64%	–0.48%
24-Dec-12	83.00%	–0.08%	–0.06%
25-Dec-12	81.00%	0.07%	0.05%
26-Dec-12	84.00%	–0.14%	–0.11%
27-Dec-12	85.00%	0.07%	0.06%
28-Dec-12	85.00%	–0.56%	–0.47%
31-Dec-12	86.00%	0.79%	0.67%

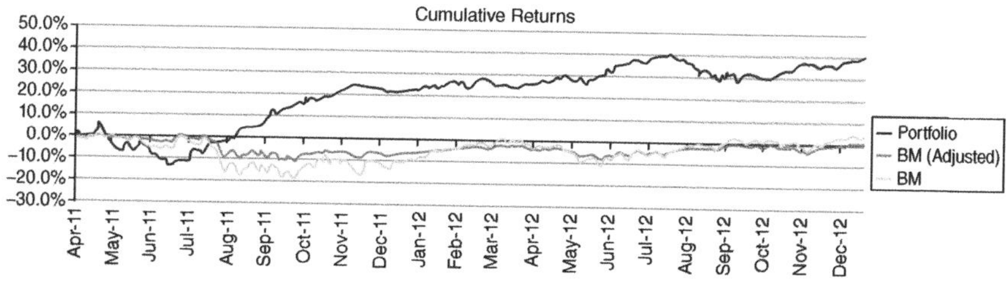

FIGURE 11.2 Cumulative return versus the benchmark and net adjusted benchmark.

	Geometric	Arithmetic
Ann. Portfolio Return	20.71%	19.74%
Ann. BM Return	2.26%	3.40%
Ann. Adj BM Return	0.47%	0.77%
Ann. Excess Return (vs. Adj BM)	20.24%	18.98%
Ann. Rf	0.60%	0.60%
Correlation	-0.05	
Beta	-0.05	
Ann. Benchmark Volatility	15.25%	
Ann. Downside Volatility	8.82%	
Ann. Portfolio Volatility	13.57%	

Ann. TE	16.05%
Skew	0.209
Kurtosis	4.770

M^2	0.232	
R-Squared	0.003	
Information Ratio	1.261	
Sharpe Ratio	1.481	
Sortino Ratio	2.280	
Treynor Ratio		N/A when Beta <0
Max Drawdown	-17.42	

FIGURE 11.3 Performance risk adjusted summary.

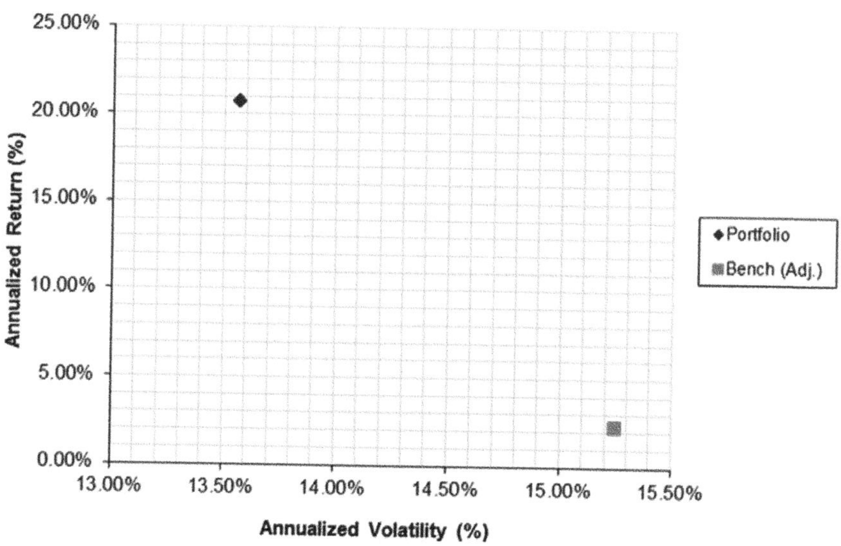

FIGURE 11.4 Efficient frontier.

FURTHER READING

Ackermann, C., McEnally, R., Ravenscraft, D., The performance of hedge funds: Risk, return, and incentives. *The Journal of Finance*, **54**(3), 1999, pp. 833–874.

The Alternative Investment Management Association (AIMA), Roadmap to hedge funds for institutional investors, November 2012.

Bacon, C., *Practical Portfolio Performance Measurement and Attribution*, 2nd edition, Wiley Finance, Hoboken, NJ, 2008.

Brown, S., Goetzmann, W., Mutual fund styles, *Journal of Financial Economics*, **43**(3), 1997, pp. 373–399.

Brown, S., Goetzmann, W., Hedge funds with style, working paper no. 00-29, Yale ICF, 2001.

Caglayan, M., Edwards, F., Hedge fund performance and manager skill, *The Journal of Future Markets*, **21**(11), 2001, pp. 1003–1028.

Crerend, W., *Fundamentals of Hedge Fund Investing*, McGraw-Hill, New York, 1998.

Fung, W., Hsieh, D., Empirical characteristics of dynamic trading strategies: The case of hedge funds, *The Review of Financial Studies*, **10**(2), 1997, pp. 275–302.

Fung, W., Hsieh, D., A primer on hedge funds, *Journal of Empirical Finance*, **6**(3), 1999, pp. 309–331.

Fung, W., Hsieh, D., The risk in hedge fund strategies: Theory and evidence from trend followers, *The Review of Financial Studies*, **14**(2), 2001, pp. 313–341.

Gregoriou, G.N., Hubner, G., Papageorgiou, N., Rouah, F., *Hedge Funds: Insights in Performance Measurement, Risk Analysis, and Portfolio Allocation*, Wiley, Hoboken, NJ, 2005.

Sharpe, W., Mutual fund performance. *Journal of Business*, **39**(1), 1996, pp. 119–138.

Szylar C., *UCITS Handbook*, ISTE/Wiley, Hoboken, NJ, 2012.

CHAPTER TWELVE

Stress Testing and Back Testing

Stress testing is especially important after long periods of benign economic and financial conditions, when fading memory of negative conditions can lead to complacency and the underpricing of risk. It is also a key risk management tool during periods of expansion, when innovation leads to new products that grow rapidly and for which limited or no loss data is available.

—Basel Committee, May 2009

All models seen previously adopt the assumption of normal conditions of market and assign a low probability of extreme events. If we want to know what the potential loss would be under extreme scenarios, then VaR is not always a reliable method, and as such it needs to be complemented with appropriate stress tests and reliable back testing.

While VaR has acquired a strong following in the risk management community, there is reason to be skeptical of both its accuracy as a risk management tool and its use in decision making. There are many dimensions on which researchers have criticized VaR, and we will categorize these issues into those dimensions. Following the financial crisis raised by the subprimes, some newspapers were clearly writing about the failure of VaR.

The technique of stress testing is a technique that is used to estimate the potential loss by submitting the model to extreme variations in the parameters, corresponding to a financial disaster scenario: stock market crash, collapse of the exchange rate, sudden increase in interest rates, and so on., within this framework can be estimate the VaR under extreme situations already produced such as the stock market crash of October 1987, the 1992 EMS crisis, or the Mexican crisis of 1995. For example, to test the impact of an extreme movement in U.S. stock prices, a manager may assume that all market variables are equal to those of October 19, 1987. If we consider this too extreme scenario, the manager could choose January 8, 1988. To test the effect of extreme movement of the rate of interest in England, the manager could assume that market variables underwent changes commensurate with those real-life stories on April 10, 1992. Stress

Handbook of Market Risk, First Edition. Christian Szylar.

testing is less recursive than back testing, but it is essential to control the behavior of the model in situations where the risk measure must be reliable; it usually does this by disrupting the variance–covariance matrix while keeping the positive semi-defined property.

This property is affected when we interfere with the correlation matrix but intact when we interfere with the matrix of volatilities. Indeed, she manages to take account of situations completely absent of historical data; and any forecast, even if it is little likely, is deemed possible. The crisis simulation method forces the risk managers to analyze the vulnerabilities of the financial institution to certain events. In situations of crisis in financial markets, the liquidity of the markets dries. This phenomenon makes it unavailable to any information price reliable enough to quantify the potential loss. In this case, a well-conducted testing stress seems to be the only method capable of assessing the risk of the financial institution. Because stress testing method suffers from a lack of scientific rigor in the calculation of the VaR in the sense that the construction of scenarios occurs completely subjectively, more extreme events against which the financial institution seeks to protect itself can hardly be anticipated; when the financial institution has a wide portfolio and complex, stress testing may experience some difficulties in managing a large mass of opportunities and a lot of correlations.

12.1 Definition and Introduction to Stress Testing

The purpose of the VaR model is the quantification of the maximum potential loss which might be generated by a portfolio in normal market conditions. This loss is estimated on the basis of a given time period and a certain confidence interval. We must complete this approach with stress tests, in order to quantify the risks associated with possible abnormal market movements. These tests evaluate the reactions of the portfolio's value to extreme financial or economic events at a given point in time.

Regulators require that a portfolio manager follow up on the risk of the occurrence of the extreme variations of the risk factors to which the portfolios might be exposed through their investments by implementing a rigorous program of stress tests. The program should cover all the risk factors having a non-negligible influence on the portfolio's value and should also deal with correlation changes between risk factors.

The scenarios defined by Risk Management must be adapted to the nature of the portfolio's positions and risks, and therefore any fundamental change in the investment strategy should be accompanied by a recalibration of the crisis scenarios.

The calculations' results must be analyzed by Risk Management and should, if need be, lead to amended measures for the purpose of adjusting the fund's risk situation.

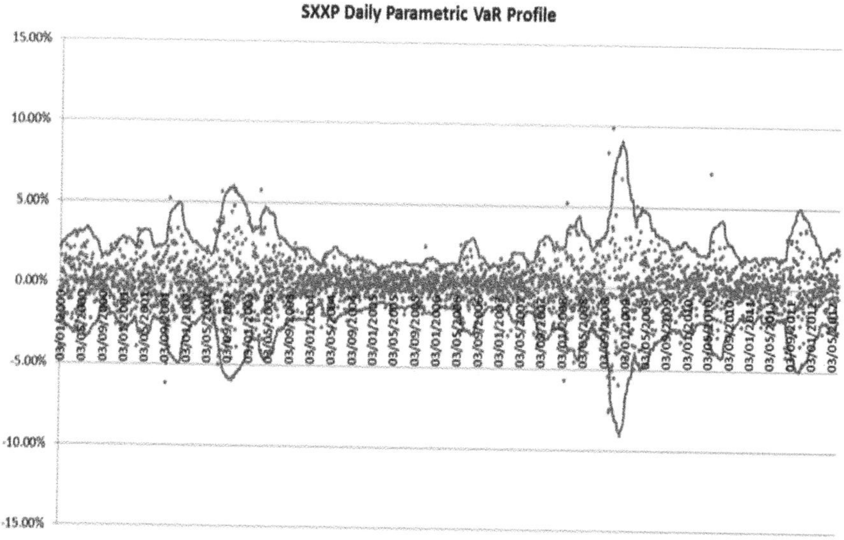

FIGURE 12.1 S&P 500 Daily parametric VaR profile with 99% confidence level.

The stress test calculations should be done with a frequency that is in line with the fund's risk profile, but, at a minimum, once per month.

VaR works under the "normal market assumption." Therefore the loss that results from the VaR calculation can be underestimated.

Just to give you an idea, let's take the S&P500 and let's use a parametric VaR (Figure 12.1). The period is from January 2000 to May 2012. Using a 99% confidence level and computing a daily parametric VaR, we would expect to have a maximum of 32 violations according to the normal distribution rule. In reality, the actual number of breaches is 100, so it is 68 more than expected by the normal distribution.

If we were using a 95% confidence level, still using daily parametric VaR, we would expect 162 breaches. Actually we faced 368 breaches of this daily VaR forecast (Figure 12.2).

To compensate the limitation inherent to any VaR approach as demonstrated above, we use stress testing. Stress testing is a useful method of determining how a portfolio will fare during a period of financial crisis. The Monte Carlo simulation is one of the most widely used methods of stress testing. One of the biggest problems faced today by fund managers is to determine the vulnerabilities in the portfolios they manage and then knowing when to act to reshape or rebalance their portfolios. Stress testing helps them.

Stress testing is defined as a generic term describing various techniques used by financial firms to gauge their potential vulnerability to exceptional but plausible events. Stress tests generally fall into two categories:

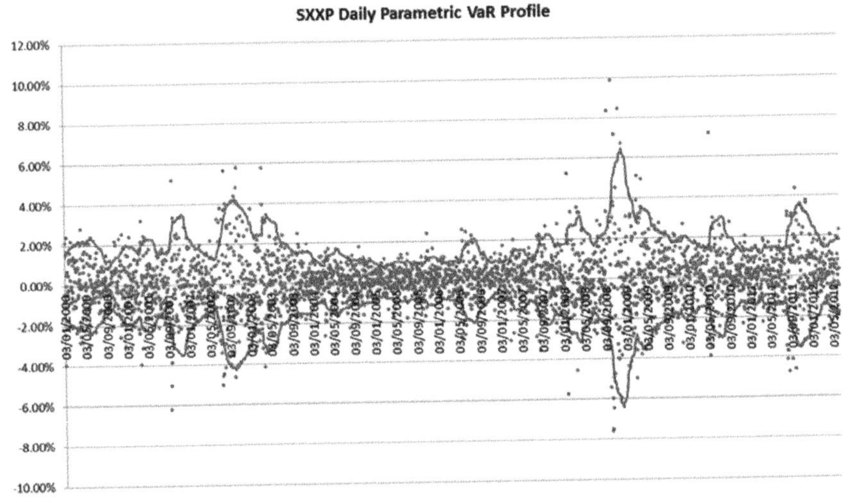

FIGURE 12.2 S&P 500 daily parametric VaR profile with 95% confidence level.

- Sensitivities (or single-factor tests), which seek to identify how portfolios respond to changes in relevant economic variables or risk parameters.
- Scenarios, which seek to assess the resilience of financial institutions and the financial system to an exceptional but plausible scenario.

Stress testing also refers to a range of techniques used to assess the vulnerability of a portfolio to "exceptional but plausible" financial shocks or sudden market falls.

Applying stress testing in the fund industry has occurred in practice since the introduction of UCITS III and for funds classified as being sophisticated. Some leading asset managers were always stress testing their portfolios to assess what can be wrong for their portfolio, but this was not something that the fund industry used to as standard. It was different in the banking industry. In alternative space, the usage of stress testing is depending on the asset management firm's risk culture, but since the 2008 financial crisis we can see an increasing usage of stress testing.

Stress tests should measure any potential major depreciation of a portfolio value as a result of unexpected changes in the relative value parameters and their correlation. Since the credit crunch crisis, stress testing on correlation change has become a very widely developed approach. The reason for this is because some financial instruments, like CDOs (Collateral Debt Obliagations) and others, were considered as non-risky because their constituents were supposed to be negatively correlated. The crisis showed at the end that they were correlated, which led to the situation we are now in. This is why completely reversing the correlation between assets, even if unlikely to happen in reality, may be a useful exercise.

It is also essential that the stress tests being applied to the portfolio are aligned with the risk factors affecting the portfolio. Applying stress test scenarios based on interest rates for an equity fund may not be particularly relevant and may even be completely useless. This is also why the risk profiling of the fund is such an important and critical step for sound and reliable risk management practices.

The stress tests must be appropriate for analyzing potential situations in which the use of derivatives would bring about a loss. Most regulators in the European Union have decided that stress tests must be carried out at least once a month and results documented.

One of the key questions related to stress test results is how to use the results. What are we doing with the results? Because there is another question behind this, which is: what is the likelihood that such a scenario used in the stress test will really happen? Stress testing reveals how well a portfolio is positioned in the event forecasts prove to be true. Stress testing also lends insight into a portfolio's vulnerabilities. Although extreme events are never certain, studying their performance implications strengthens understanding.

Stress testing is an important and evolving tool in risk mitigation, and regulators increasingly look for its use in institutions of all sizes. It is important to view stress testing as a supplement to risk management—not a catch-all—and to know which tests are most appropriate for a given portfolio. Stress testing involves examining an alternative future that could cause problems in a portfolio. It enables the manager to determine how bad those problems could become and prepare for them if that scenario develops. It also enables the manager to verify whether the institution would be able to handle the problems. We can also test alternative scenarios based on what the portfolio manager put in the portfolio, and how he or she manages the portfolio. It is therefore not just a regulatory requirement to comply with stress testing, but is also definitively a key management tool.

The Bank for International Settlements (BIS) has issued several papers and guidance notes on what should be considered as state-of-the-art stress testing, along with a report summarizing stress tests being applied by banks that can constitute practical guidelines for those who want to learn more about stress tests.[1] Even if these documents are intended for banks, it is still worth reading them because many of their recommendations can be adopted for fund stress testing.

In May 2004, the Committee on the Global Financial System initiated an exercise on stress tests undertaken by banks and securities firms. The exercise had two main aims. The first was to conduct a review of what financial institutions perceived to be the main risk scenarios for them at that time, based on the type of enterprise-wide stress tests that they were running. The second aim was

[1]Working group established by the Committee on the Global Financial System, *Stress Testing at Major Financial Institutions: Survey Results and Practice*, Bank for International Settlements (BIS), available at: http://www.bis.org/publ/cgfs24.pdf (accessed February 17, 2010), January 2005.

to explore some of the more structural aspects of stress testing and examine how practices had evolved.

In May 2009, because of the financial crisis due to the credit, BIS issued *Principles for Sound Stress Testing Practices and Supervision.* Stress testing is a critical tool used by banks as part of their internal risk management and capital planning. The guidances give a comprehensive set of principles for the sound governance, design, and implementation of stress testing programs at banks.

12.2 Stress Test Approaches

Two main methodological approaches to stress testing can be considered.

12.2.1 PIECEWISE APPROACH

A "piecewise approach" evaluates the vulnerability of a fund to single risk factors by forecasting several "financial soundness indicators" (such as exposure to exchange rate or interest rate risks) under various stress scenarios.

The benefits of stress testing (Figure 12.3) using a single risk factor approach are that:

- It can be run relatively quickly.
- It allows an intuitive link between the factor and outcome of the test.
- It can be used by senior managers to form an initial view of the impact of a move in a financial variable on the firm.

There are several approaches: either risk parameters are moved instantaneously by a unit amount (e.g., a parallel shift in interest rates by 200 bp (basis points)) or worst-case historical movements for each risk factor (e.g., the most significant fall in house prices in last 40 years) are used.

Another variant of this stress test is to apply a half standard deviation shock to a certain number of market variables (from indices, indices subsectors, commodities, currencies, and emerging versus developed countries) and check what would be the impact on the fund's return considering its current sensitivities to these variables. Figure 12.4 summarizes the impact on the fund and on the benchmark after all variables have been shocked based on half of an annual standard deviation. All of the variables are shocked for a downside return based on half of

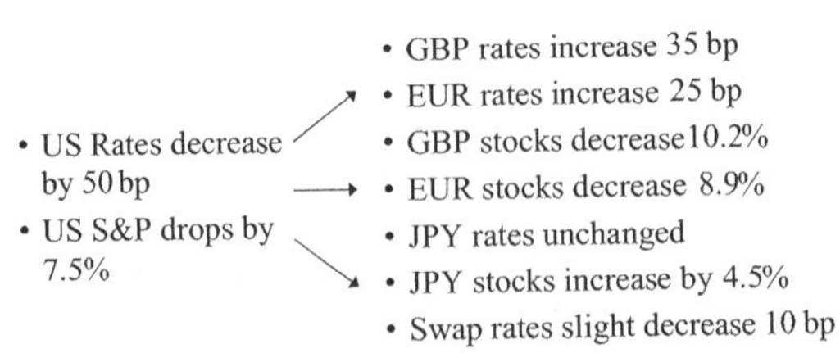

FIGURE 12.3 Stress test using various factors.

Impact on Return from Market Indices

Stressed Variable	Chg	Ret	Rank
MSCI AC EUROPE	-14.66	-1.50	1
MSCI WORLD/FINANCE	-13.78	-1.50	2
MSCI World (USD)	-10.54	-1.49	4
DAX INDEX	-14.64	-1.47	5
FTSE 100 INDEX	-10.35	-1.40	10
MSCI UK	-10.32	-1.40	11
STXE 600 EUR Pr	-11.19	-1.39	12
Euro Stoxx 50 Pr	-14.31	-1.39	14
MSCI EUROPE	-11.08	-1.38	16
MSCI PAN-EURO	-10.94	-1.38	17
FTSE MIB index	-17.77	-1.37	20
MSCI AC AMERICAS	-11.07	-1.37	21
MSCI EM LATIN AMERICA	-13.68	-1.36	24
CAC 40 INDEX	-14.33	-1.36	25
S&P 500 INDEX	-11.00	-1.31	36
RUSSIAN RTS INDEX $	-16.38	-1.23	43
IBEX 35 INDEX	-14.01	-1.19	46
DOLLAR INDEX SPOT	-4.38	1.19	47
JPMorgan Monthly EMBIs PI	-18.14	1.19	48
NASDAQ 100 STOCK INDEX	-11.10	-1.14	53

Impact on Return from Volatility Indices

Stressed Variable	Chg	Ret	Rank
GERM VDAX VOLATILITY IDX	-42.93	1.31	34
FTSE100 Volatility Index	-55.05	1.23	44
CBOE SPX VOLATILITY INDX	-54.03	1.14	51
Volatility Index Japan	-37.22	0.28	110

Impact on Return from Commodities

Stressed Variable	Chg	Ret	Rank
MS Cmdty Index	-15.44	-1.35	30
LMEX LONDON METALS INDEX	-12.93	-1.14	54
Copper	-14.39	-1.08	61
Copper (3m)	-14.61	-1.05	64
Crude Oil	-15.50	-0.91	78
Brent Oil	-13.00	-0.81	80
Silver	-21.98	-0.79	81
Soybean	-9.94	-0.66	87
Gold	-10.10	-0.63	89
Corn (No.2)	-13.98	-0.48	99
Coal	-8.07	-0.47	100
Raw Sugar	-17.13	-0.43	103
Wheat	-17.03	-0.43	104
Orange Juice	-15.60	-0.12	117
Natural Gas	-16.88	-0.04	120

Impact on Return from World Sectors

Stressed Variable	Chg	Ret	Rank
Financials	-11.15	-1.45	6
Health Care	-7.32	-1.44	7
Materials Sector	-10.50	-1.39	13
Industrial	-9.89	-1.39	15
Consumer Staples	-5.37	-1.37	19
Energy Sector	-11.39	-1.35	27
Consumer Discretionary	-9.22	-1.35	29
Telecomm Services Sector	-5.93	-1.33	32
Utility Sector	-7.17	-1.29	38
Information Technology	-9.55	-1.17	49

Impact on Return from FX Rates

Stressed Variable	Chg	Ret	Rank
EUR-USD X-RATE	-5.60	-1.30	37
AUD-USD X-RATE	-6.91	-1.27	40
USD-CAD X-RATE	-4.87	1.26	42
NZD-USD X-RATE	-6.75	-1.12	56
USD-BRL X-RATE	-7.42	1.10	59
AUD-JPY X-RATE	-7.76	-1.02	69
EUR-JPY X-RATE	-5.90	-1.01	71
GBP-USD X-RATE	-4.48	-0.97	74
USD-THB X-RATE	-2.54	0.92	77
EUR-KRW X-RATE	-6.83	-0.73	84
EUR-GBP X-RATE	-3.66	-0.69	86
EUR-SEK X-RATE	-3.25	0.60	93
EUR-CHF X-RATE	-4.59	-0.59	94
EUR-NOK X-RATE	-3.03	0.46	101
EUR-AUD X-RATE	-4.99	0.43	102
USD-KRW X-RATE	-5.09	0.43	105
USD-MYR X-RATE	-3.55	0.38	107
USD-JPY X-RATE	-3.16	0.24	111
USD-IDR X-RATE	-2.83	-0.24	112
EUR-CAD X-RATE	-4.35	-0.09	119

Impact on Return from Style Indices

Stressed Variable	Chg	Ret	Rank
US Govt 10y Yld	-22.61	-1.05	65
US Govt 5y Yld	-33.80	-0.82	79
Global Em-Dm Financials Spread	-4.85	0.62	92
US Govt 2y Yld	-45.58	-0.36	108
Global Emerging-Developed Spread	-3.97	0.32	109

Impact on Return from STOXX Sector Index

Stressed Variable	Chg	Ret	Rank
STXE 600 Chem EUR Pr	-13.26	-1.49	3
STXE 600 Au&Pt EUR Pr	-20.03	-1.44	8
STXE 600 FnSv EUR Pr	-12.94	-1.38	18
STXE 600 Pr&Ho EUR Pr	-8.62	-1.37	22
STXE 600 Ins EUR Pr	-17.37	-1.36	23
STXE 600 Bnk EUR Pr	-17.96	-1.36	26
STXE 600 BsRs EUR Pr	-17.82	-1.35	28
STXE 600 ReEs EUR Pr	-11.96	-1.34	31
STXE 600 Ig&S EUR Pr	-13.48	-1.32	33
STXE 600 Cn&Mt EUR Pr	-15.96	-1.31	35
STXE 600 Mda EUR Pr	-10.79	-1.28	39
STXE 600 Oil&G EUR Pr	-11.80	-1.20	45
STXE 600 Tech EUR Pr	-12.51	-1.15	50
STXE 600 Util EUR Pr	-11.78	-1.14	52
STXE 600 Tr&Ls EUR Pr	-9.91	-1.11	57

Impact on Return from MSCI EM Sectors

Stressed Variable	Chg	Ret	Rank
Consumer Staples	-5.14	-1.26	41
Materials Sector a	-9.91	-1.12	55
Utilities Sector a	-5.50	-1.05	63
Energy Sector a	-10.53	-1.05	66
Telecomm Services a	-5.24	-1.04	67
Financials	-9.41	-1.02	70
Consumer Discretionary	-9.71	-1.00	72
Health Care	-6.20	-0.94	76
Industrials	-11.25	-0.77	82
Information Technology	-10.84	-0.40	106

FIGURE 12.4 Sensitivity stress test summary. **Source:** Marshall Wace LLP.

TABLE 12.1 Impact on Return: Top 10 Variables

Stress Description	Stressed Variable	Change	Return	Rank
World sector index	Consumer staples	−5.66	−1.42	1
World sector index	Health care	−7.77	−1.39	2
World sector index	Utility sector	−7.57	−1.36	3
World sector index	Telecomm services sector	−6.20	−1.33	4
STOXX sector index	STXE 600 Chem EUR Pr	−13.71	−1.33	5
Market index	DAX index	−15.22	−1.32	6
Market index	MSCI World (USD)	−11.18	−1.30	7
Market index	MSCI PAN-EURO	−11.52	−1.30	8
Market index	STXE 600 EUR Pr	−11.97	−1.29	9
Market index	MSC Europe	−11.67	−1.29	10

an annual standard deviation. The nature of these tests is such that in the absence of derivatives the results can be interpreted in either direction. For example, the largest impact after half a standard deviation shock to each variable on the portfolio is coming from a −14.66% drop in the MSCI All Countries Europe, resulting in a −1.50% portfolio return. This can also be interpreted as a +14.66% shock leading to a +1.50% return. In this example the portfolio is a long/short equity fund hence losing less than the benchmark.

Table 12.1 lists the top 10 variables which have the highest impact on the fund's return.

The stress test assumes that the covariance structure remains constant. The effect of a shock to a given market (emerging markets consumer staples in the above example) is assessed by the correlated impact expected by the underlying assets in the fund.

The nonlinear expected stress returns from option positions are calculated by fully re-pricing each option with updated model inputs. The inputs are conditionally updated with the expected spot price of the underlying position and short term volatility forecast. The option modeling uses a proprietary internal pricing model (used for risk purposes only) and is used for both listed and OTC options.

12.2.2 INTEGRATED APPROACH

An "integrated approach" combines the analysis of sensitivity of the fund to multiple risk factors into a single estimate of the probability distribution of aggregate losses that could materialize under any given stress scenario (Figure 12.5).

Types of Scenarios.[2] There are several points to consider before running stress tests:

- *Time Horizon:* The horizon normally used is near term rather than long term. A longer time horizon may be more appropriate, because some macroeconomic impact may take more than a year to filter through.

[2]**Source:** PWC.

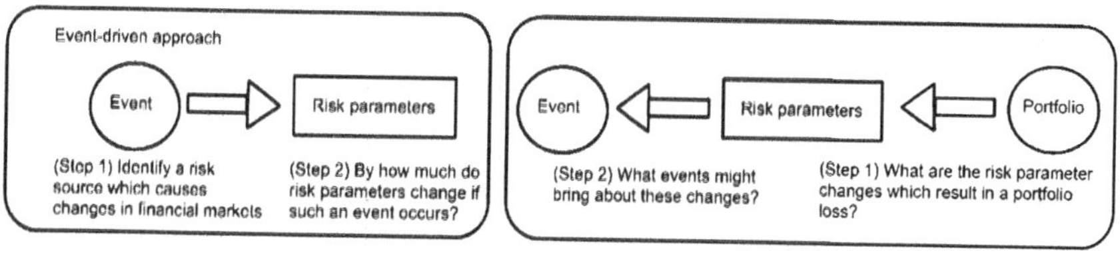

FIGURE 12.5 **Stress testing approaches. Source: Stress testing at major financial institutions: survey results and practice (BIS).**

- *Unexpected Illiquidity:* Many crises are characterized by an abrupt lack of liquidity in financial markets.
- *Lack of Hedges:* Hedging instruments may be rendered invalid during stress events.
- *Aggregation:* The process of aggregating the effects of stress tests performed at a risk type or business unit level raises issues regarding diversification benefits and second-round effects.
- *Correlations:* Levels that prevail in ordinary conditions may cease to exist during exceptional events.

While substantial progress has been made in developing quantitative techniques that help assess the vulnerability of portfolios, a number of methodological challenges still need to be overcome. In particular, stress-testing needs to pay closer attention to the correlation of risks and risk measures over time and across assets. It needs to focus on the length of the time horizon used for simulations and to the potential instability of all reduced-form parameter estimates because of feedback effects.

Stress tests are performed in a number of stages (Figure 12.6), including:

- Defining the scope of the analysis in terms of the relevant set of assets and portfolios.
- Designing and calibrating a stress scenario.
- Quantifying the direct impact of the simulated scenario on the balance sheet of a portfolio. This can be done either by focusing on forecasting single financial soundness indicators under stress or by integrating the analysis of market and credit risks into a single estimate of the probability distribution of aggregate losses that could materialize in the simulated stress scenario.
- Interpreting results to evaluate the overall risk-bearing capacity of a portfolio.
- Accounting for potential feedback effects within the portfolio.

Aggregate stress tests can usefully complement VaR for market monitoring, because they provide forward-looking information on the impact of possible extreme events on the portfolio.

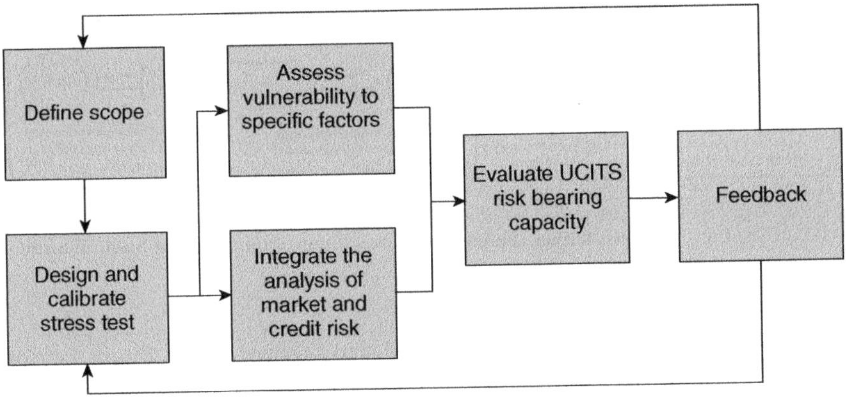

FIGURE 12.6 The various stages of stress testing.

12.2.3 DESIGNING AND CALIBRATING A STRESS TEST

There are a number of elements involved in the design of any stress scenario, including:

- The choice of the type of risks to analyze (market, credit, interest rate, liquidity, etc.).
- Whether single or multiple risk factors are to be shocked.
- What parameter(s) to shock (prices, volatilities, correlations).
- By how much (based on historical or hypothetical scenarios).
- Over what time horizon.

The analysis of a wide range of risk factors enhances the predictive power of the stress test—at the cost, however, of an increased computational burden. Similarly, simulating a comprehensive scenario including multiple shocks allows more realistic predictions than focusing on *ad hoc* sensitivities of single parameters.

One of the key decisions is how to calibrate the size of the shocks used for stress testing. Setting the hurdle too low or too high might make the whole exercise meaningless. In general, shocks can be calibrated to the largest past movement in the relevant risk variables over a certain horizon (change from peak to trough or deviation from trend) or be based on historical variance (unconditional or conditional). Alternatively, with sufficient data, we can attempt to estimate the joint empirical distribution of past deviations from the trend of the relevant risk variables and use its quantiles for simulating the stress scenario.

It is important to capture in the simulated scenario the second-round effects on any other variable that might be affected by the original shock (for example, a severe oil shock is likely to affect stock prices, interest rates, etc.). Ideally, models should be employed to fully characterize the interacting shocks affecting key factors or asset prices that define the scenario of interest.

In fact, identifying all second-round effects of a given set of shocks is among the major challenges encountered in designing a comprehensive and internally consistent stress scenario.

Assessing Vulnerability to Specific Risk Factors. Having selected the scope of the portfolio and designed a stress scenario, the impact of shocks can be measured using a number of different indicators. Indicators comprise sensitivity to market risk (including interest rate and foreign exchange risk) as well as indicators of market liquidity.

The sensitivity of these indicators to adverse changes in fundamentals can be estimated on historical data and then used to simulate the impact of possible stress scenarios in the future on the portfolio. Depending on data availability, the econometric analysis could exploit both the time series and cross-sectional dimensions. Time series analysis is useful for assessing the buildup of UCITS vulnerabilities over time.

Integrating the Analysis of Market and Credit Risks. The various risks monitored through indicators may all be correlated and are certainly not mutually exclusive (e.g., an oil price shock is likely to have repercussions on inflation and interest rates and therefore can be a source of interest rate risk as well as credit risk, commodity price risk, etc.). Therefore, in order to evaluate the vulnerability of a portfolio to a given stress scenario, risk managers should look for an integrated risk model that jointly accounts for multiple sources of risk as opposed to relying on different indicators that separately quantify the impact of individual risk factors.

In essence, a risk model is an analytical tool that maps a given macro scenario and relevant portfolio into a probability distribution of losses, from which various risk measures can be derived.

Under specific distributional and parameter assumptions, it provides a common metric by which to compare the vulnerability of different portfolios to a given shock or the impact of different stress scenarios on a given portfolio.

Aggregation and Interpretation of Results. In interpreting the results, we must consider:

- *Non-additivity of Risks and of Risk Measures.* A correlated set of shocks to the pace of interest rates or asset prices may be a source of market and credit risk and counterparty for the portfolio. In this sense, given their joint likelihood of occurrence, risks should not be analyzed using separate models and then simply added up. A superior approach consists of integrating models of market and credit risks.
- *Length of Time Horizon.* Historical experience suggests that both the buildup and resolution of macrofinancial imbalances may span several years.

Macroeconomic shocks are likely to be serially correlated over time. In fact, systemic vulnerabilities arise from the progressive erosion of capital reserves as a result of financial strains that persist over multiple years. Therefore, measuring only the first-year impact of a given stress scenario may underestimate the full impact on the vulnerability of the financial system. Moreover, because the response time necessary for policy makers to deal with potential financial imbalances often exceeds one year, their "risk measurement horizon" should be lengthened accordingly.

Feedback Effects. The degree to which a portfolio might respond to any given shock depends on the nature and timing of the shock itself, the size and diversification of the portfolios, and liquidity in the market.

12.3 Historical Stress Testing

Historical stress tests or scenarios intend to test the healthiness of a portfolio by analyzing what would happen to the portfolio if particularly adverse and unexpected movements which occurred in the past would hit the portfolio in the near future. Some well-known examples of historical scenarios are the Russian Crisis, the attacks of 9/11, and more recently the Sub-Prime Crisis. Some of these historical scenarios could last only a few days, such as the Black Monday (October 19th, 1987) scenario. Some others like the Dotcom Bubble spanned over several months. The main advantage of these types of scenarios is that they really did happen! But even if the temptation is great to use these historical scenarios off the shelf and to systematically apply them on any types of portfolio, the risk manager should choose his historical scenarios very carefully and review them on a regular basis as the composition of the portfolio changes, but also because of a few dangers.

Extreme events can be characterized by volatility jumps, increased risk aversion, negative returns for risky assets, and increased correlation across asset classes. Such events actually happen more often than is commonly perceived. In just the last 21 years, we have experienced major market events:

- Black Monday (1987)
- Gulf War (1990)
- European ERM crisis (1992)
- Mexican crisis (1994)
- Asian crisis (1997)
- Long-Term Capital Management (LTCM) (1998)
- The dot.com internet business crisis (2000)
- September 11 (2001)
- Credit crisis (2008)

12.3.1 SOME EXAMPLES OF HISTORICAL STRESS TEST SCENARIOS

Black Monday (1987). Black Monday refers to Monday, October 19, 1987, when stock markets around the world crashed, shedding huge value in a very short time. The crash began in Hong Kong and then spread west through international time zones to Europe, hitting the United States after other markets had already declined by a significant margin. The Dow Jones industrial average dropped by 508 points to 1738.74 (22.61%). The stock market crash of 1987 was the largest one-day stock market crash in history. The Dow lost 22.6% of its value, or $500 billion, on October 19, 1987!

European ERM Crisis (1992). Black Wednesday refers to the events of September 16, 1992, when the Conservative Government was forced to withdraw the pound sterling from the European Exchange Rate Mechanism (ERM) after they were unable to keep sterling above its agreed lower limit. The most high-profile of the currency market investors, George Soros, made over $1 billion profit by short-selling sterling. In 1997 the UK treasury estimated the cost of black Wednesday at £3.4 billion.

Mexican Crisis (1994). The 1994 economic crisis in Mexico, widely known as the Mexican peso crisis, started with the sudden devaluation of the peso in December 1994.

After nearly a decade of stagnant economic activity and high inflation in Mexico, the Mexican government liberalized the trade sector in 1985, adopted an economic stabilization plan at the end of 1987, and gradually introduced market-oriented institutions. These reforms led to the resumption of economic growth, which averaged 3.1% per year between 1989 and 1994. In 1993, inflation was brought down to single-digit levels for the first time in more than two decades.

As its economic reforms advanced, Mexico began to attract more foreign investment, a development helped by the absence of major restrictions on capital inflows, especially in the context of low U.S. interest rates. Indeed, large capital inflows began in 1990, when a successful foreign debt renegotiation was formalized. The devaluation of the peso in December 1994 put an abrupt end to these capital inflows and precipitated the financial crisis.

LTCM. LTCM was a U.S. hedge fund that used trading strategies such as fixed income arbitrage, statistical arbitrage and pairs trading, combined with high leverage. It failed spectacularly in the late 1990s, leading to a massive bailout by other major banks and investment houses, which was supervised by the Federal Reserve. The core strategy of LTCM consisted of "convergence-arbitrage" trades, trying to take advantage of small differences in prices among near-identical bonds.

LTCM was founded in 1994 by John Meriwether, the former vice-chairman and head of bond trading at Salomon Brothers. Board of directors' members included Myron Scholes and Robert C. Merton, who shared the 1997 Nobel Memorial Prize in Economic Sciences. Initially enormously successful with annualized returns of over 40%[3] (after fees) in its first years, in 1998 it lost $4.6 billion in less than four months following the Russian financial crisis and became a prominent example of the risk potential in the hedge fund industry.

With losses of capital by LTCM, its bank lenders became worried about the security of their loans. In the fall of 1998 when LTCM was on the brink of failure, the Federal Reserve Bank of New York brought the lenders together and brokered a bailout. Some 14 or so banks contributed about $300 million each to raise a $3.65 billion loan fund. That fund, along with the equity still held by LTCM, enabled it to withstand the turmoil in the markets.

Another financial crisis occurred in the form of unusually high spreads on swaps. LTCM was reorganized and continued to operate. By the next year it had paid off its loans and was effectively liquidated by early 2000.

12.3.2 OTHER STRESS TEST SCENARIOS

12.3.2.1 Interest Rate Scenarios. Interest scenarios are relative and additive to the current yield curve. This means that each point of the yield curve constitutes the sum of the current yield curve value and a relative base point shift of the respective yield curve point.

12.3.2.2. Relative FX Scenarios. Relative FX scenarios refer to the price quotations of the respective currency compared to the leading currency. This signifies for the above example that the current currency relationship in the price format,

$$1\,\text{CAD} = \text{FX}(\text{EUR}, \text{CAD}) \times \text{EUR}$$

where FX(CAD,EUR) represents the current CAD exchange rate, has been integrated in the scenario relationship:

$$1\,\text{CAD} = (100\% - 13\%) \times \text{FX}(\text{EUR}; \text{CAD}) \times \text{EUR}$$

12.3.2.3 Dynamic FX Scenarios. With dynamic FX scenarios, the scenario effect consists of two components: the risk factor RF (volatility of the respective FX rate) and the scenario factor (SF) editable in the scenario. If a dynamic FX scenario has been defined for a foreign exchange rate, the scenario value is calculated as follows:

$$\text{FX rate}_{\text{scenario}} = \text{FX rate}_{\text{current}} \times (1 + \text{SF} \times \text{RF})$$

12.3.2.4 Progression Scenarios. The analysis type is enabled for bonds, credits, participation certificates, caps, floors, and structured bonds. It computes net present values for future points in time, hence allowing an estimation of the

[3]The portfolio had to be heavily leveraged to create a 30–40% return. LTCM choose to limit its risk by targeting a level of volatility similar to a position in U.S. equities, at 15% per year.

value development of specific instruments or particular portfolios. This calculation requires that future development scenarios be defined for all relevant evaluation interest curves.

These development scenarios are presupposed between (today's) value date and the (future) analysis date. The calculation for the analysis date is made on the basis of the scenario curves for this date. Payments that are due prior to the future evaluation date are prolonged as a virtual zero bond until the analysis date; the prolongation is based on the corresponding instrument evaluation curve and the corresponding development scenario.

12.4 Reverse Stress Test

Reverse stress tests try to identify the risks that would lead an institution to fail. This is an appealing idea in the sense that instead of starting from the existing standpoint and seeing how close we can go toward the ridge of the cliff without falling, reverse stress testing tells you what risks you could take to fall directly off the cliff. That makes so much sense that you may wonder why we have not carried out reverse stress tests for ages. The main problem with reverse stress testing is "how" to do it. There are so many reasons why an institution would fail that it may take some time to determine meaningful stress tests. When we conduct other types of stress testing, we always start from the known—the portfolio itself and its VaR—and try to progress more or less in the dark to gauge the risks ahead. With a reverse stress test, we start from the unknown and try to figure out how we became lost on the way home. This intellectually challenging thought could soon become a tedious task where one tries to assess which events could have triggered the failure and how this event has contaminated the entire system. There is no easy answer to this problem, but since contagion is the result of increasing correlation, working with copula statistical analysis could be a starting point.

In reverse stress testing, one has to identify a range of adverse circumstances that would cause a firm's business plan to become unviable and assess the likelihood that such events could crystallize. The factors that can lead to business model failure can be either idiosyncratic or systemic. An idiosyncratic event could be for example an internal fraud which can lead to loss of reputation or exhaustion of capital and finally a wind down. Systemic factors can be for example a sharp increase in unemployment which leads to high defaults and reduced capital and business model failure.

12.5 Stress Testing Correlation and Volatility

Every portfolio is usually managed according to a predefined volatility band. So for example a portfolio manager has decided that his portfolio volatility will not exceed a volatility band of 8–15%. Correlation is a critical component of the resulting volatility for a portfolio. Therefore it is important to stress test how the stock's volatility and the pairwise correlation can move before they may breach the volatility band defined by the portfolio manager. The purpose of this stress test is to have a visual representation based on current risk and level of correlation of the fund before breaching its risk budget and the volatility range of the fund. The report shows a matrix of the predicted volatilities we can expect given a change in the level of portfolio stock correlation (horizontal) and level of market volatility (vertical). The gray-shaded cell in Figure 12.7 highlights the current level of predicted volatility, while blue and red regions show when the predicted volatility would be, respectively, below and above the volatility target range. In this sample, the volatility band of the fund is 8–10%.

Suppose that market volatility increases to 1.5 times its current level independently of correlation. The matrix in Figure 12.7 can be used to forecast how the predicted volatility may change by moving vertically down the matrix to the row corresponding to a volatility multiplier of 1.5; that is, the volatility moves from 5.52% to 8.27%.

Now suppose that stock correlation independently moves higher from its current level of 0.37—for example to 0.70. Moving across the matrix to the corresponding correlation column the portfolio volatility increases from 5.52% to 6.81%.

12.6 Multivariate Stress Testing

The above types of stress tests are a useful and a necessary part of a firm's risk framework. However, they are limited in several respects. Market sensitivity tests are useful in understanding the impact of a single market/sector/asset class move on a portfolio, but they only allow for a single driver of returns at a time. Historic stress tests incorporate all drivers of return, but they relate only to a single period in history. Given the current market situation characterized by multiple events (U.S. Fiscal Cliff, EU Sovereign Debt Crisis, . . .), firms may consider that they need an additional type of stress test that allows them to simultaneously input multiple assumptions on:

- Moves in multiple asssets: for example, Eurostoxx index declines 25% while FTSE UK index declines 15%.
- Currency moves: EURUSD declines 25%.
- Single position moves: the group of periphery exposed banks decline by 45%.
- Changes to correlations: average stock correlations move to 0.8.
- Changes to volatilities: Eurozone stock volatilities double, while UK volatilities increase by 50%.
- Confidence.

The multiviariate stress testing tool allows all of these inputs (Table 12.2). It utilizes a Bayesian approach to allow the firms to specify a range of events, along with confidence in each of these events to predict the impact on key portfolio characteristics. The results are considered in context with the

Stressed V olatility

Stock Volatility Multiplier	Implied Average Portfolio Stock Correlation 0.00	0.10	0.20	0.30	0.37	0.40	0.50	0.60	0.70	0.80	0.90	1.00
0.25	1.17	1.23	1.29	1.34	1.38	1.41	1.52	1.61	1.70	1.79	1.87	1.95
0.50	2.34	2.46	2.57	2.68	2.76	2.82	3.03	3.22	3.41	3.58	3.75	3.90
0.75	3.51	3.69	3.86	4.03	4.14	4.24	4.55	4.84	5.11	5.37	5.62	5.85
1.00	4.68	4.92	5.15	5.37	5.52	5.65	6.06	6.45	6.81	7.16	7.49	7.81
1.25	5.85	6.15	6.44	6.71	6.89	7.06	7.58	8.06	8.52	8.95	9.36	9.76
1.50	7.02	7.38	7.72	8.05	8.27	8.47	9.09	9.67	10.22	10.74	11.24	11.71
1.75	8.19	8.61	9.01	9.39	9.65	9.88	10.61	11.28	11.92	12.53	13.11	13.66
2.00	9.36	9.84	10.30	10.74	11.03	11.30	12.12	12.90	13.63	14.32	14.98	15.61
2.25	10.54	11.07	11.59	12.08	12.41	12.71	13.64	14.51	15.33	16.11	16.85	17.56
2.50	11.71	12.30	12.87	13.42	13.79	14.12	15.15	16.12	17.03	17.90	18.73	19.52

Above upper Vol target of 10%

Below lower Vol target of 8%

Correlation and Volatility Levels as of: 30 Dec 11

FIGURE 12.7 Correlation and volatility stress test versus risk budget. **Source:** Marshall Wace LLP.

TABLE 12.2 Example of Multivariate Eurozone Economics Stress Test

Possible Scenarios	Characteristics	Implications
Eurozone breakup	• Dissolution of monetary union • Reversion to national currencies • Conversion of all assets and liabilities to national currencies	• Capital flight and financial systematic distress • Plunging consumer and business confidence • Further fiscal tightening • Huge impacts on main financial indices • Increase in volatility • Increase in correlations
A managed exit for Greece	• Greece is the only country to exit the eurozone • Departure is far less disruptive compared to a bigger economy • Back-stop funding is put in place to limit contagion	• The notion of the irreversibility of EMU would be shattered forever • EUR/USD slumps to parity • Real estate and FI investments suffer one off losses on Greek debt devaluation

probability of such a scenario occurring and risk adjusted accordingly. These multivariate stress tests are run on an *ad hoc* basis when markets are characterized by a high level of uncertainty or when there is an event (e.g., QE, elections like in Greece in June 2012) that may severely affect equities price on the downside or upside. These multivariate stress tests will also highlight where a book would breach its upper risk target limit.

12.7 What Is Back Testing?

Since the VaR is an indicator of risk, which is also used to calculate the minimum of capital, regulatory bodies have adopted, in addition to the criterias of degree of confidence, the period detention—tests that must verify the models VaR. Among these tests is back testing, which is used to validate the relevance of these models—that is, the adequacy of the VaR to the risks actually supported. Depending on the model, back testing can take different forms. It aims, for example, to check the percentage of defaults per tranches or level risk which are not deviating from the original forecast. It can also aim to ensure that the number of exceedances of the limit set by the VaR over time does not exceed a certain threshold.

Model validation is the general process of checking whether a model is adequate. This can be done with a set of tools, including *back testing*, *stress testing*, and *independent review and oversight*.

Back testing is a formal statistical framework that consists of verifying that actual losses are in line with projected losses. This involves systematically comparing the history of VaR forecasts with their associated portfolio returns.

The quality of the VaR model must be demonstrably determined by means of a daily comparison between the potential market risk amount calculated by the model and the actual change in the value of the portfolio (back testing). If the latter exceeds the former, we must take appropriate action immediately.

The use of VaR as a risk disclosure or risk management tool will be scrutinized internally but also by external parties, such as regulators, auditors, investors, creditors and credit rating agencies. To make it simple, back testing intends to provide estimates of the accuracy of the risk models being used.

With the latest market turmoil stemming from the U.S. sub-prime mortgage crises, it is clear that there is a need for an approach that comes to terms with problems posed by extreme event estimation. VaR is not a "coherent" risk measure because it does not necessarily satisfy the sub-additivity condition.[4]

The choice of a VaR model comprises a cost–benefit analysis with respect to the accuracy, type of data to be retrieved, and ease of implementation. A wide range of simplifying assumptions is usually used in VaR models (distributions of returns, historical data window defining the range of possible outcomes, etc.); and as the number of assumptions grows, the accuracy of the VaR estimates tends to decrease.

It is essential that the risk numbers provide accurate information and that someone in the organization is accountable for producing the best possible risk estimates. In order to ensure the accuracy of the forecasted risk numbers, risk managers should regularly back-test the risk models being used, as well as evaluate alternative models if the results do not provide full satisfaction and confidence.

VaR models provide a framework to measure risk, and if a particular model does not perform its intended task properly, it should be refined or replaced. Risk managers should be accountable for implementing the best possible framework to measure risk, even if it involves introducing subjective judgment into the risk calculations.

The back-testing methodology should answer the following questions:

- How well does the model measure a particular percentile of or the entire profit and-loss distribution?
- How well does the model predict the size and frequency of losses?

Many standard back-tests of VaR models compare the actual portfolio losses for a given horizon versus the estimated VaR numbers. In its simplest form, the back-testing procedure consists of calculating the number or percentage of times that the actual portfolio returns fall outside the VaR estimate and comparing that number to the confidence level used. For example, if the confidence level were 99%, we would expect portfolio returns to exceed the VaR numbers on about 1% of the days.

[4]Sub-additivity means that a portfolio will risk an amount, which is at most the sum of the separate amounts risked by its subportfolios.

12.7.1 VAR IS NOT ALWAYS AN ACCURATE MEASURE[5]

VaR is only a first-order approximation of downside risk. It is not a magic tool. Users, including the regulators, of VaR should not be lulled into a state of complacency, but recognize its inherent limitation. Having said that, VaR may not be correct also because of some wrong settings within the risk engine. VaR can also be inaccurate if the wrong VaR model has been applied—for example a parametric VaR for a portfolio containing a lot of nonlinear instruments such as options. VaR can also be wrong because of abnormal market conditions. It is then therefore important to back-test the model on a regular basis and assess whether the VaR errors are coming from its inherent limitations or if they are simply because of wrong settings or parameterizations or because of the inaccuracy of risk models of a risk engine. Even if VaR is not a perfect measure, the greatest benefit of VaR is that it forces the fund to focus on risk.

There is no precise measure of VaR, and each measure comes with its own limitations. The end result is that the VaR that we compute for an asset, portfolio, or firm can be wrong, and sometimes the errors can be large enough to make VaR a misleading measure of risk exposure. The reasons for the errors can vary across firms and for different measures and include the following:

Return Distributions. Every VaR measure makes assumptions about return distributions that, if violated, result in incorrect estimates of the VaR. With delta-normal estimates of VaR, we are assuming that the multivariate return distribution is the normal distribution, since the VaR is based entirely on the standard deviation in returns. With Monte Carlo simulations, we get more freedom to specify different types of return distributions, but we can still be wrong when we make those judgments. Finally, with historical simulations we are assuming that the historical return distribution (based upon past data) is representative of the distribution of returns looking forward.

There is substantial evidence that returns are not normally distributed and that outliers are not only more common in reality, but are much larger than expected, given the normal distribution.

History May Not a Good Predictor. All measures of VaR use historical data to some degree or the other. In the variance–covariance method, historical data are used to compute the variance–covariance matrix that is the basis for the computation of VaR. In historical simulations, the VaR is entirely based upon the historical data with the likelihood of value losses computed from the time series of returns. In Monte Carlo simulations, the distributions do not have to be based upon historical data, but it is difficult to see how else they can be derived. In short, any VaR measure will be a function of the time period over which the historical data are collected. If that time period was a relatively stable one, the computed VaR will be a low number and will understate the risk looking

[5]Aswath Damodaran from a Stern School of Business Working Paper.

forward. Conversely, if the time period examined was volatile, the VaR will be set too high.

Nonstationary Correlations. Measures of VaR are conditioned on explicit estimates of correlation across risk sources (in the variance–covariance and Monte Carlo simulations) or implicit assumptions about correlation (in historical simulations). These correlation estimates are usually based upon historical data and are extremely volatile. One measure of how much they move can be obtained by tracking the correlations between widely following asset classes over time.

Short Term. VaR can be computed over a quarter or a year, but it is usually computed over a day, a week, or a few weeks. In most real-world applications, therefore, the VaR is computed over short time periods rather than longer ones. There are three reasons for this short-term focus. The first is that the financial service firms that use VaR often are focused on hedging these risks on a day-to-day basis and are thus less concerned about long-term risk exposures. The second is that the regulatory authorities, at least for financial service firms, demand to know the short-term VaR exposures at frequent intervals. The third is that the inputs into the VaR measure computation, whether it is measured using historical simulations or the variance–covariance approach, are easiest to estimate for short periods. In fact, as we noted in the last section, the quality of the VaR estimates quickly deteriorate as you go from daily, weekly, and monthly to annual measures.

Absolute Value. The output from a VaR computation is not a standard deviation or an overall risk measure but is stated in terms of a probability that the losses will exceed a specified value. As an example, a VaR of $100 million with 95% confidence implies that there is only a 5% chance of losing more than $100 million. The focus on a fixed value makes it an attractive measure of risk to financial service firms that worry about their capital adequacy. By the same token, it is what makes VaR an inappropriate measure of risk for firms that are focused on comparing investments with very different scales and returns; for these firms, more conventional scaled measures of risk (such as standard deviation or betas) that focus on the entire risk distribution will work better.

In short, VaR measures look at only a small slice of the risk that an asset is exposed to, and a great deal of valuable information in the distribution is ignored. Even if the VaR assessment that the probability of losing more than $100 million is less than 5% is correct, would it not make sense to know what the most you can lose in that catastrophic range (with less than 5% probability) would be? It should, after all, make a difference whether your worst possible loss was $1 billion or $150 million.

Suboptimal Decisions. Even if VaR is correctly measured, it is not clear that using it as the measure of risk leads to more reasoned and sensible decisions on the part of managers and investors. In fact, there are two strands of criticism against the use of VaR in decision making. The first is that making investment decisions based upon VaR can lead to overexposure to risk, even when the decision makers are rational and VaR is estimated precisely. The other is that managers who understand how VaR is computed can manipulate the measure to report superior performance while exposing the firm to substantial risks.

Overexposure to Risk. Assume that managers are asked to make investment decisions while having their risk exposures measured using VaR. Basak and Shapiro (2001) note that such managers will often invest in more risky portfolios than managers who do not use VaR as a risk assessment tool. They explain this counterintuitive result by noting that managers evaluated based upon VaR will be much more focused on avoiding the intermediate risks (under the probability threshold), but that their portfolios are likely to lose far more under the most adverse circumstances. Put another way, by not bringing in the magnitude of the losses once you exceed the VaR cutoff probability (90% or 95%), you are opening yourself to the possibility of very large losses in the worst-case scenarios.

Agency Problems. Like any risk measure, VaR can be manipulated by managers who have decided to make an investment and want to meet the VaR risk constraint. Since VaR is generally measured using past data, traders and managers who are evaluated using the measure will have a reasonable understanding of its errors and can take advantage of them.

Consider the example of the VaR from oil price volatility that we estimated using historical simulation earlier in the chapter; the VaR was understated because it did not capture the increasing volatility in oil prices toward the end of the time period. A canny manager who knows that this can take on far greater oil price risk than is prudent while reporting a VaR that looks like it is under the limit.

It is true that all risk measures are open to this critique; but by focusing on an absolute value and a single probability, VaR is more open to this game playing than other measures.

12.8 Back Testing: A Rigorous Approach Is Required

Back testing can be as much an art as a science. It is important to incorporate rigorous statistical tests with other visual and qualitative tests.

The simplest back test consists of counting the number of exceptions (losses larger than estimated VaR) for a given period and comparing them to the expected number for the chosen confidence interval.

The back test compares whether the observed percentage of outcomes covered by the risk measure is consistent with a 99% level of confidence. That is, they attempt to determine whether a portfolio's 99th percentile risk measures truly cover 99% of the portfolio's returns.

VaR provides no handle on the extent of the losses that might be suffered beyond a certain threshold. VaR is incapable of distinguishing between situations where losses in the tail are only a bit worse and those where they are overwhelming. An alternative measure that is coherent and quantifies the losses that might be encountered in the tail is the expected tail loss (ETL).

A more rigorous way to perform the back-testing analysis is to determine the accuracy of the model predicting both the frequency and the size of expected losses. Back-testing ETL or expected tail gain numbers can provide an indication of how well the model captures the size of the expected loss (gain) beyond VaR, and therefore can enhance the quality of the back-testing procedure. The field of ETL estimation and model comparison is just beginning to develop, and there is an obvious lack of empirical research.

Artzner et al. (1999) introduced the expected shortfall risk measure, which equals the expected value of the loss, given that a VaR violation occurred. Yamai and Yoshiba (2002) compared the two measures and argued that VaR is not reliable during market turmoil, whereas ETL can be a better choice overall. Angelidis and Degiannakis (2006) tested the performance of various parametric VaR and ETL models. They found that different volatility models are "optimal" for different assets.

Statistics enable us to check whether the risk model is accurately capturing the frequency, independence, or magnitude of exceptions, which are defined as losses (gains) exceeding the VaR estimate for the selected period.

Tests in statistics can be categorized in two types of errors:

- Type 1 errors occur when the model that is correct is rejected.
- Type 2 errors occur when the wrong model is not rejected.

It is clear that in risk management, it can be much more costly to incur Type II errors, and therefore a high threshold should be defined in order to accept the validity of any risk model.

The implications for the choice confidence level for the VaR calculations is that the larger the confidence level for the VaR estimates, the fewer the number of "exceptions" and therefore the more difficult it is to validate the model. A 95% VaR level means that more "exception" points will be observed than with the 99% level, and the accuracy of the resulting model will be better assessed.

Many statistical tests are based on the frequency and time dynamics of exceptions.

We will now briefly discuss the most common ones.

12.8.1 TEST OF FREQUENCY OF TAIL LOSSES OR KUPIEC'S TEST

Kupiec's test attempts to determine whether the observed frequency of exceptions is consistent with the frequency of expected exceptions according to the VaR model and chosen confidence interval. Under the null hypothesis, the correct number of exceptions follows a binomial distribution. The probability of experiencing x or more exceptions if the model is correct is given by:

$$\Pr\left(\frac{x}{n}, p\right) = \binom{n}{x} p \times (1-p)^{n-x}$$

where x is the number of exceptions, p is the probability of an exception for a given confidence level, and n is the number of trials.

If the estimated probability is above the desired "null" significance level (usually 5–10%), the model is accepted. If the estimated probability is below the significance level, the model is rejected. This test determines how well the model predicts the frequency of losses and gains beyond VaR numbers.

12.8.2 CONDITIONAL COVERAGE OF FREQUENCY AND INDEPENDENCE OF TAIL LOSSES[6]

Kupiec's test only focuses on the frequency of exceptions and ignores the time dynamics of those exceptions. VaR models assume that exceptions should be independently distributed over time. If the exceptions exhibit some type of "clustering," then the VaR model may fail to capture the variability of profits and losses under certain conditions.

The Christoffersen test enables us to test sub-hypotheses regarding the frequency and independence of exceptions, as well as test the joint hypothesis that the VaR model has the right frequency of independent exceptions.

An additional benefit is that it generates some additional useful information, such as (a) the conditional probabilities of experiencing an exception followed by an exception in the risk model and (b) the average number of days between exceptions.

The standard tests that focus on frequency and independence of exceptions are weak and often fail to properly exclude the null hypothesis and are therefore likely to result in a type II error. Moreover, the "true" null probability is not known. As a consequence, it is difficult to know whether the wrong model can be accepted or whether a good model can be rejected because the null probability can be wrong.

Dowd suggests using a bootstrapping mechanism to construct a sample of null hypothesis probabilities that can then be used as back-testing input. Bootstrapping involves creating alternative samples by drawing observations from the original sample of VaR and profits and losses and then replacing the observation in the sample pool after it has been drawn. The process can be repeated to create alternative samples from which the p-values for the Kupiec and Christoffersen tests can be estimated.

The bootstrapped values can provide a confidence band around the results of statistical tests.

In addition to back testing the traditional interval and point risk measures such as VaR and ETL, we may also be interested in back testing how well the

[6]Christoffersen, P., Evaluating interval forecasts, *International Economic Review*, vol. 39, 1998, pp. 841–862.

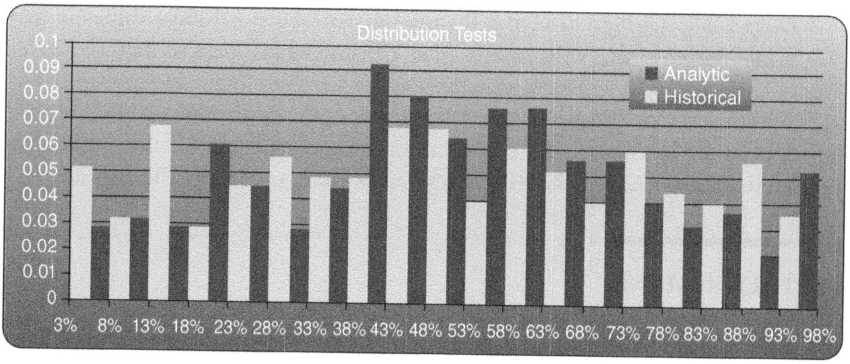

FIGURE 12.8 Histogram of time series of observed probabilities. Source: Blanco, C., Oks, M., Backtesting VaR models: Quantitative and qualitative tests, accessed 18 March 2010, http://www.fea.com/resources/pdf/Backtesting1.pdf.

model predicts the entire distribution of profits and losses. This has an added benefit of further rejecting bad models.

In this approach, forecasts at many quantiles are compared to the actual data and the probability of observing a return below the actual data is calculated.

If the risk model is correct, then the time series of observed probabilities should be independent and identically distributed as a uniform (0, 1) variable. We can then perform a graphical analysis by simply constructing a histogram of these probabilities and checking that it looks reasonably flat (Figure 12.8).

12.8.3 CLEAN AND DIRTY BACK TESTING

With empirical testing of statistical forecasts that have been created via appropriate risk analysis tools at the beginning of the historical analysis period, the risk forecast may be created for instance on the basis of an internal model (VaR model) or similar models (German principle 1, scenario matrix approach, stress tests, or historical simulation). In this sense, the back-testing values assessed according to the "clean P&L (Profit and Loss)" concept (clean in so far as it does ***not*** take transaction movements within the back-testing period into consideration).

Back-testing analysis can be performed for all types of financial instruments and, where possible, can examine the development of the specific market values within the analysis period. There are basically two main approaches to perform back testing on VaR: clean and dirty. We describe the two techniques as follows:

Clean Back Testing. Hypothetical fluctuations of the portfolio's value on day T are calculated by assuming that the portfolio constituents from close of business of day $T-1$ are held constant over day T. The portfolio is revalued using the change in prices of the underlying securities. The hypothetical fluctuation in portfolio value is compared to the VaR calculated using positions as of close of business of day $T-1$.

Dirty Back Testing. Effective fluctuations of the portfolio's value on day T compared to the VaR calculated as of close of business of day $T - 1$.

Selecting the one to be used for internal purpose or for any external reporting depend on the portfolio turnover. In the case of a portfolio with non-negligible daily turnover, the dirty back test is the standard method to use.

FURTHER READING

Alexander, C., Sheedy, E. A., Model-based stress tests: Linking stress tests to VaR for market risk, working document, Macquarie Applied Finance Center, 2008.

Angelidis, T., S. Degiannakis, S., Backtesting VaR models: an expected shortfall approach, Athens University of Economics and Business, Department of Statistics, Technical Report no. 223, 2006.

Aragonés, J. R., Blanco, C., Dowd, K., Incorporating stress tests into market risk modeling, *Derivatives Quarterly*, **7**, 2001, pp. 44–49.

Aragonés, J. R., Blanco, C., Dowd, K., Stress tests, market risk measures, and extremes: bringing stress tests to the forefront of market risk management, in Rösch, D., Scheule, H. (eds.), *Stress Testing for Financial Institutions: Applications, Regulations, and Techniques*, Risk Books, London, 2008, chapter 2.

Artzner, P., Delbaen, F., Eber, J.-M., Heath, D., Coherent measures of risk, *Mathematical Finance*, **9**(3), 1999, pp. 203–228.

Basak, S., Shapiro, A., Value-at-risk based risk management: optimal policies and asset prices, *Review of Financial Studies*, **14**(2), Summer 2001, pp. 371–405.

Basel Committee on Bank Supervision, Principles for Sound Stress Testing Practices and Supervision, Consultative document, January 2009.

Berkowitz, J., A coherent framework for stress, *Journal of Risk*, **2**(2), Winter 1999–2000, pp. 5–15.

Bogle, J. C., Black Monday and black swans, *Financial Analyst Journal*, **64**(2), March–April 2008, pp. 30–40.

Cornish, E. A., Fisher, R. A., Moments and cumulants in the specification of distributions, *Review of the International Statistical Institute*, **5**, 1937, pp. 307–320.

Dowd, K., *Measuring Market Risk*, Wiley, Hoboken, NJ, 2007.

Goldberg, L., et al., Beyond value at risk: Forecasting portfolio loss at multiple horizons, *Journal of Investment Management*, **6**(2), 2008, pp. 73–98.

Maillard, D., *A User's Guide to the Cornish Fisher Expansion*, SSRN 1997178.

McNeil, A., *Extreme Value Theory for Risk Managers*, ETH Zentrum, Zurich, 1999.

Rebonato R., *Coherent Stress Testing; A Bayesian Approach to the Analysis of Financial Risk*, Wiley, Hoboken, NJ, 2010.

Sorge, M., Stress-testing financial systems: An overview of current methodologies, Working Papers, no. 165, Bank for International Settlements (BIS), December 2004.

Taleb, N. N., *The Black Swan: The Impact of the Highly Improbable*, Random House, New York, 2007.

Yamai, Y., Yoshiba, T., Comparative analyses of expected shortfall and value-at-risk, working paper, Research Division, Bank of Japan, Monetary and Economic Studies, April 2002.

CHAPTER THIRTEEN

Banks and Basel II/III

Banks play a special role of intermediation, by facilitating payment flows across customers, and maintain markets for financial instrument. The purposes of banks can make their failures much more disruptive for the economy than the failure of other businesses. The threat here of a failure of a bank is that of a systemic risk.

Systemic risk can be defined as the risk of a sudden shock, which would damage the financial system to such an extent that economic activity would suffer. Systemic risk involves contagious transmission of the shock due to actual or suspected exposure to a failing bank. This is usually accompanied by a flight-to-quality, which reflects an increased demand for government securities, pushing up the relative cost of capital to the corporate sector.

Failures in the banking system have been particularly damaging, as we have been witnessing since the bankruptcy of Lehman, which plunged the world economy into recession, with several domestic banking systems being rescued by their respective governments.

In order to avoid systemic risk, regulators around the world worked together along with local governments and supra-national agencies to develop a set of tools and regulations to keep banks regulated. Systemic risk can come from two sources:

- Panicky behavior of depositors or investors, which would lead to a bank run in most cases
- Interruption in the payment system.

In this chapter, first we will provide a brief historical perspective and evolution of market risk for banks over time, and the development of regulation within that period. We will then look at the first Basel Capital Accord, with the introduction of the credit risk charge for the capital requirements for banks. Thereafter, we will develop the methodology under Basel for the calculation of the

Handbook of Market Risk, First Edition. Christian Szylar.

market risk charge, first under the standardized approach, followed by the Internal Models Approach. Finally, we will look at the development under Basel III, taking into account market risk development as well as liquidity ratios.

13.1 A Brief History of Banking Regulations

The history of banking regulation is largely correlated to a history of government and private responses to banking panics. The first of banking panics was bank runs, when depositors lost faith in the ability of their banks to make full payment and "ran to the banks" to withdraw their money. In response to banking runs, most countries adopted a compulsory deposit insurance scheme, eliminating the possibility of the bank run. We shall see later that it still happened in the UK with Northern Rock, at the height of the 2008 financial crisis.

The other type of systemic risk, arising from the interruption in the payment system, forced regulators to look into the issue more carefully after the Bankhaus Herstatt bank problem in June 1974. Bankhaus Herstatt was a small German bank active in the foreign exchange market, with several U.S. counterparties. When the bank closed down at noon, U.S. time, after receiving payments in German marks, the U.S. counterparty banks never received payments in U.S. dollars in the afternoon, creating substantial losses for the counterparties, on top of a liquidity squeeze for the U.S. banks. This event caused severe disruption in the payment system and was perhaps the most extreme shock experienced in the foreign exchange market.

Bank regulators led a concerted effort in order to avoid such situations, which ultimately led to the creation of the Basel Committee on Banking Supervision (BCBS).

The BCBS consists of senior officials from the G-10 (Group of Ten) countries (Belgium, Canada, France, Germany, Italy, Japan, the Netherlands, United Kingdom, United States, and Sweden, plus Luxembourg and Switzerland).

Though business activities have always been exposed to risks, the formal study of managing risk started in the latter half of the twentieth century.

The market risk capital standards are intended to ensure that banks hold capital sufficient to cover their market risks in their trading portfolios. While market risk can arise from the full range of banking activities, it is most prominent in trading activities, where positions were market to market daily. Thus the market risk capital standards concentrate on positions in banking organizations' trading portfolios.

Following from the credit risk charges in the Basel Accord of 1988, regulators focused their attention on market risk in banks due to the increased activities of proprietary trading in commercial and investment banks. Market risk can be defined as the loss incurred to the bank due to changes in market variables. It is the risk that the value of on/off balance sheet positions will be adversely affected by market movements in underlying factors (equity prices, interest rates, FX rates, and commodity prices).

Interest Rate Risk. Interest rate exposure can be described as the risk of the reduction in a projected or anticipated measure of net interest income, resulting from changes in market interest rates. The Basel Committee on Banking Supervision bases its definition on the different effects of interest rate exposure:

> Interest rate risk is the exposure to the bank's financial condition to adverse movement in interest rates. Changes in interest rates affect a bank's earnings by changing its net interest income and the level of other interest sensitive income and operating expenses. Changes in interest rates also affect the underlying value of the bank's liabilities, assets, and off-balance sheet instruments because of the economic value of future cash flow.

With a view to capturing interest rate risk, the Basel Committee on Banking Supervision breaks it down into four main types:

- Repricing risk, which arises from mismatch in interest rate fixation periods.
- Yield curve risk, which is caused by changes in the slope and shape of the yield curve.
- Basis risk, which arises from an imperfect correlation in the adjustment of the rates earned and paid on different products. When interest rates changes, these differences can give rise to unexpected changes in the cash flows and earnings spread among assets, liabilities, and off-balance sheet instrument of similar maturities or repricing frequencies.
- Optionality risk, which arises primarily from options (gamma and vega effect) that are embedded in many banking book positions.

Commodity Risk. A commodity is defined as a physical product that is or can be traded on a secondary market—for example, agricultural products, minerals (including oil), and precious metals. Commodity risk arises when a bank has open positions (long or short), in a commodity, where the price can be affected due to movements in the markets. Commodity risk is also affected by basis risk, forward gap risk, and interest rate risk.

FX Risk. Foreign exchange risk is the risk that a bank may suffer loss as a result of adverse exchange rate movements during a period in which it has an open position, either spot or forward in a foreign currency.

Equity Risk. Equity risk applies when a bank has open positions in the equity market, which can be affected by price movements in the underlying equities.

13.2 The 1988 Basel Accord

The Basel Capital Accord was concluded on 15 July 1988, representing a milestone for financial regulation of international banks. For the first time, minimum level of capital requirement to be held by banks against financial risks were instituted as regulatory requirements. The Basel Accord was reinforced by the Basel Committee in 2001, also known as Basel II, which allowed greater flexibility and more reliance on the bank's internal methodologies. Following the latest financial crisis that began in 2008 led to some more rules and regulations leading the Basel Committee to release a new set of rules, or Basel III, which intensified the capital requirements to be held by international banks.

13.2.1 DEFINITION OF CAPITAL

Published by the Basel Committee on Banking Supervisions in 1988, the Basel Capital Accord put in writing the agreement between the G10 central banks to apply common minimum capital standards to their banking industries. The requirements fitted the objective of introducing international convergence of capital measurements and capital standards.

The agreement defined a common measure of capital requirement. The Basel Accord requires capital to be equal to at least 8 percent of its total risk-weighted assets. However, the word "capital" here has a broader interpretation than the usual definition of equity book value. Because the capital requirement's aim is to protect deposits, for it to be effective, the capital requirement must be permanent. Capital consists of two components:

Tier 1 Capital: Tier 1 capital includes only permanent shareholder's equity (issued and fully paid ordinary shares/common stock and perpetual noncumulative preference shares), and disclosed reserved. As stated above, such capital is permanent, which is set aside as a buffer to cushion future losses. This basic definition of capital excludes revaluation reserves and cumulative preference shares.

Tier 2 Capital: Also known as supplementary capital. This includes all other capital and components of the balance sheet that provide some protection, yet representing instruments that can cover potential losses. These include undisclosed reserves (consisting of the part of the accumulated after-tax surplus of retained profits) that are not identified in the balance sheet, yet should have the same high quality and character as a disclosed capital reserve. Revaluation reserves are also accounted for in Tier 2 capital. General provisions/general loan-loss reserves, which are provisions, held against future unidentified losses qualify for inclusion within Tier 2 capital. Hybrid capital instruments are also included in the definition of Tier 2 capital. This includes a range of instruments that combine characteristics of equity capital and of debt. Some requirements need to be met in order to qualify instruments under hybrid capital instruments (unsecured, not redeemable, available to participate in losses). Finally, subordinated term debt should be included in the calculation for Tier 2 capital. It consists of conventional unsecured debt capital instruments with a fixed term to maturity of over five years.

There are limits and restrictions into the calculation of the credit risk charge from the capital elements as described above, such as:

- The total of Tier 2 elements is limited to a maximum of 100 percent of the total of tier 1 elements.
- During the last five years to maturity, a cumulative discount factor of 20 percent will be applied to the subordinated term debt. Furthermore, the instruments falling in this category will be limited to a maximum of 50 percent of tier 1.
- The general loan-loss reserves are limited to a maximum of 1.25 percentage points.
- The asset revaluation reserves take the form of latent gains on unrealized securities subject to a discount of 55 percent to be applied between historical cost book and market value to reflect the potential volatility of this form of capital.

13.2.2 CREDIT RISK CHARGE

The Basel Accord consolidated the movement toward risk weighting of assets. The assignment of assets was principally based on the generic nature of the borrower (or underlying instruments) rather than the borrower's credit worthiness (and financial characteristics). Risk capital weights were classified into four different categories, depending on the nature of the asset for on-balance sheet items (BS). Table 13.1 is a summary of the risk weight classification and the corresponding asset classes that define the calculation of the credit risk charge for BS items.

As described in Table 13.1, only four risk weights applied to BS items for the calculation of the credit risk charge. For instance, a treasury bond does not have any risk associated with it from a Basel Accord (because U.S. Treasuries are obligations emanating from an Organization for Economic Cooperation and Development (OECD)), while a municipal bond from the US would have a 20% risk weight. Furthermore, following the risk weighting factors, a bond issued by a AAA-rated institution (not a bank), would have the same risk weight of 100% compared to a loan to a sub-investment grade corporation.

The credit risk charge from balance sheet items must be 8% times the risk-weighted assets for the calculation of the capital requirements for the Basel Accord.

The following equation applies:

$$\text{Credit risk charge} = 8\% \times \text{RWA} = 8\%\left(\sum_i w_i \times \text{Notional of instrument}\right)$$

Let's go through a simple example where a bank's balance sheet contains only three securities. Say that the bank holds \$10 million in U.S. Treasury bonds, has a \$5 million loan to a corporate firm, and also holds a \$1 million mortgage

TABLE 13.1 **Risk-Weighting Factors and Their Corresponding Asset Classes**

Risk Weight	Asset Class
0%	Cash held
	Gold held
	Claims on central governments and central banks denominated in national currency
	Claims on OECD central governments
20%	Cash items in process of collection
	Claims on multilateral development banks
	Claims on banks incorporated in the OECD and loans guaranteed by OECD incorportated banks
	Claim on banks incorporated in countries outside the OECD with a residual maturity of up to one year
	Claims on nondomestic OECD public-sector entities
50%	Residential mortgage loans
100%	Claims on the private sector (corporate debt, for example)
	Claims on banks incorporated outside the OECD with maturity over I year
	Claims on central governments outside the OECD
	Claims on commercial companies owned by public sector
	Real estate
	Premises, plant, and equipments along with other fixed assets All other assets

TABLE 13.2 **A Worked Example for the Credit Risk Charge**

	Notional	Risk Weight	Risk-Weighted Assets
U.S. Treasury:	10,000,000	0%	0
Mortgage Loan:	1,000,000	50%	500,000.00
Corporate Loan:	5,000,000	100%	5,000,000.00
Credit Risk Charge at 8%:			440,000.00

on the borrower's principal residence. As described in Table 13.1, the U.S. Treasury bonds have a risk weight of 0%, while a 50% risk weight would apply to the residential mortgage, and finally a 100% risk weight would apply to the corporate loan. The risk-weighted assets in this example would correspond to the data in Table 13.2.

The total risk-weighted capital of the bank would then be \$5.5 million. The bank would have to hold at least \$440,000 in total capital in order to comply with the Basel Accord (8% × 5,500,000).

13.2.3 OFF-BALANCE SHEET ITEMS

The Basel Committee also focused on off-balance sheet items (OBS) to be accounted for within the capital adequacy framework. The accord dealt with the OBS items in a two-step process.

The Basel Accord computes a credit exposure that is equivalent to the notional of debt instrument, through credit conversion factors. The second step would assign the "new" asset to one of the risk categories based on the type of customer/borrower, just as a balance sheet item would be treated. The Basel Accord divides the different instruments and techniques into five broad categories:

1. Direct credit substitutes (letters of credits serving as financial guarantees for loans and securities, guarantees of indebtedness, bankers' acceptances). These types of instruments will carry a 100% credit conversion factor. This is due to the possibility of the full notional being at risk from, say, the letter of credit.
2. Certain transaction-related contingent items such as performance bonds, bid bonds, and warranties will carry a 50% credit conversion factor.
3. Short-term, self-liquidating trade-related contingent liabilities arising from the movement of goods (e.g., documentary credits collateralized by the underlying shipments) will carry a 20% credit risk conversion factor.
4. Commitments with an original maturity exceeding one year and all NIFs and RUFs will carry a 50% credit risk conversion factor.
5. Interest and exchange rate-related items (e.g., swaps, options, futures), where the credit risk equivalent amount will be calculated in one of two ways that we will explain below.

The treatment of foreign exchange and interest rate-related items require a special treatment given the complexity of their exposures. The accord stated that banks are not exposed to credit risk for the full face value of these contracts, but only to the potential cost of replacing the cash flow (on contracts with positive value), if the counterparty defaults. The credit equivalent amounts depends on the maturity of the contract and on the volatility of the rates underlying that type of instrument. The accord calculates the credit equivalent amount of its OBS interest rate and foreign exchange rate instruments to be the sum of the current, net replacement value, and an add-on to reflect the potential future exposure over the remaining life of the contract.

$$\text{Credit exposure} = \text{Net replacement value} + \text{Add-on}$$

The total replacement costs are obtained by marking-to-market the contracts that fall under this category.[1] The add-on factor depends on the maturity of the contract and the type of contract These are shown in Table 13.3.

[1]Since exchange rate contracts involve an exchange of principal on maturity, higher conversion factors applied. Interest rate contracts are defined to include single-currency interest rate swaps, basis swaps, FRAs, interest rate futures, and interest rate options. Exchange rate contracts include cross-currency interest rate swaps, forward foreign exchange contracts, currency futures, and currency options.

TABLE 13.3 **Add-On Factors**

	(SI) Contract				
Residual Maturity	Interest Rate (%)	Exchange Rate and Gold (%)	Equity (%)	Precious Metals except Gold (%)	Other Commodities (%)
Less than 1 year	0	1.0	6	7	10
One year and less than 5 years	0.5	5.0	8	7	12
Over 5 years	1.50	7.50	10	8	15

The add-on that constitutes part of the formula for the credit exposure for off-balance sheet Exposure can be decomposed into 3 steps: the notional, the add-on factor and finally the NGR (net to gross ratio). The formula for the add-on is

$$\text{Add-on} = \text{Notional} \times \text{Add-on factor} \times (0.4 + 0.6 \times \text{NGR})$$

The NGR represents the net-to-gross ratio, which is the level of the net replacement cost over the level of gross replacement cost for transactions subject to legally enforceable netting agreements. The ratio is always between 0 and 1 (the level of the net replacement cost cannot be greater than the level of the gross replacement cost). The purpose of this factor is to reduce the capital requirements for contracts that are subject to legally enforceable netting agreements.

The computation of the risk-weighted assets off the balance sheet is then obtained by applying counterparty risk to the credit exposure. Since most counterparty institutions that operate in such transactions are of significant credit safeness, the risk weights (by type of assets) are multiplied by 50%.The credit risk charge for off-balance sheet items is then defined as

$$\text{CRC(off-balance sheet)} = 8\% \times \left(\sum_i w_i \times 50\% \times \text{Credit exposure}\right)$$

Let us consider an example for the calculation of an off-balance sheet item into the credit risk charge for the financial institution.

Consider a $10 million interest rate swap with a national corporation for hedging purposes. Let's consider that the maturity left of the swap is 3 years and that the current marked-to-market value of the swap is $500,000. Furthermore, let us consider that the financial institution also has another interest rate swap with the same counterparty with 4 years of maturity left, along with the same notional of $10 million.

Since the financial institution only has this outstanding interest swap with the corporation, there is no netting possible, hence the factor (0.4 + 0.6 × NGR) = 1.

13.2.4 DRAWBACKS FROM THE BASEL ACCORD

The Basel Accord and regulations of 1988 have been subject to criticism from different sources. First, because Basel I only covered credit risk and targeted G-10 countries, it was seen as too narrow in its scope to ensure adequate financial stability in the international financial system.

The main criticism that can be drawn on the Basel Accord was the possibility of regulatory arbitrage by financial institutions. Opportunities for forms of regulatory arbitrage are inherent in the Basel I approach due to the limited number of risk weightings. The assignment of all exposures involving a particular type of counterparty to a single-risk bucket provides the possibility to assign the same risk weighting to both a large profitable and stable firm and to a high-risk borrow. This posed the problem that the four risk weights were too simplified in order to stop any arbitrage opportunities that financial institutions will use in order to have a lesser capital requirement.

For instance, consider a situation where XYZ Bank can make a loan of $50 million to an investment grade company rated AA, called ABC Electric, or to a subinvestment grade firm rated CCC, BNM Cars. XYZ Bank is forced by the Basel Accord to hold 8% of regulatory capital, or $4 million. In order to make the loan, it has to borrow $46 million.

Now suppose that the AA loan to to ABC Electric returns 5% and the financial institution's rate of borrowing is, say, 4.5%. Here XYZ would make a profit in this transaction of $430,000. Comparing this profit to the regulatory capital requirement of $4 million, this profit would translate into a 10.8% rate of return.

However, by making the same loan of $50 million to BNM Cars (and excluding the expected credit risk from the rate of return), at 6%, XYZ would make a profit of $930,000, which would correspond to a rate of return of 23.3% with regard to the capital requirement held by the firm.

Table 13.4 represents the calculation done in order to find the rate of return, along with profits made by XYZ Bank in both cases.

This example shows that capital regulatory requirements can perversely induce banks to shift their lending patterns from investment grade companies to lower-rated borrowers, in order to bring the economic capital more in line with the regulatory capital requirement. (Shareholders may also think that a

TABLE 13.4 **Capital Requirement Arbitrage Example**

XYZ Bank	ABC Electric		BNM Cars	
Loan	50,000,000.00		50,000,000.00	
Capital requirement	4,000,000.00	**8%**	4,000,000.00	**8%**
Bank borrowing	46,000,000.00		46,000,000.00	
Rate of borrowing (Bank)	2,070,000.00	**4.5%**	2,070,000.00	**4.5%**
Rate of lending	2,500,000.00	**5%**	3,000,000.00	**6%**
Total profit	430,000.00	**10.8%**	930,000.00	**23.3%**

10.8% rate of return is not sufficient enough for the financial institution, hence driving the bank to take on more credit risk by lending to lower-rated firms.)

Generally viewed, the 1988 Basel Accord pitfalls consisted of four major points:

1. Limited differentiation of credit risks. The four risk-weight categories were viewed as too simplistic. The example above gave an example of the same risk-weight and regulatory capital being applied to both investment grade firms and sub-investment grade firms.
2. No recognition of the term structure effects of credit risk. The maturity of the loan made to a firm has no effect in Basel I. The capital charges are set at the same level for a 1-year loan as for a 20-year loan, which inherently does not have the same credit risk (default risk goes up as the maturity of the loan gets longer).
3. Lack of recognition of portfolio diversification effects. Credit risk can be mitigated as any other type of risks, through the use of diversification effects. However, the Basel Accord does not recognize the diversification effects and sums all the individual risk exposures, which would overstate the risk.
4. Finally, one very important criticism of the Basel Accord was its lack of market risk assumed by financial institutions and banks. This was later amended in the 1996 Amendment by the Basel Committee.

The 1988 Basel Accord was a first step to tighter international capital requirements, remaining a milestone in the financial regulation.

13.2.5 1996 AMENDMENT

Due to the lack of market risk assumed by financial institutions in the Basel Accord of 1988, the Basel Committee decided to amend the Basel Accord in order to incorporate a charge for market risk. The amendment that was passed at the end of 1997 added a capital charge for market risk based on either of two approaches: the standardized approach or the internal models method. Market risk is defined as the risk of losses in on and off-balance sheet positions arising in movements in market prices. The risk subjects in the requirements for the 1996 Amendment are:

- The risk pertaining to *interest rate related instruments* and *equities* in the trading book.
- Foreign exchange risk and commodities throughout the bank.

The amendments separate the bank's assets into two categories, the trading book, and the banking book. The trading book represents the bank portfolio with financial instruments that are willingly held for short-term resale and typically marked-to-market. The banking book consists of other instruments, mainly loans, that are held to maturity and typically valued on a historical cost basis.

Overall, since the Capital Accord was first put in place by the Basel Committee on the Banking Supervision, there have been tighter international capital requirements. However, capital markets changed dramatically between 1988 and the early 2000s, with the credit risk charge appearing outdated. In June 2004, the Basel Committee finalized a comprehensive revision to the Basel Accord, in order to keep up with the rapidly changing financial markets.

13.3 Basel II

Basel II was intended to create an international standard for banking regulators to control how much capital banks need to put aside to guard against the types of financial and operational risks banks. One focus was to maintain sufficient consistency of regulations so that this does not become a source of competitive inequality amongst internationally active banks. In theory, Basel II attempted to accomplish this by setting up risk and capital management requirements designed to ensure that a bank has adequate capital for the risk the bank exposes itself to through its lending and investment practices.

Basel II's framework is based on a three-pillar concept, where the pillars are mutually supporting: minimum capital requirements, supervisory review, and market discipline. We will develop each pillar below.

Pillar 1: Minimum Capital Requirements. The first pillar deals with the maintenance of regulatory capital calculated for the three major components of risk that a bank faces: credit risk, market risk, and operational risk. This is a development from the Basel Accord, to add onto more risk charges, in order to better encompass the risks faced by banks. Furthermore, banks now have a wider choice of models for computing their risk charges. We will develop all the different approaches in more detail.

Pillar 2: Supervisory Review. Supervisors are given more improved "tools" compared to the previous Basel Framework, in order to ensure that the banks have a process in place for assessing their capital in relation to risks, operate above their minimum capital ratios, and take corrective actions where problems arise.

Pillar 3: Market Discipline. The aim of Pillar 3 is to promote greater stability in the financial system. Market discipline supplements regulation because sharing information facilitates the assessment of the banks by external parties. The aim of Pillar 3 is to allow market discipline to operate by requiring lenders to publicly provide details of their risk management activities, risk rating processe, and risk distributions. It sets out the public disclosures that banks must make in order to lend greater insight into the adequacy of their capitalization. Banks that fail to meet disclosure requirements under Pillar 3 will not qualify for using internal models (which tend to lead to lower capital charges).

The capital ratio is calculated using the definition of regulatory capital and risk-weighted assets. The total capital ratio must be no lower than 8%. We will develop here the different risk charges that form the first pillar of the Basel II framework.

13.3.1 THE CREDIT RISK CHARGE

As with the Basel Accord, the Basel Committee on the Banking Supervision left the credit risk charge to be computed as the sum of the individual credit charges:

$$\text{Credit risk charge} = 8\% \times \text{RWA} = 8\% \left(\sum_i w_i \times \text{Notional of instrument} \right)$$

However, the committee permits banks to choose between two broad methodologies for calculating their capital requirements for credit risk.

13.3.1.1 The Standardized Approach. The Standardized Approach extends the 1998 Basel Accord, with finer classification of categories for credit risk, based on external credit ratings, provided by external credit assessment institutions. However, unlike in the Basel Accord, the new risk weightings for assets are more granular and are broken down according to external credit ratings. Table 13.5 represents a summary of the new risk weightings.

From the grid above,it is clear that higher-rated corporate and financial institutions will benefit from the new risk-weightings to be introduced under

TABLE 13.5 **New Risk Weighting under Basel II**[a]

Obligors	AAA to AA– (%)	A+ to A– (%)	BBB+ to BBB– (%)	BB+ to BB– (%)	B+ to B– w.s. (%)	Below B– (%)	Unrated (%)
Sovereigns	0	20	50	100	100	150	100
Banks (Option 1)[b]	20	50	100	100	100	150	100
Banks (Option 2)[b]	20	50	50	100	100	150	50
Banks (Option 2 short-term claims)	20	20	20	50	50	150	20
Corporates	20	50	100	100	150	150	100
Securitzation tranches	20	50	100	350	Deducted	Deducted	Deducted

Source: BIS, International Convergence of Capital Measurement and Capital Standards, June 2004.
[a]In case of split ratings, the higher risk-weighting applies if the bank has two split ratings; if a bank has three ratings, the risk-weighting is based on the two highest ratings.
[b]Option 1: Risk weight for a bank is derived from the external rating of the sovereign of the country in which the bank is incorporated. Option 2: Risk weight is determined by the bank's external credit rating.

Basel II. However, lower-rated sovereigns, lower-rated banks, and noninvestment grades corporate will suffer, with a new risk weighting of 150% to be introduced. This is one of the main differences from the Basel Accord, because credit rating was not taken into account.

Short-term claims under Option 2 are defined as having an original maturity of three months or less. Banks can apply a preferential risk weight for short-term domestic currency claims, assigning a risk weight that is one category less favorable than that assigned to claims on sovereign, subject to a floor of 20%. Banks not using Option 2 have to use the following short-term exposure approach, under which A1/P1-rated short-term bank debt incurs a risk-weighting of 20%, A2/P2-rated 50%, and A3/P3-rated 100% (under Option 1). It is clear that risk weights under this approach will be higher for banks rated lower than A1/P1. Currently, the majority of European banks have a short-term rating of A1/P1 and would therefore be 20% risk-weighted for short-term facilities under the BIS II standardized approach (Option 1). Banks using Option 2 have to apply the above short-term ratings-driven credit assessment approach for short-term exposures greater than three months, but less than one year.

There are also various special categories under the standardized approach, such as the following:

- Preferential risk-weightings for lower risk retail lending (75% for non-mortgage retail loans).
- 35% risk-weighting for residential mortgages fully secured on residential property (down from 50% currently), although these are weighted 100% once they are 90 days past due).
- Commercial mortgages will generally remain 100% risk-weighted, but, subject to the discretion of the relevant authority, can be 50% risk-weighted (150% risk-weighted when 90 days past due); the UK will continue to risk-weight commercial mortgages 100%.
- Loans to SMEs will be included in retail lending (subject to a limit of €1m).
- Commercial mortgages that meet strict criteria in well-developed and established markets, where loss rates meet low thresholds that may be weighted at 50% for the first tranche of loans on qualifying commercial properties.
- Past due loans,—that is, past due for more than 90 days (other than a residential mortgage)—risk-weighted 150% when the specific risk provisions are less than 20% of the outstanding amount of the loan; 100% risk-weighted when the specific risk provisions are no less than 20% of the outstanding amount of the loan; 100% risk-weighted when the specific provisions are no less than 50% of the outstanding amount of the loans, but with supervisory discretion to reduce the risk weight to 50%.
- Other assets: Investments in equity or regulatory capital instruments issued by banks or securities firms will be risk-weighted at 100%, unless deducted from the capital base as described above.

- Off-balance sheet commitments: These will be converted into credit exposure equivalents through the use of credit conversion factors (CCF). The most important ones are as follows:
  - Commitments with an original maturity of up to one year and commitments with an original maturity over on year will receive a CCF of 20% and 50%, respectively.
  - Lending of banks' securities or the posting of securities as collateral will receive a CCF of 100%.
  - Short-term self-liquidating trade letters of credit will receive a CCF of 20%.

Banks, whose risk management procedures and internal models do not satisfy the minimum criteria required by the Internal Ratings-Based Approach (IRB), have to use the standardized approach.

13.3.1.2 The Internal Ratings-Based (IRB) Approach. Subject to certain minimum conditions and disclosure requirements, banks that have received supervisory approval to use the IRB approach may rely on their own internal estimates of risk components in determining the capital requirement for a given exposure. The risk components include measures of the profitability of default (PD), loss given default (LGD), exposure at default (EAD), and effective maturity (M).

Under the IRB approach, banks must categorize banking-book exposures into broad classes of assets with different underlying risk characteristics, subject to definitions set out in the Basel II treaty. The classes are corporate, sovereign, banks, retail, and equity. Within the corporate asset class, five sub classes of specialized lending are separately identified. Within the retail class, three subclasses are separately identified. Within the retail and corporate classes, a distinct treatment for purchased receivables may also apply, provided certain conditions are met.

The IRB model assumes a confidence level of 99.9%, and covers only unexpected losses (UL)—that is, losses that are not covered by provisions. Credit risk mitigation techniques will be allowed for the IRB approach.

Despite a potential loosening of capital requirements in certain areas under Basel II, banks will have to continue to include rating agency considerations into their capital structure decision-making, in order to maintain ratings. For instance, Basel II reinforces the role of tier 2 capital, to the extent that the use of tier 2 capital is allowed to underpin substantial potential sources of risk in the banking sector, such as underprovisioned expected loan losses, insurance subsidiaries, and investment in deeply subordinated tranches of securitizations. S&P has pointed out that the policy to make regulatory capital deductions in equal parts from tier 1 and tier 2 capital for risks in these areas may lead the banking industry to build a proportionally greater reserve of tier 2 capital. However, the agency points out that certain tier 2 capital instruments lack the permanency and loss absorption features that are required to include it into the agency's core capital calculation and will therefore continue to require sufficient levels of tier 1 core capital.

Moreover, S&P points out that Basel II makes only minor changes to the existing guidelines for assessing market risk capital charges for securities classified as trading assets. The agency believes that Basel II understates the amount of capital required to prudently support market, operational, and business risk in underwriting and trading securities. While this creates opportunities for trading-oriented banking groups to increase capital leverage, S&P said that it does not expect the banks to materially reduce capital as a result of Basel II. The agency clearly stated that it requires banks to have a cushion in capital resources above a worst-case scenario on a liquidation basis. We therefore expect banks' capital levels to continue to depend on regulatory considerations, investor expectations, and peer pressure, as well as on the credit ratings the banks want to maintain.

The BIS clearly states that overall minimum capital requirements for the banking system are expected to remain unchanged as a result of Basel I. Rather, the main purpose of Basel II is to ensure better alignment of capital requirements with the underlying risk of their portfolios. Under the new rules, banks are therefore expected to redistribute capital according to risk profiles and business activities.

Once a bank adopts an IRB approach, it is expected to extend it across all asset classes and across the entire banking group.

The Basel Committee on Banking Supervision also recognizes credit risk mitigation techniques, which were not present in the first Basel Accord from 1988. Techniques such as collateralization, third-party guarantees, credit derivates, and netting are allowed to mitigate the credit risk charge.

13.3.2 OPERATIONAL RISK CHARGE

One of the main areas of change of the new Accord compared to the 1988 Basel Accord is the addition of an operational risk charge. The Basel Committee expects that the ORC will represent on average 12% of the total capital charge.

The Basel Committee defines operational risk as "the risk of loss resulting from inadequate or failed internal processes, people and systems or from external events." The definition includes legal risk, but excludes strategic and reputational risk. The Committee's framework to quantify operational risk is based on three different methods, each increasing the sophistication and the risk sensitivity: the Basic Indicator Approach; the Standardized Approach, and the Advanced Measurement Approach.

13.3.2.1 The Basic Indicator Approach. The Basic Indicator Approach is based on aggregate measures of business activity. Banks using this approach must hold capital for operational risk equal to the average over the previous three years of a fixed percentage (alpha) of annual gross income (the negative values are excluded). The charge is expressed as

$$\text{BIA(ORC)} = \sum \alpha \times \text{GI}_i$$

where α is in the fixed percentage set out at 15% and GI is the annual gross income of the bank.

Gross income is defined as net interest income plus net non-interest income. The advantage of using this method is it simplicity, and it uses available data. Because the Basel Committee recommends sophisticated banks to move along the spectrum of complexity to calculate their operational risk charge, the Basic Indicator Approach should be mainly used by nonsophisticated banks.

13.3.2.2 The Standardized Approach. In the standardized approach, the bank's activities are divided into eight business lines: corporate finance, trading & sales, retail banking, commercial banking, payment & settlement, agency services, asset management, and retail brokerage. Within each business line, gross income is a broad indicator that serves as a proxy for the scale of business operations and thus the likely scale of operational risk exposure within each of these business lines. The capital charge for each business line is calculated by multiplying gross income by a factor (denoted beta) assigned to that business line. Beta serves as a proxy for the industry-wide relationship between the operational risk loss experience for a given business line and the aggregate level of gross income for that business line. It should be noted that in the Standardised Approach, gross income is measured for each business line, not the whole institution; that is, in corporate finance the indicator is the gross income generated in the corporate finance business line.

The total capital charge is calculated as the three-year average of the simple summation of the regulatory capital charges across each of the business lines in each year. In any given year, negative capital charges (resulting from negative gross income) in any business line may offset positive capital charges in other business lines without limit. However, where the aggregate capital charge across all business lines within a given year is negative, the input to the numerator for that year will be zero. The total capital charge may be expressed as

$$\mathrm{SA(ORC)} = \sum_{i=1}^{8} \beta_i \times \mathrm{GI}_i$$

where β is a fixed percentage, relating to the level of required capital to the level of the gross income for each of the eight business lines. The different betas are set out in Table 13.6.

The final approach described by the Basel Committee in order to calculate the operational risk charge for banks is the Advanced Measurement Approach.

13.3.2.3 The Advanced Measurement Approach. Under the AMA, the regulatory capital requirement will equal the risk measure generated by the bank's internal operational risk measurement system using the quantitative and qualitative criteria for the AMA discussed below. Use of the AMA is subject to supervisory approval. (It can only be used if the bank demonstrates effective management and control of operational risk.) In order to qualify for the use of the AMA, a bank must satisfy its supervisor such that, at a minimum:

TABLE 13.6 Beta Factors

Business Lines	Beta Factors (%)
Corporate finance	18
Trading and sales	18
Retail banking	12
Commercial Banking	15
Payment and settlement	18
Agency services	15
Asset management	12
Retail brokerage	12

Source: BIS.

- Its board of directors and senior management, as appropriate, are actively involved in the oversight of the operational risk management framework.
- It has an operational risk management system that is conceptually sound and implemented with integrity; and it has sufficient resources in the use of the approach in the major business lines as well as the control and audit areas.

Once these criteria are satisfied, the risk charge is obtained from the unexpected loss (UL), or VaR at the 99.9% confidence level over a one-year horizon:

$$\text{AMA(ORC)} = \text{UL(1 year, 99.9\% confidence)}$$

Basel II's requirement for operational risk can be described as a tradeoff between efficiency and complexity. The Accord represents a major step forward for the measurement and management of banking risk.

After the credit risk charges were implemented along with the operational risk charge, the Basel Committee focused its attention toward market risk in response to the increased trading activities (like proprietary) of commercial banks.

13.3.3 THE MARKET RISK CHARGE

Market risk refers to the risk to an institution resulting from movements in market prices—in particular, changes in interest rates, foreign exchange rates, and equity and commodity prices. Market risk is often propagated by other forms of financial risk such as credit and market-liquidity risks. A bank should develop a sound and well-informed strategy to manage market risk. The strategy should first determine the level of market risk the institution is prepared to assume. This level should be set with consideration given to, among other factors, the amount of market risk capital set aside by the institution.

Once its market risk tolerance is determined, the institution should develop a strategy that balances its business goals with its market risk appetite. A bank should consider the following factors: economic and market conditions and their impact on market risk; whether the institution has the expertise to profit in specific markets and is able to identify, monitor, and control the market risk in those markets; and the institution's portfolio mix and how it would be affected if more market risk was assumed.

We will develop here the Market Risk Charge as set out by Basel Committee on Banking Supervision. The capital charge for market risk can be computed using two methods. The first is based on a "standardized" method, similar to the credit risk system, while the second method is called the internal model approach (IMA) and is based on the bank's own risk management systems, which are more adaptable than the rigid set of standardized rules. For the first time in financial regulation, banks are allowed to use their own internal models, which can be seen as a breakthrough.

13.3.3.1 The Standardized Method. The objective of the market risk amendment was "to provide an explicit capital cushion for the price risk to which banks are exposed." The original proposal was based on a prespecified building block approach, consisting of attaching add-ons to all positions (as in the Credit Risk Charge for the first Basel Accord).

Specific guidelines are issued to compute the bank's market risk for portfolios exposed to interest rate risk, equity risk, foreign exchange risk, commodity risk, and option risk. The bank's total risk is obtained from the sum of the difference risk charges:

$$MRC = MRC(IR) + MRC(ER) + MRC(OR) + MRC(CR) + MRC(FX)$$

We will develop here each approach to the different risk types.

13.3.3.1.1 Interest Rate Risk. This section describes the standard framework for measuring the risk of holding or taking positions in debt securities and other interest-rate-related instruments in the trading book. The instruments covered include all fixed-rate and floating-rate debt securities and instruments that behave like them, including nonconvertible preference shares. Convertible bonds—that is, debt issues or preference shares that are convertible, at a stated price, into common shares of the issuer—will be treated as debt securities if they trade like debt securities and as equities if they trade like equities.

The minimum capital requirement is expressed in terms of two separately calculated charges, one applying to the *specific risk* of each security, whether it is a short or a long position, and the other to the interest rate risk in the portfolio (termed *general market risk*) where long and short positions in different securities or instruments can be offset.

The capital charge for specific risk is designed to protect against an adverse movement in the price of an individual security owing to factors related to the individual issuer. In measuring the risk, offsetting will be restricted to matched positions in the identical *issue* (including positions in derivatives). Even if the

TABLE 13.7 Specific Risk Capital Charge

Categories	External Credit Assessment	Specific Risk Capital Charge
Government	AAA to AA– A+ to BBB–	0%
		0.25% (residual term to final maturity 6 months or less)
		1.00% (residual term to final maturity greater than 6 and up to and including 24 months)
		1.60% (residual term to final maturity exceeding 24 months)
	BB+ to B– Below B–	8.00%
	Unrated	12.00%
		8.00%
Qualifying		0.25% (residual term to final maturity 6 months or tess)
		1.00% (residual term to final maturity greater than 6 and up to and including 24 months)
		1.60% (residual term to final maturity exceeding 24 months)
Other	Similar to credit risk charges under the standardized approach of the Basel II Framework—for example:	
	BB+ to BB–	8.00%
	Below BB–	12.00%
	Unrated	8.00%

Source: BIS.

issuer is the same, no offsetting will be permitted between different issues since differences in coupon rates, liquidity, call features, and so on, mean that prices may diverge in the short run.

The specific risk capital charges for "government," which include all forms of government paper, are listed in Table 13.7. The "qualifying" category includes securities issued by public sector entities, along with securities that are rated investment-grade by at least two credit rating agencies.

The capital requirements for general market risk are designed to capture the risk of loss arising from changes in market interest rates. A choice between two methods is permitted to measure the general market risk: a duration band method and a maturity band method. However, in each method, the capital charge is the sum of four components:

- The net short or long position in the whole trading book.
- A small proportion of the matched positions in each time band (the *vertical disallowance*).

- A larger proportion of the matched positions across different time-bands (the *horizontal disallowance*).
- A net charge for positions in options where appropriate.

Let us first have a look at the maturity band method, to calculate the general market risk for interest rate risk charge. For the maturity band method, long or short positions in debt securities and other sources of interest rate exposures including derivative instruments are inputted into a maturity ladder containing 13 time bands (or 15 for low-coupon instruments). Fixed-rate instruments are allocated according to their residual term maturity, while floating-rate instruments are allocated in the maturity ladder according to the residual term to the next repricing date.

The first step in the calculation is to weight the positions in each time band by a factor designed to reflect the price sensitivity of those positions to assumed changes in interest rates. The different weights for each time band is described in Table 13.8.

The next step in the calculation is to offset the weighted long and shorts in each time band, resulting in a single position (whether short or long) for each time band. Since, however, each band would include different instruments and different maturities, a 10% capital charge to reflect basis risk and gap risk will be levied on the smaller of the offsetting positions, be it long or short.

In addition, the rules have vertical and horizontal disallowances that increase the risk charge. Within each band, these disallowances are given by the product of a weight applied to the minimum of the absolute value of the sum of long and short positions. The horizontal disallowance scale is shown in Table 13.9.

TABLE 13.8 **Maturity Time Bands**

Coupon 3% or More	Coupon Less than 3%	Risk Weight (%)	Assumed Changes in Yield
1 month or less	1 month or less	0.00	1.00
1–3 months	1–3 months	0.20	1.00
3–6 months	3–6 months	0.40	1.00
6–12 months	6–12 months	0.70	1.00
1–2 years	1.0–1.9 years	1.25	0.90
2–3 years	1.9–2.8 years	1.75	0.80
3–4 years	2.8–3.6 years	2.25	0.75
4–5 years	3.6–4.3 years	2.75	0.75
5–7 years	4.3–5.7 years	3.25	0.70
7–10 years	5.7–7.3 years	3.75	0.65
10–15 years	7.3–9.3 years	4.50	0.60
15–20 years	9.3–10.6 years	5.25	0.60
Over 20 years	10.6–12 years	6.00	0.60
	12–20 years	8.00	0.60
	Over 20 years	12.50	0.60

Source: BIS.

TABLE 13.9 Horizontal Disallowance

Zones	Time Band	Within the Zone	Between Adjacent Zones	Between Zones 1 and 3
Zone 1	0–1 month 1–3 months 3–6 months 6–12 months	40%		
			40%	
Zone 2	1–2 years 2–3 years 3–4 years	30%		100%
			40%	
Zone 3	4–5 years 5–7 years 7–10 years 10–15 years 15–20 years Over 20 years	30%		

Source: BIS.

Thus, if the sum of the weighted longs in a time band is $100 million and the sum of the weighted shorts $90 million, the so-called "vertical disallowance" for that time band would be 10% of $90 million (i.e., $9.0 million).

For the duration band method, banks with the necessary capability may, with a prior approval of their regulators, use a more accurate method of measuring all of their general market risk by calculating the price sensitivity of each position separately.

Duration is a measure of the average cash-weighted term to maturity of a bond. There are two types of duration:

Macaulay Duration. This measures the weighted average of the time of each payment;

Modified Duration. This measures the sensitivity of a bond price to yield changes by detailing the bond pice change, given a certain change in the bond's yield.

While all bond prices are sensitive to changes in yields (or interest rates), duration tends to be greater for longer-term bonds.

The method is designed as follows:

1. Calculate the price sensitivity of each instrument in terms of a change in interest rate of between 0.6 and 1.0 percentage points, depending on the maturity of the instrument. The assumed changed in yields are represented in Table 13.10.
2. Slot the resulting sensitivity measures into a duration-based ladder according to 15 time bands.

TABLE 13.10 **Duration Method**

	Assumed Change in Yield		Assumed Change in Yield
Zone 1		**Zone 3**	
1 month or less	1.00	3.6–4.3 years	0.75
1–3 months	1.00	4.3–5.7 years	0.70
3–6 months	1.00	5.7–7.3 years	0.65
6–12 months	1.00	7 3–9.3 years	0.60
		9.3–10.6 years	0.60
Zone 2		10.6–12 years	0.60
1.0–1.9 years	0.90	12–20 years	0.60
1.9–2.8 years	0.80	Over 20 years	0.60
2.8–3.6 years	0.75		

Source: BIS.

3. Subject to long and short positions in each time band to a 5% vertical disallowance designed to capture basis risk.
4. Carry forward the net positions in each time band for horizontal offsetting subject to the disallowance shown in Table 13.9.

The measurements system (unrelated to the method of measure of general market risk) should include all interest rate derivatives and off-balance sheet items in the trading book, which react to interest rate movements. General market risk applies to positions in all derivative products in the same manner as for cash positions, subject only to an exemption for fully or very closely matched positions in identical instruments. The different types of interest rate derivatives, along with their respective treatments into the calculation of the interest rate risk charge, are listed in Table 13.11.

Let us consider the worked example given by the Basel Committee in Amendment to the Capital Accord to incorporate market risks.

Consider a bank that has the following positions:

- A "qualifying" bond, with residual maturity of 8 years, coupon of 8%, and a $13.33 million market value.
- A government bond, with residual maturity of 2 years, coupon of 7%, and a $75 million market value.
- An interest-rate swap, where the bank received floating rate interest and pays fixed, next interest fixing date after 9 months, with a residual life of 8 years and a value $150 million.
- A long position in interest rate futures, with a notional of $50 million, and a delivery date after 6 months; the life of underlying government bond is 3.5 years.

TABLE 13.11 Interest Rate Derivatives

Instrument	Specific Risk Charge	General Market Risk Charge
Exchange-traded future		
Government debt security	No	Yes, as two positions
Corporate debt security	Yes	Yes, as two positions
Index on interest rates (e.g., LIBOR)	No	Yes, as two positions
OTC forward		
Government debt security	No	Yes, as two positions
Corporate debt security	Yes	Yes, as two positions
Index on interest rates	No	Yes, as two positions
FRAs, swaps	No	Yes, as two positions
Forward foreign exchange	No	Yes, as one position in each currency
Options		Either
Government debt security	No	(a) Carve out together with the associated hedging positions • Simplified approach • Scenario analysis • Internal models (Part B)
Corporate debt security	Yes	(b) General market risk charge according to the delta-plus method (gamma and vega should receive separate capital charges)
Index on interest rates	No	
FRAs Swaps	No	

Source: BIS.

First, we need to slot the positions into the appropriate time band, which is done in Table 13.12. For the swap, this includes a short position of $150 million in the 7–10 years band, and a long position of $150 million on the 6- to 12-month band. On the same basis, the futures position is separated into two legs: a long position of $50 million on the 3- to 4-year band (representing the underlying government bond), along with a short position on the 3- to 6-month band.

We then need to assign a risk weight to each position and sum them across all assets. Table 13.12 lists the risk weight for each position. After weighting the positions, the next steps in the calculation will be to calculate the following:

The Vertical Disallowance in the 7- to 10-year Band: The matched position in this time band is 0.5 (the lesser of the absolute values of the added long or short positions in the time band), which leads to a capital charge of 10% of 0.5, which is $50,000. The remaining net position is −5.125.

The Horizontal Disallowances within the Zones Have to Be Calculated as Well: Because there is more than one position only in zone 1, a horizontal disallowance can only be calculated in this zone. In doing this, the matched position is calculated as 0.2 (the lesser of the absolute values of the added

TABLE 13.12 Example from the BIS

	Zone 1				Zone 2			Zone 3					
Time band	**0–1**	**1–3**	**3–6**	**6–12**	**1–2**	**2–3**	**3–4**	**4–5**	**5–7**	**7–10**	**10–15**	**15–20**	**over 20**
	Months				**Years**								
Position		+75 Gov.	−50 Fut.	+150 Swap			+50 Fut.			−150 Swap +13.33 Qual.			
Weight (%)	0.00	0.20	0.40	0.70	1.25	1.75	2.25	2.75	3.25	3.75	4.50	5.25	6.00
Position × Weight		+0.15	−0.20	+1.05			+1.125			−5.625 + 0.5			
Vertical disallowance										0.5 × 10% = 0.05			
Horizontal disallow 1	0.20 × 40% = 0.08												
Horizontal disallowance 2					1.125 × 40% = 0.45								
Horizontal disallowance 3	1.0 × 100% = 1.0												

long and short positions in the same zone). The capital charge for the horizontal disallowance within zone 1 is 40% of 0.2 = 0.08 = $80,000. The remaining net (long) position in zone 1 is +1.00.

The *horizontal disallowances between adjacent zones* have to be calculated: After calculating the net position within zone 1, the following positions remain: zone 1, +1.00; zone 2, +1.125; zone 3, –5.125. The matched position between zones 2 and 3 is 1.125 (the lesser of the absolute values of the long and short positions between adjacent zones) The capital charge in this case is 40% of 1.125 = 0.45 = $450,000.

The *horizontal disallowance between zones 1 and 3* has to be calculated: The remaining net (long) position in zone 1 is +1.00, and in zone 3 the net (short) position is –4.00. If there were no offsetting between zones 1 and 3 allowed the capital charge would be 5.00 = $5,000,000. However, the horizontal disallowance between the distant zones is 100% of the matched position, which leads to a capital charge of 100% of 1.00 = 1.00 = $1,000,000.

The overall net position is 3.00, leading to a capital charge of $3,000,000.

Adding up the base risk charge to the disallowance, we have a general market risk charge of $4.58 million:

The Total Capital Charge in this example is:

for the certical disallowance	$50,000
for the horizontal disallowance in zone 1	$80,000
for the horizontal disallowance between adjacent zones	$450,000
for the horizontal disallowance between zones 1 and 3	$1,000,000
for the overall net open position	$3,000,000
	$4,580,000

The market risk charge for interest rate risk at each time t is the sum of the general market risk charge and specific risk charges:

$$\mathrm{IR(MRC)}t = \mathrm{IR(GMRC)t} + \mathrm{IR(SMRC)}t$$

The next step in calculating the market risk charge with respect to the Standardized Approach is to look at the other types of risk that a bank may face.

13.3.3.1.2 Equity Risk. The minimum capital standards to cover the risk of holding or taking positions in equities in the trading book are set out below. It applies to all long and short positions in all instruments that exhibit market behavior similar to equities. Long and short position by the same issuer may be reported on a net basis. The instruments covered include common stocks, whether voting or non-voting, convertible securities that behave like equities, and commitments to buy or sell equity securities.

As with debt securities, the minimum capital standard for equities is expressed in terms of two separately calculated charges for the "specific risk" of holding a long or short position in an individual equity and for the "general market risk" of holding a long or short position in the market as a whole. Specific risk is defined as the bank's gross equity positions (i.e., the sum of all long equity positions and of all short equity positions), and general market risk is defined as the difference between the sum of the longs and the sum of the shorts (i.e., the overall net position in an equity market). The long or short position in the market must be calculated on a market-by-market basis; that is, a separate calculation has to be carried out for each national market in which the bank holds equities.

Regarding the specific risk charge, the Basel Accord differentiates between liquid and diversified portfolios, to normal portfolios along with equity index derivatives, in order to take into account the benefits of diversification in the equity trading book. The capital charge for *specific* risk will be 8%, unless the portfolio is both liquid and well-diversified, in which case the charge will be 4%. Given the different characteristics of national markets in terms of marketability and concentration, national authorities will have discretion to determine the criteria for liquid and diversified portfolios. The *general market risk* charge will be 8%.

In order to calculate the standard formula for specific and general market risk, positions in derivatives should be converted into notional equity positions:

- Futures and forwards contracts relating to individual equities should, in principle, be reported at current market prices.
- Futures relating to stock indices should be reported as the marked-to-market value of the notional underlying equity portfolio.
- Equity swaps are to be treated as two notional positions.
- Equity options and stock index options should be either "carved out" together with the associated underlying or be incorporated in the measure of general market risk described in this section according to the delta-plus method.

Besides general market risk, a further capital charge of 2% will apply to the net long or short position in an index contract comprising a diversified portfolio of equities. This capital charge is intended to cover factors such as execution risk. National supervisory authorities will take care to ensure that this 2% risk weight applies only to well-diversified indices and not, for example, to sectoral indices.

Table 13.13 is a summary of treatment of equity derivates with regard to their calculation of specifc risk and general market risk.

To calculate the total market risk charge for equities, we then sum the general market risk charge to the specific market risk charge.

Let's consider an example for the equity risk charge calculation. Consider a portfolio that contains long 10,000 shares of company A, short 20,000 shares of company B, short 5000 shares of company C, long 15,000 shares of company D, and short 2000 shares of company E.

TABLE 13.13 Treatment of Equity Derivatives

Instrument	Specific Risk	General Market Risk
Exchange-trated or OTC-Future		
Individual equity	Yes	Yes, as underlying
Index	2%	Yes, as underlying
Options		
Individual equity	Yes	Either (a) Carve out together with the associated hedging positions • simplified approach • scenario analysis • internal models (Part B)
Index	2%	(b) General market risk charge according to the delta-plus method (gamma and vega should receive separate capital charges)

TABLE 13.14 Example of Equity Risk Charge

	Position	Quantity	Market Price	Market Value
Company A	Long	10,000	35	350,000
Company B	Short	20,000	25	500,000
Company C	Short	5,000	50	250,000
Company D	Long	15,000	20	300,000
Company E	Short	2,000	60	120,000
			Gross	1,520,000
			Net	–220,000

Table 13.14 represent a summary of the equity book. Firstly, we must determine the overall net open position. To do that, just take the sum of the long position minus the sum of the short positions. The overall net short open position is $220,000. Considering the capital charge is 8% for equity positions in the Basel Accord, the capital charge for general risk is USD 17,600. Now we must work out the specific risk of the positions.

Gross position of the portfolio is USD 1,520,000. Hence the specific risk charge for the portfolio in the example is USD 60,800. Hence the overall equity risk charge for the portfolio is USD 78,400.

13.3.3.1.3 Commodity Risk Charge. This section establishes a minimum capital standard to cover the risk of holding or taking positions in commodities, including precious metals, but excluding gold (which is treated as a foreign currency). A commodity is defined as a physical product that is or can be traded on a secondary market—for example, agricultural products, minerals (including oil), and precious metals.

The price risk in commodities is often more complex and volatile than that associated with currencies and interest rates. Commodity markets may also be less liquid than those for interest rates and currencies; as a result, changes in supply and demand can have a more dramatic effect on price and volatility.

These market characteristics can make price transparency and the effective hedging of commodities risk more difficult. For spot or physical trading, the directional risk arising from a change in the spot price is the most important risk.

However, banks using portfolio strategies involving forward and derivative contracts are exposed to a variety of additional risks, which may well be larger than the risk of a change in spot prices. These include:

- Basis risk (the risk that the relationship between the prices of similar commodities alters through time)
- Interest rate risk (the risk of a change in the cost of carry for forward positions and options)
- Forward gap risk (the risk that the forward price may change for reasons other than a change in interest rates)

Three different alternatives are available to measure the commodity position risk within the Standardized Approach Framework. Commodity risk can be measured in a standardized manner, using either a simple framework or a measurement system that captures forward gap and interest rate risk separately by basing the methodology on seven time bands. We will develop all three different approaches here.

For the maturity ladder approach and the simplified approach, long and short positions in each commodity may be reported on a net basis for the purposes of calculating open positions. However, positions in different commodities will as a general rule not be offsettable in this fashion. Nevertheless, national authorities will have discretion to permit netting between different subcategories of the same commodity in cases where the subcategories are deliverable against each other. Commodities can be grouped into clans, families, subgroups, and individual commodities. For example, a clan might be Energy Commodities, within which hydrocarbons are a family with crude oil being a subgroup and West Texas Intermediate, Arabian Light, and Brent being individual commodities.

They can also be considered as offsettable if they are close substitutes against each other and a minimum correlation of 0.9 between the price movements can be clearly established over a minimum period of one year. However, a bank wishing to base its calculation of capital charges for commodities on correlations would have to satisfy the relevant supervisory authority of the accuracy of the method which has been chosen and obtain its prior approval. Where banks use the models approach, they can offset long and short positions in different commodities to a degree which is determined by empirical correlations, in the same way as a limited degree of offsetting is allowed, for instance, between interest rates in different currencies.

The first approach that banks are allowed to use in determining their commodity position risk is to use the models described later in this chapter regarding the use of internal models to measure market risks. However, the Basel Committee considers it as essential that the following elements are part of the methodology that will be used by these banks:

- Directional risk, to capture the exposure from changes in spot prices arising from open net positions.
- Forward gap and interest rate risk, to capture the exposure to changes in forward prices arising from maturity mismatches.
- Basis risk, to capture the exposure to changes in the price relationships between two similar, but not identical, commodities (e.g., jet oil and heating oil).

The Maturity Ladder Approach. We will develop first the maturity ladder approach, where banks will first have to express each commodity position in terms of standard unit of measurements (barrels, kilos, etc.). The net open position will then be converted into national currency at current spot rates.

Second, in order to capture forward gap and interest rate risk within a time band (which, together, are sometimes referred to as curvature/spread risk), matched long and short positions in each time band will carry a capital charge. The methodology will be rather similar to that used for interest rate-related instruments. Positions in the separate commodities (expressed in terms of the standard unit of measurement) will first be entered into a maturity ladder while physical stocks should be allocated to the first time band.

A separate maturity ladder will be used for each commodity as defined in paragraph 5 above. For markets which have daily delivery dates, any contracts maturing within ten days of one another may be offset. For each time band, the sum of short and long positions that are matched will be multiplied first by the spot price for the commodity, and then by the appropriate spread rate for that band. Table 13.15 contains time bands and spreads.

The residual net positions from nearer time bands may then be carried forward to offset exposures in time bands that are further out. However, recognizing that such hedging of positions among different time bands is imprecise, a surcharge equal to 0.6% of the net position carried forward will be added with respect to each time band that the net position is carried forward. The capital charge for each matched amount created by carrying net positions forward will be calculated as in paragraph 8 above. At the end of this process, a bank will have either only long or only short positions, to which a capital charge of 15% will apply.

TABLE 13.15 Time Bands and Spread Rate

Time Band	Spread Rate (%)
0–1 month	1.5
1–3 months	1.5
3–6 months	1.5
6–12 months	1.5
1–2 years	1.5
2–3 years	1.5
Over 3 years	1.5

Source: BIS.

All commodity derivatives and off-balance-sheet positions that are affected by changes in commodity prices should be included in this measurement framework. This includes commodity futures, commodity swaps, and options where the "delta plus" method is used (developed later). In order to calculate the risk, commodity derivatives should be converted into notional commodities positions and assigned to maturities as follows:

- Futures and forward contracts relating to individual commodities should be incorporated in the measurement system as notional amounts of barrels, kilos, and so on, and should be assigned a maturity with reference to expiry date.
- Commodity swaps where one leg is a fixed price and the other the current market price should be incorporated as a series of positions equal to the notional amount of the contract, with one position corresponding with each payment on the swap and slotted into the maturity ladder accordingly. The positions would be long positions if the bank is paying fixed and receiving floating, and short positions if the bank is receiving fixed and paying floating.
- Commodity swaps where the legs are in different commodities are to be incorporated in the relevant maturity ladder. No offsetting will be allowed in this regard except where the commodities belong to the same subcategory.

We will now explain how to use the maturity ladder approach (Table 13.16) following the example described by the Basel Committee.

Let us assume that all positions are in the same commodity and converted to national currency at current spot rates as described above. The basic charge for the net position is 15% of notional. Positions can be offset, subject to a spread risk weight of 1.5% (third column). Positions can be offset across bands, subject to a carry-forward weight of 0.6%. The portfolio in Table 13.16 assumes that there are $800 million long position in the 3- to 6-month time band, along with $1000 million short position in the same time band. The portfolio also contains a long $600 million position in the 1- to 2-year time band, and finally a short $600 million position in the over-3-year time band.

TABLE 13.16 Commodity Maturity Ladder Approach

Time Band	Position	Spread Rate	Capital Calculation	
0–1 month		1.5%		
1–3 months		1.5%		
3–6 months	Long 800 US $ Short 1000 US $	1.5%	800 long + 800 short (matched) × 1.5% =	24
			200 short carried forward to 1–2 years, capital charge: 200 × 2 × 0.6% =	2.4
6–12 months		1.5%		
1–2 years	Long 600 US $	1.5%	200 long + 200 short (matched) × 1.5% =	6
			400 long carried forward to over 3 years. capital charge: 400 × 2 × 0.6% =	4.8
2–3 years		1.5%		
Over 3 years	Short 600 US $	1.5%	400 long + 400 short (matched) × 1.5% =	12
			net position: 200 capital charge: 200 × 15% =	30

Source: BIS.

For the 3- to 6-month time band, we can match the long position with some of the short position to get a net short open position of $200 million that can be carried forward to the 1- to 2-year band, which is subject to a carry-forward weight of 0.6%, giving $2.4 million in the capital calculation charge for the commodity risk. Also, we have the gross long position of $800 million, along with the gross position of short $800 million that is subject to a spread weight of 1.5%, giving $24 million in the capital charge for that time band. Hence, for the 3–6 months time band, we have a capital charge of $26.4 million.

Working our way down the maturity ladder, the time bands, and the matching position that can be offset, following the same methodology as for the 3 to 6-month time band, we have a final commodity risk charge for this portfolio of $79.2 million.

The Simplified Approach. In the simplified approach, calculating the capital charge for directional risk, the same procedure is applied as in the maturity ladder approach. The capital charge will equal 15% of net position, long or short, in each commodity. On top of the capital charge, an additional capital charge of 3% of the bank's gross position (long plus short) is added, in order to protect the bank against basis risk, interest rate risk, and forward gap risk. Hence the formula for each commodity in the simplified approach is

$$\text{Commodity risk}_i\,(\text{MRC}) = 15\% * (\text{Long} - \text{Short}) + 3\% \times (\text{Long} + \text{Short})$$

Finally, the market risk charge applies separately to each commodity, so that for each type of commodity the simplified approach, or the maturity ladder approach, must be used. This will give a total commodity risk charge if the bank held N commodities:

$$\text{Commodity risk charge} = \sum_{i=1}^{N} \text{CO}_i$$

Let us now have a look at the capital charge under the standardized method for foreign exchange positions.

13.3.3.1.4 ***Foreign Exchange Risk.*** Let us now have a look at the capital charge under the standardized method for foreign exchange positions. Foreign exchange risk is the risk that the value of foreign exchange positions may be adversely affected by movements in currency exchange rates.

Foreign exchange risk incurs only general market risk charge and no specific market risk. The capital charge for foreign exchange risk may also include a charge for gold, because it is not included in the commodity risk charge. The capital requirement for positions held in foreign currencies is calculated at 8% of the overall net open positions. The Basel Committee sets out two processes to calculate the capital requirement for foreign exchange risk. The first is to measure the exposure in any single currency position, whereas the second is to measure the risks inherent in a bank's mix of long and short positions in different currencies.

A bank net open position in a single currency should be calculated by summing the following:

- The net spot position (i.e., all asset items less all liability items, including accrued interest, denominated in the currency in question)
- The net forward position (i.e., all amounts to be received less all amounts to be paid under forward foreign exchange transactions, including currency futures and the principal on currency swaps not included in the spot position)
- Guarantees (and similar instruments) that are certain to be called and are likely to be irrecoverable
- Net future income/expenses not yet accrued but already fully hedged (at the discretion of the reporting bank)
- depending on particular accounting conventions in different countries, any other item representing a profit or loss in foreign currencies
- The net delta-based equivalent of the total book of foreign currency options.

Some exceptions are also dealt with, by the Basel Committee. For example, in certain cases, the national supervisory authority may allow banks to exclude

FX positions from the capital charges calculation. Banks with positions taken deliberately to hedge against an adverse exchange rate movement on its capital ratio may exclude these positions, provided that:

- The position is of a structural nature.
- The excluded position protects only the bank's capital adequacy ratio.
- The exclusion of the position is applied adequately and consistently.

Banks with negligible business in foreign currencies and with no FX positions taken for their own account may exclude their FX positions if they meet both of the following requirements:

- Their FX business (the greater of the sum of their gross long positions and the sum of their gross short positions) does not exceed 100% eligible capital.
- Its overall net position does not exceed 2% of its eligible capital.

In order to measure the foreign exchange risk in a portfolio of foreign currency positions and gold, banks will have the choice between two alternatives measures, a "shorthand" method, which treats all the currencies with the same weight, and the use of the internal model, which takes into account the actual degree of risk dependent on the composition of the bank's portfolio. We will develop here the shorthand method that can be used.

Under the shorthand method, the nominal amount (or net present value) of the net position in each foreign currency and in gold is converted at spot rates into the reporting currency. The overall net open position is measured by aggregating the following:

- The greater of
  - the sum of the net short positions or
  - the sum of the net long positions.
- The net position (short or long), in gold.

Let us take an example of calculating the capital charge for FX risk following the above method. Consider that a bank has the following positions that have been converted into its reporting currency, say Swiss francs (CHF), at spot rates.

Currency:	JPY	EUR	GBP	USD	AUD	Gold
Net position (CHF in m):	50	100	150	−20	−180	−35

Here, we need to take the sum of the long positions and the sum of the short positions to determine which is greater in order to take it into account in the calculation. Following the data below, we see that the sum of the long positions is greater than the sum of the short positions.

Sum of long posotion:	300
Sum of short posotion:	−200
Gold	−35

The capital charge is therefore calculated as 8% of the sum of the long positions, plus 8% of the gold positions. Hence the capital charge in this example is CHF 26.8 m (300 × 8% + 35 × 8%).

Finally, we need to have a look at the treatment of options using the Standardized Approach. In recognition of the wide diversity of banks' activities in options and the difficulties of measuring price risk for options, several alternatives have been put in place by the Basel Committee on Banking Supervision.

13.3.3.1.5 Option Risk. Banks that only use purchased options will be able to use a simplified method, while banks who also write options will be expected to use one of the intermediate approaches or a comprehensive risk management model under the terms of the internal models approach.

The Simplified Approach. The market risk charge under the simplified approach is described in Table 13.17 below. In this approach, the positions for the options and the associated underlying are not subject to the standardized methodology but rather are "carved out" and subject to separately calculated capital charges that incorporate both general market risk and specific market risk. As an example of how the calculation would work, consider the case where a holder of 100 shares valued at $10 each holds an equivalent put option to protect against downside risk, with a strike at $11; the capital charge would then be $100 × 10 × 16% = $160, less the amount that the put is in the money (K-S here is 11–10, 1 × 100 = $100, giving a final capital charge of $60.

The Intermediate Approach. The intermediate approach accounts for optionality and can be measured using two methods, the delta-plus method, or the scenario-based method. The delta-plus method uses the sensitivity parameters

TABLE 13.17 Simplified Approach for the Treatment of Options

Position	Treatment
Long cash and long put or short cash and long call	The capital charge will be the market value of the underlying security multiplied by the sum of specific and general market risk charges the underlying less the amount the option is in the money (if any) bounded at zero
Long call or long put	The capital charge will be the lesser of (i) the market value of the underlying security multiplied by the sum of specific and general market risk charges for the underlying and (ii) the market value of the option.

Source: BIS.

or "Greeks," associated with options to measure their market risk and capital requirements. Under the delta-plus method, the delta equivalent position of each equivalent amount subject to the applicable general market risk charges. Separate capital charges are then applied to the gamma and vega risks of the option positions. The *scenario approach* uses simulation techniques to calculate changes in the value of an options portfolio for changes in the level and volatility of its associated underlying. Under this approach, the general market risk charge is determined by the scenario "grid" (i.e., the specified combination of underlying and volatility changes) that produces the largest loss. For the delta-plus method and the scenario approach the specific risk capital charges are determined separately by multiplying the delta-equivalent of each option by the specific risk weights.

Delta-Plus Approach. Five coefficients are used to help explain how option values behave in relation to changes in market parameters:

- Price of the underlying asset
- Strike price
- Volatility of the underlying
- Time to maturity
- Risk-free interest rate

These are represented by the Greek letters delta, gamma, lambda, theta, and rho, and are referred to as the "option Greeks."

- Delta (Δ) measures the rate of change in the value of an option with respect to a change in the price of the underlying asset.
- Gamma (Γ) measures the rate of change in the delta of an option with respect to a change in the price of the underlying asset.
- Vega (ν) measures the rate of change in an option price with respect to a change in market volatility for the underlying asset price.
- Theta (Θ) measures the rate of change in an option value with respect to a change in the remaining maturity (time) of the option.
- Rho (ρ) measures the rate of change in the value of an option with respect to a change in the risk-free interest rate.

Delta-weighted positions with debt securities or interest rates as the underlying will be slotted into the interest rate time bands as set out in the requirements for interest rate risk for capital charge. A two-legged approach should be used as for other derivatives, requiring one entry at the time the underlying contract takes effect and requiring a second entry at the time the underlying contract matures. For instance, a bought call option on a June three-month interest-rate future will in April be considered, on the basis of its delta-equivalent value, to be a long position with a maturity of five months and a short position with a maturity of two months. The written option will be similarly slotted as a long position with a maturity of two months and a short position with a maturity of five months. Floating rate instruments with caps or floors will be treated as a combination of floating rate securities and a series of European-style options. For example, the holder of a three-year floating rate bond indexed to six-month LIBOR with a cap of 15% will treat it as:

- A debt security that reprices in six months.
- A series of five written call options on a FRA with a reference rate of 15%, each with a negative sign at the time the underlying FRA takes effect and a positive sign at the time the underlying FRA matures.

The net delta of options positions is computed first, which is factored into the standard risk charge for the relevant category of underlying (i.e., foreign exchange risk, equity risk, commodity risk). In addition to the capital charges arising from delta risk, there will be further capital charges for gamma and vega risk. The capital charge should be calculated the following way:

- For each individual option, a "gamma impact" should be calculated according to a Taylor series expansion as:

$$\text{Gamma impact} = \frac{1}{2} \times \text{Gamma} \times \text{VU}^2$$

  where VU is the variation of the underlying of the option.
- VU needs to be calculated as follows:
  - For interest rate options if the underlying is a bond, the market value of the underlying should be multiplied by the risk weights set out for the interest rate risk charge.
  - For options on equity and equity indices, the market value of the underlying should be multiplied by 8%.
  - For foreign exchange and gold options, the market value of the underlying should be multiplied by 8%.
  - For options on commodities, the market value of the underlying should be multiplied by 15%.

Options with the same underlying will have a gamma impact that is either positive or negative. Banks need to sum the individual gamma impact, resulting in a net gamma impact that is either positive or negative. Only negative gamma impacts will be included in the final calculation. The total gamma capital charge will then be the sum of the absolute value of the net gamma impacts.

To this total gamma impact, banks will be required to calculate the capital charges by multiplying the sum of the vegas for all options on the same underlying, by a proportional shift in volatility of ±25%. The total capital charge for vega risk will then be the sum of the absolute value of the individual capital charges that have been calculated for vega risk.

The Basel Committee on Banking Supervision sets out a worked example for the calculation of the delta-plus method for options, which we will describe below.

Assume a bank has an European short call option on a commodity with an exercise price of 490 and a market value of the underlying 12 months from the expiration of the option at 500, a risk-free interest rate at 8% per annum, and the volatility at 20%. The current delta for this position is according to the Black–Scholes formula −0.721 (i.e., the price of the option changes by −0.721 if the price of the underlying moves by 1).The gamma is −0.0034 (i.e., the delta changes by −0.0034—from −0.721 to −0.7244—if the price of the underlying moves by 1). The current value of the option is 65.48.

The first step under the delta-plus method is to multiply the market value of the commodity by the absolute value of the delta.

$$500 \times 0.721 = 360.5$$

The delta-weighted position then has to be incorporated into the measure described above. If the bank uses the maturity ladder approach and no other positions exist, the delta-weighted position has to be multiplied by 0.15 to calculate the capital charge for delta.

$$360.5 \times 0.15 = 54.075$$

The capital charge for gamma has to be calculated according to the formula described above.

$$1/2 \times 0.0034 \times (500 \times 0.15)^2 = 9.5625$$

The capital charge for vega has now to be calculated. The assumed current (implied) volatility is 20%. Because only an increase in volatility carries a risk of loss for a short call option, the volatility has to be increased by a relative shift of 25%. This means that the vega capital charge has to be calculated on the basis of a change in volatility of 5 percentage points from 20% to 25% in this example. According to the Black–Scholes formula used here, the vega equals 168. Thus a 1% or 0.01 increase in volatility increases the value of the option by 1.68. Accordingly a change in volatility of 5 percentage points increases the value by

$$5 \times 1.68 = 8.4$$

which is the capital charge for vega risk. Finally, the nonlinear portion of the market risk charge is obtained by summing both the vega and gamma impact together, which is then 9.56 + 8.40 = 17.96.

The Scenario Approach. Banks, who deal in more sophisticated options strategies, will have the right to base their market risk capital charge for their options portfolios on a scenario matrix analysis.

This will be accomplished by specifying a fixed range of changes in the option portfolio's risk factors and calculating changes in the value of the option portfolio at various points along this "grid." For the purpose of calculating the capital charge, the bank will revalue the option portfolio using matrices for simultaneous changes in the option's underlying rate or price and in the volatility of that rate or price. A different matrix will be set up for each individual underlying.

The options and related hedging positions will be evaluated over a specified range above and below the current value of the underlying. Those banks using the alternative method for interest rate options should use, for each set of time bands, the highest of the assumed changes in yield applicable to the group to which the time bands belong. The other ranges are ±8% for equities, ±8% for foreign exchange and gold, and ±15% for commodities. For all risk categories, at least seven observations (including the current observation) should be used to divide the range into equally spaced intervals.

The second dimension of the matrix entails a change in the volatility of the underlying rate or price. A single change in the volatility of the underlying rate or price equal to a shift in volatility of +25% and −25% is expected to be sufficient in most cases. After calculating the matrix, each cell contains the net profit or loss of the option and the underlying hedge instrument. The capital charge for each underlying will then be calculated as the largest loss contained in the matrix.

13.3.3.2 The Internal Models Approach. In contrast with the Standardized Approach, the Internal Models Approach relies on banks' internal risk management systems to compute the market risk charge. For a bank to use its own risk management system to evaluate the market risk charge it would be required to hold for capital requirements, it has first to be explicitly approved by its regulator, along with the bank satisfying qualitative requirements. The Basel Committee saw this method as a possibility for banks to have an incentive to develop more robust risk management systems, because it would lead to lower capital requirements.

13.3.3.2.1 Qualitative Requirements. Supervisory authorities need to be able to assure themselves that banks are using models that have market risk management systems that are conceptually sound and implemented with integrity, in order for these banks to be using the internal model approach. Accordingly, banks need to be able to satisfy a number of qualitative criteria before they are permitted to use the model. These criteria are as follows:

- The bank should have an independent risk control unit that is responsible for the design and implementation of the bank's risk management system. The unit should produce and analyze daily reports on the output of the bank's risk measurement model. This unit must be independent from business trading and should report directly to the senior management of the bank.

- The independent risk control unit should conduct a regular backtesting programme, which will provide feedback as to the accuracy of the internal VaR models.
- The unit should be involved in the initial and ongoing validation of the risk models.
- Board of directors and senior management should be actively involved in the risk control process and must regard risk control as an essential aspect of the business. As a consequence, the daily reports produced by the risk control unit should be reviewed by management with authority to enforce reductions in the bank's risk profile.
- The bank's internal risk model must be integrated into day-to-day risk management process. Its output should be an integral part of the process of planning, monitoring, and controlling the bank's risk profile.
- The risk management framework should be used in conjunction with internal trading limits and exposures.
- The risk management framework should also be complemented with a routine and rigorous programme of stress testing. The result of the stress testing should be reviewed periodically by senior management, used in the internal assessment of capital adequacy, and reflected in the policies and limits set out by the board of directors.
- Banks using the internal model approach should ensure compliance with a documented set of internal policies, controls, and procedures regarding the operation of the risk management system.
- Last but not least, an independent review of the risk measurement system should be carried out regularly in the bank's own internal auditing process, which should take place at least once a year. This independent review will include the adequacy of the documentation put in place, the organization of the risk unit, the integration of market risk measures into daily risk management, the approval process for risk pricing models, the validation of any significant change in the risk measurement process, the integrity of the management information system, and the verification of the model's accuracy through frequent back testing.

13.3.3.2.2 Specification of Market Risk Factors On top of following the qualitative criteria set up by the Basel Committee, a bank using the internal model approach also needs to follow a sufficient number of specifications for their market risk factors. The risk factors contained in a market risk measurement system should be sufficient to capture the risks inherent in the bank's portfolio of on- and off-balance sheet trading positions. Although banks will have some discretion in specifying the risk factors for their internal models, the following guidelines should be fulfilled.

For interest rates exposure, there must be a set of risk factors corresponding to interest rates in each currency the banks has exposure to. The risk measurement system should model the yield curve using one of a number of generally accepted approaches, for example, by estimating forward rates of zero coupon yields. The yield curve should be divided into various maturity segments in order to capture variation in the volatility of rates along the yield curve; there will typically be one risk factor corresponding to each maturity segment. For material exposures to interest rate movements in the major currencies and markets, banks must model the yield curve using a minimum of six risk factors. However, the number of risk factors used should ultimately be driven by the nature of the bank's trading strategies. For instance, a bank with a portfolio of various types of securities across many points of the yield curve and that engages in complex arbitrage strategies would require a greater number of risk factors to capture interest rate risk accurately. The risk measurement system must incorporate separate risk factors to capture spread risk (e.g., between bonds and swaps). A variety of approaches may be used to capture the spread risk arising from less than perfectly correlated movements between government and other fixed-income interest rates, such as specifying a completely separate yield curve for non-government fixed-income instruments (for instance, swaps or municipal securities) or estimating the spread over government rates at various points along the yield curve.

For *exchange rates* (which may include gold), the risk measurement system should incorporate risk factors corresponding to the individual foreign currencies in which the bank's positions are denominated. Since the value-at-risk figure calculated by the risk measurement system will be expressed in the bank's domestic currency, any net position denominated in a foreign currency will introduce a foreign exchange risk. Thus, there must be risk factors corresponding to the exchange rate between the domestic currency and each foreign currency in which the bank has a significant exposure.

For equity prices, there should be risk factors corresponding to each of the equity markets in which the bank holds significant positions: At a minimum, there should be a risk factor that is designed to capture market-wide movements in equity prices. The sophistication and nature of the modeling technique for a given market should correspond to the bank's exposure to the overall market as well as concentration in individual equity issues in that market.

For *commodity prices*, there should be risk factors corresponding to each of the commodity markets in which the bank holds significant positions. For banks with relatively limited positions in commodity-based instruments, a straightforward specification of risk factors would be acceptable. Such a specification would likely entail one risk factor for each commodity price to which the bank is exposed. In cases where the aggregate positions are quite small, it might be acceptable to use a single risk factor for a relatively broad subcategory of commodities. For more active trading, the model must also take account of variation in the "convenience yield" between derivatives positions such as forwards and swaps and cash positions in the commodity.

Once these requirements are satisfied, banks have the flexibility to devise the precise nature of their models, yet need to follow minimum standards for the purpose of calculating their capital charge. These are defined as quantitative requirements, and are set out below:

- The computation of the "value-at-risk," or VaR, must be done on a daily basis.
- In calculating the VaR, a 99th percentile, a one-tailed confidence interval shall be used.
- In calculating the VaR, an instantaneous, price shock equivalent to a 10-day movement in prices is to be used (holding period will then be 10 working days). However, banks can rescale their daily VaR using the square root of time.
- The historical sample period for calculating the VaR should be constrained to at least one year of data; however, for banks that use a weighting scheme, the weighted average time lag cannot be less than 6 months.
- The data sets used in the calculation of VaR must be updated at least every quarter, or whenever market prices are subject to material changes.
- The methodology for the calculation of VaR can be any of the three main models: historical simulations, Monte Carlo simulations, or variance–covariance matrices, as long as the bank's model capture all the material risks run by the bank.
- For the measurements of options risk, banks must capture the nonlinearity characteristics of options positions and must have a set of risk factors that captures the volatility of the rates and prices underlying the positions (vega risk).

The general market risk charge should be calculated on a daily basis and shall be set at the higher of the previous day's VaR, or the average of the daily value-at-risk measures on each of the preceding 60 business days, multiplied by a multiplication factor. The multiplication factor will be set by individual supervisory authorities on the basis of their assessment of the bank's own internal models, subject to an absolute minimum of 3.

Furthermore, banks will be required to add to the multiplication factor a "plus" factor directly related to the performance of the model, introducing a positive incentive to maintain the predictive quality of the model. The purpose of this factor is to penalize a bank that provides an overly optimistic projection of its market risk.

Banks using models will also be subject to a capital charge to cover *specific risk* (as defined under the standardized approach for market risk) of interest rate-related instruments and equity securities. Where a bank has a VaR measure that incorporates specific risk and that meets all the qualitative and quantitative requirements for general risk models, it may base its charge on modeled estimates, provided that the measure is based on models that meet the additional criteria and requirements set out below. Banks that are unable to meet these additional criteria and requirements will be required to base their specific risk capital charge on the full amount of the specific risk charge calculated under the standardized method. The model must capture all material components of price risk and be responsive to changes in market conditions, and it also must explain the historical price variation of the portfolio, capture concentrations, be robust to an adverse environment, capture name-related basis risk, capture event risk, and be validated through back testing.

The market risk charge using the Internal Model Approach is then on any given day *t*:

$$\text{IMA(MRC)} = \text{Max}\left(k\frac{1}{60}\sum_{i=1}^{60}\text{VaR}_{t-i};\ \text{VaR}_{t-1}\right) + \max(s\text{VaR}_{t-1}, kS\text{VaR}_{\text{avg}})$$

where k represents both the multiplication factor and the plus factor, and SvaR represents the stressed VaR described below.

In addition to the calculation of a normal value-at-risk, the Basel Committee also implemented the need to compute a stressed value at risk.

*13.3.3.2.3 **Stressed VaR.*** The stressed VaR measure is intended to replicate the value-at-risk measure that would be generated on the bank's current portfolio if the relevant market factors were experiencing a period of stress and should therefore be based on the 10-day, 99th percentile, one-tailed confidence interval value-at-risk measure of the current portfolio, with model inputs calibrated to historical data from a continuous 12-month period of significant financial stress relevant to the bank's portfolio.

In order to choose a historical period for calibration purposes, banks should formulate a methodology for identifying a stress period relevant to their current portfolios, based on one of the following two approaches:

- Judgment-based approach, which does not use a detailed quantitative analysis, but relies on a high-level analysis of the risks inherent in the current portfolio, and past periods of stress related to those risk factors.
- Formulaic approach, which applies a more systematic quantitative analysis to identify the historical period representing a significant stress for a current portfolio.

While either approach can be used by banks, it is preferable for the identification of the historical period, that the formulaic approach should be used. Banks may also combine both approaches, to limit the computational burden of the formulaic approach. The stressed value at risk should be calculated at least weekly.

One of the qualitative requirements for using the Internal Model Approach is that banks need to have a robust and rigorous stress testing programme. Stress testing is a key component of a bank risk measurement system to assess its capital position.

*13.3.3.2.4 **Stress Testing.*** The purpose of stress testing is to identify events that could greatly impact the bank and are presumably not captured in VaR measures. A major goal of stress testing is to "evaluate the capacity of the bank's capital to absorb large potential losses," if and when such events should happen.

Stress testing is described as a process to identify and manage situations that could cause extraordinary losses. A bank's stress scenarios must cover a range of factors including low-probability events in all major types of risks.

Banks' stress tests should be of both a quantitative and qualitative nature, incorporating both market risk and liquidity aspects of market disturbances. Quantitative criteria should identify plausible stress scenarios to which banks could be exposed. Qualitative criteria should emphasize that two major goals of stress testing are to evaluate the capacity of the bank's capital to absorb potential large losses and to identify steps the bank can take to reduce its risk and conserve capital. This assessment is integral to setting and evaluating the bank's management strategy, and the results of stress testing should be routinely communicated to senior management and, periodically, to the bank's board of directors.

The Basel Committee suggest that banks should combine the use of supervisory stress scenarios along with scenarios developed by the bank. Scenario analysis consists of evaluating a portfolio under different states of the economy (worst-case analysis). Stress testing is available in three different categories:

- *Scenarios Requiring No Simulation by the Bank.* Banks should have the information on the largest losses experienced during the reporting period to gain a better understanding of the vulnerabilities of the bank.
- *Scenarios Requiring Simulations by the Bank.* Banks should subject their portfolios to a series of simulated stress scenarios, which should include the 1987 stock market crash, the ERM crisis in 1992, the 1998 Russian financial crisis, the 2000 tech bubble burst, or the 2007/2008 subprime crisis, incorporating both the large prices movements and the sharp reduction in liquidity associated with these events.
- *Scenarios Developed by the Bank Itself to Capture the Specific Characteristics of Its Portfolio.* These scenarios would be driven by the current position of the bank, instead at looking at past events or past losses of the bank (e.g., problems in a key region of the world combined with a sharp move in oil prices). In order to use scenarios developed inhouse, banks need to provide regulators with the documentation of the methodology used to carry out and identify these scenarios.

The assessment of stress testing is of importance to evaluate the risk profile of institutions, along with their risk management systems. Results of the stress testing analysis should be reported and reviewed periodically to senior management and should be reflected in the policies and limits set by the management or the board of directors. If the stress testing analysis reveals particular vulnerability to a given set of circumstances, the bank should take prompt action to manage these risks appropriately.

Finally, in order to have access to the internal model approach in the Market Risk framework, banks need to be able to verify the accuracy of their risk models.

13.3.3.2.5 Back Testing. It is important that banks have processes in place to ensure that their internal models have been adequately validated by suitably qualified parties independent of the development process to ensure that they are conceptually sound and adequately capture all material risks. This validation should be conducted when the model is initially developed and when any significant changes are made to the model. The validation should also be conducted on a periodic basis but especially where there have been any significant structural changes in the market or changes to the composition of the portfolio which might lead to the model no longer being adequate. More extensive model validation is particularly important where specific risk is also modeled and is required to meet the further specific risk criteria. As techniques and best practices evolve, banks should avail themselves of these advances.

Back testing is a statistical testing framework that consists of checking whether trading losses are in line with VaR forecasts. The essence of all back testing efforts is the comparison of actual trading results with model-generated risk measures. If this comparison is close enough, the back testing raises no issues regarding the quality of the risk measurement model. The value-at-risk measures are intended to be larger than all but a fraction of the trading outcomes, where the fraction is determined by the confidence interval level of the value-at-risk measure.

An additional consideration for back testing arises because the value-at-risk approach to risk is generally based on the sensitivity of a static portfolio to instantaneous price shocks. Hence the inclusion of fee income together with trading gains and losses should not be included in the definition of trading outcome. In particular, in any given 10-day period, significant changes in portfolio composition relative to the initial positions are common at major financial institutions. Hence, the back-testing framework described by the Basel Committee involves the use of risk measures calibrated to a one-day holding period.

The Basel Committee framework around back testing recommends banks to use both a hypothetical approach and actual trading outcomes in back-testing results. Hypothetical portfolios are constructed as to match the VaR measure exactly, meaning that their returns are obtained by freezing the positions of the portfolios from one day to the next, to compare their real gains or losses. The two approaches are likely to provide complementary information on the quality of the risk management system.

The framework adopted by the Committee, which is also the most straightforward procedure for comparing the risk measures with the trading outcomes, is simply to calculate the number of times that the trading outcomes are not covered by the risk measures ("exceptions"). For example, over 200 trading days, a 99% daily risk measure should cover, on average, 198 of the 200 trading outcomes, leaving two exceptions.

The Basel Committee back-testing framework consists of recording daily exceptions of the 99 percent VaR over the last year (250 trading days). On average, we could expect 1% of 250 days, or 2.5 instances of exceedances of the value-at-risk over the last year. More exceptions of the VaR would be either (a) a fault in the model understating the value-at-risk of the bank or (b) market conditions such that the bank is unlucky in its record of exceptions.

Such statistical testing framework must account for two types of errors:

- *Type 1 Errors.* The probability that selecting a given number of exceptions as a threshold for rejecting the accuracy of the model will result in an erroneous rejection of the model. For example, if the threshold is set as low as one exception, then an accurate model will be rejected fully 91.9% of the time.
- *Type 2 Errors.* These describe the probability of not rejecting a model that is false. For example, if the model's actual level of coverage is 97%, and the threshold for rejection is set at seven or more exceptions, then this model would be erroneously accepted 37.5% of the time.

Usually, one has to trade off one type of error against another. Most statistical tests fix the type 1 error and structure the test as to minimize type 2 errors. If we define x as the number of exceptions, n as the total number of observations, and p as the confidence level interval, then the random variable x follows a binomial distribution. The number of exceptions is a random variable X, which is the result of T independent Bernoulli trials, where each trial results in an outcome of $y = 0$ or $y = 1$. The binomial variable has mean and variance $E[X] = pT$, and $V[X] = p(1 - p)T$. So calculating the probability of observations occurring, we can use the binomial distribution.

The Penalty Zones. With the statistical consideration for a back-testing framework, the Basel Committee has put in place a three-zone approach, distinguished by colors into a hierarchy of responses. Table 13.18 shows the three zones, with the number of exceptions in each zone and their equivalent potential increase multiplicative factor (the plus factor described above).

The Basel Committee decided that up to four exceptions is acceptable, which falls into the green zone. A bank reporting a number of exceptions of its VaR risk measurement model will not be faced with an increase of the plus factor. If the number of exceptions is between 5 and 9, the bank falls into the yellow zone, which would incur a progressive penalty, where the multiplicative factor k

TABLE 13.18 **The Basel Penalty Zones**

Zone	Number of Exceptions	Potential Increase in Plus Factor
Green	0–4	0.00
Yellow	5	0.40
	6	0.50
	7	0.65
	8	0.75
	9	0.85
Red	>10	1.00

described above is increased from 3 to 4. If the number of exceptions is over 9 (non-inclusive), the bank falls in the red zone, generating an automatic nondiscretionary penalty.

In practice, there are several possible explanations for a back-testing exception, some of which go to the basic integrity of the model, some of which suggest an underspecified or low-quality model, and some of which suggest either bad luck or poor intra-day trading results. Classifying the exceptions generated by a bank's model into these categories can be a very useful exercise.

- *Basic Integrity of the Model.* The deviations occurred due to incorrectly reported positions, or errors in the program code. This would be considered as a very serious fault, in which case a penalty should apply and corrective action should be taken.
- *Model's Accuracy Could Be Improved.* The risk measurement model is not assessing the risk of some instruments with sufficient precision. This would also be considered as a serious fault, in which case a penalty should apply and corrective action should be taken.
- *Bad Luck or Markets Moved in Fashion Unanticipated by the Model.* This is described by random chance (which is a very low probability event), or that markets moved by more than the model predicted. These exceptions "should be expected to occur at least some of the time."
- *Intra-day Trading.* There was a large change in the bank's positions or some other income event between the end of the first day, and the end of the second day. This problem should not occur while using hypothetical portfolios as described before.

Finally, the Basel Committee sees that a bank market risk capital requirement will be calculated using either the Standardized Method, the Internal Model Approach, or a combination of both approaches. Conditions apply for using a combination of both approaches, which are listed below:

- Each broad risk factor category must be assessed using a simple approach.
- No elements of market risk may escape measurement.
- The capital charges assessed under the standardized approach and under the internal model approach are to be aggregated according to a simple sum method.

We will now look at the treatment of illiquid positions within the market risk framework set out by the Basel Committee, because this is an important part in order to calculate the capital charge requirement for a bank with such positions.

13.3.3.2.6 Treatment of Illiquid Positions. We will now look at the treatment of illiquid positions within the market risk framework set out by the Basel

Committee, because this is an important part in order to calculate the capital charge requirement for a bank with such positions. The main difference is that the guidance for the prudent valuation now accounts for positions that are either in the trading book or in the banking book. A bank must establish adequate systems and controls sufficient to give management the confidence that their valuation estimates are prudent and reliable. Such systems must include documented policies and procedures for the process of valuation, clear and independent reporting lines for the department accountable for the valuation process.

Different valuation methodologies exist in order to price illiquid positions, such as marking-to-market or marking-to-model. We will briefly describe both approaches, as proposed by the Basel Committee.

Marking to Market. Marking to market is the process of a daily valuation of positions at readily available close price in orderly transactions that are sourced independently. Banks must marked-to-market as often as possible. A more prudent side of bid/offer spread should be used unless the institution is a significant market maker in a particular position type and it can close-out at mid market.

Banks should maximize the use of relevant observable inputs and minimize the use of unobservable inputs when estimating fair value using a valuation technique. However, observable inputs or transactions may not be relevant, such as in a forced liquidation or distressed sale, or transactions may not be observable, such as when markets are inactive. In such cases, the observable data should be considered, but may not be determinative.

Marking to Model. Where marking to market is not a possibility, banks can use a model of marking to model. Marking-to-model is defined as any valuation which has to be benchmarked, extrapolated, or otherwise calculated from a single market input. When marking to model, an extra degree of conservatism is appropriate.

13.3.3.2.7 Incremental Risk Charge. The Basel Committee/IOSCO Agreement reached in July 2005 contained several improvements to the capital regime for trading book positions. Among these revisions was a new requirement for banks that model specific risk to measure and hold capital against default risk that is incremental to any default risk captured in the bank's value-at-risk (VaR) model. The incremental default risk charge was incorporated into the trading book capital regime in response to the increasing amount of exposure in banks' trading books to credit risk-related and often illiquid products whose risk is not reflected in VaR. In October 2007, the Basel Committee on Banking Supervision (the Committee) released guidelines for computing capital for incremental default risk for public comments. At its meeting in March 2008, it reviewed comments received and decided to expand the scope of the capital charge. The decision was made in light of the recent credit market turmoil where a number of major banking organizations had experienced large losses, most of which were sustained in banks' trading books. Most of those losses were not captured in the

99%/10-day VaR. Since the losses have not arisen from actual defaults but rather from credit migrations combined with widening of credit spreads and the loss of liquidity, applying an incremental risk charge covering default risk only would not appear adequate. For example, a number of global financial institutions commented that singling out just default risk was inconsistent with their internal practices and could be potentially burdensome.

The incremental risk charge represents an estimate of the default and migration risks of unsecuritized credit products over a one-year horizon period at 99.9% confidence level, taking into account the liquidity horizons of individual positions or sets of positions. The newly implemented incremental risk charge only applies to banks that are subject to the MRA and that seek to model specific risk in the trading book.

Under the proposal, the trading book capital charge for a firm modeling specific risk would consist of three components: a general market risk charge, a specific market risk charge (both measured using the 10-day VaR at the 99% confidence interval), and the incremental risk charge (IRC).

The incremental risk charge would encompass all positions subject to the MRA, regardless of their perceived liquidity, except the positions whose valuations depend solely on commodity prices, foreign exchange rates, or the term structure of default-free interest rates. Example of IRC products include debt securities, equities, securitizations of commercial and consumer products, collateralized debt obligations, and other structured products. The incremental risk charge captures the potential for direct/indirect losses from internal/external rating migrations and obligor's defaults.

The Basel Committee also proposed key supervisory parameters for computing the incremental risk charge. Specifically, for all incremental risk-charges-covered positions, a bank's IRC model must measure all losses at the 99.9% confidence interval over a capital horizon of one year, taking into account the liquidity horizons applicable to the positions. This constant level of risk assumption implies that a bank would rebalance, or roll over, its trading positions over the one-year capital horizon in a manner that maintains the initial risk level, as indicated by a metric such as VaR or the profile of the exposure by credit rating and concentration.

Particular attention needs to be paid to the liquidity assumptions in the IRC model, especially with regard to a stressed market. The Basel Committee proposes a floor with regard to the liquidity horizon for certain product groups: equities one month, re-securitizations one year, and three months for all other positions.

Economic and financial dependence among obligors causes a clustering of default and migration events. Accordingly, the IRC charge includes the impact of correlations between default and migration events among obligors, and a bank's IRC model must include the impact of such clustering of default and migration events.

A bank's IRC model must appropriately reflect issuer and market concentrations. Thus, other things being equal, a concentrated portfolio should attract a higher capital charge than a more granular portfolio. Concentrations that can arise within and across product classes under stressed conditions must also be reflected.

Within the IRC model, exposure amounts may be netted only when long and short positions refer to the same financial instrument. Otherwise, exposure amounts must be captured on a gross (i.e., non-netted) basis. Thus, hedging or diversification effects associated with long and short positions involving different instruments or different securities of the same obligor ("intraobligor hedges"), as well as long and short positions in different issuers ("interobligor hedges"), may not be recognized through netting of exposure amounts. Rather, such effects may only be recognized by capturing and modeling separately the gross long and short positions in the different instruments or securities.

It is expected that banks will develop their own models for the incremental risk charge and that the models will be consistent with the "use test." If internal models developed by the bank do not map directly to supervisory principles, then the bank must prove that the capital charge calculated by their model is comparable; otherwise they may be subject to a capital adjustment factor.

The Basel Committee on Banking Supervision released a quantitative impact study (QIS), in October 2009, showing a significant increase in capital requirements. The impact study includes data from 43 banks across 10 countries. The results of the impact study indicates an average increase of at least 11.5% of overall capital requirements and of 223.7% of market risk capital requirements. Looking to different sources for the increase on a bank's market risk requirements, the largest contribution to the average increase can be attributed to the stressed VaR (110.8%), followed by the incremental risk charge (102.7%).

The estimated size of the incremental risk charge is reported in Table 13.19 as a fraction of market risk capital requirements for liquidity horizons. We can see that the size of the IRC depends on the assumed liquidity horizon, as we

TABLE 13.19 Incremental Risk Capital Charge for Different Liquidity Horizons Compared with the Overall Market Risk Capital Requirements, in Percent

	Capital Charge SMM (Fallback Option)	Specific Risk Surcharge	Incremental Risk Capital Charge Including Default and Migration Risk for a Liquidity Horizon of . . .			Default-Only Charge 3 m Liquidity Horizon
			1 m	3 m	6 m	
Mean	422	23	136	126	156	97
Median	181	17	92	84	98	66
StDev	714	20	131	132	159	92
Min	26	1	9	5	5	7
Max	2973	78	522	565	613	375

Source: BIS.

note an increase to the charge the higher the horizon is, but the results varies significantly, as the standard deviation shows.

13.4 Example of the Calculation of the Capital Ratio

If a bank has tier 1 capital of 700, tier 2 capital of 100, tier 3 capital of 600, weighted risk assets for credit risk of 7500, and a market risk capital charge of 350, it first has to multiply the measure of market risk by 12.5 to create trading book notional risk weighted assets. By doing this, the bank creates a numerical link between the calculation of the capital requirement for credit risk, where the capital charge is based on the risk-weighted assets, and the capital requirement for market risk, where instead the capital charge itself is calculated directly on the basis of the measurement systems. After the calculation of the minimum capital charge, the amount of capital that is eligible for meeting those requirements must be computed, starting with credit risk, covered in this example by 500 tier 1 capital and 100 tier 2 capital. This leaves 200 tier 1 capital available to support the bank's market risk requirements, which—because of the 250% rule—means that only 500 of the tier 3 capital is eligible. Because this bank only needs to use 100 tier 1 capital and 250 tier 3 capital to meet its market risk capital requirement, the bank has 100 tier 1 capital and 250 tier 3 capital that is unused but eligible for future market risk requirements.

For calculating the capital ratio, excess tier 1 capital should be taken into account because it can be used to meet credit and/or market risk requirements (Table 13.20). Therefore, the capital ratio is calculated by dividing the eligible capital (excluding unused tier 3) by the total (notional) risk assets (1050/

TABLE 13.20 Example of Calculation of Capital Ratio

Risk Assets	Minimum Capital Charge	Available Capital	Minimum Capital for Meeting Requirement	Eligible Capital (Excluding Unused Tier 3)	Unused but Eligible Tier 3	Unused but Not Eligible Tier 3
Credit risk 7500	600	tier 1 700 tier 2 100	tier 1 500 tier 2 100	tier 1 700 tier 2 100		
Market risk 4 375 (i.e., 350 × 12.5)	350	tier 3 600	tier 1 100 tier 3 250	tier 3 250	tier 3 250	tier 3 100
				Capital ratio: 1050/11,875 = 8.8%	Excess tier 3 Capital ratio: 250/11, 875 = 2.1 %	

11,875 = 8.8%). Excess tier 3 capital that is unused but eligible can also be calculated as an excess tier 3 capital ratio (250/11,875 = 2.1%).

13.5 Basel III and the New Definition of Capital; The Introduction of Liquidity Ratios

According to the Basel Committee on Banking Supervision, the Basel III proposal has two main objectives: (a) to strengthen the regulations regarding capital base and liquidity of banks with the goal of promoting a more resilient banking sector and (b) to improve the banking' sector ability to absorb shocks arising from financial and economic stress. These twin objectives are proposed to be achieved by modifying some of the existing norms in the following main areas: capital reforms, liquidity reforms, and other elements relating to the general improvement in the stability for the financial system.

The original Basel II guidelines in the Basel Committee document *International Convergence of Capital Measurement and Capital Standards: A Revised Framework* June 2006 established capital adequacy requirements for the interest rate and other market risks of financial instruments held in a bank's trading book. Under Basel II, the interest rate and other market risk capital requirements for the trading book are calculated under either the Standardized Measurement Method (SMM) or the Internal Models Approach (IMA). Under the IMA, the capital requirement is defined in a probabilistic framework involving changes in the aggregate economic value of financial instruments in a bank's portfolio over an analysis horizon period. In particular, the capital requirement is a function of the value-at-risk (VaR) metrics for the portfolio calculated daily over the 60 preceding business days using a 99% one-tail confidence interval based upon an instantaneous shock equivalent to a 10-day movement in underlying market rates or prices. To determine the capital requirement, the higher of the value of the daily VaR metric for the preceding business day and the average of the daily VaR metric values over the preceding 60-business-day period is calculated, and this result is multiplied by a factor specified by the bank's regulator that has a minimum value of 3. This results in a market-risk-equivalent asset amount equal to the market risk capital requirement times 12.5, which is required for calculation of the bank's capital adequacy ratio.

The market risk capital requirements guidelines under the IMA are discussed in "International Convergence of Capital Measurement and Capital Standards: A Revised Framework," June 2006, and were updated in two Basel Committee documents: "Revisions to the Basel II Market Risk Framework," July 2009, and "Guidelines for Computing Capital for Incremental Risk in the Trading Book," July 2009. These updated guidelines impose additional requirements on the calculation of the Market risk capital requirement: a stressed, long-term capital requirement, a long-term incremental risk charge, a specific risk charge, and a comprehensive risk capital requirement. The sum of the original capital requirement plus these additional requirements is considered the new market risk capital requirement under these guidelines. Collectively, the updated guidelines are considered as part of the Basel III capital adequacy guidelines.

The Basel III market risk capital requirements also include a comprehensive risk capital requirement. The comprehensive risk capital requirement covers comprehensive risk, which represents an estimate of all price risks of the bank's portfolio of correlation trading positions over a one-year capital horizon at a 99.9% confidence level, assuming a constant level of risk exposure over the capital horizon. A correlation trading position is: (i) a securitization position for which all or substantially all of the value of the underlying exposures is based on the credit quality of a single company for which a two-way market exists, or on commonly traded indices based on such exposures for which a two-way market exists, or (ii) a position that is not a securitization position that hedges a position described in (i). Resecuritization positions, derivatives of a securitization position that do not provide a pro rata share in the proceeds of a securitization tranche, and securitization positions for which the underlying assets or reference exposures are retail exposures, residential mortgage exposures, or commercial mortgage exposures are not correlation trading positions.

Under the Basel III market risk measurement framework, market risk is defined as the risk of losses in on- and off-balance-sheet positions arising from movements in market prices. The risks subject to this requirement are the risks pertaining to interest-rate-related instruments and equity securities in the trading book and foreign exchange risk and commodities risk throughout the bank on a worldwide net consolidated basis irrespective of where the instruments are booked. The trading book consists of positions in financial instruments and commodities held either with trading intent or in order to hedge other elements of the trading book. Positions held with trading intent are those held intentionally for short-term resale and/or with the intent of benefiting from actual or expected short-term price movements or locking in arbitrage profits and may include, for example, proprietary positions, positions arising from client servicing (e.g., matched principal broking) and market making.

Securitization positions are covered by the Basel III market risk measurement framework. Securitization positions include securitization tranche instruments created by a securitization transaction in which (i) all or a portion of the credit risk of one or more underlying exposures is transferred to one or more third parties, (ii) the credit risk associated with the underlying exposures has been separated into at least two tranches that reflect different levels of seniority, (iii) performance of the securitization exposures depends upon the performance of the underlying exposures, (iv) all or substantially all of the underlying exposures are financial exposures (such as loans, commitments, credit derivatives, guarantees, receivables, asset-backed securities, mortgage-backed securities, other debt securities, or equity securities), and (v) for nonsynthetic securitizations, the underlying exposures are not owned by an operating company. Securitization positions also include market risk exposures that reference underlying securitization tranche instruments.

The market risk capital requirements for securitization positions that are correlation trading positions are addressed by the IMA. A correlation trading position is (i) a securitization position for which all or substantially all of the value of the underlying exposures is based on the credit quality of a single company for which a two-way market exists, or on commonly traded indices based on such exposures for which a two-way market exists on the indices, or (ii) a position that is not a securitization position that hedges a securitization position described in (i). Correlation trading positions may include CDO index tranches, customized CDO tranches, and *n*th-to-default credit derivatives, and hedges of these positions may include standardized CDS index and single-name CDS positions. The market risk capital requirements for securitization positions that are not correlation trading positions are addressed under the SMM, so these securitization positions are not modeled and analyzed under the IMA.

Changes in the capital reform, redefining both the quantity and quality of capital, are also present in the new regulations.

Tier 1 capital requirement has been increased from 4% to 6% of the total capital requirement of 8%. Under tier 1 capital, the minimum capital of common equity (core capital), the highest form of loss absorbing capital, is raised from the current level of 2% to 4.5%. This is to be adhered to after making the necessary regulatory adjustments (after subtracting perpetual debts, from tier 1). This increase will be phased in to apply from 2016, and it will come into full effect in 2019. In addition to the increased core capital, an additional core capital of 2.5% is recommended as a capital conservation buffer. This will take the minimum core equity requirement to 7%. Table 13.21 gives an overview of the

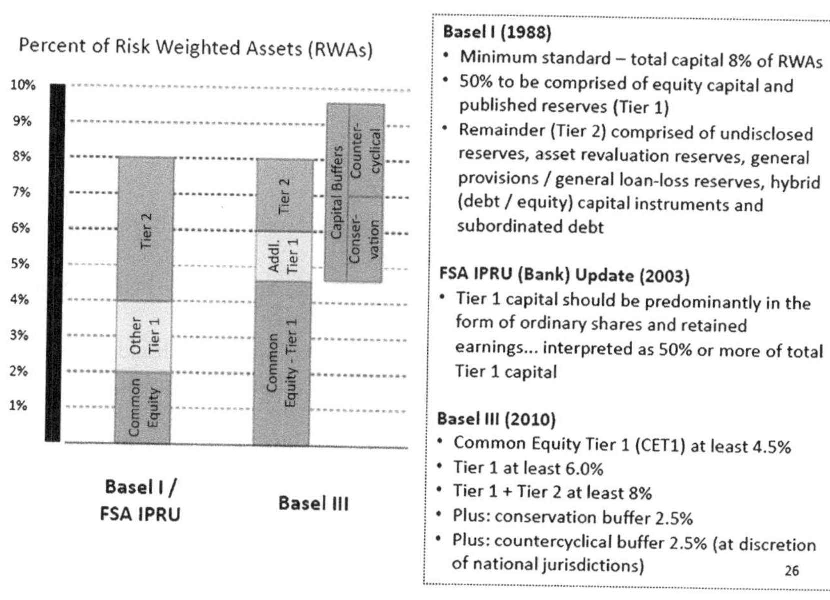

FIGURE 13.1 Summary of the minimum standards from Basel I to Basel III.

TABLE 13.21 Key Criteria for the Definition of Tier 1 and Tier 2 Capital

	Key Criteria	
Common equity tier 1 (CET1)	• Most subordinated—highest capacity to absorb losses • Common shores (Basel III criteria are highly prescriptive) • No circumstances under which distributions are obligatory • Disclosed reserves with regulatory adjustments (highly prescriptive) aimed at optimizing loss absorbability	
Additional tier 1	• Subordinated to "subordinated debt" • Primary preferred stock but also includes hybirds (Basel III criteria are highly prescriptive) • Maturity is perpetual . . . no step-ups or other incentives to redeem • Full discretion to cancel dividends coupons • Liabilities with prespecified conversion triggers	• Callable with supervisory approval after minimum 5 years and with certain assurances • Not secured or guaranteed by issuer • No issuer influence . . . directly purchased and independently funded • Instrument cannot have a credit sensitive dividend feature • Specific criteria for SPVs
tier 2	• Subordinated to depositors and general creditors • Primarily subordinated debt • Maturity is minimum 5 years (regulatory capital recognized on straight-line amortization basis over remaining 5 years) • No step-ups or other incentives to redeem • Certain loan loss provisions	

change from the 1998 Basel Accord for the capital ratios, to the Basel III capital ratios.

Table 13.21 gives an overview of the classes of capital and their respective criteria.

Some components of the existing tier 1 capital are disqualified under the new regime, including investment in financial subsidiaries, goodwill, and other intangibles assets, deferred tax assets, and so on.

One of the main changes of the new Basel III framework is the introduction of a global liquidity standard, because strong capital requirements are a necessary condition for banking sector stability. The Basel Committee developed two minimum standards for funding liquidity. These standards have been developed to achieve the objective "to promote resilience of a bank's liquidity risk profile by ensuring that it has sufficient high-quality resources to survive an acute stress scenario." These two standards are:

- Liquidity coverage ratio (LCR), for short-term resilience
- The net stable funding ratio, for longer time horizon resilience

Liquidity Coverage Ratio. The liquidity coverage ratio is intended to promote resilience to potential liquidity disruptions over a 30-day horizon. It requires a bank to maintain an adequate level of unencumbered, high-quality assets that can be converted into cash to meet its liquidity, under an acute liquidity stress scenario. The ratio has been developed following the extreme circumstances witnessed during the global financial crisis that began in 2007.

The following equation shows how the liquidity coverage ratio would work:

$$\text{LCR} = \frac{\text{Stock of highly liquid assets}}{\text{Net cash outlfow over the next30 days}} > 100\%$$

Net cash outflows are defined as the total expected cash outflows minus total expected cash inflows during the 30-day period of stress. Cash outflows are subject to prescribed "run-off" rates, while cash inflows are subject to prescribed inflow factors.

The ratio requires a higher liquidity buffer even for banks that match their outflows with sufficient inflows according the ratio assumptions, because there is a cap of 75% on inflows. High-quality assets should comprise at least 60% level 1 assets (cash, central banks reserves, and sovereign debt qualifying for the 0% risk weight under the standardized approach for credit risk) and no more than 40% of level 2 assets (sovereign debt qualifying for a 20% risk weight under the standardized approach for credit risk, as well as qualifying for corporate bonds of at least AA rating).

The Net Stable Funding Ratio. The net stable funding ratio requires a minimum amount of stable resources of funding at a bank relative to the liquidity profiles of assets. It aims to limit over-reliance on short-term wholesale funding during times of buoyant market liquidity and encourage better assessment of liquidity risk across all on- and off-balance sheet items. The amount of stable funding available is calculated through applying weightings to different categories of liability, which is then compared with the amount of stable funding required, calculated by applying weightings to the institutions assets and off-balance sheet items, including potential liquidity exposure. The formula used to calculate the net stable funding ratio is

$$\text{NSFR} = \frac{\text{Available stable funding}}{\text{Required stable funding}} > 100\%$$

Stable funding is defined as the portion of those types of equity and liability financing expected to provide reliable sources of funds over a one-year time horizon to cover conditions of extended stress. The available amount of stable funding is calculated by first assigning the carrying value of an institution's equity and liabilities to one of five categories below. The amount assigned to each

TABLE 13.22 Phase-In Arrangements

	2011	2012	2013	2014	2015	2016	2017	2018	As Of 1* Jan 2019
Leverage Ratio	Supervisory Monitoring		Parallel Run 1/1/2013 to 1/1/2017 Disclosure starts 1/1/2025					Migrate Pillar 1	
Minimum common equity capital ratio			3.5%	4.0%	4.5%	4.5%	4.5%	4.5%	4.5%
Capital conservation buffer						0.625%	1.25%	1.875%	2.5%
Minimum common equity plus capital conservation buffer			3.5%	4.0%	4.5%	5.125%	5.75%	6.375%	7.0%
Phase-in of deductions from CET1 (including amounts exceeding the limit for DTAs, MSRs and financials)				20%	40%	60%	80%	100%	100%
Minimum tier 1 capital			4.5%	5.5%	6.0%	6.0%	6.0%	6.0%	6.0%
Minimum total capital			8.0%	8.0%	8.0%	8.0%	8.0%	8.0%	8.0%
Minimum total capital plus conservation buffer			8.0%	8.0%	8.0%	8.625%	9.125%	9.875%	10.5%
Capital instruments that no longer qualify as non-core tier 1 capital or tier 2 capital			Phased over 10-year horizon beginning 2013						
Liquidity coverage ratio (LCR)	1				2				
Net stable funding ratio (NSF)		1						2	

category is to be multiplied by an ASF factor ranging from 0% to 100%, and the total ASF is the sum of the weighted amounts.

The amount of stable funding required by supervisors is to be measured using supervisory assumptions on the broad characteristics of the liquidity risk profiles of an institution's assets and off-balance sheet (OBS) exposures. The required amount of stable funding is calculated as the sum of the value of assets held and funded by the institution, multiplied by a specific required stable funding (RSF) factor assigned to each particular asset type, added to the amount of off-balance sheet activity (or potential liquidity exposure) multiplied by its associated RSF factor(s).

As the Basel Committee issued the latest set of guidelines in December 2010, it has permitted a phase-in arrangement over the next few years for banks to follow the capital requirements developed in this chapter. Table 13.22 describes the Phase-in Arrangements as required by the Basel Committee for the implementation of Basel III.

FURTHER READING

The following texts have been used to write this chapter. Most of the examples and situations are from these texts.

Basel Committee on Banking Supervision, *Risk Management Guidelines for Derivatives*, www.bis.org/publ/bcbsc211.pdf, 1994.

Basel Committee on Banking Supervision, *Amendment to the Capital Accord of July 1988*, www.bis.org/publ/bcbs12b.pdf, 1995a.

Basel Committee on Banking Supervision, *An Internal Model-Based Approach to Market Risk Capital Requirements*, www.bis.org/publ/bcbs19.pdf, 1995b.

Basel Committee on Banking Supervision, *Framework for Supervisory Information About the Derivatives Activities of Banks and Securities Firm (Joimt Report by the Basel Committee and the Technical Committee of the IOSCO)*, www.bis.org/publ/bcbs17.pdf, 1995c.

Basel Committee on Banking Supervision, *Planned Supplement to the Capital Accord to Incorporate Market Risk*, www.bis.org/publ/bcbs16.pdf, 1995d.

Basel Committee on Banking Supervision, *Amendment to the Basel Capital Accord to Incorporate Market Risk*, www.bis.org/publ/bcbs24.pdf, 1996a.

Basel Committee on Banking Supervision, *Amendment to the Basel Capital Accord to Incorporate Market Risk*, www.bis.org/publ/bcbs24a.pdf, 1996b.

Basel Committee on Banking Supervision, *Supervisory Framework for the Use of "Backtesting" in Conjunction with the Internal Models Approach to Market Risk Capital Requirements*, www.bis.org/publ/bcbs22.pdf, 1996c.

Basel Committee on Banking Supervision, *International Convergence of Capital Measurement and Capital Standards*, www.bis.org/publ/bcbs04a.pdf, 1998.

Basel Committee on Banking Supervision, *A New Capital Adequacy Framework*, www.bis.org/publ/bcbs50.pdf, 1999.

Basel Committee on Banking Supervision, *Basel II: International Convergence of Capital Measurement and Capital Standards: A Revised Framework*, www.bis.org/publ/bcbs107.pdf, 2004a.

Basel Committee on Banking Supervision, *Implementation of Basel II: Practical Considerations*, www.bis.org/publ/bcbs109.pdf, 2004b.

Basel Committee on Banking Supervision, *Amendment to the Capital Accord to Incorporate Market Risks*, www.bis.org/publ/bcbs119.pdf, 2005.

Basel Committee on Banking Supervision, *Proposed Revisions to the Basel II Market Risk Framework*, www.bis.org/publ/bcbs140.pdf, 2008.

Basel Committee on Banking Supervision, *Analysis of the Trading Book Quantitative Impact Study*, www.bis.org/publ/bcbs163.pdf, 2009a.

Basel Committee on Banking Supervision, *Guidelines for Computing Capital for Incremental Risk in the Trading Book*, www.bis.org/publ/bcbs159.pdf, 2009b.

Basel Committee on Banking Supervision, *Revisions to the Basel II Market Risk Framework*, www.bis.org/publ/bcbs158.pdf, 2009c.

Basel Committee on Banking Supervision, *Basel III: A Global Regulatory Framework for More Resilient Banks and Banking Systems*, www.bis.org/publ/bcbs189_dec2010.pdf, 2010a.

Basel Committee on Banking Supervision, *Basel III: International Framework for Liquidity Risk Measurement, Standards and Monitoring*, www.bis.org/publ/bcbs188.pdf, 2010b.

Basel Committee on Banking Supervision, *The Basel Committee's Response to the Financial Crisis: Report to the G20*, www.bis.org/publ/bcbs179.pdf, 2010c.

Basel Committee on Banking Supervision, *Results of the Comprehensive Quantitative Impact Study*, www.bis.org/publ/bcbs186.pdf, 2010d.

Basel Committee on Banking Supervision, *Revisions to the Basel II Market Risk Framework—Updated as of 31 December 2010*, www.bis.org/publ/bcbs193.pdf, 2011.

Basel Committee on Banking Supervision, *A Framework for Dealing with Domestic Systematically Important Banks*, www.bis.org/publ/bcbs224.pdf, 2012a.

Basel Committee on Banking Supervision, *Results of the Basel III Monitoring Exercise as of 30 June 2011*, www.bis.org/publ/bcbs217.pdf, 2012b.

Belmont D. P., *Value Added Risk Management in Financial Institutions: Leveraging Basel II*, John Wiley & Sons, 2004.

CHAPTER FOURTEEN

Conclusion

Almost five years after the start of the credit crunch, the financial sector is now under more scrutinity than ever. In 2008 we were close to Armagedon. The banking system was saved from collapse by billions of taxpayer's money, which in turn led to anger that the public was having to bail out bankers, who were finally perceived as just unreasonably risk-taking, gambling, and greedy. Following this crisis, significant changes to the regulatory systems have been done with the objective to make financial institutions more robust in case of another systemic crisis. Parallel additional controls and a better risk governance have been implemented. Some regulators in Europe announced tougher restrictions on the bonuses in order to limit risk-taking. Some of these new regulations are still under discussion, and probably more will come. It is important to secure the financial markets from system risk, but we also have to make sure that new regulations will just stop this industry from functioning, especially in Europe. I see regulations as brakes for a car, but we just have to make sure that the brakes do stop the car completely.

In the last 20 years, the financial risk management has gained an important role for the companies and financial instruments as demonstrated in this book. Financial innovations have imposed new challenges for market participants and their superviors in the areas of systemic risk. The world of capital markets is very fast-moving, especially the increased innovation in financial products and their growing complexity. The need for sound risk management has never been so important as today. The current financial crisis has revealed significant weaknesses in risk management practices across the financial services industry.[1] I certainly believe that the ability to manage properly market risk will become a source of competitive advantage among financial institutions: firstly, investors, shareholders, and regulators are expecting strong and efficient risk management

[1]Hull, J. C., Rethinking Risk Management, PRMIA presentation, April 2009.

Handbook of Market Risk, First Edition. Christian Szylar.

practices; secondly, successful managers will be those who will be able to capture and properly manage the new markets characteristics.

A holistic development of a global, systemic approach to hazards and perils is at the center of the new science of cindynics. Risk management's future development may be greatly aided by cindynics. Cindynics is derived from "kindunos," the Greek word for danger, and refers to the new science of hazard identification. The latest developments in cindynics now include financial cyndinics.

To conclude, we also would like to end on a positive note. Risk is usually perceived in a negative way. The dictionary usually defines risk as an exposure to a danger or to chance. The Chinese symbol representing risk is interesting. The first symbol represents "danger," while the second one is the symbol for "opportunity." This makes risk a combination of danger and opportunity.

危機

We do believe that the world, as resulting from the financial crisis, will also set new opportunities for those who will able to translate the lessons we learned into their daily practices when investing. Risk does not have to be considered a negative aspect but can certainly also be something positive and used in a constructive manner. UCITS, for example, is all about opportunities as long as risks are identified, measured, properly monitored, and managed, as well as reported to the senior person with the ultimate responsibilities, such as the board of directors. Risk management is linked with strategic management, but it is also a matter of added value. Proper and sound risk management creates added value when used and integrated in a convenient way.

Risk management is first a question of consciousness and needs the top management support. Too often in the past, risk has been seen as a cost of complying with regulatory requirements. Firms managing their risk in a systematic can actually improve their competitiveness and ensure sustainable development.

The final aim is not to eliminate risk. It is to assist personnel in managing the risks involved in all investment activities to maximize opportunities and minimize adverse consequences. Consequently, effective risk management requires:

- Identifying and taking opportunities to improve performance, as well as taking action to avoid or reduce the chances of something going wrong.
- A systematic process that can be used when making decisions to improve the effectiveness and efficiency of performance.

- Forward thinking and active approaches to management.
- Effective communication.
- Accountability in decision making.
- Balance between the cost of managing risk and the anticipated benefits.

In a rapidly changing and increasingly challenging world, every organization is facing more complex risks that carry greater severity. Leading organizations have been surveyed to find out (a) their views of emerging and escalating risks and (b) the steps they are taking to address these challenges.

Our experience of regulations for banks has changed dramatically over the last 20 years. Due to financial innovation and a few banking crises, regulators have tried to put in place international regulatory standards in order to protect the banking sector against various risks inherent in the day-to-day management of banks. The 1998 Basel Accord was a first step toward international requirements standards, and it has since been developed to incorporate most of the financial innovations designed by banks. From a pure credit risk framework at the start, the Basel Committee on Banking Supervision has incorporated market risk and operational risk as capital charge for bank capital requirements. This has now been extended over liquidity risk, with the introduction of liquidity ratios under Basel III, in order to safeguard banks against a potential crisis in liquidity funding, as was experienced during the global financial crisis beginning in 2007. At the height of the crisis, financial systems all over the world were close to collapse due to the complexity of the systems created. Today, regulators

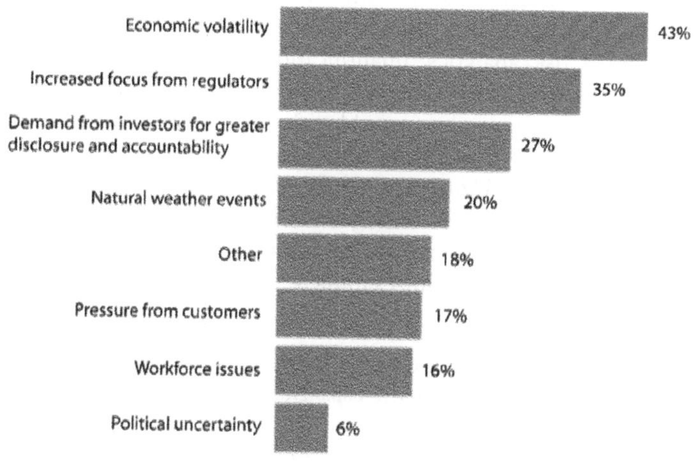

FIGURE 14.1 External drivers strengthening risk management (2008–2009). *Source:* AON Global Risk Management Survey 2009.

and banks are under the spotlight due the economic situation in most countries, and they are working together in order to provide their respective economies with a more robust and sound financial system.

The report of the Counterparty Risk Management Policy Group III recommends that "each institution ensure that the risk tolerance of the firm is established or approved by the highest levels of management and shared with the boards."[2]

The *Global Risk Management Survey* by Deloitte highlights (its respondents being mostly international banks) that 77% have clearly stated risk framework oversight by the board of directors. Furthermore, in its study, Deloitte shows that 73% of these respondents have chief risk officers that report to the board of directors directly. This shows the tendency in institutions to create foundational elements of an effective integrated risk management to face today's challenges in an enterprise-wide risk management.

One theme recurring in the surveys is the significant regulatory and legislative changes affecting risk management. As the *AON Global Risk Management Survey* shows,[3] the cost, quantity, and complexity of regulations presents serious challenges in terms of managing compliance with regulatory risks. Businesses are spending considerable time and resources in the pursuit of compliance with various types of regulations.

This has consequences regarding their reputational risk (which is recurrent in the top risk level in the surveys), because the early signs show the difficulty of quantifying this risk. The AON survey tells us that, "even if an organization is innocent, its business can be affected by an event that even remotely ties it to wrongdoing."

One other risk that stands out from the surveys is credit/counterparty risk (or third-party liability). According to the survey by Deloitte, "there is a broad consensus among the institutions, about the responsibilities of the independent credit risk management. Eighty percent of institutions said that primary responsibilities included risk analytics, quantification, and portfolio risk reporting, monitoring of risk exposures compared to limits, etc." This demonstrates that the need for more accurate and responsible risk management is increasing rapidly.

However, there is a downside to having all these risks: *Cost*. According to the Accenture survey on *Managing Risk for High Performance in Extraordinary Times*,[4] the cost of effective risk management has increased by more than 25% for almost half of the firms, due to the need for more competent staff and more compliant-monitoring process, for example.

[2]Counterparty Risk Management Policy Group (CRMPG) III, *Containing Systemic Risk: The Road to Reform*, available at: http://www.crmpolicygroup.org/docs/CRMPG-III.pdf (accessed March 16, 2010), August 2008.

[3]Aon, *The Definitive Report on Risk—Aon's 2009 Global Risk Management Survey*,

[4]Accenture, Managing risk for high performance in extraordinary time, *Report on the Accenture 2009 Global Risk Management Study*, available at http://www.accenture.com/NR/rdonlyres/78589759-FE29-43E3-AFDF-171D1B9F2587/0/Accenture_Managing_Risk_for_High_Performance_in_Extraordinary_Times.PDF (accessed 16 March 2010), 2009.

One of the preferred solutions for firms in most of the surveys to tackle cost and time consumption is outsourcing. It provides them with the elimination of time-consuming management for IT applications, a unified risk procedure across all sites, an improved process and a better turn-around time of risk responses, and an improved ability to deal with regulatory requirements.

A brief summary of the future of risk management reveals the increasing importance of:

- Developing more integrated risk management capabilities.
- Improving the quality and relevance of information and the frequency of risk reporting.
- Creating risk-adjusted companies' performance management processes increasing the involvement of risk management in driving value creation. Optimism still exists about a strong and efficient risk management.

"Managing risk is the main task ahead," says a recent *Financial Times* article.[5] "The main challenges for asset managers in the coming decade is understanding, managing and communicating risk."

We hope that this handbook on market risk can provide a useful contribution to the debate on how a financial institution can create a well-governed risk management infrastructure with the flexibility to stand up to future volatility and changing conditions.

[5]Grene S., "FM", *Financial Times*, 4 January, 2010.

Index

Note: Page numbers in *italics* refer to figures; those in **bold** to tables.

Wiley Handbooks in

FINANCIAL ENGINEERING AND ECONOMETRICS

Advisory Editor

Ruey S. Tsay

The University of Chicago Booth School of Business, USA

The dynamic and interaction between financial markets around the world have changed dramatically under economic globalization. In addition, advances in communication and data collection have changed the way information is processed and used. In this new era, financial instruments have become increasingly sophisticated and their impacts are far-reaching. The recent financial (credit) crisis is a vivid example of the new challenges we face and continue to face in this information age. Analytical skills and ability to extract useful information from mass data, to comprehend the complexity of financial instruments, and to assess the financial risk involved become a necessity for economists, financial managers, and risk management professionals. To master such skills and ability, knowledge from computer science, economics, finance, mathematics and statistics is essential. As such, financial engineering is cross-disciplinary, and its theory and applications advance rapidly.

The goal of this Handbook Series is to provide a one-stop source for students, researchers, and practitioners to learn the knowledge and analytical skills they need to face today's challenges in financial markets. The Series intends to introduce systematically recent developments in different areas of financial engineering and econometrics. The coverage will be broad and thorough with balance in theory and applications. Each volume will be edited by leading researchers and practitioners in the area and covers state-of-the-art methods and theory of the selected topic.

Published Wiley Handbooks in Financial Engineering and Econometrics

Bauwens, Hafner, and Laurent · *Handbook of Volatility Models and Their Applications*

Chan and Wong · *Handbook of Financial Risk Management: Simulations and Case Studies*

James, Marsh, and Sarno · *Handbook of Exchange Rates*

Viens, Mariani, and Florescu · *Handbook of Modeling High-Frequency Data in Finance*

Szylar · *Handbook of Market Risk*

Forthcoming Wiley Handbooks in Financial Engineering and Econometrics

Bali and Engle · *Handbook of Asset Pricing*

Brandimarte · *Handbook of Monte Carlo Simulation*

Chacko · *Handbook of Credit and Interest Rate Derivatives*

Cruz, Peters, and Shevchenko · *Handbook of Operational Risk*

Florescu, Mariani, Stanley, and Viens · *Handbook of High-Frequency Trading and Modeling in Finance*

Jacquier · *Handbook of Econometric Methods for Finance: Bayesian and Classical Perspecitves*

Longin · *Handbook of Extreme Value Theory and Its Applications to Finance and Insurance*

Starer · *Handbook of Equity Portfolio Management: Theory and Practice*

Veronesi · *Handbook of Fixed-Income Securities*

Printed and bound by CPI Group (UK) Ltd, Croydon, CR0 4YY
16/09/2026
14963423-0004